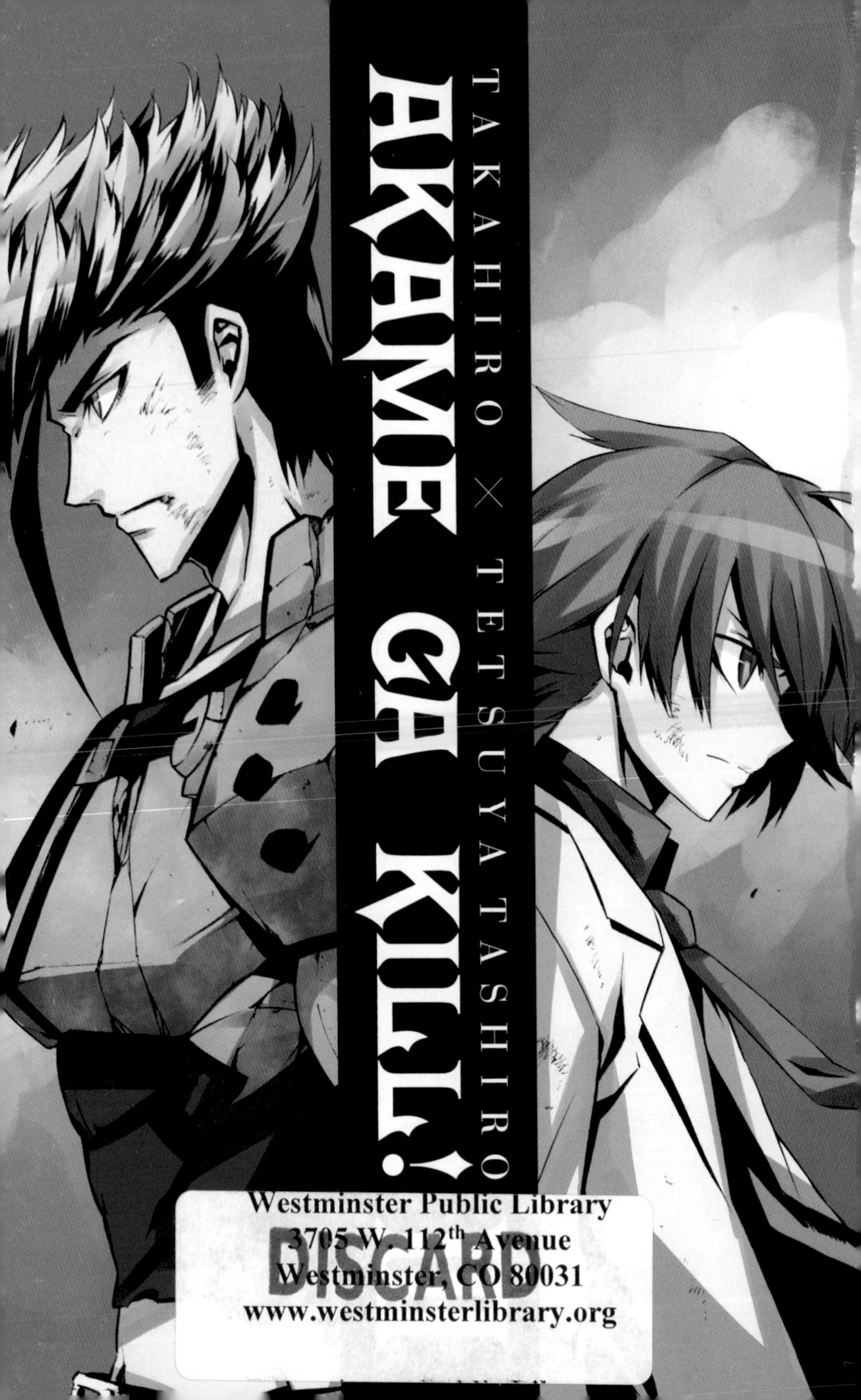
TAKAHIRO × TETSUYA TASHIRO
AKAME GA KILL!

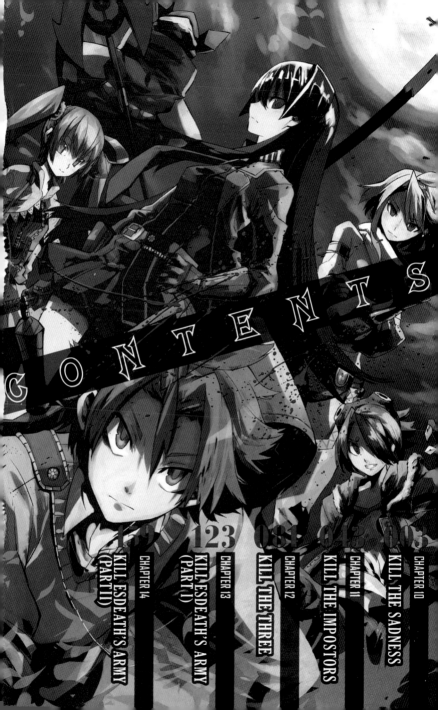

CONTENTS

159 123 081 043 003

CHAPTER 14
KILL ESDEATH'S ARMY
(PART II)

CHAPTER 13
KILL ESDEATH'S ARMY
(PART I)

CHAPTER 12
KILL THE THREE

CHAPTER 11
KILL THE IMPOSTORS

CHAPTER 10
KILL THE SADNESS

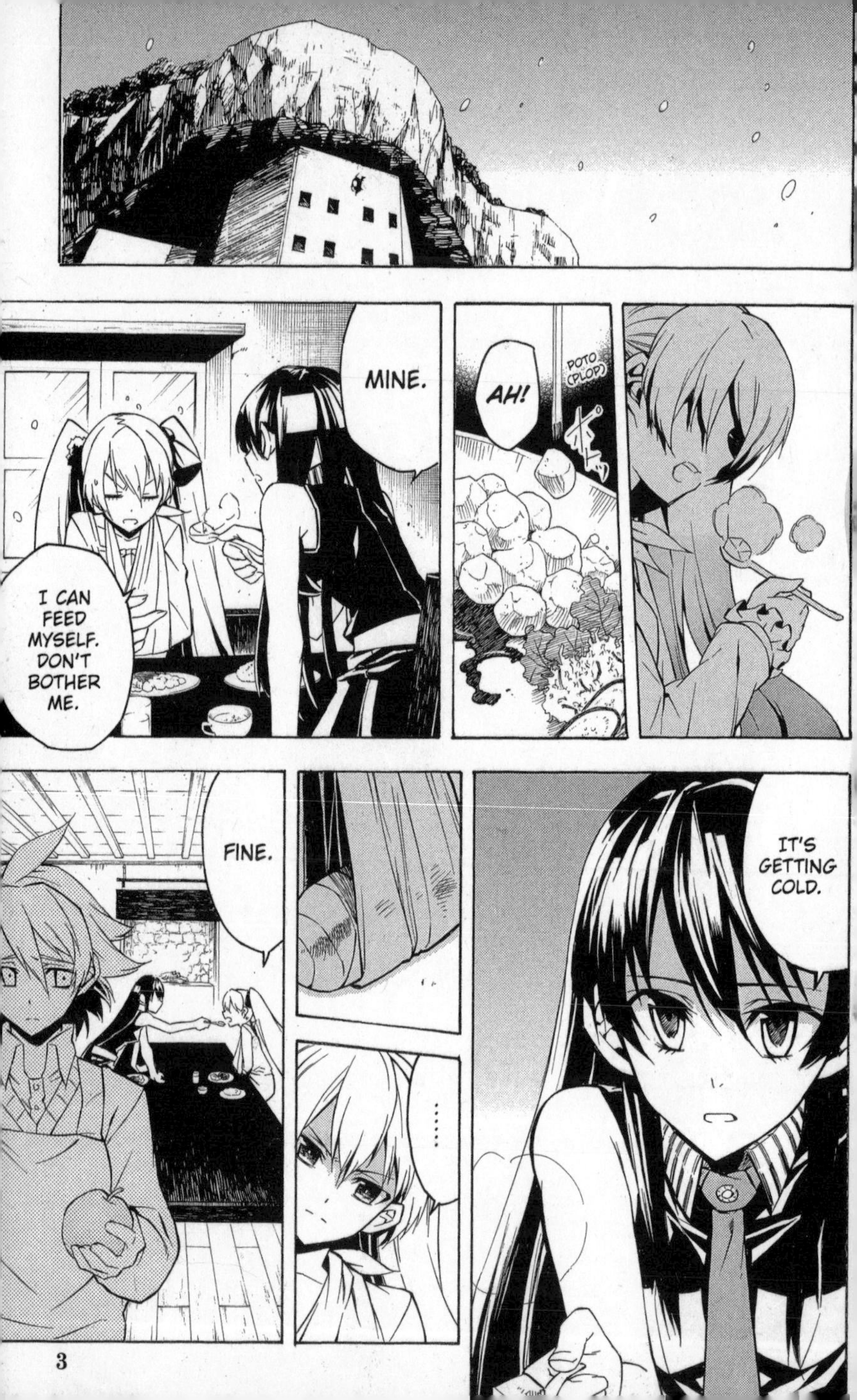
AH!
POTO (PLOP)
MINE.
I CAN FEED MYSELF. DON'T BOTHER ME.
IT'S GETTING COLD.
......
FINE.

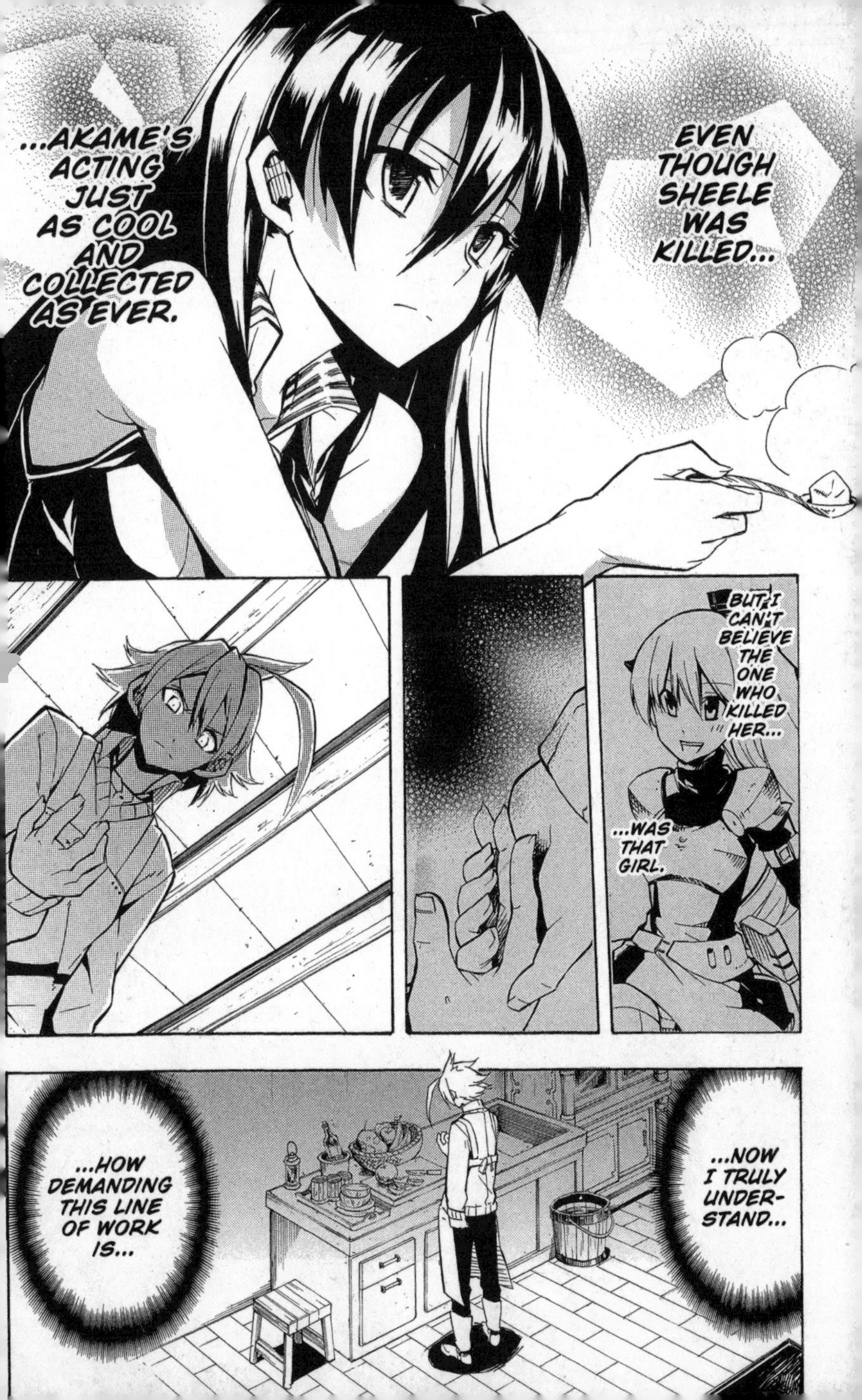
EVEN THOUGH SHEELE WAS KILLED...
...AKAME'S ACTING JUST AS COOL AND COLLECTED AS EVER.
BUT I CAN'T BELIEVE THE ONE WHO KILLED HER...
...WAS THAT GIRL.
...NOW I TRULY UNDER-STAND...
...HOW DEMANDING THIS LINE OF WORK IS...

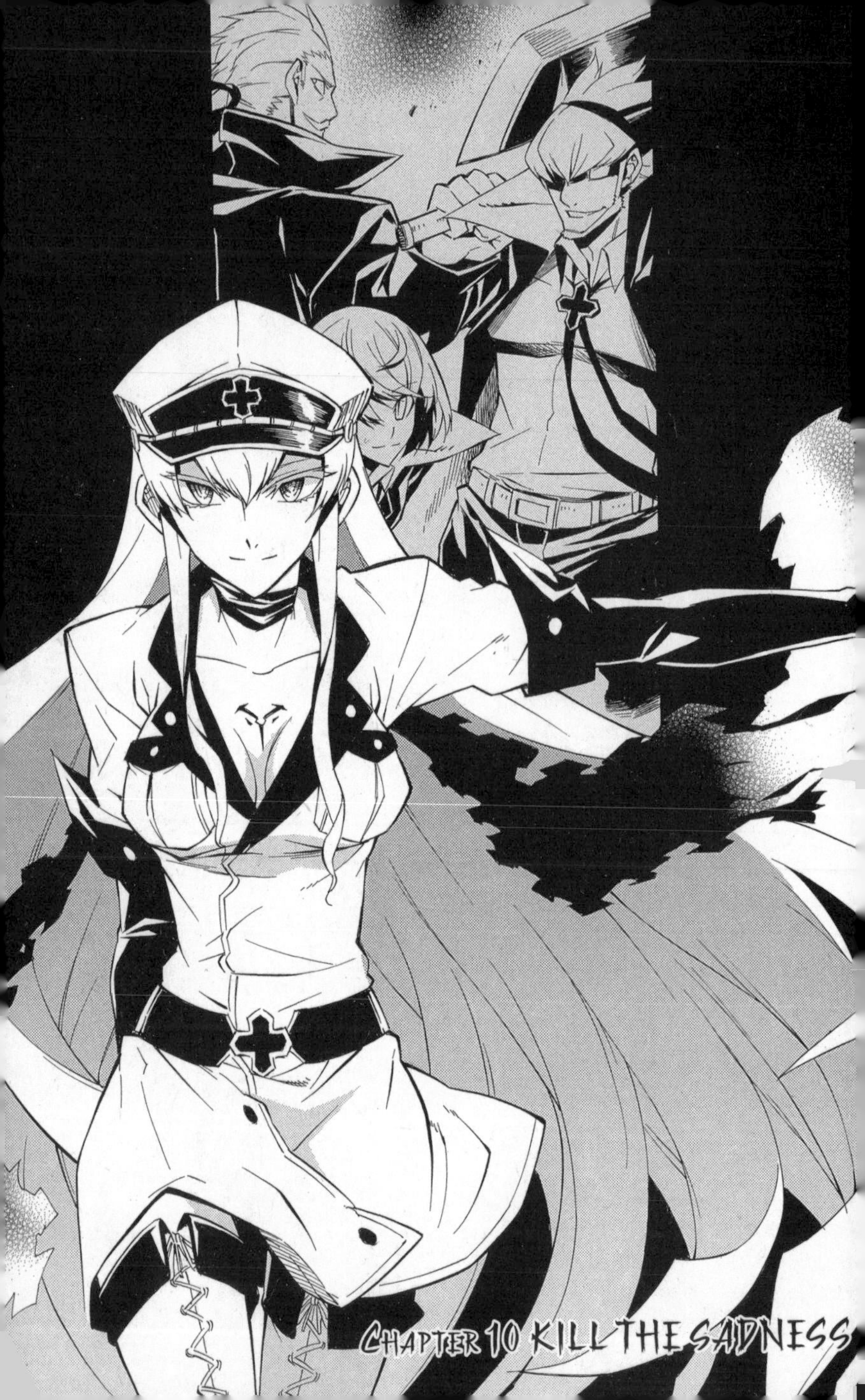
CHAPTER 10 KILL THE SADNESS

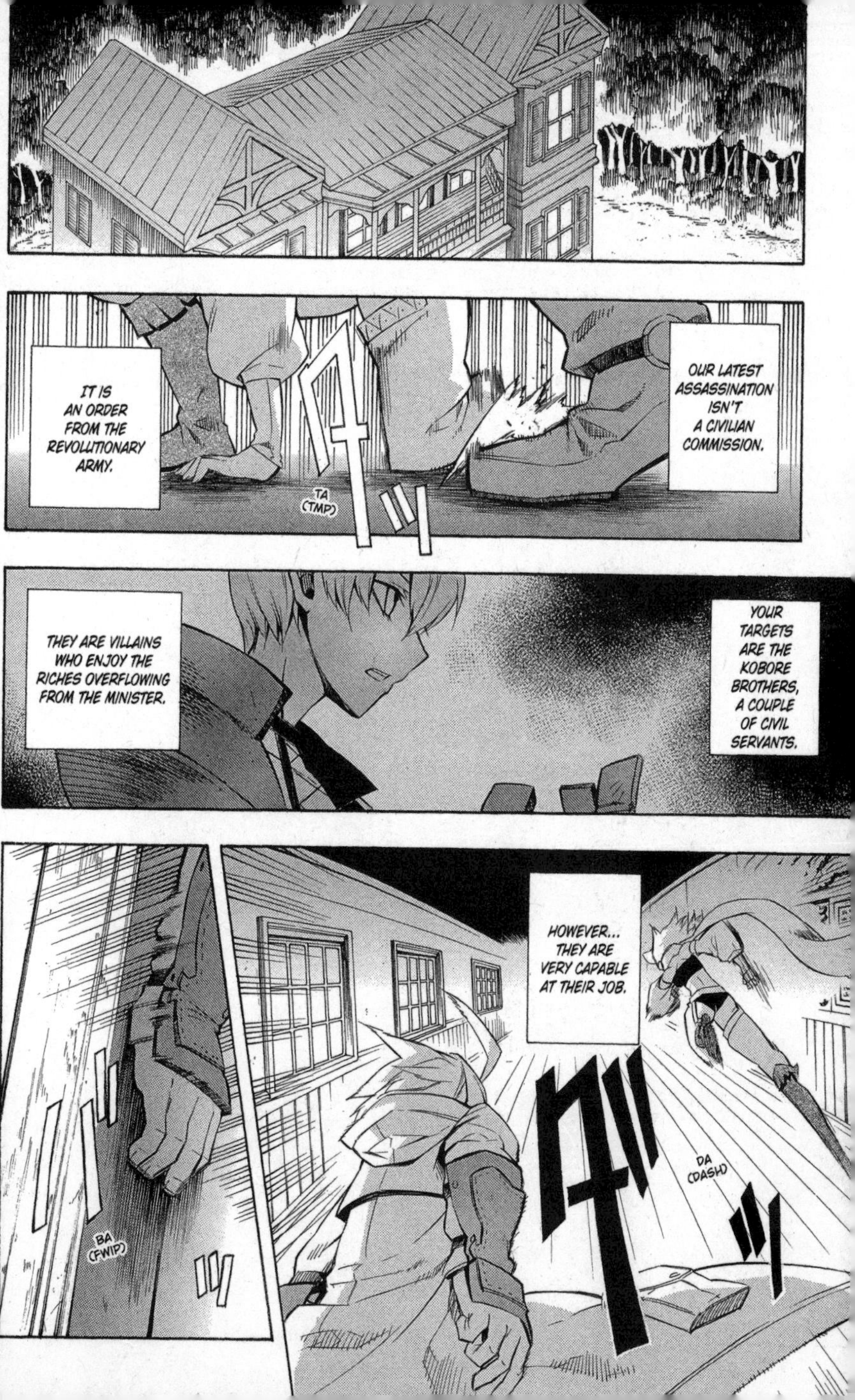
OUR LATEST ASSASSINATION ISN'T A CIVILIAN COMMISSION.
IT IS AN ORDER FROM THE REVOLUTIONARY ARMY.
TA (TMP)
YOUR TARGETS ARE THE KOBORE BROTHERS, A COUPLE OF CIVIL SERVANTS.
THEY ARE VILLAINS WHO ENJOY THE RICHES OVERFLOWING FROM THE MINISTER.
HOWEVER... THEY ARE VERY CAPABLE AT THEIR JOB.
DA (DASH)
BA (FWIP)

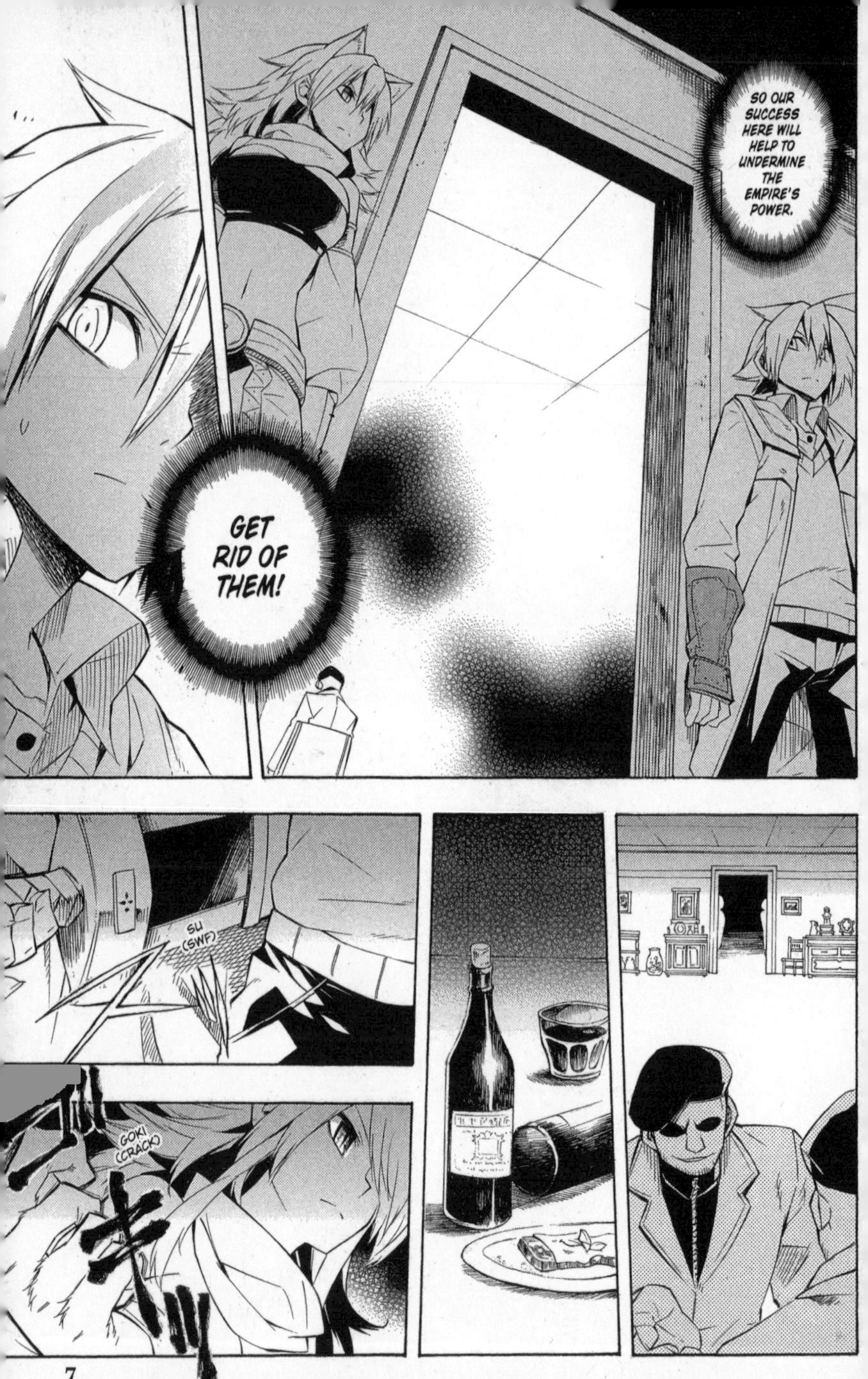
SO OUR SUCCESS HERE WILL HELP TO UNDERMINE THE EMPIRE'S POWER.
GET RID OF THEM!
...
SU (SWF)
GOKI (CRACK)

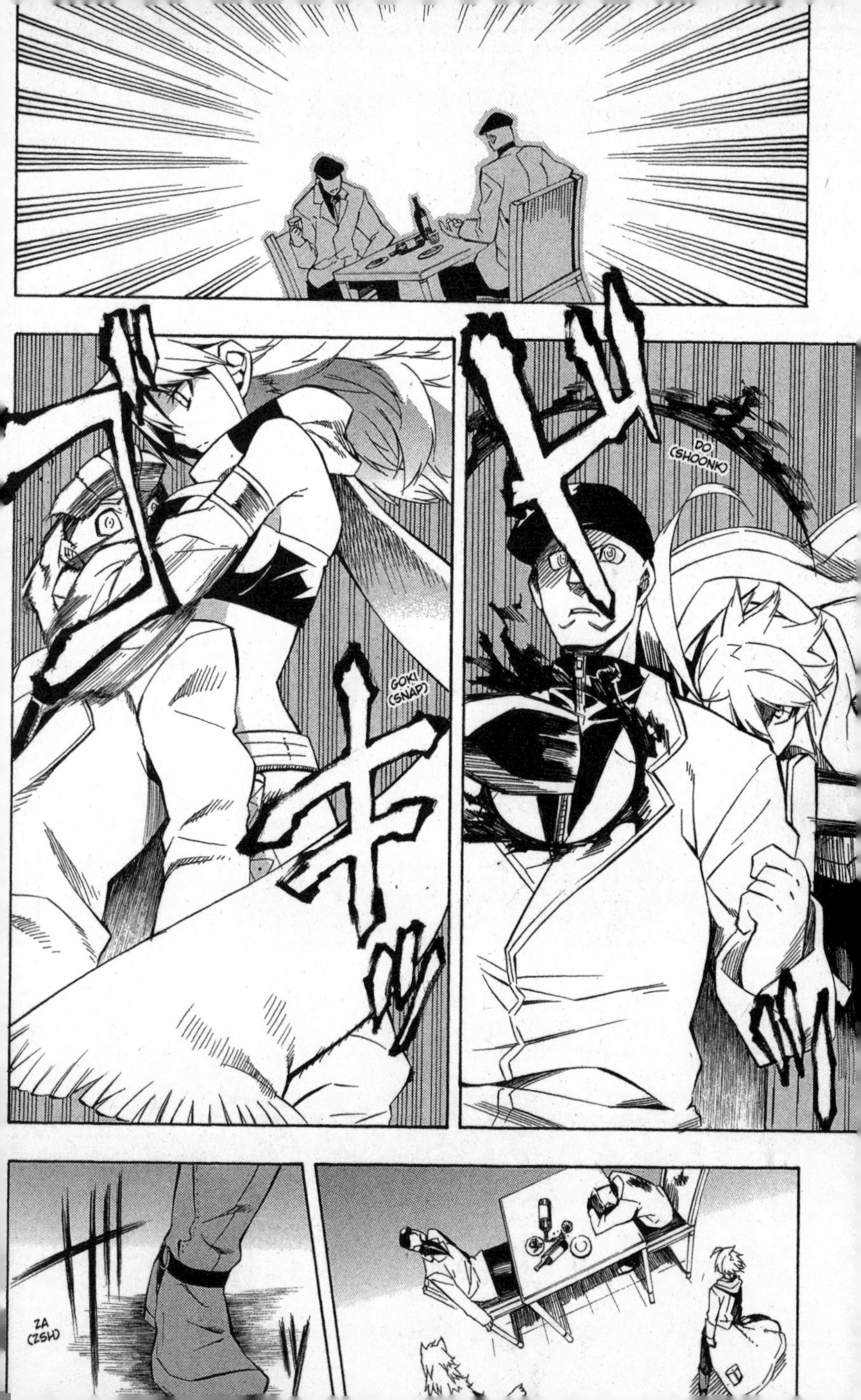
DO
(SHOONK)
GOKI
(SNAP)
ZA
(ZSH)

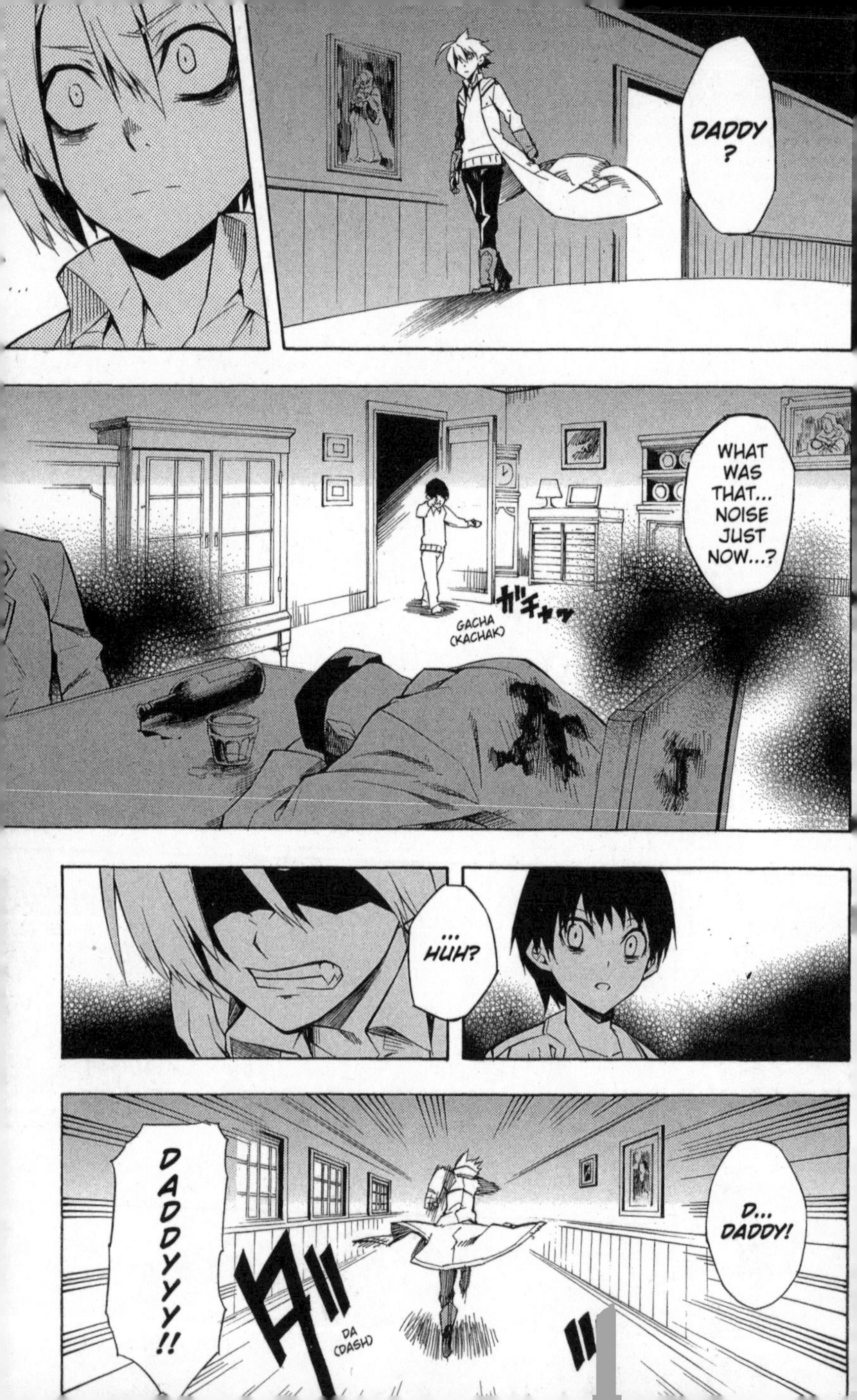
DADDY ?
...
WHAT WAS THAT... NOISE JUST NOW...?
ガチャッ
GACHA (KACHAK)
... HUH?
D... DADDY!
DADDYYY!!
DA (DASH)

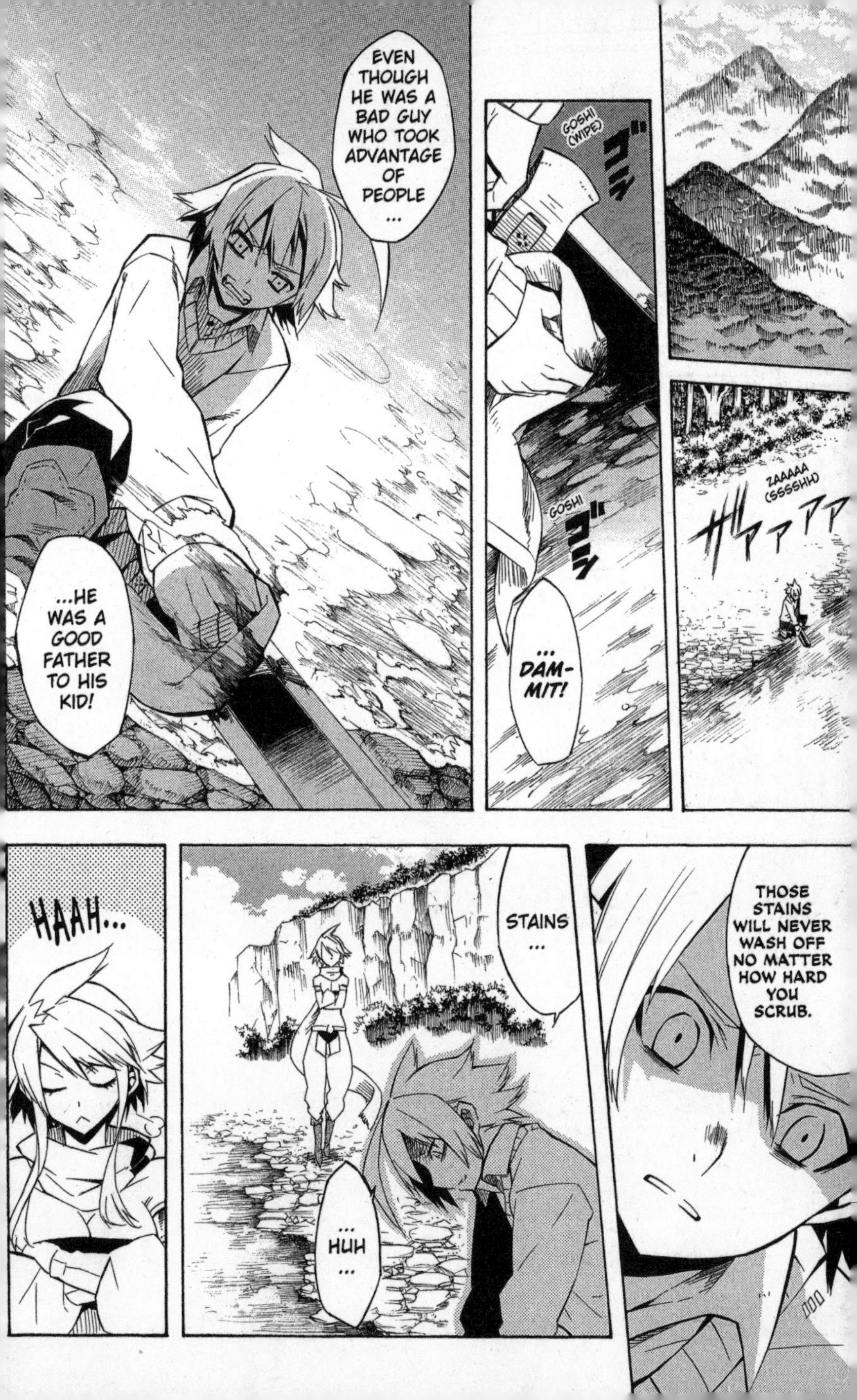
ZAAAAA (SSSSSHH)
GOSHI (WIPE)
GOSHI
... DAM-MIT!
EVEN THOUGH HE WAS A BAD GUY WHO TOOK ADVANTAGE OF PEOPLE ...
...HE WAS A GOOD FATHER TO HIS KID!
THOSE STAINS WILL NEVER WASH OFF NO MATTER HOW HARD YOU SCRUB.
STAINS ...
... HUH ...
HAAH...

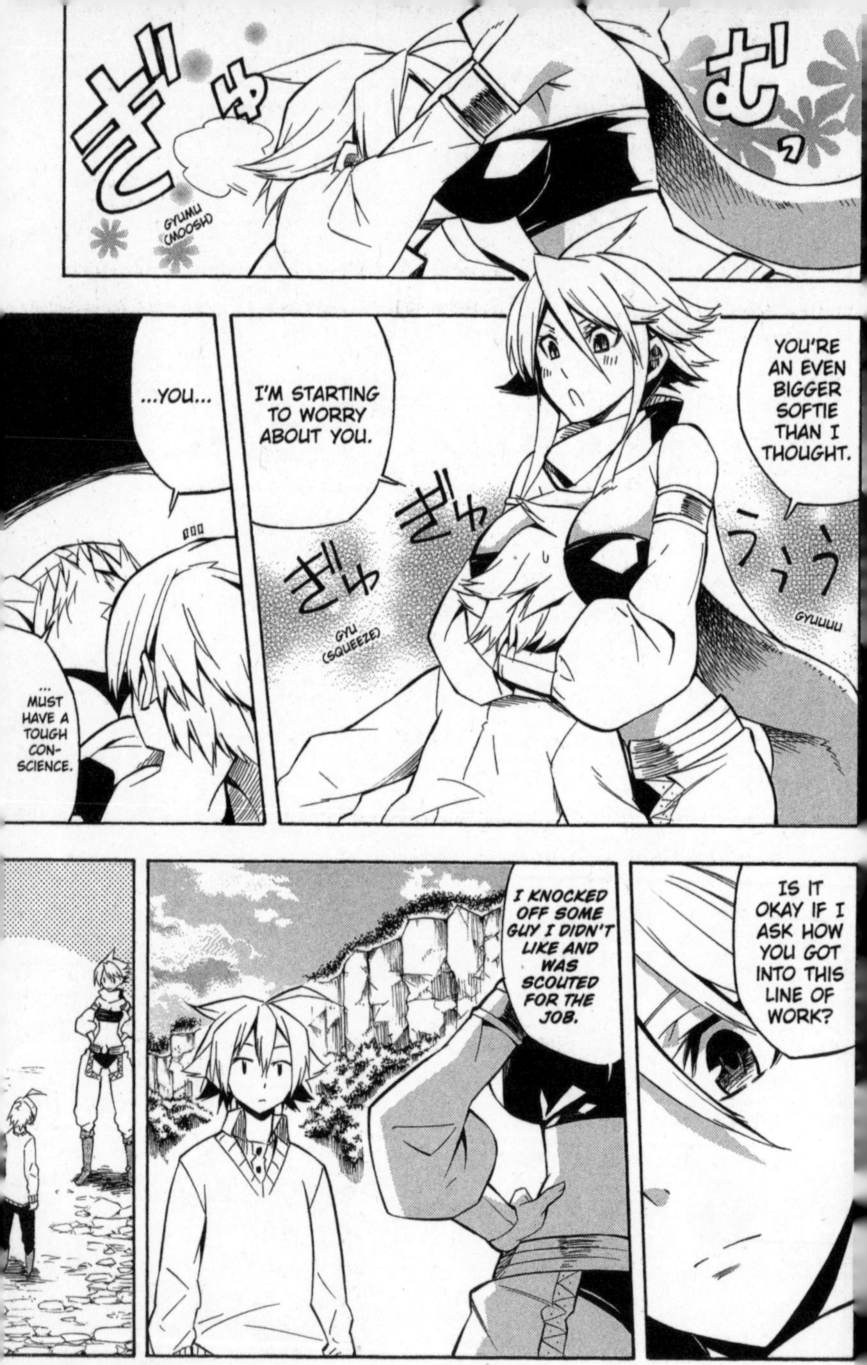
GYUMU (MOOSH)
YOU'RE AN EVEN BIGGER SOFTIE THAN I THOUGHT.
GYUUUU
I'M STARTING TO WORRY ABOUT YOU.
GYU (SQUEEZE)
...YOU...
... MUST HAVE A TOUGH CON-SCIENCE.
IS IT OKAY IF I ASK HOW YOU GOT INTO THIS LINE OF WORK?
I KNOCKED OFF SOME GUY I DIDN'T LIKE AND WAS SCOUTED FOR THE JOB.

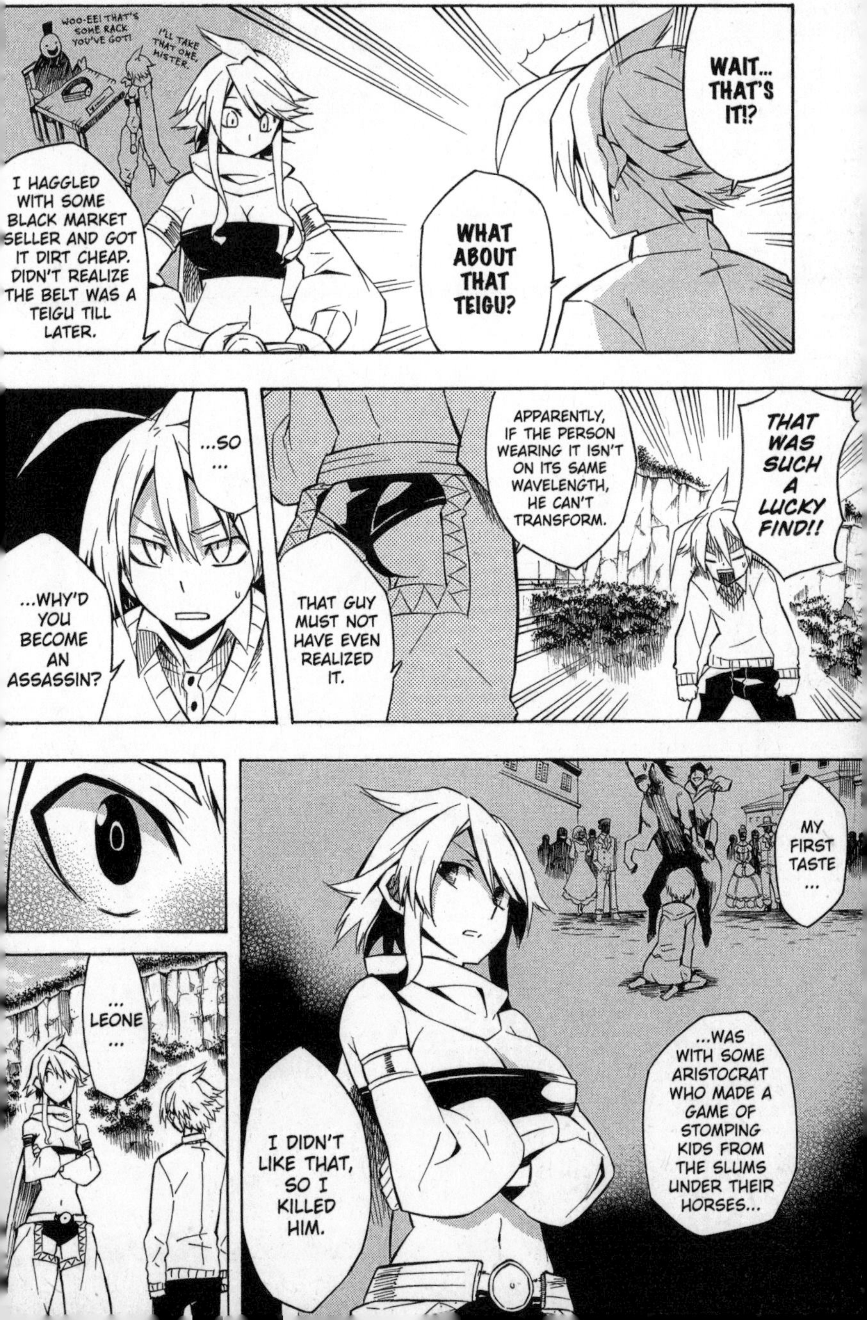
WAIT... THAT'S IT!?
WHAT ABOUT THAT TEIGU?
WOO-EE! THAT'S SOME RACK YOU'VE GOT!
I'LL TAKE THAT ONE, MISTER.
I HAGGLED WITH SOME BLACK MARKET SELLER AND GOT IT DIRT CHEAP. DIDN'T REALIZE THE BELT WAS A TEIGU TILL LATER.
THAT WAS SUCH A LUCKY FIND!!
APPARENTLY, IF THE PERSON WEARING IT ISN'T ON ITS SAME WAVELENGTH, HE CAN'T TRANSFORM.
THAT GUY MUST NOT HAVE EVEN REALIZED IT.
...SO ...
...WHY'D YOU BECOME AN ASSASSIN?
MY FIRST TASTE ...
...WAS WITH SOME ARISTOCRAT WHO MADE A GAME OF STOMPING KIDS FROM THE SLUMS UNDER THEIR HORSES...
I DIDN'T LIKE THAT, SO I KILLED HIM.
... LEONE ...

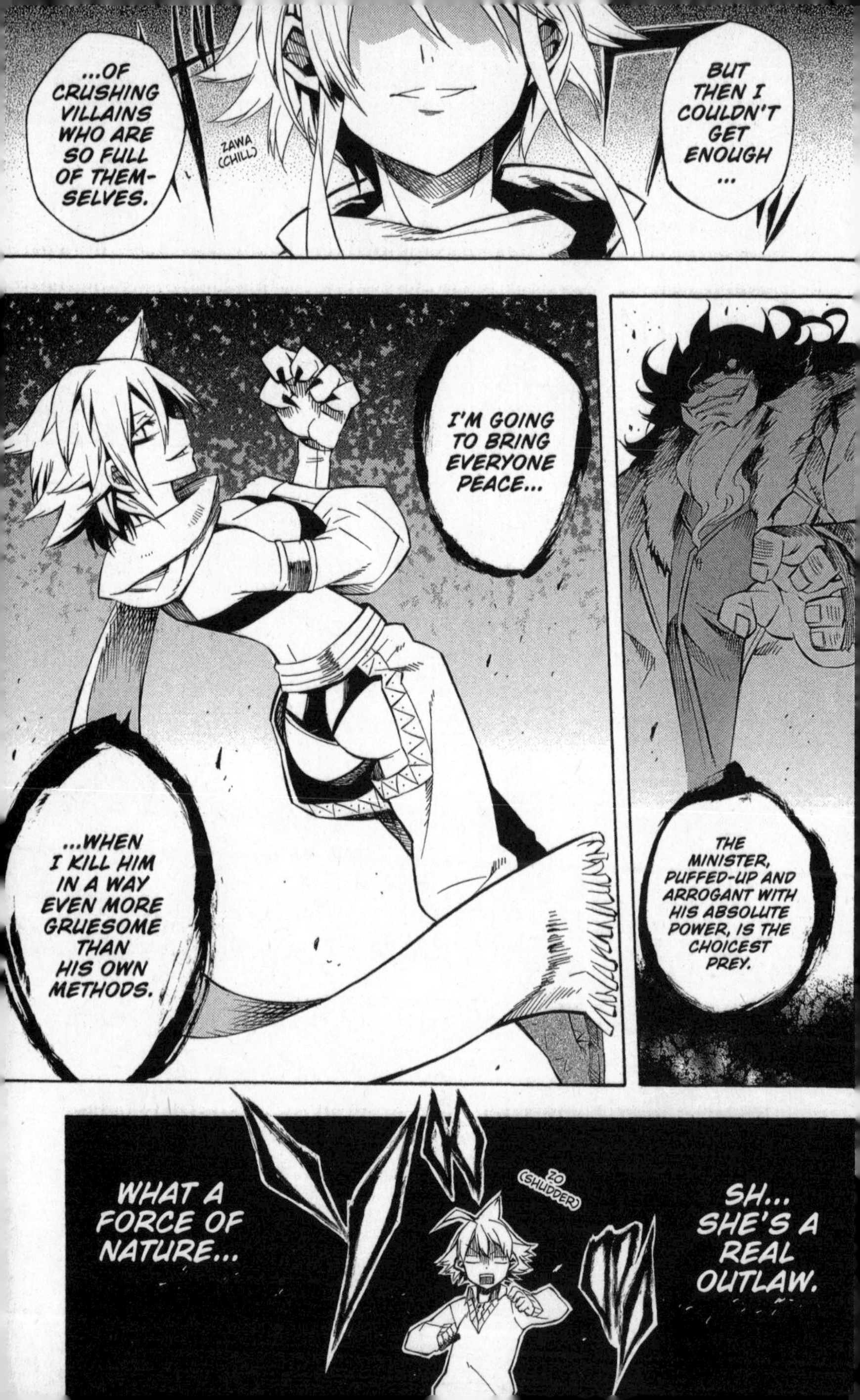
BUT THEN I COULDN'T GET ENOUGH...
ZAWA (CHILL)
...OF CRUSHING VILLAINS WHO ARE SO FULL OF THEM-SELVES.
THE MINISTER, PUFFED-UP AND ARROGANT WITH HIS ABSOLUTE POWER, IS THE CHOICEST PREY.
I'M GOING TO BRING EVERYONE PEACE...
...WHEN I KILL HIM IN A WAY EVEN MORE GRUESOME THAN HIS OWN METHODS.
SH... SHE'S A REAL OUTLAW.
ZO (SHUDDER)
WHAT A FORCE OF NATURE...

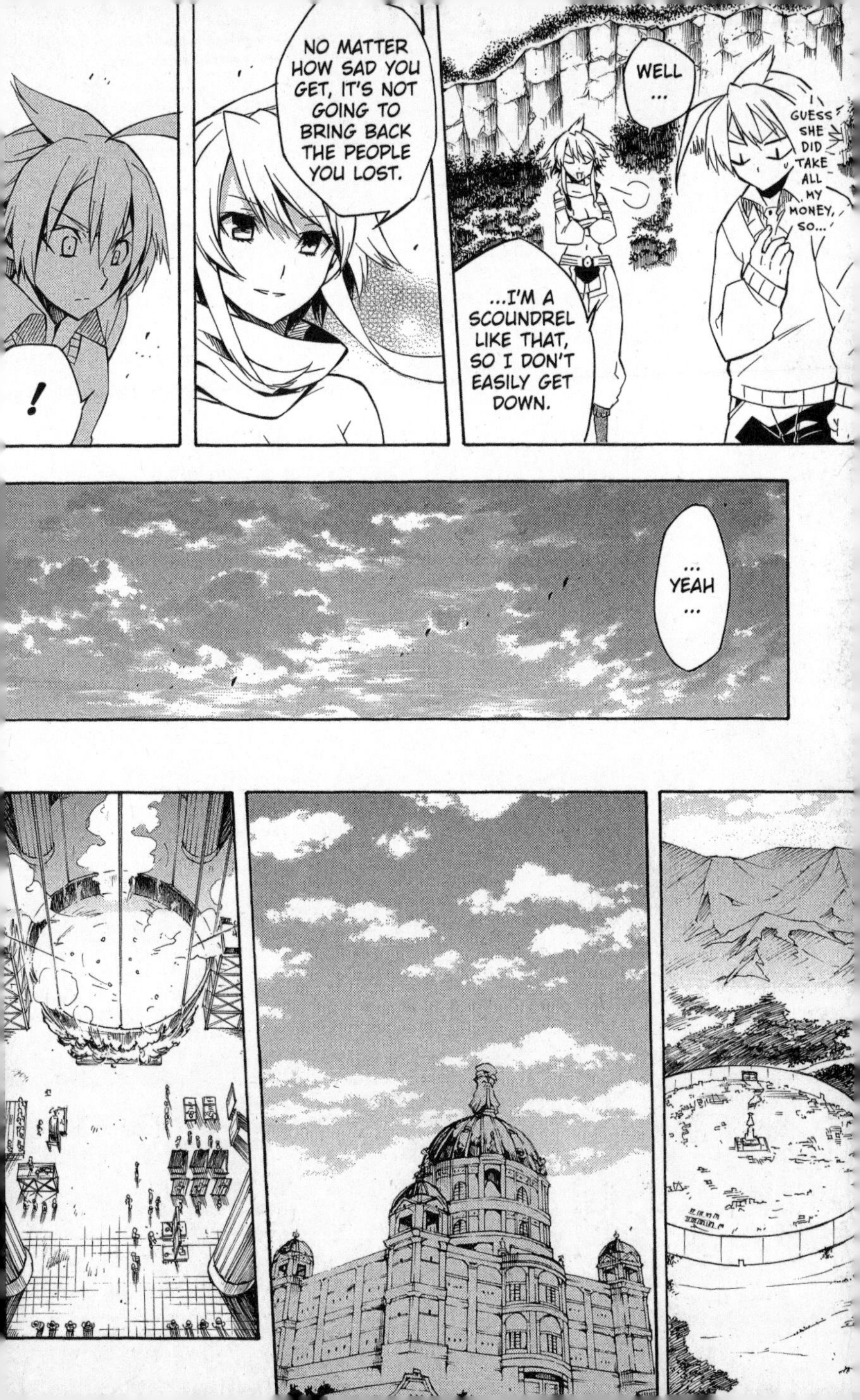
WELL ...
I GUESS SHE DID TAKE ALL MY MONEY, SO...
...I'M A SCOUNDREL LIKE THAT, SO I DON'T EASILY GET DOWN.
NO MATTER HOW SAD YOU GET, IT'S NOT GOING TO BRING BACK THE PEOPLE YOU LOST.
!
... YEAH ...

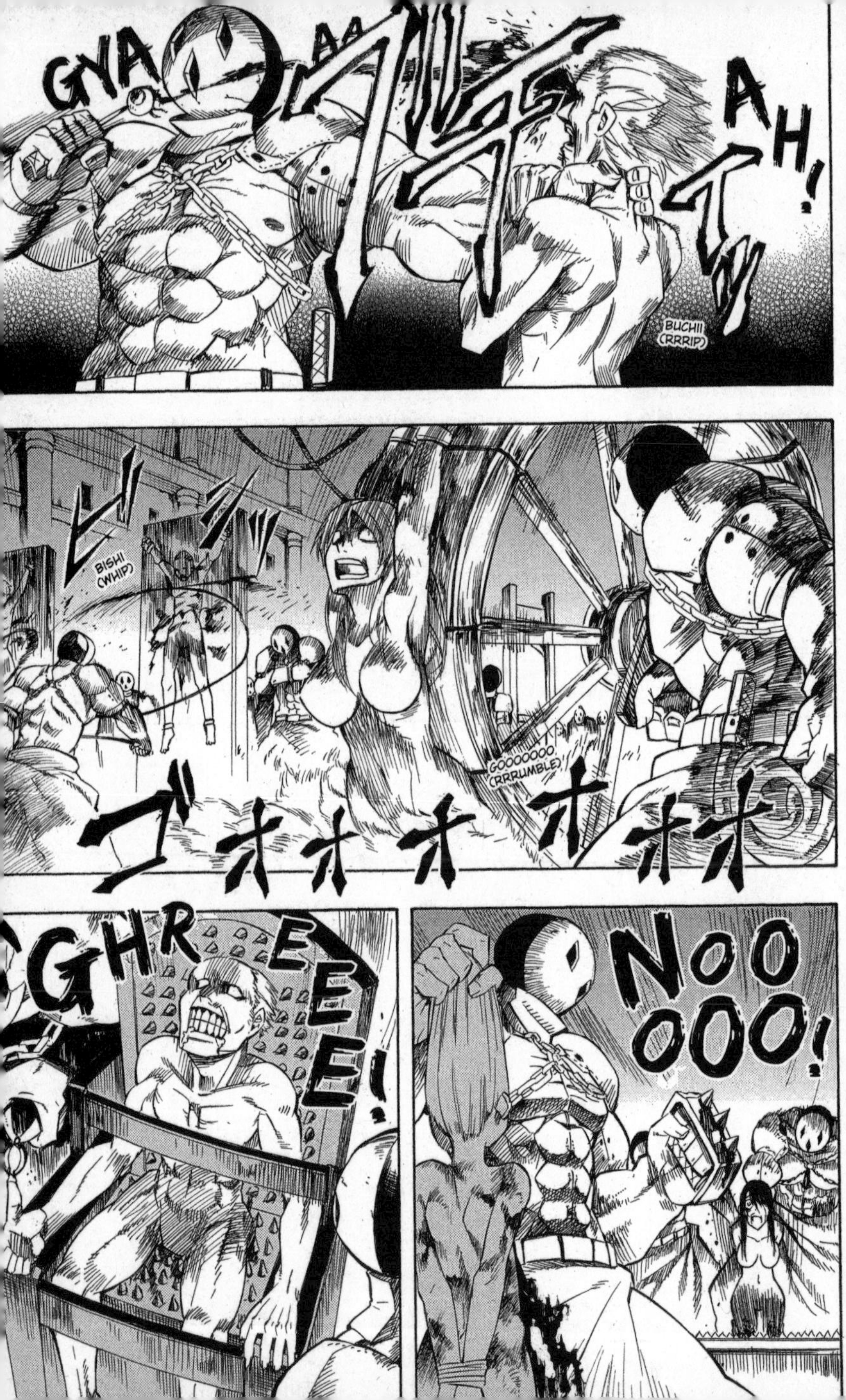
GYAAAAAH!
BUCHII (RRRIP)
BISHI (WHIP)
GOOOOOOO (RRRUMBLE)
ゴオオオオ
NOOOOOO!
GHREEE!

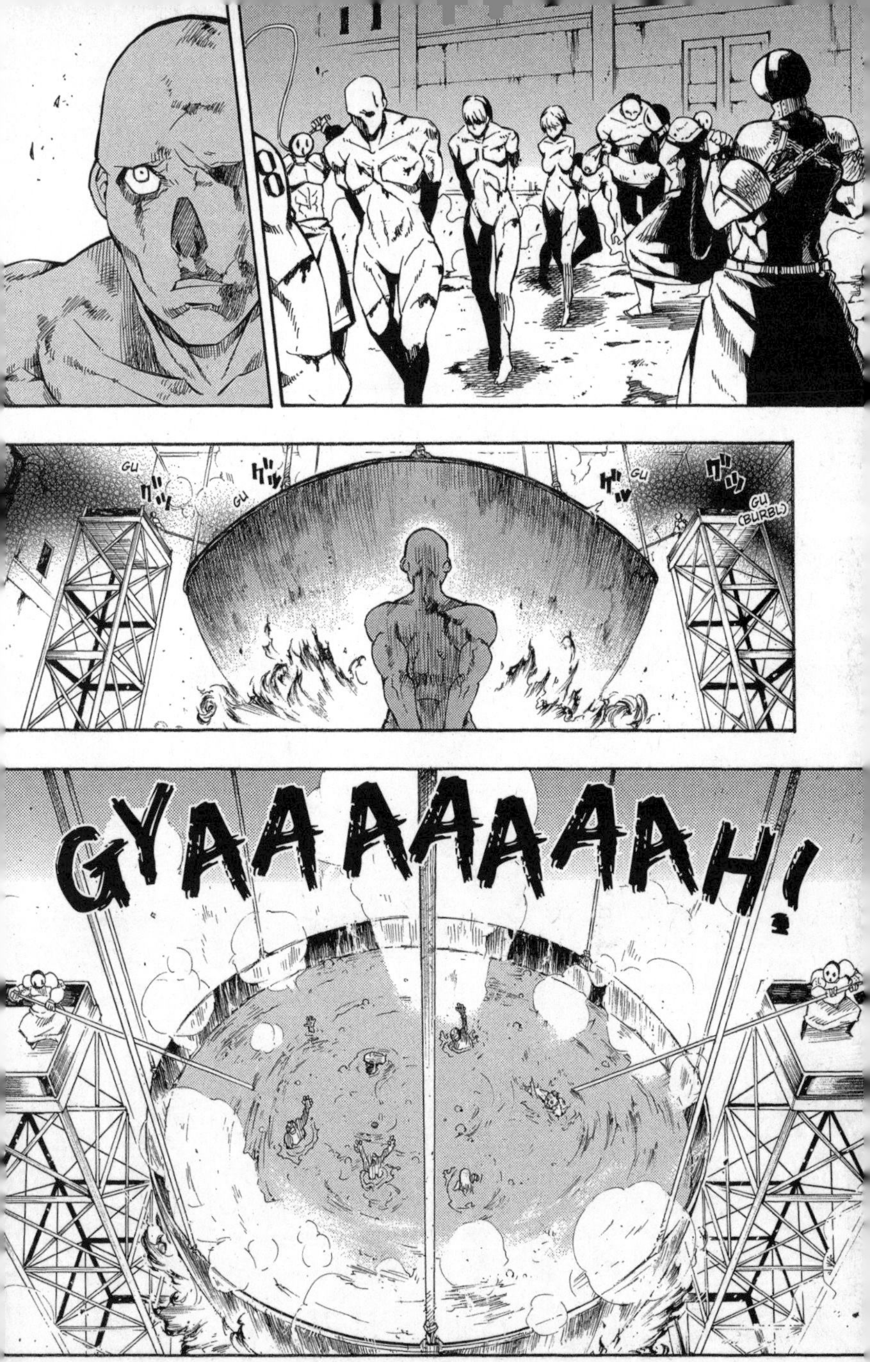
GU (BURBL)
GU
GU
GU
GYAAAAAAAH!

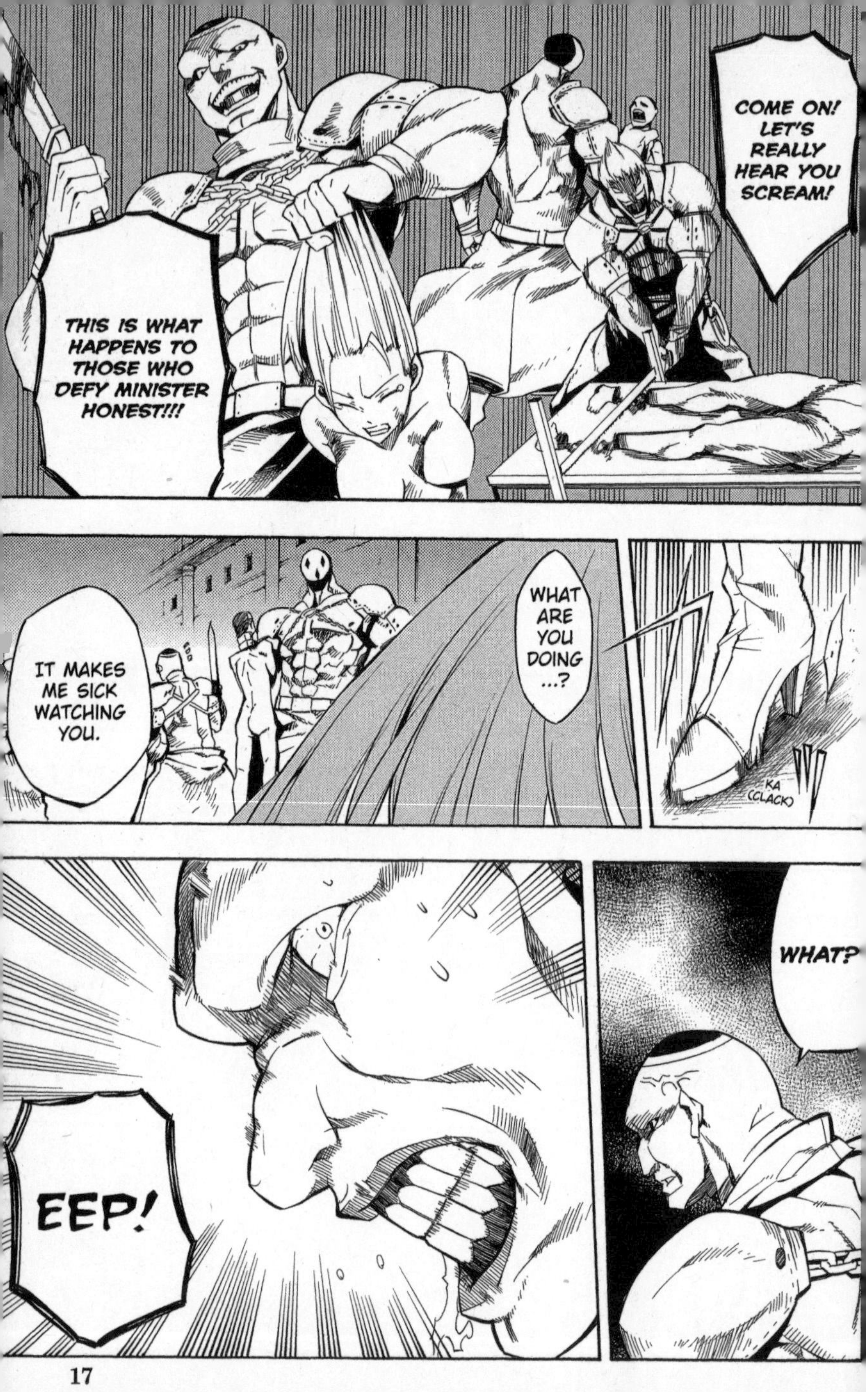
COME ON! LET'S REALLY HEAR YOU SCREAM!
THIS IS WHAT HAPPENS TO THOSE WHO DEFY MINISTER HONEST!!!
KA (CLACK)
WHAT ARE YOU DOING ...?
IT MAKES ME SICK WATCHING YOU.
WHAT?
EEP!

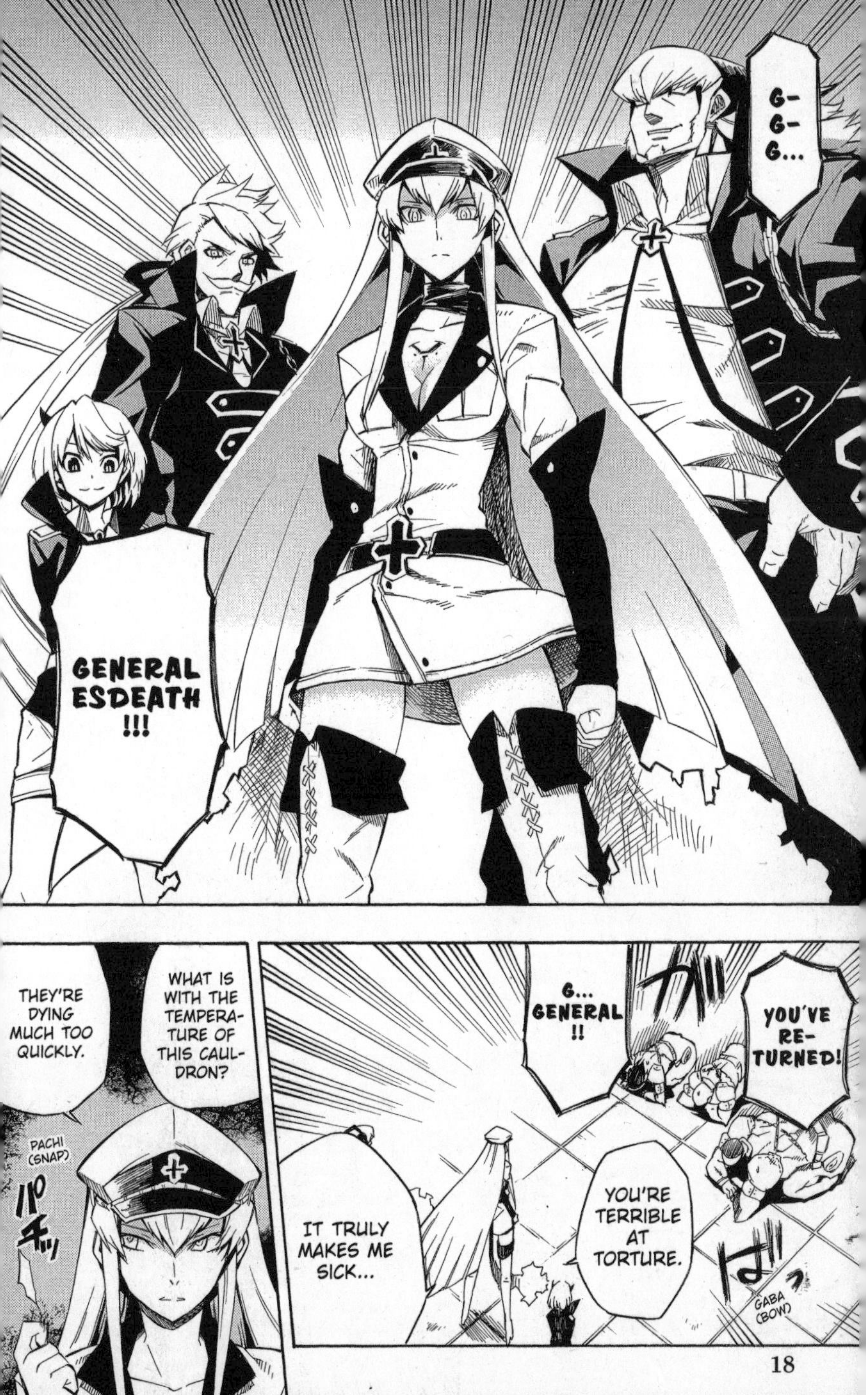
G- G- G...
GENERAL ESDEATH!!!
YOU'VE RE-TURNED!
G... GENERAL!!
GABA (BOW)
YOU'RE TERRIBLE AT TORTURE.
IT TRULY MAKES ME SICK...
WHAT IS WITH THE TEMPERA-TURE OF THIS CAULD-RON?
THEY'RE DYING MUCH TOO QUICKLY.
PACHI (SNAP)

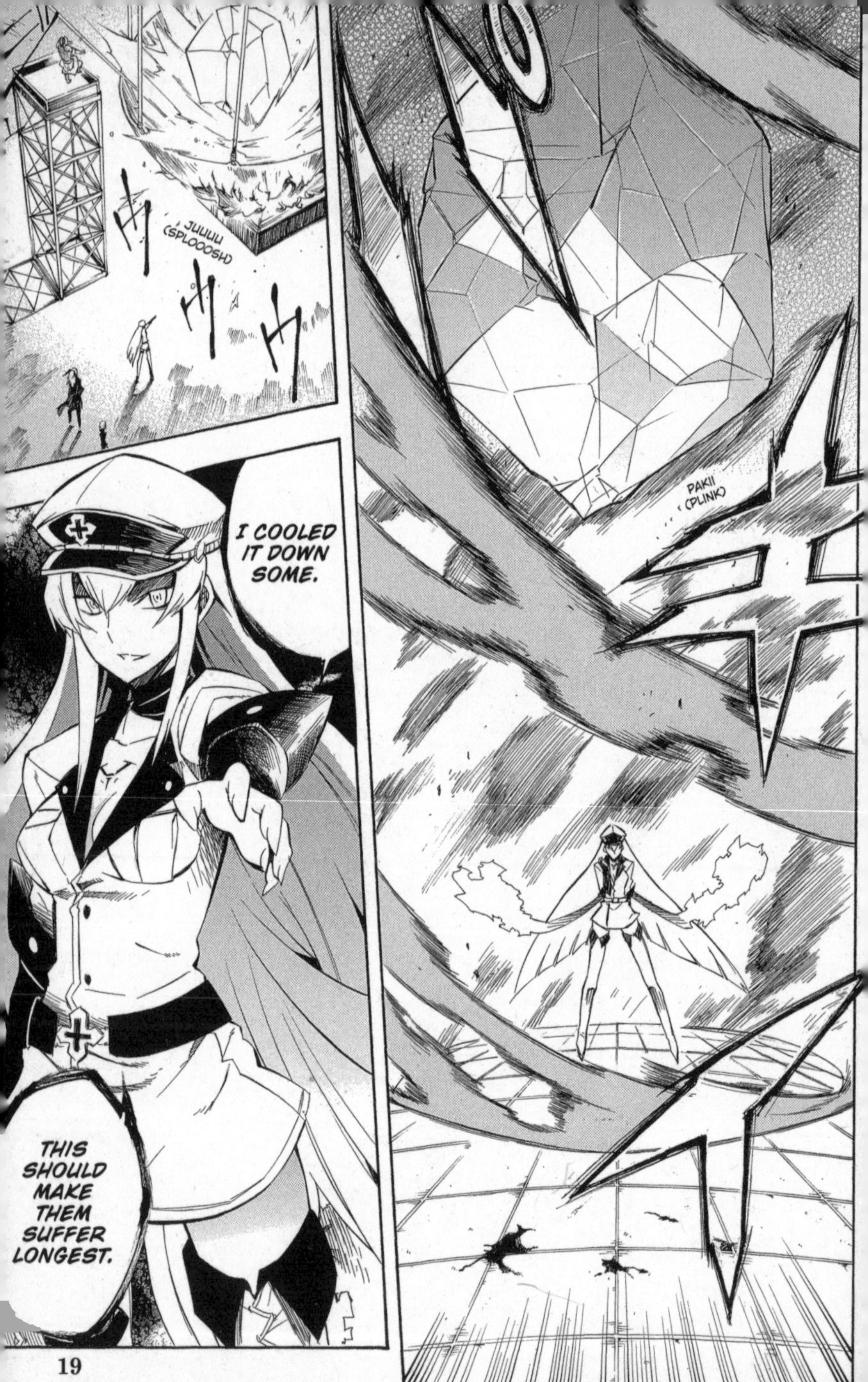
PAKII (PLINK)
JUUUU (SPLOOOSH)
I COOLED IT DOWN SOME.
THIS SHOULD MAKE THEM SUFFER LONGEST.

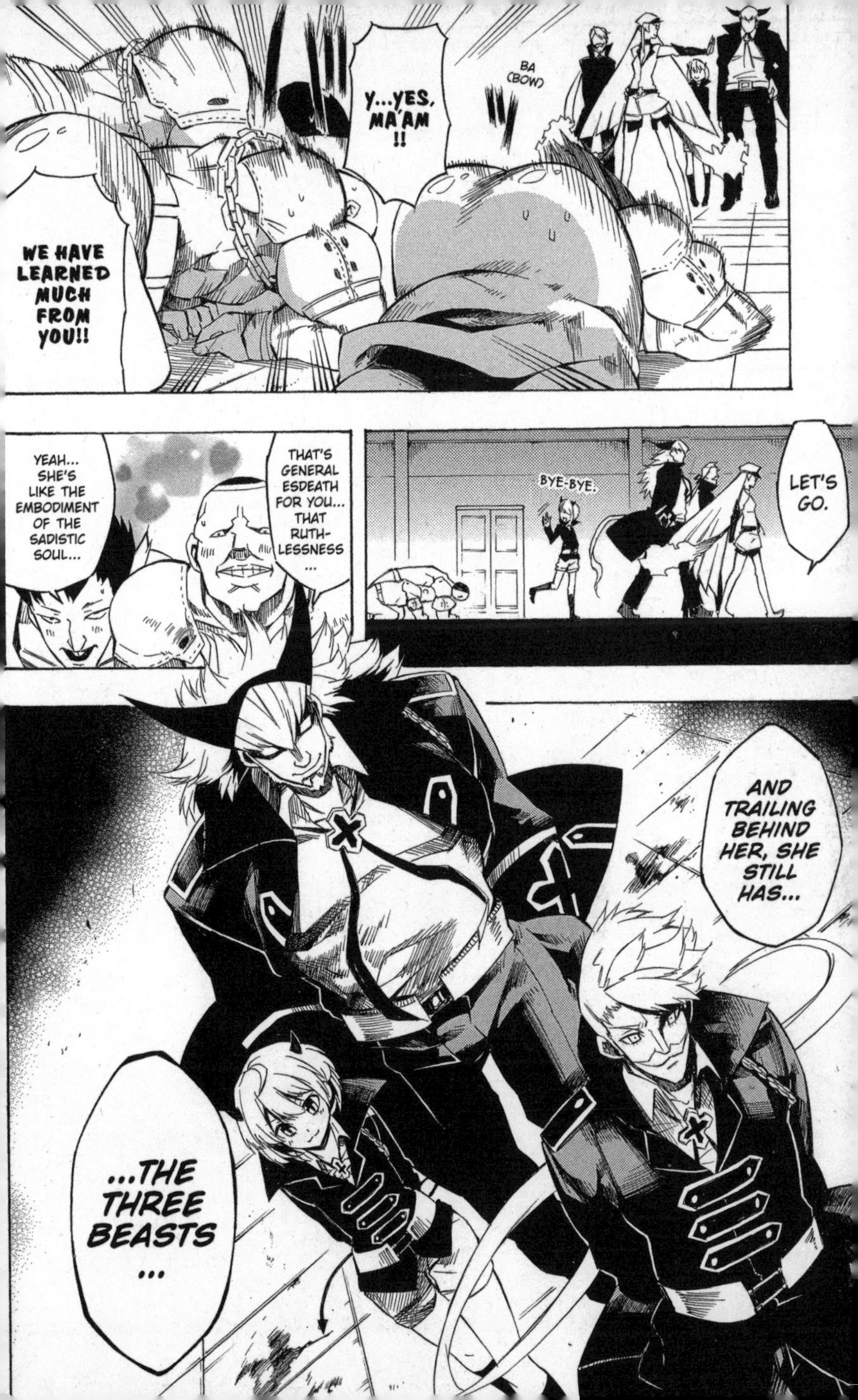
BA (BOW)
Y...YES, MA'AM!!
WE HAVE LEARNED MUCH FROM YOU!!
LET'S GO.
BYE-BYE.
THAT'S GENERAL ESDEATH FOR YOU... THAT RUTHLESSNESS...
YEAH... SHE'S LIKE THE EMBODIMENT OF THE SADISTIC SOUL...
AND TRAILING BEHIND HER, SHE STILL HAS...
...THE THREE BEASTS...

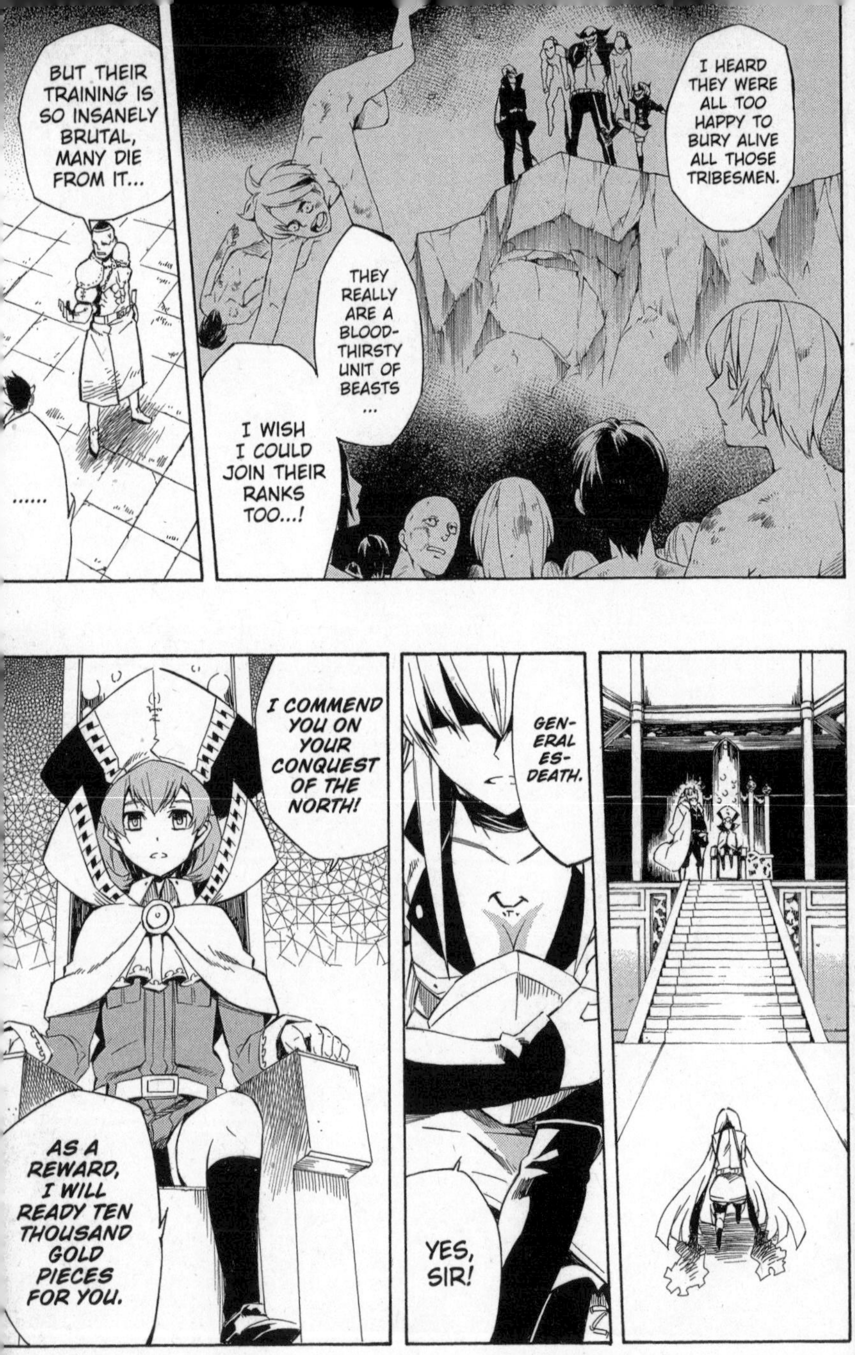
I HEARD THEY WERE ALL TOO HAPPY TO BURY ALIVE ALL THOSE TRIBESMEN.
THEY REALLY ARE A BLOOD-THIRSTY UNIT OF BEASTS ...
I WISH I COULD JOIN THEIR RANKS TOO...!
BUT THEIR TRAINING IS SO INSANELY BRUTAL, MANY DIE FROM IT...
......
GEN-ERAL ES-DEATH.
YES, SIR!
I COMMEND YOU ON YOUR CONQUEST OF THE NORTH!
AS A REWARD, I WILL READY TEN THOUSAND GOLD PIECES FOR YOU.

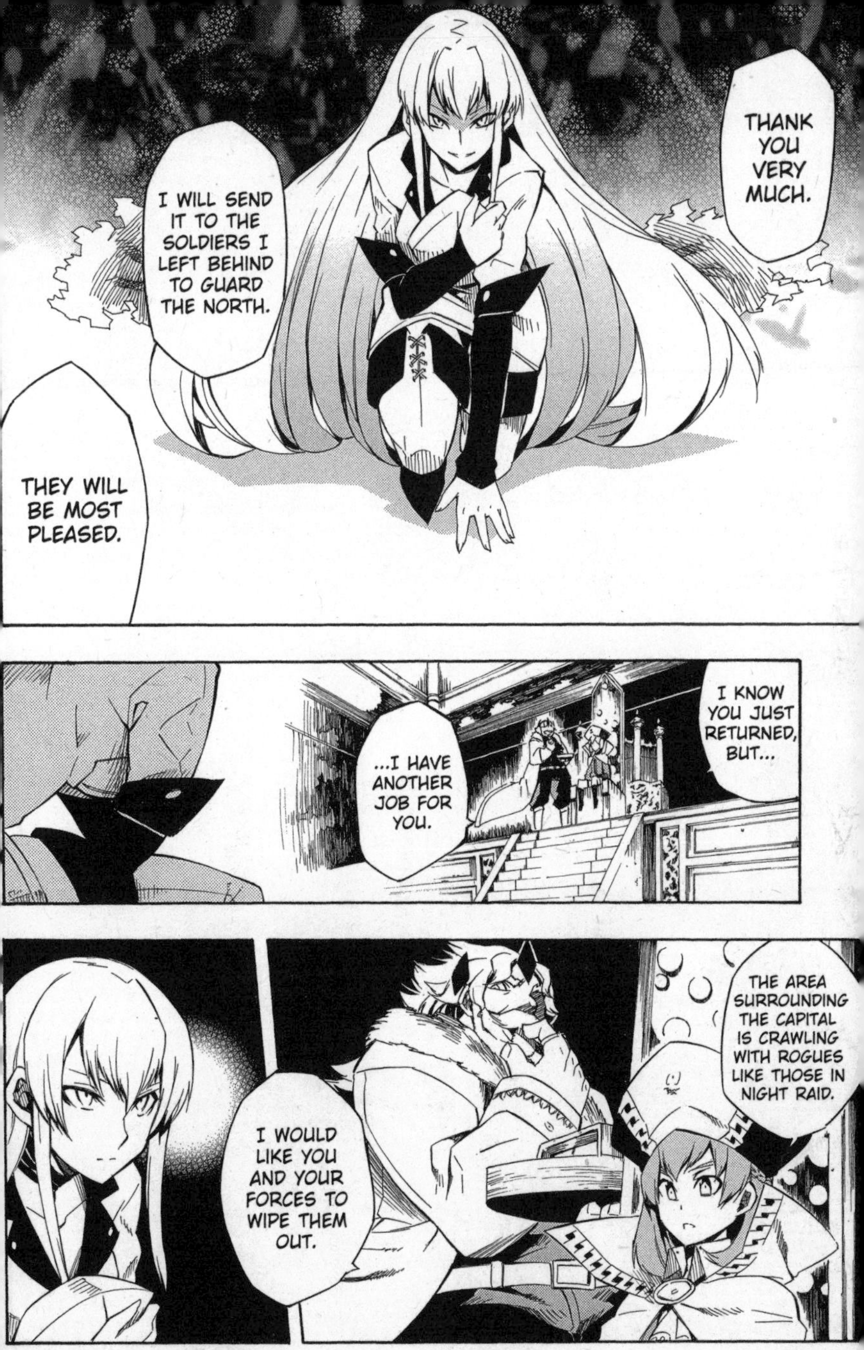
THANK YOU VERY MUCH.
I WILL SEND IT TO THE SOLDIERS I LEFT BEHIND TO GUARD THE NORTH.
THEY WILL BE MOST PLEASED.
I KNOW YOU JUST RETURNED, BUT...
...I HAVE ANOTHER JOB FOR YOU.
THE AREA SURROUNDING THE CAPITAL IS CRAWLING WITH ROGUES LIKE THOSE IN NIGHT RAID.
I WOULD LIKE YOU AND YOUR FORCES TO WIPE THEM OUT.

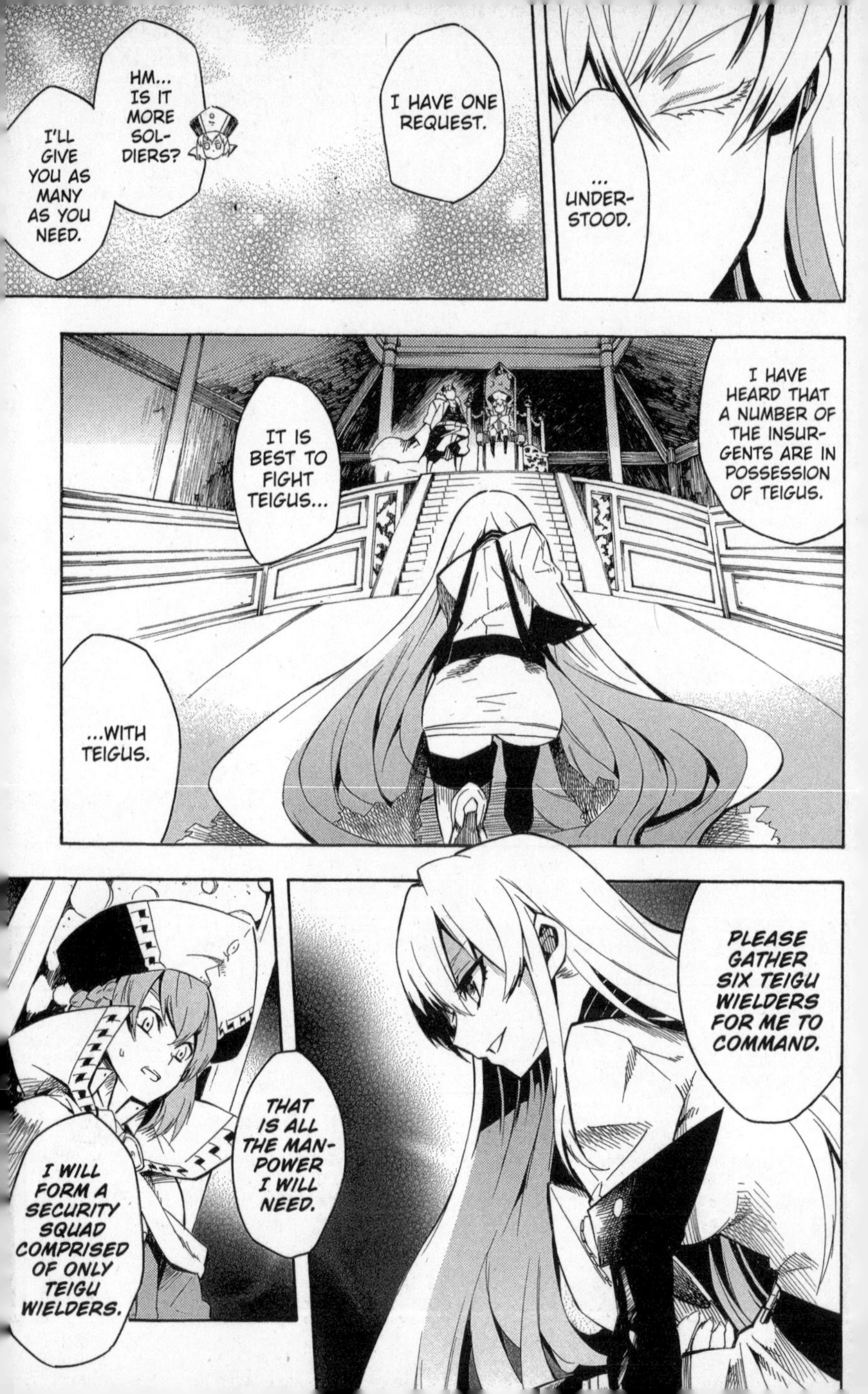

...UNDERSTOOD.
I HAVE ONE REQUEST.
HM... IS IT MORE SOLDIERS?
I'LL GIVE YOU AS MANY AS YOU NEED.
I HAVE HEARD THAT A NUMBER OF THE INSURGENTS ARE IN POSSESSION OF TEIGUS.
IT IS BEST TO FIGHT TEIGUS...
...WITH TEIGUS.
PLEASE GATHER SIX TEIGU WIELDERS FOR ME TO COMMAND.
THAT IS ALL THE MANPOWER I WILL NEED.
I WILL FORM A SECURITY SQUAD COMPRISED OF ONLY TEIGU WIELDERS.

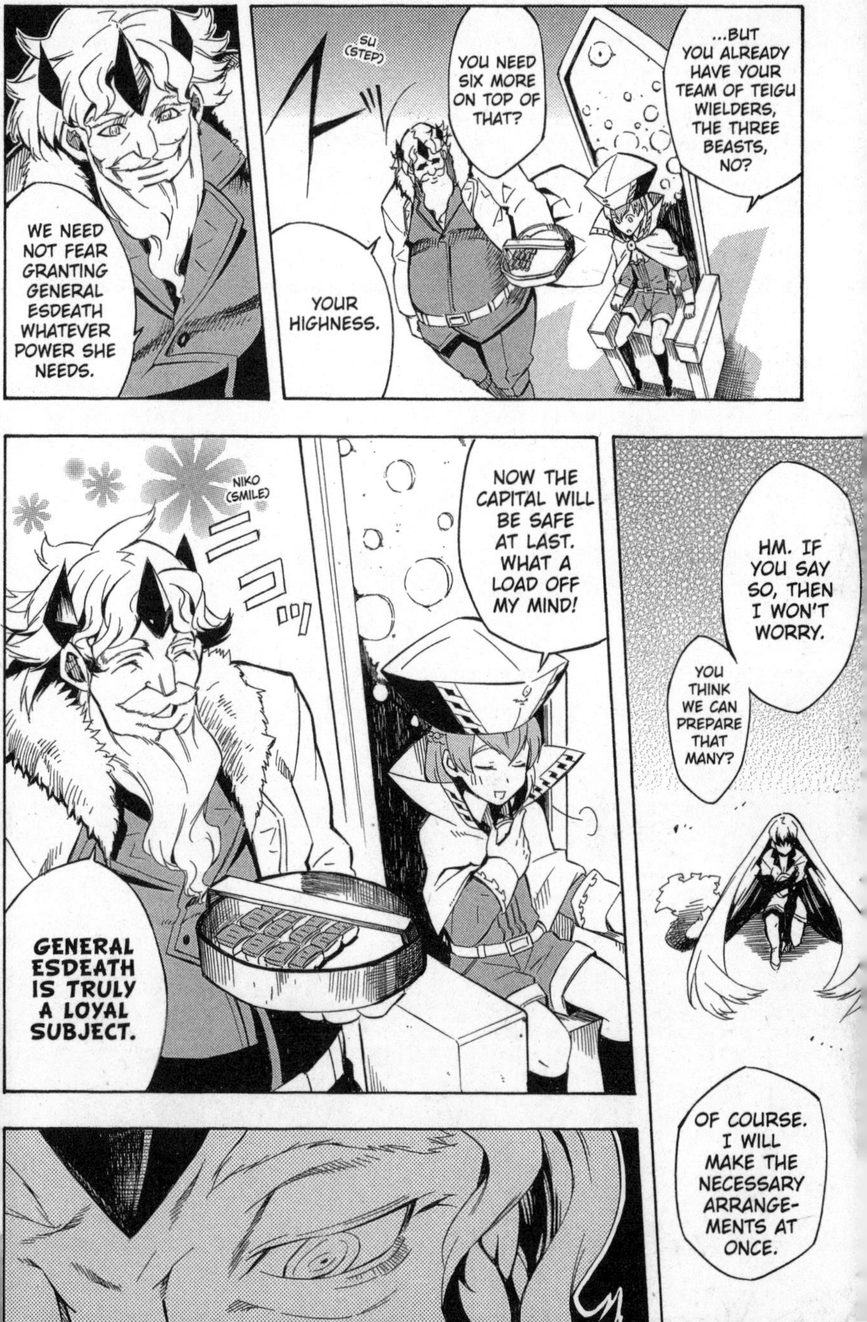
...BUT YOU ALREADY HAVE YOUR TEAM OF TEIGU WIELDERS, THE THREE BEASTS, NO?
YOU NEED SIX MORE ON TOP OF THAT?
SU (STEP)
YOUR HIGHNESS.
WE NEED NOT FEAR GRANTING GENERAL ESDEATH WHATEVER POWER SHE NEEDS.
HM. IF YOU SAY SO, THEN I WON'T WORRY.
YOU THINK WE CAN PREPARE THAT MANY?
OF COURSE. I WILL MAKE THE NECESSARY ARRANGEMENTS AT ONCE.
NOW THE CAPITAL WILL BE SAFE AT LAST. WHAT A LOAD OFF MY MIND!
NIKO (SMILE)
GENERAL ESDEATH IS TRULY A LOYAL SUBJECT.

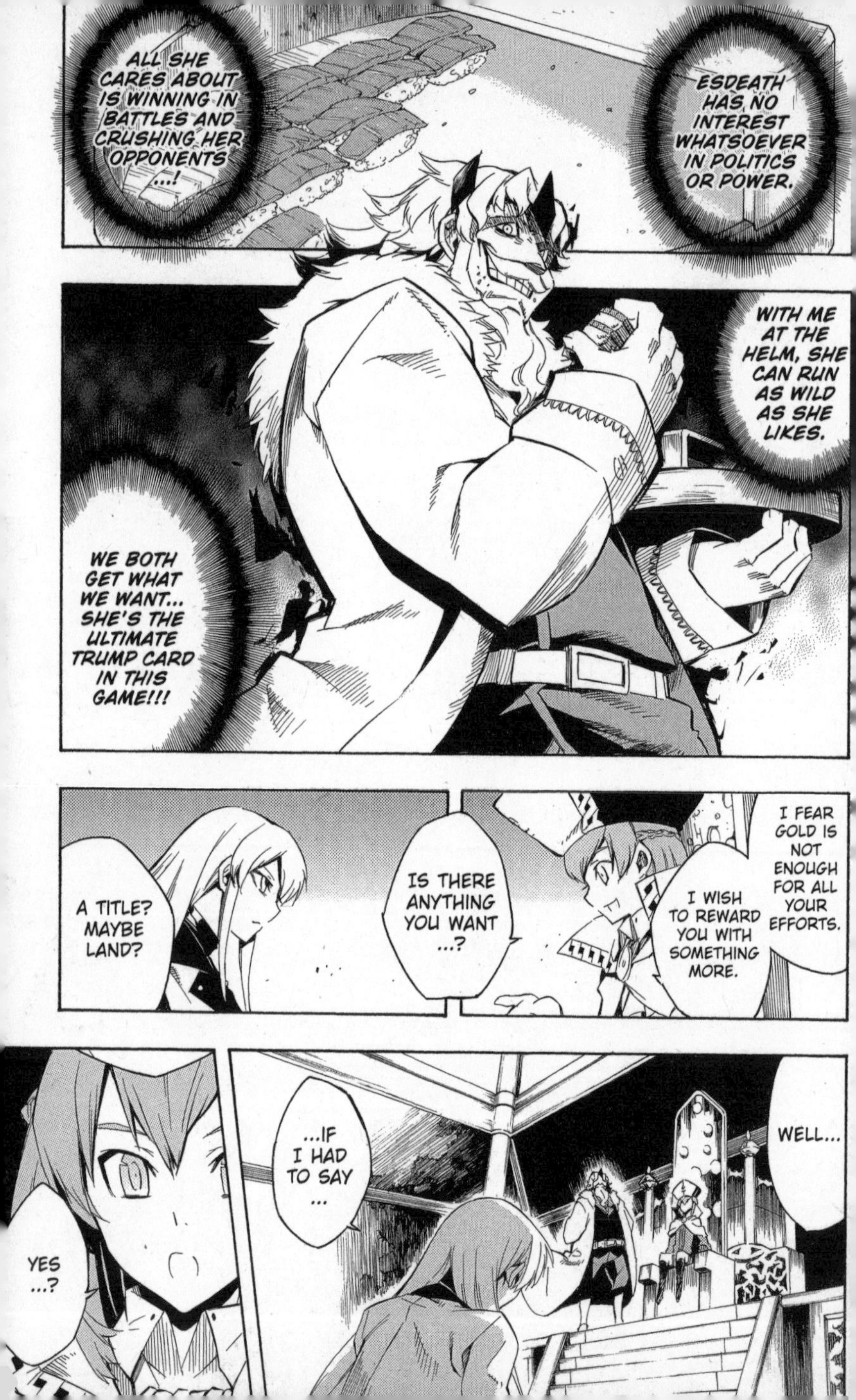
ESDEATH HAS NO INTEREST WHATSOEVER IN POLITICS OR POWER.
ALL SHE CARES ABOUT IS WINNING IN BATTLES AND CRUSHING HER OPPONENTS ...!
WITH ME AT THE HELM, SHE CAN RUN AS WILD AS SHE LIKES.
WE BOTH GET WHAT WE WANT... SHE'S THE ULTIMATE TRUMP CARD IN THIS GAME!!!
I FEAR GOLD IS NOT ENOUGH FOR ALL YOUR EFFORTS.
I WISH TO REWARD YOU WITH SOMETHING MORE.
IS THERE ANYTHING YOU WANT ...?
A TITLE? MAYBE LAND?
WELL...
...IF I HAD TO SAY ...
YES ...?

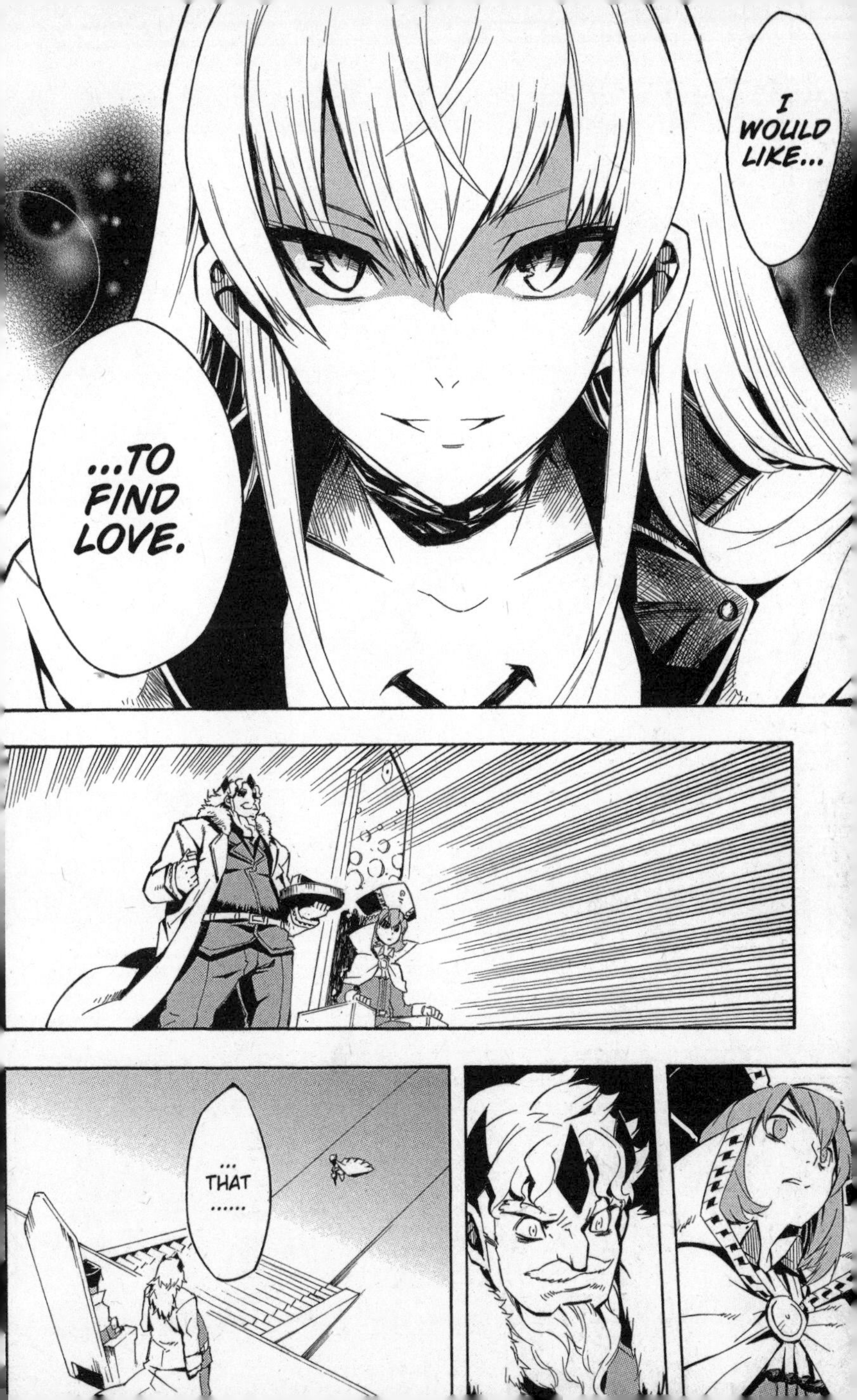
I WOULD LIKE...
...TO FIND LOVE.
... THAT ......

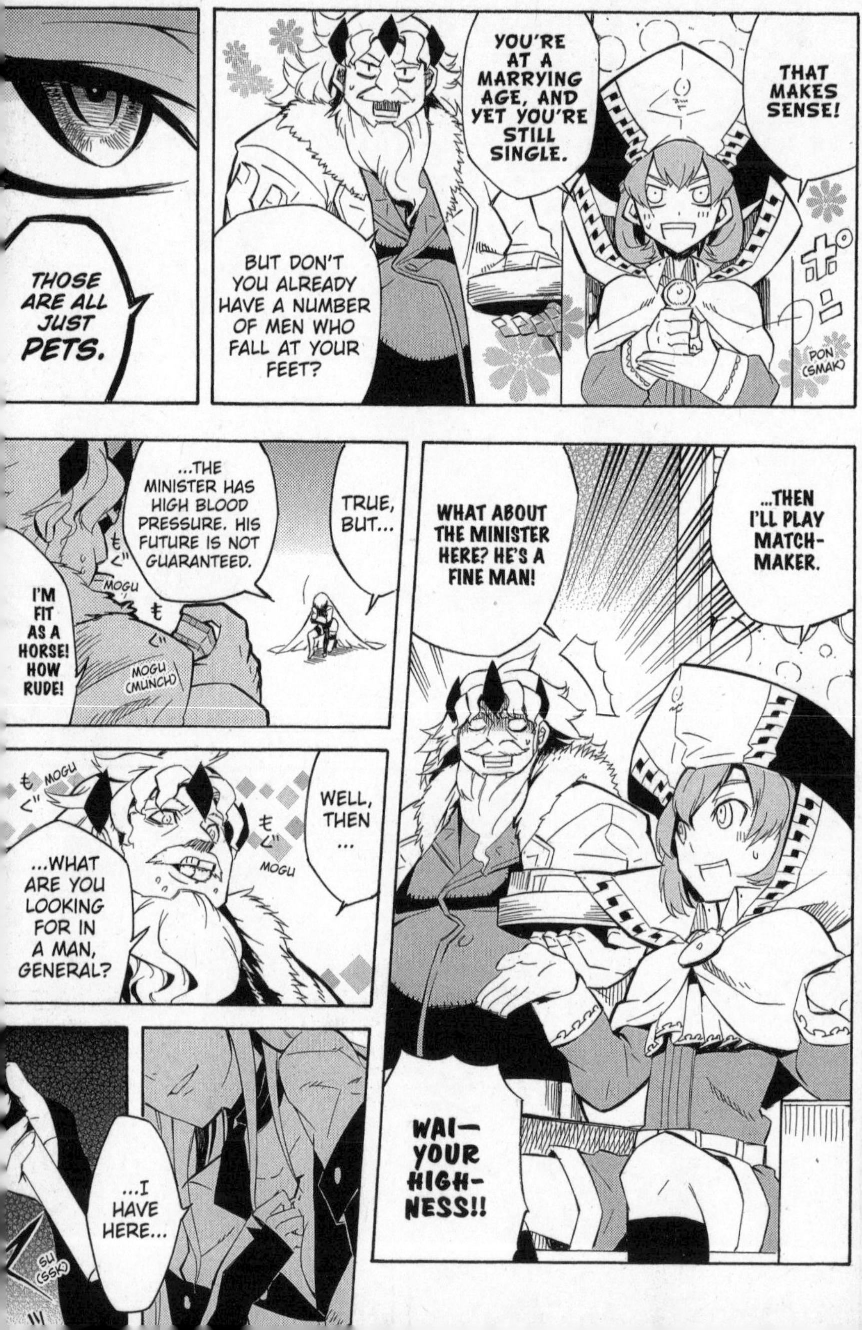
THAT MAKES SENSE!
PON (SMAK)
YOU'RE AT A MARRYING AGE, AND YET YOU'RE STILL SINGLE.
BUT DON'T YOU ALREADY HAVE A NUMBER OF MEN WHO FALL AT YOUR FEET?
THOSE ARE ALL JUST PETS.
...THEN I'LL PLAY MATCH-MAKER.
WHAT ABOUT THE MINISTER HERE? HE'S A FINE MAN!
WAI— YOUR HIGH-NESS!!
TRUE, BUT...
...THE MINISTER HAS HIGH BLOOD PRESSURE. HIS FUTURE IS NOT GUARANTEED.
MOGU
I'M FIT AS A HORSE! HOW RUDE!
MOGU (MUNCH)
WELL, THEN...
MOGU
MOGU
...WHAT ARE YOU LOOKING FOR IN A MAN, GENERAL?
...I HAVE HERE...
SU (SSK)

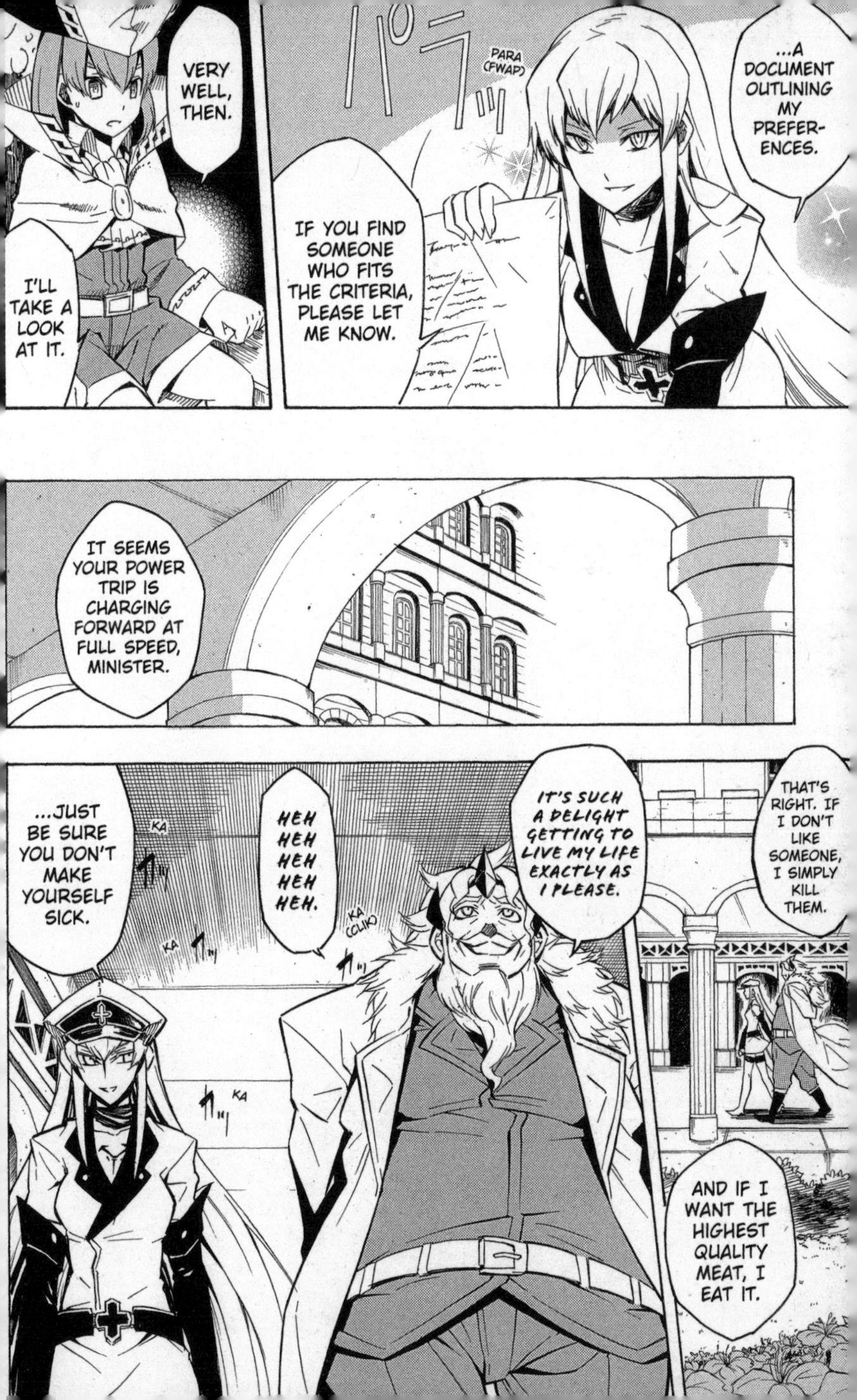
PARA (FWAP)
...A DOCUMENT OUTLINING MY PREFERENCES.
IF YOU FIND SOMEONE WHO FITS THE CRITERIA, PLEASE LET ME KNOW.
VERY WELL, THEN.
I'LL TAKE A LOOK AT IT.
IT SEEMS YOUR POWER TRIP IS CHARGING FORWARD AT FULL SPEED, MINISTER.
THAT'S RIGHT. IF I DON'T LIKE SOMEONE, I SIMPLY KILL THEM.
AND IF I WANT THE HIGHEST QUALITY MEAT, I EAT IT.
IT'S SUCH A DELIGHT GETTING TO LIVE MY LIFE EXACTLY AS I PLEASE.
KA (CLIK)
HEH HEH HEH HEH HEH.
KA
KA
KA
...JUST BE SURE YOU DON'T MAKE YOURSELF SICK.

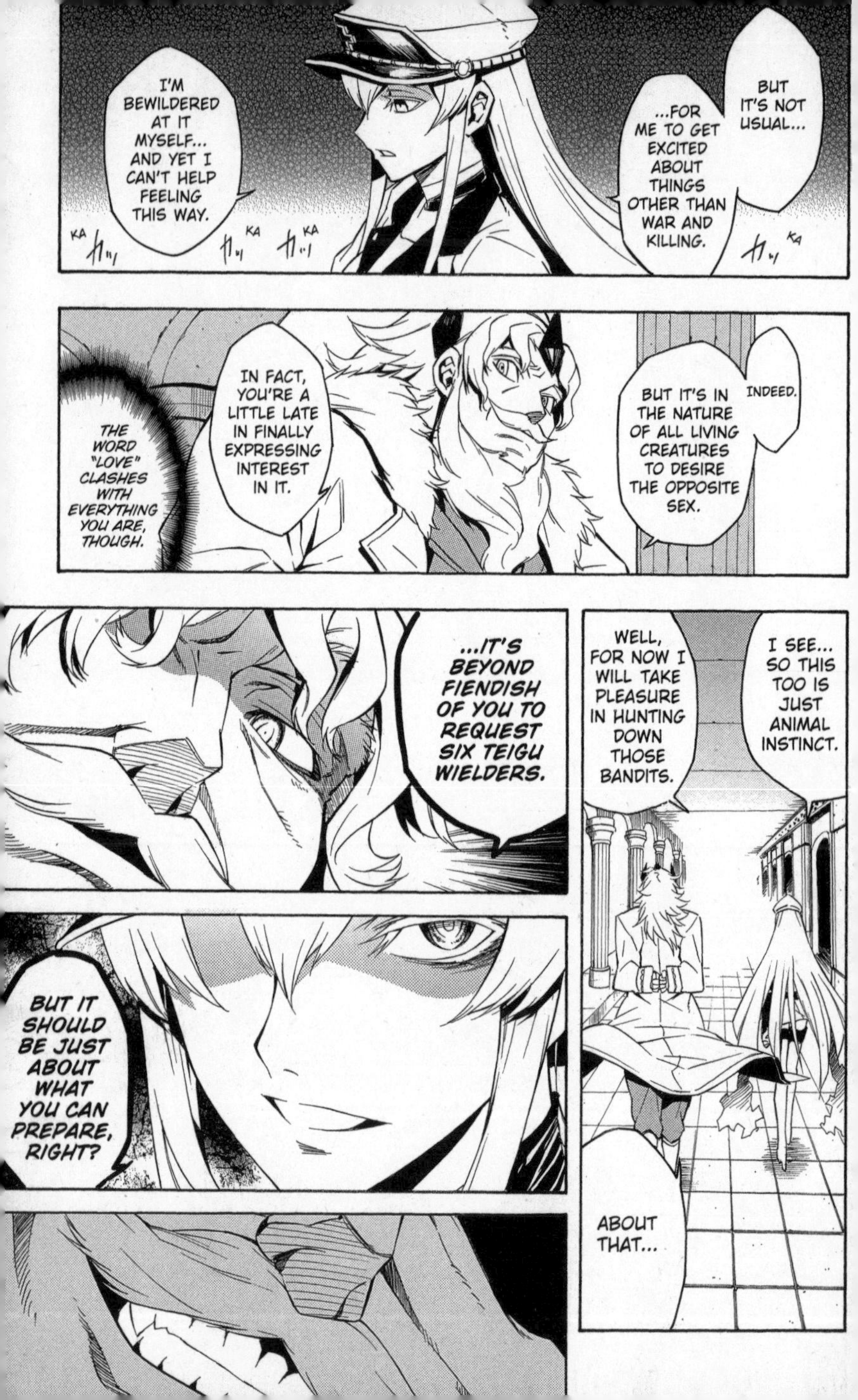
BUT IT'S NOT USUAL...
...FOR ME TO GET EXCITED ABOUT THINGS OTHER THAN WAR AND KILLING.
KA
I'M BEWILDERED AT IT MYSELF... AND YET I CAN'T HELP FEELING THIS WAY.
KA
KA
KA
INDEED.
BUT IT'S IN THE NATURE OF ALL LIVING CREATURES TO DESIRE THE OPPOSITE SEX.
IN FACT, YOU'RE A LITTLE LATE IN FINALLY EXPRESSING INTEREST IN IT.
THE WORD "LOVE" CLASHES WITH EVERYTHING YOU ARE, THOUGH.
I SEE... SO THIS TOO IS JUST ANIMAL INSTINCT.
WELL, FOR NOW I WILL TAKE PLEASURE IN HUNTING DOWN THOSE BANDITS.
ABOUT THAT...
...IT'S BEYOND FIENDISH OF YOU TO REQUEST SIX TEIGU WIELDERS.
BUT IT SHOULD BE JUST ABOUT WHAT YOU CAN PREPARE, RIGHT?

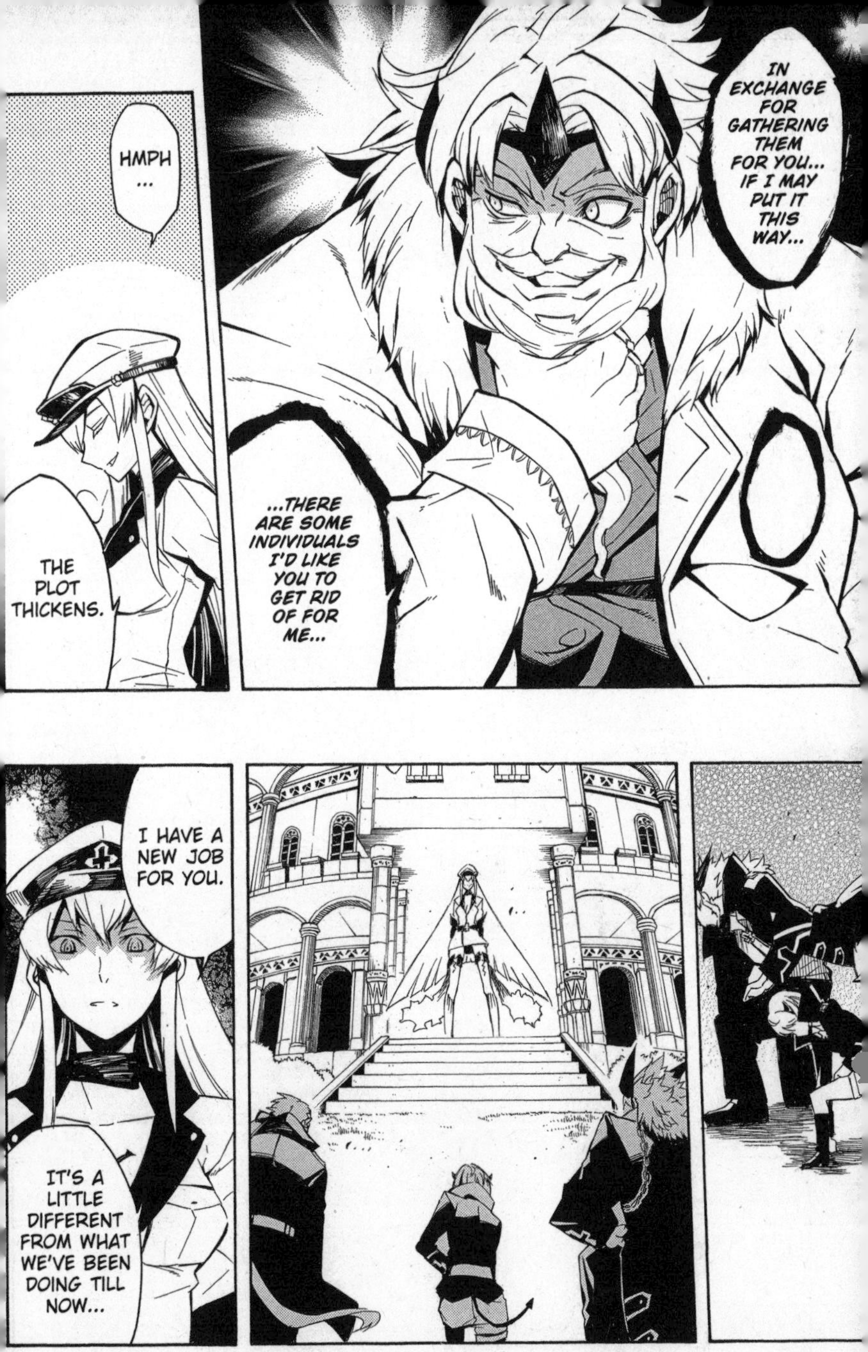
IN EXCHANGE FOR GATHERING THEM FOR YOU... IF I MAY PUT IT THIS WAY...
...THERE ARE SOME INDIVIDUALS I'D LIKE YOU TO GET RID OF FOR ME...
HMPH...
THE PLOT THICKENS.
...
I HAVE A NEW JOB FOR YOU.
IT'S A LITTLE DIFFERENT FROM WHAT WE'VE BEEN DOING TILL NOW...

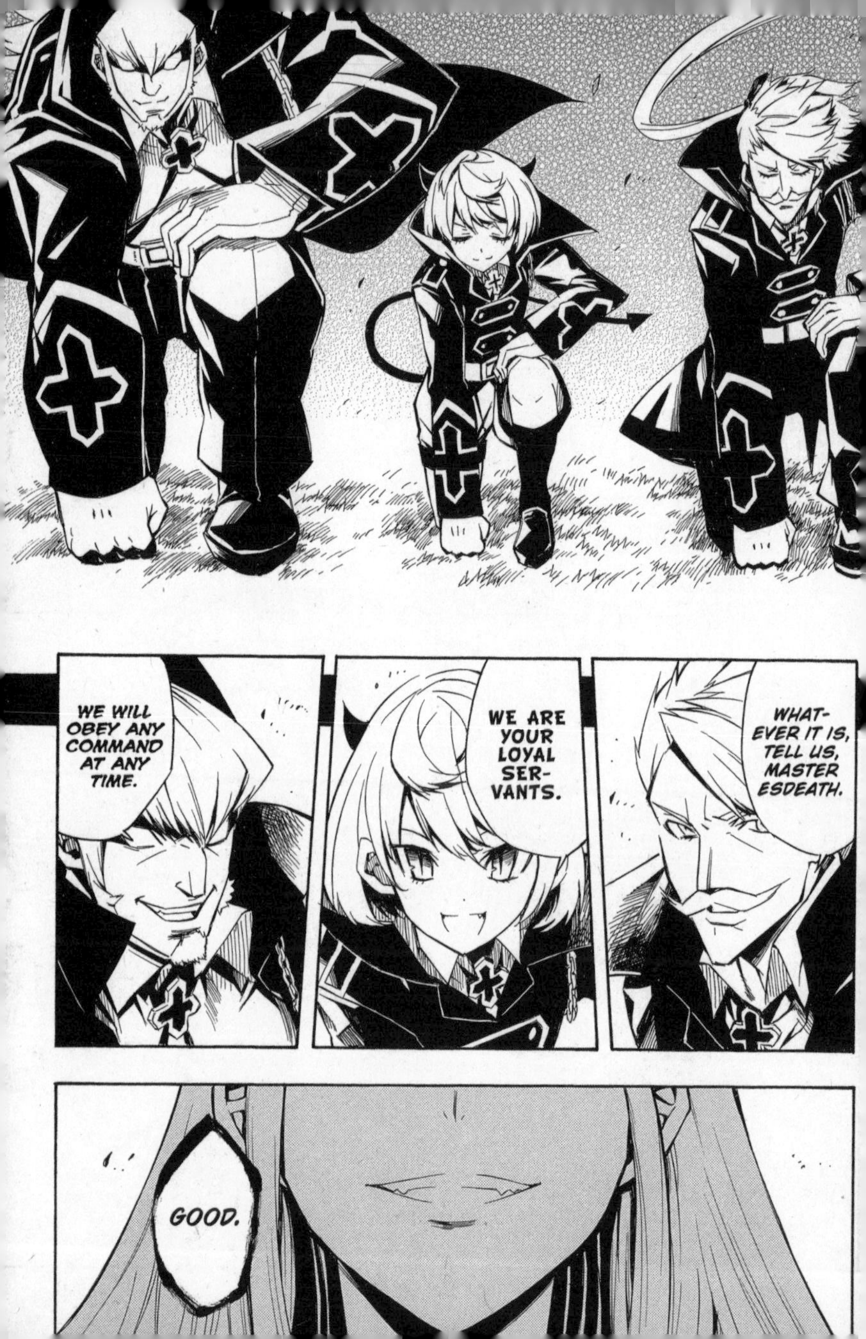
WHATEVER IT IS, TELL US, MASTER ESDEATH.
WE ARE YOUR LOYAL SERVANTS.
WE WILL OBEY ANY COMMAND AT ANY TIME.
GOOD.

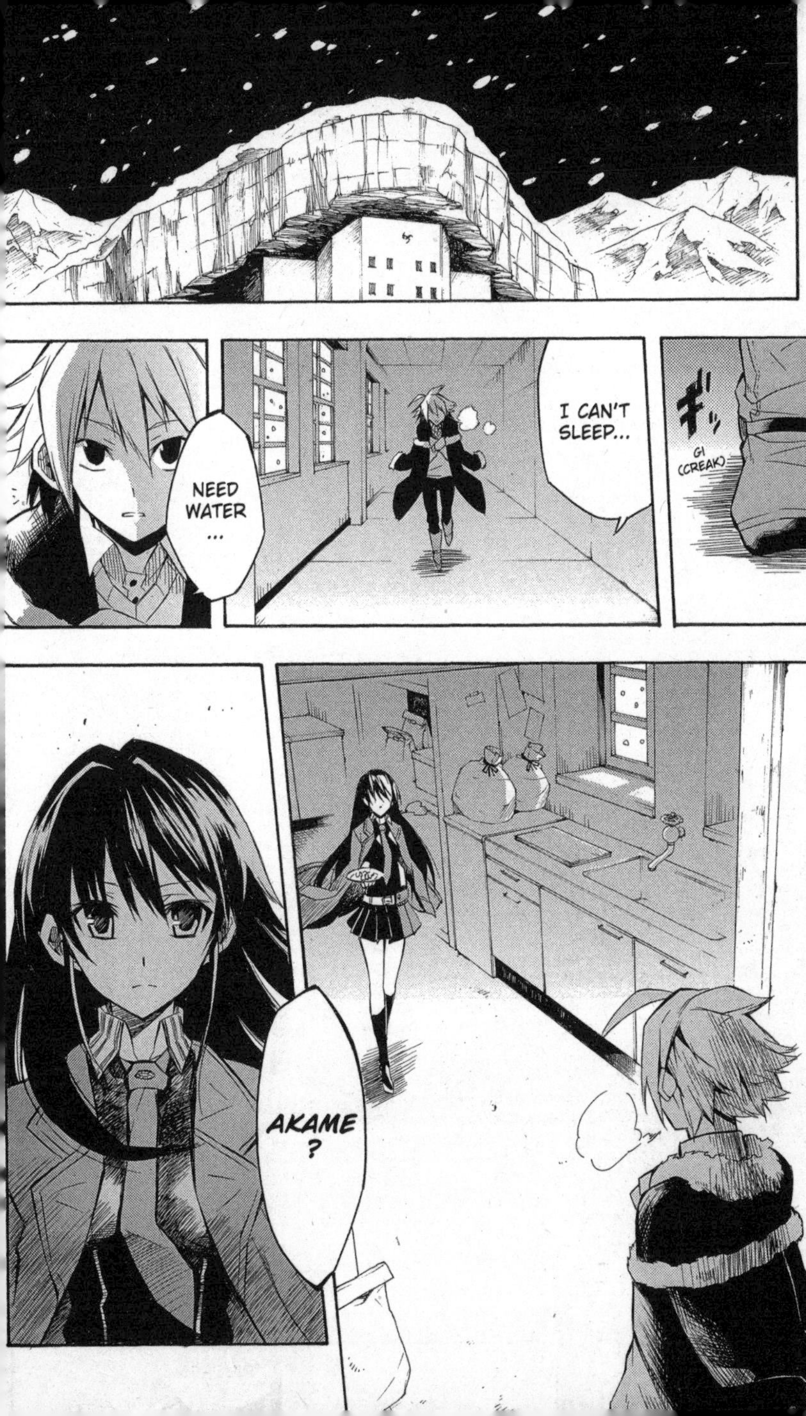
ギッ
GI (CREAK)
I CAN'T SLEEP...
NEED WATER ...
AKAME ?
...

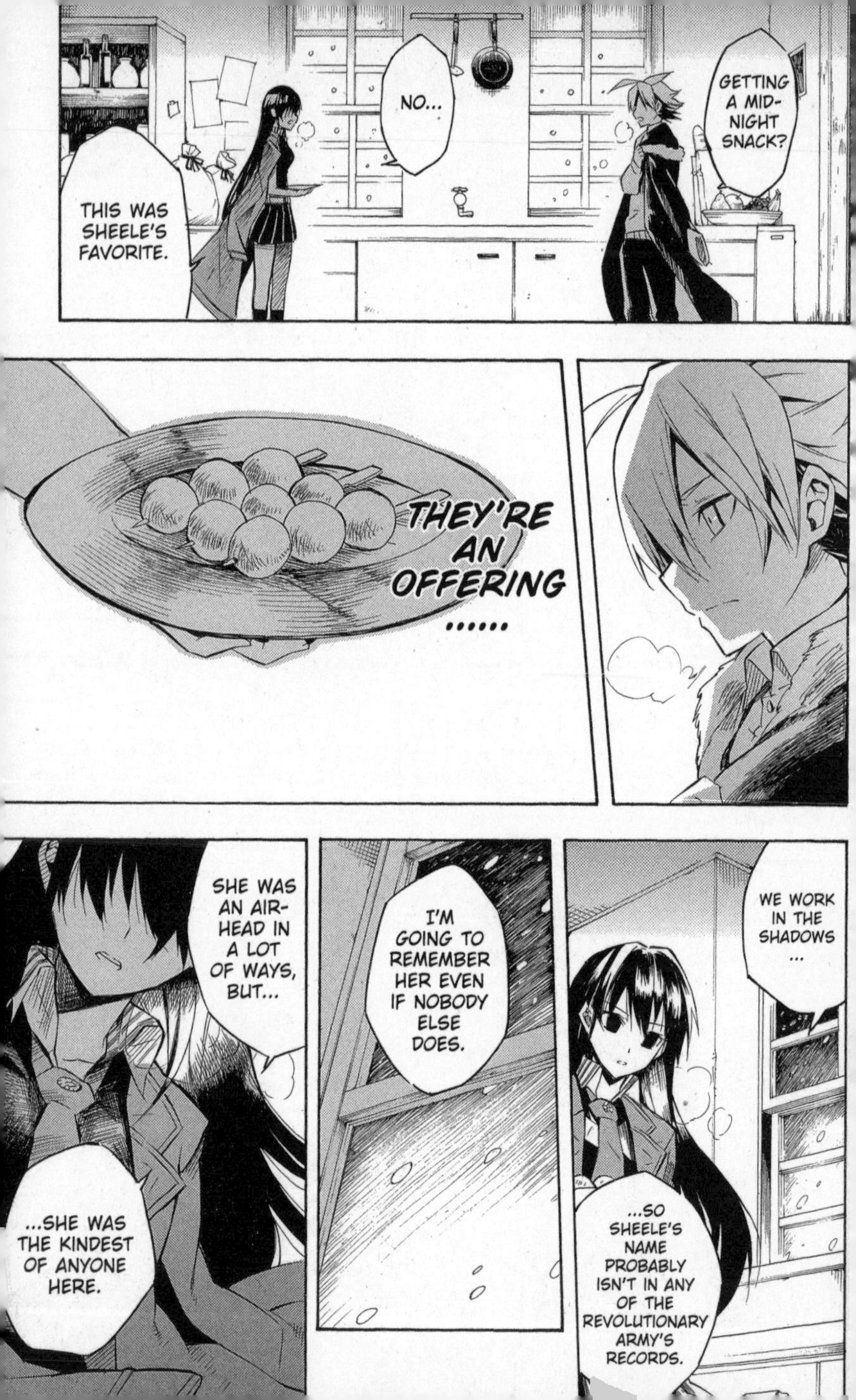
GETTING A MID-NIGHT SNACK?
NO...
THIS WAS SHEELE'S FAVORITE.
THEY'RE AN OFFERING......
WE WORK IN THE SHADOWS...
...SO SHEELE'S NAME PROBABLY ISN'T IN ANY OF THE REVOLUTIONARY ARMY'S RECORDS.
I'M GOING TO REMEMBER HER EVEN IF NOBODY ELSE DOES.
SHE WAS AN AIR-HEAD IN A LOT OF WAYS, BUT...
...SHE WAS THE KINDEST OF ANYONE HERE.

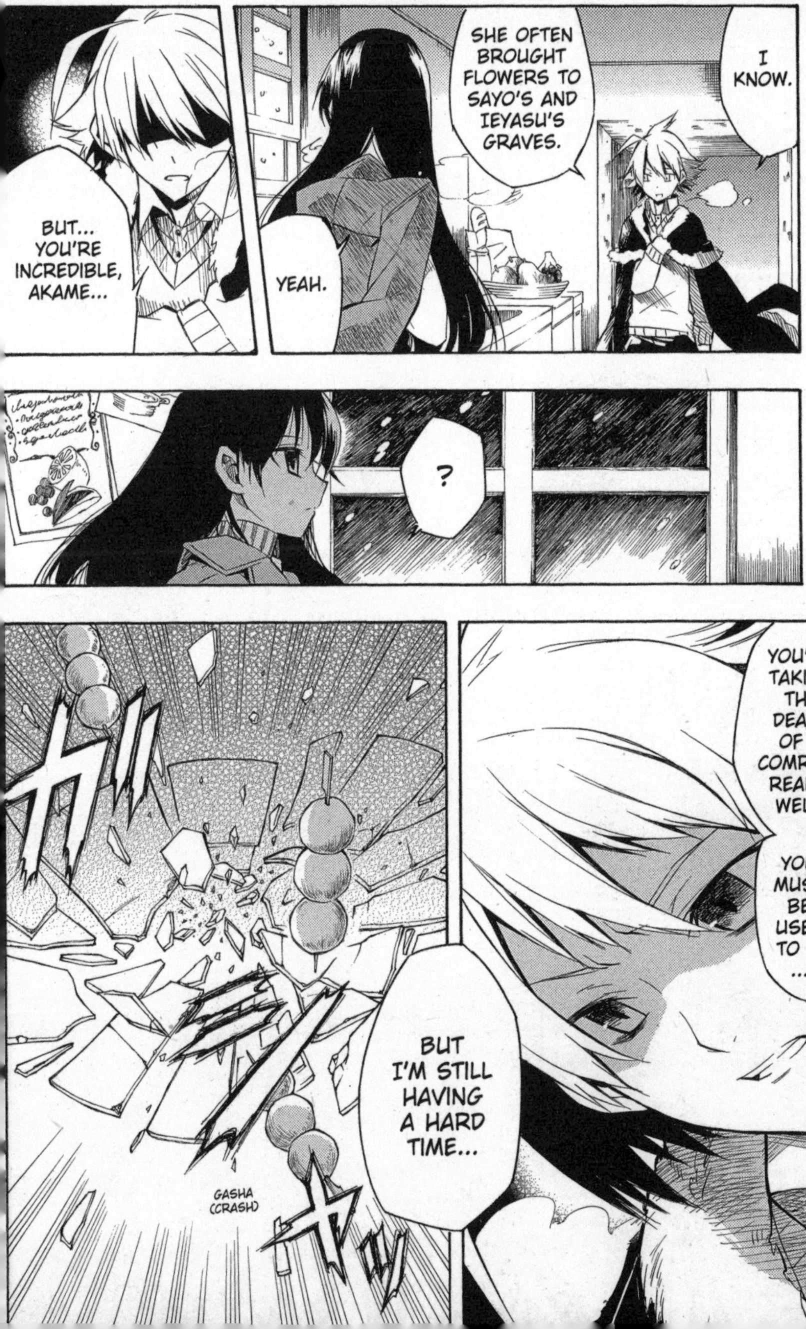
I KNOW.
SHE OFTEN BROUGHT FLOWERS TO SAYO'S AND IEYASU'S GRAVES.
YEAH.
BUT... YOU'RE INCREDIBLE, AKAME...
?
YOU'RE TAKING THE DEATH OF A COMRADE REALLY WELL.
YOU MUST BE USED TO IT ...
BUT I'M STILL HAVING A HARD TIME...
GASHA (CRASH)

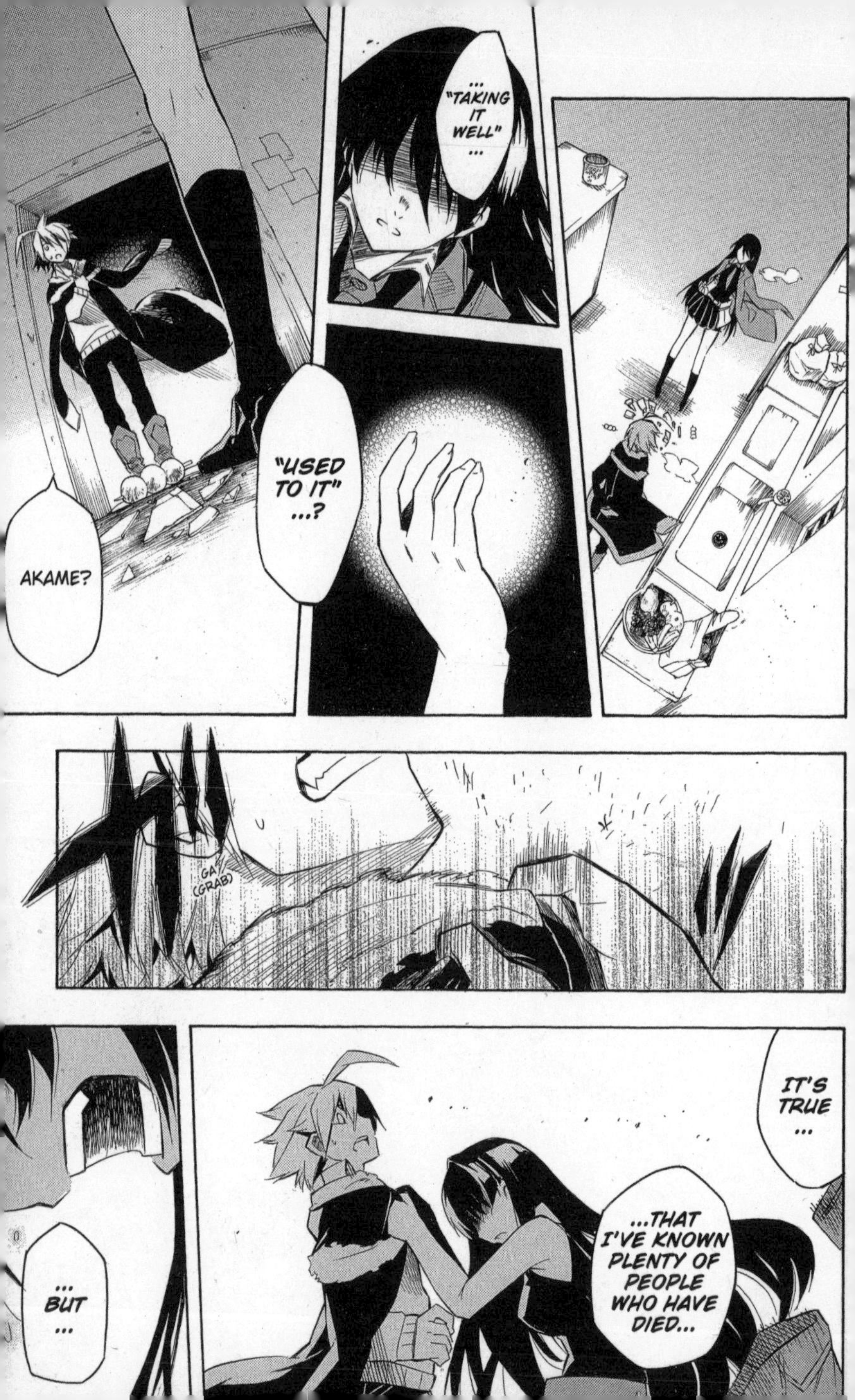
..."TAKING IT WELL"...
"USED TO IT" ...?
AKAME?
GA (GRAB)
IT'S TRUE...
...THAT I'VE KNOWN PLENTY OF PEOPLE WHO HAVE DIED...
...BUT...

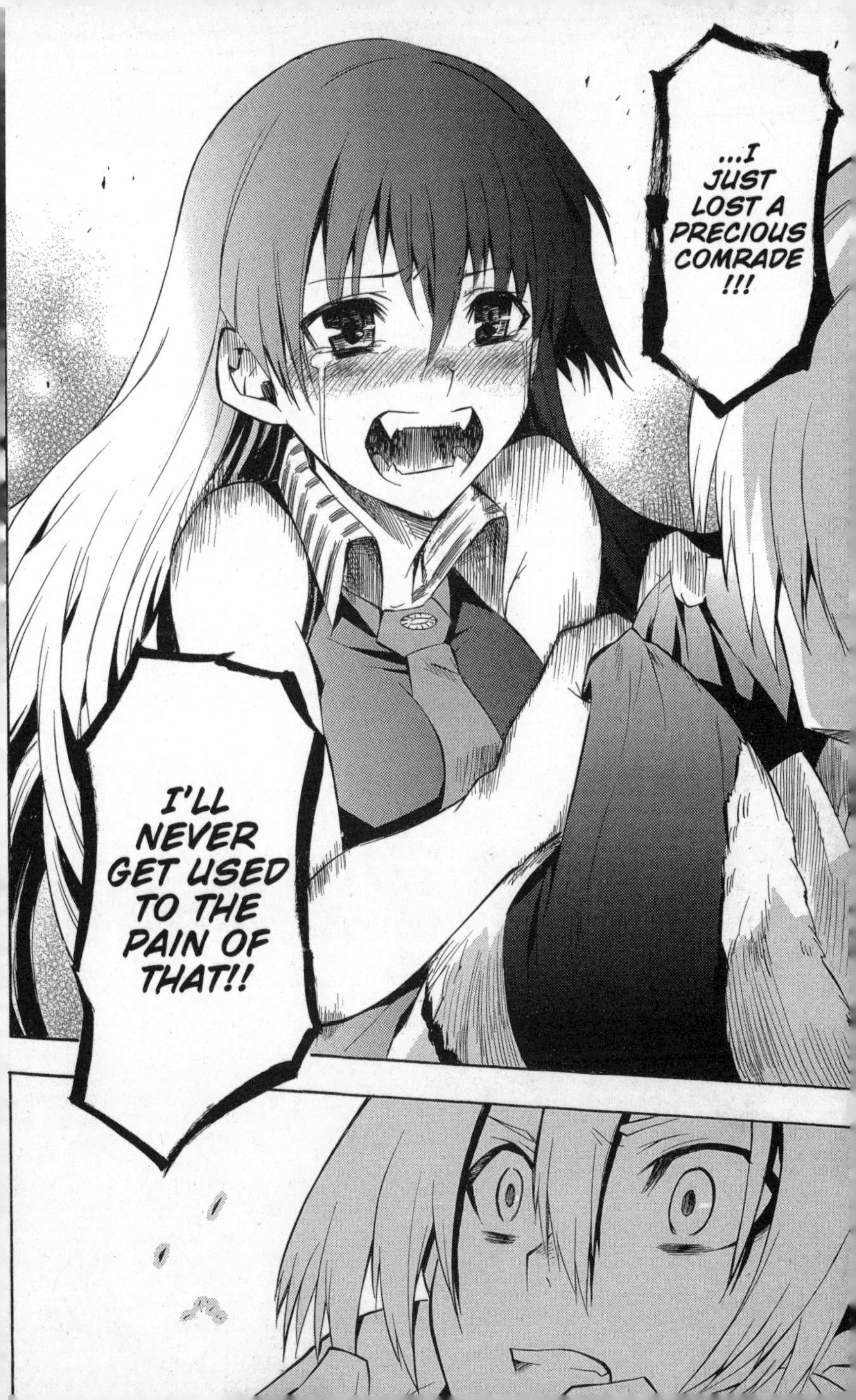
...I JUST LOST A PRECIOUS COMRADE!!!
I'LL NEVER GET USED TO THE PAIN OF THAT!!

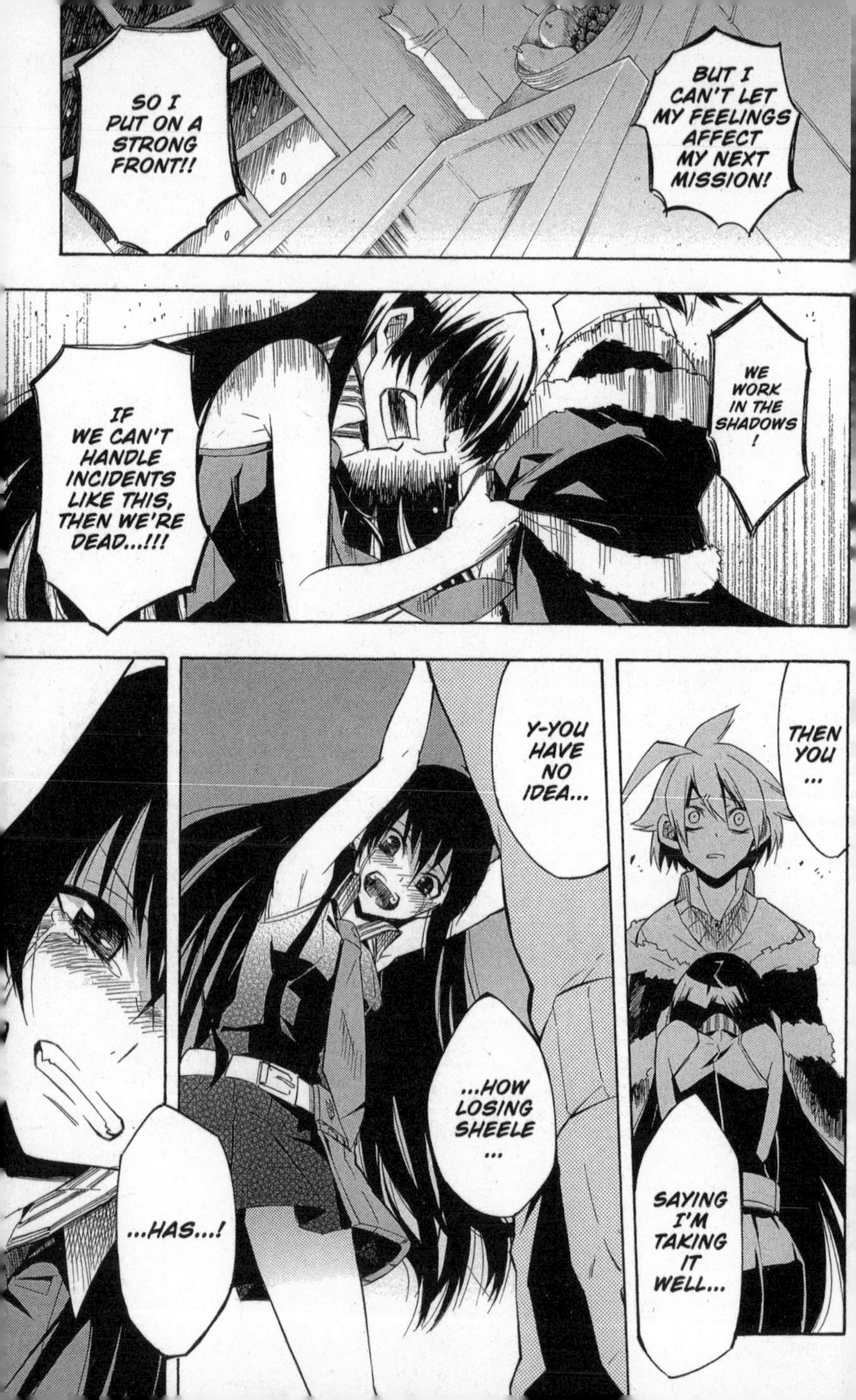
BUT I CAN'T LET MY FEELINGS AFFECT MY NEXT MISSION!
SO I PUT ON A STRONG FRONT!!
WE WORK IN THE SHADOWS!
IF WE CAN'T HANDLE INCIDENTS LIKE THIS, THEN WE'RE DEAD...!!!
THEN YOU...
SAYING I'M TAKING IT WELL...
Y-YOU HAVE NO IDEA...
...HOW LOSING SHEELE...
...HAS...!

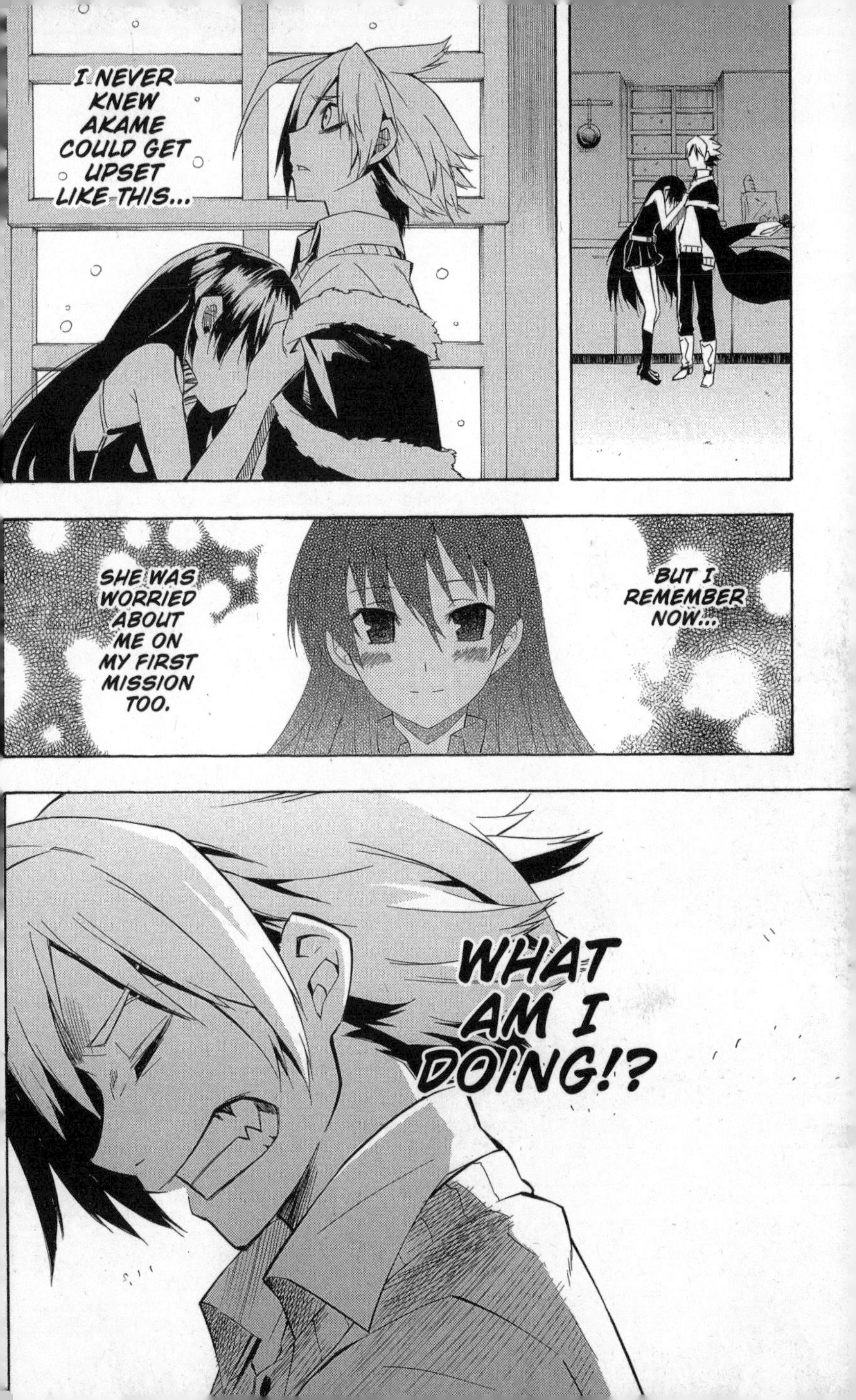
I NEVER KNEW AKAME COULD GET UPSET LIKE THIS...
BUT I REMEMBER NOW...
SHE WAS WORRIED ABOUT ME ON MY FIRST MISSION TOO.
WHAT AM I DOING!?

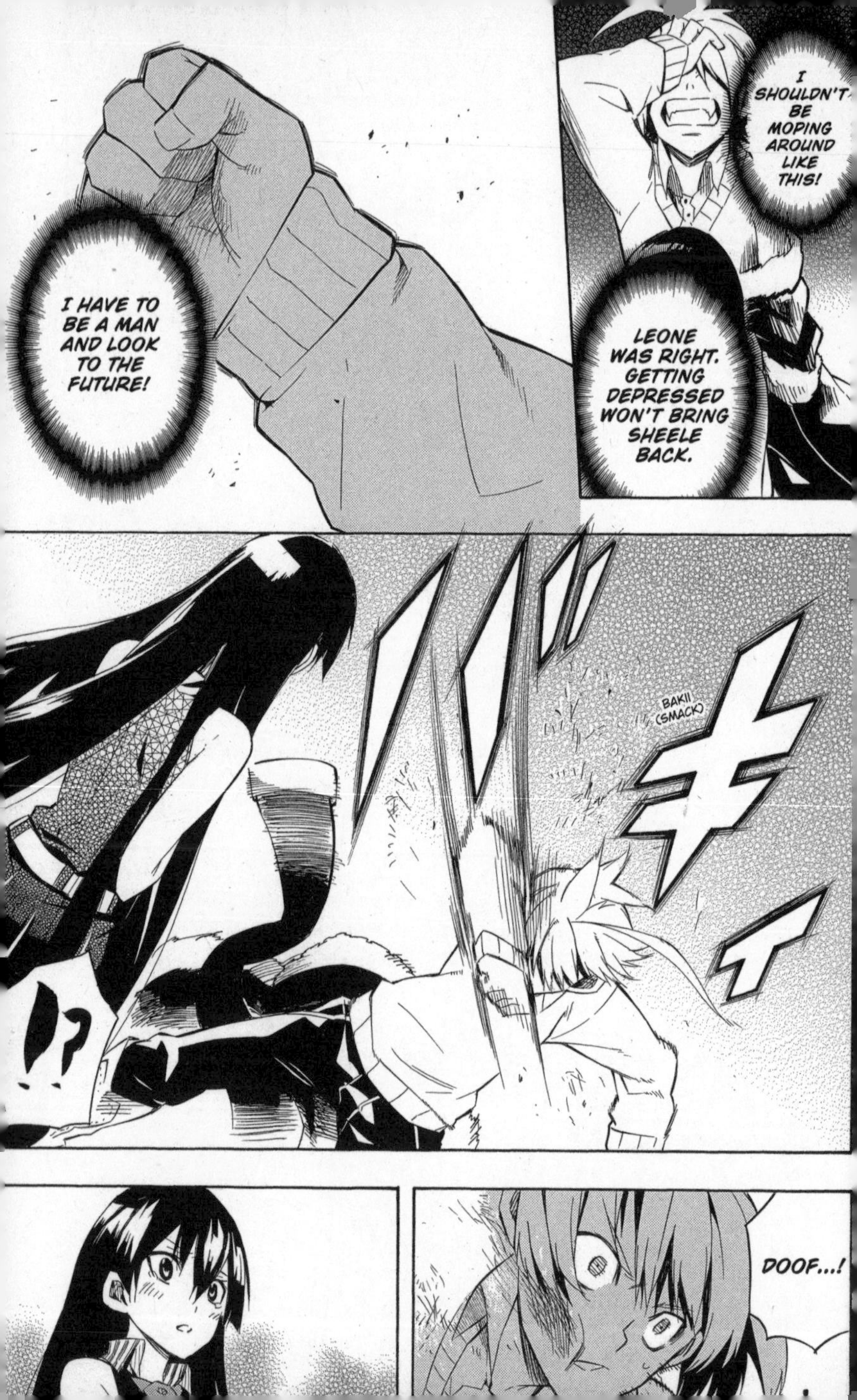
I SHOULDN'T BE MOPING AROUND LIKE THIS!
LEONE WAS RIGHT. GETTING DEPRESSED WON'T BRING SHEELE BACK.
I HAVE TO BE A MAN AND LOOK TO THE FUTURE!
BAKII (SMACK)
!?
DOOF...!

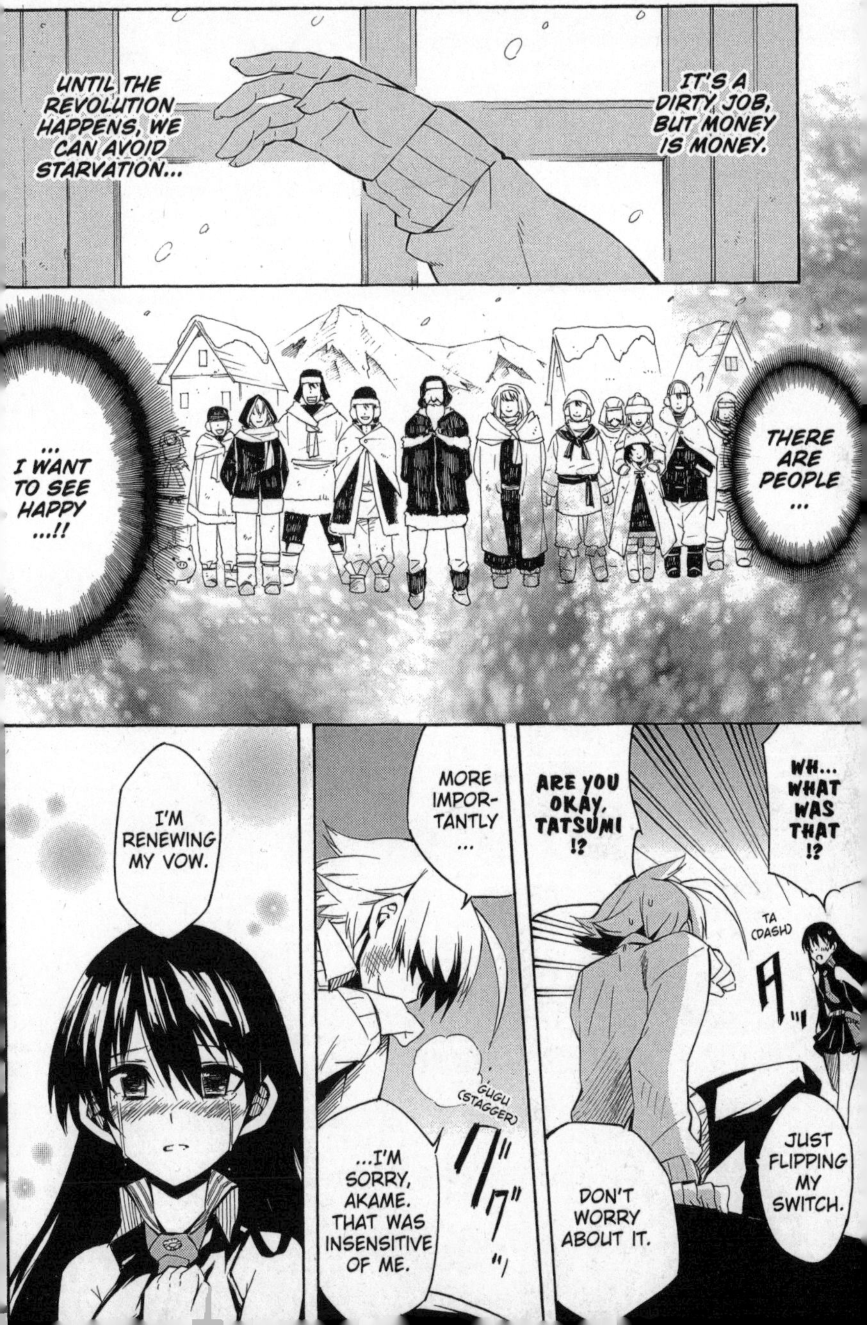
IT'S A DIRTY JOB, BUT MONEY IS MONEY.
UNTIL THE REVOLUTION HAPPENS, WE CAN AVOID STARVATION...
THERE ARE PEOPLE ...
... I WANT TO SEE HAPPY ...!!
WH... WHAT WAS THAT !?
ARE YOU OKAY, TATSUMI !?
TA (DASH)
JUST FLIPPING MY SWITCH.
DON'T WORRY ABOUT IT.
MORE IMPOR-TANTLY ...
GUGU (STAGGER)
...I'M SORRY, AKAME. THAT WAS INSENSITIVE OF ME.
I'M RENEWING MY VOW.

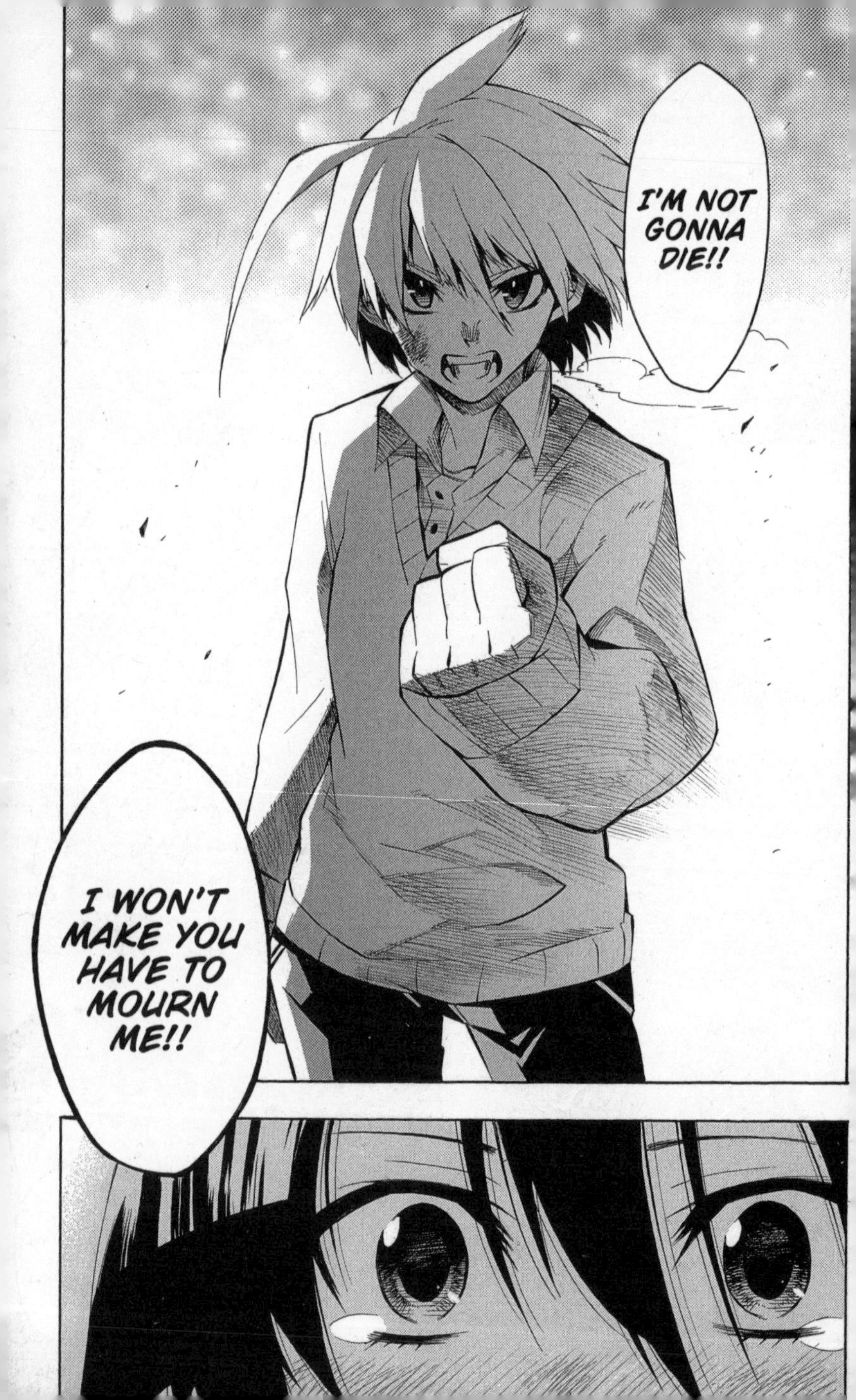
I'M NOT GONNA DIE!!
I WON'T MAKE YOU HAVE TO MOURN ME!!

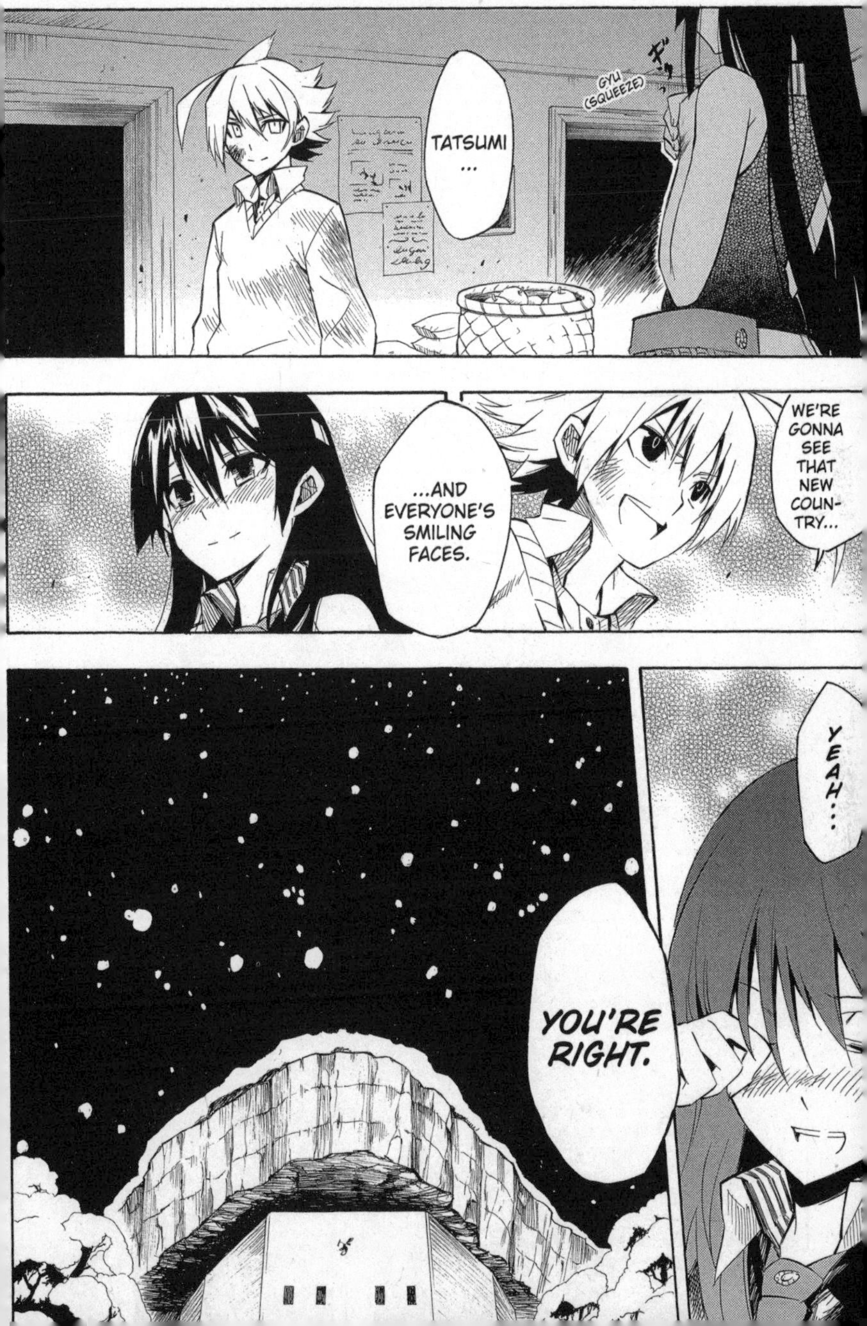
GYU (SQUEEZE)
TATSUMI ...
WE'RE GONNA SEE THAT NEW COUNTRY...
...AND EVERYONE'S SMILING FACES.
YEAH...
YOU'RE RIGHT.

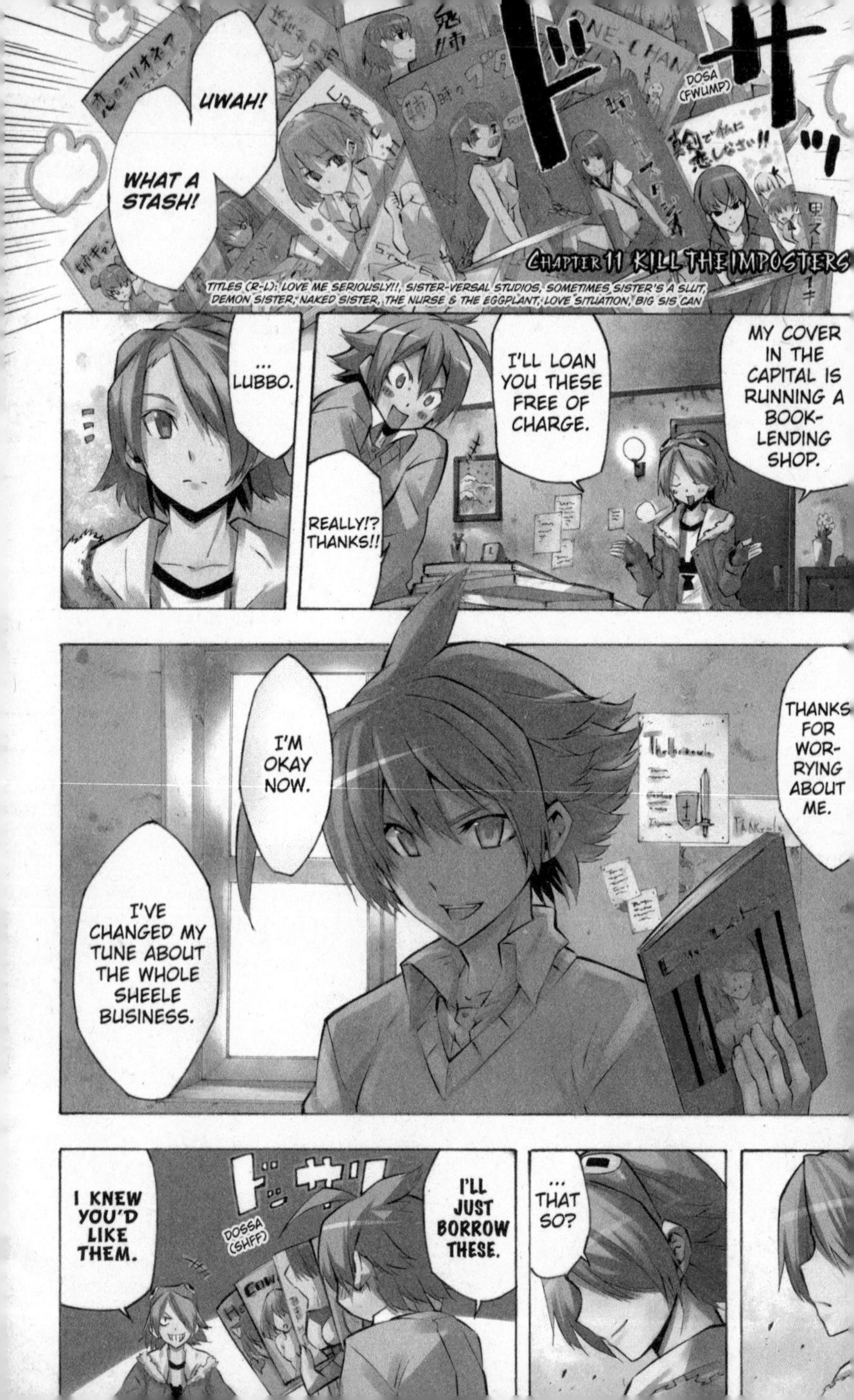
DOSA (FWUMP)
UWAH!
WHAT A STASH!
CHAPTER 11 KILL THE IMPOSTERS
TITLES (R-L): LOVE ME SERIOUSLY!!, SISTER-VERSAL STUDIOS, SOMETIMES SISTER'S A SLUT, DEMON SISTER, NAKED SISTER, THE NURSE & THE EGGPLANT, LOVE SITUATION, BIG SIS CAN
MY COVER IN THE CAPITAL IS RUNNING A BOOK-LENDING SHOP.
I'LL LOAN YOU THESE FREE OF CHARGE.
REALLY!? THANKS!!
... LUBBO.
THANKS FOR WORRYING ABOUT ME.
I'M OKAY NOW.
I'VE CHANGED MY TUNE ABOUT THE WHOLE SHEELE BUSINESS.
... THAT SO?
I'LL JUST BORROW THESE.
DOSSA (SHFF)
I KNEW YOU'D LIKE THEM.

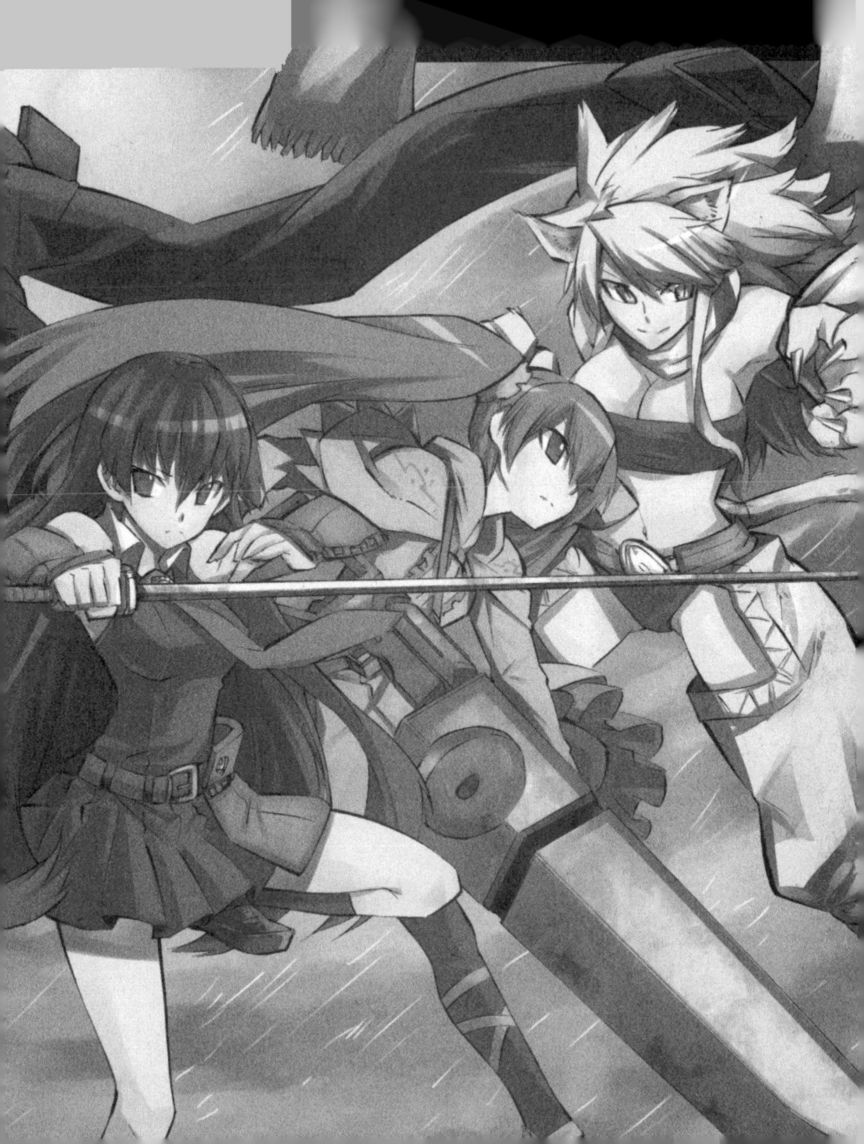

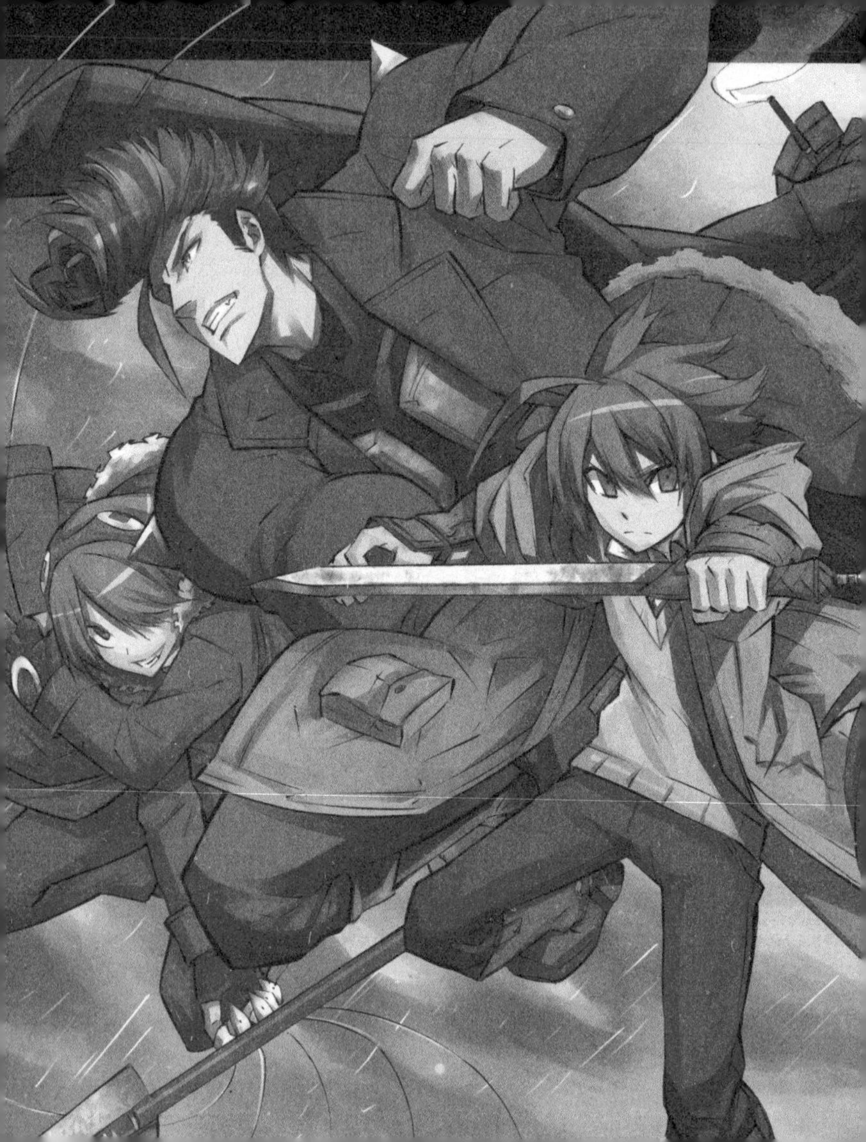

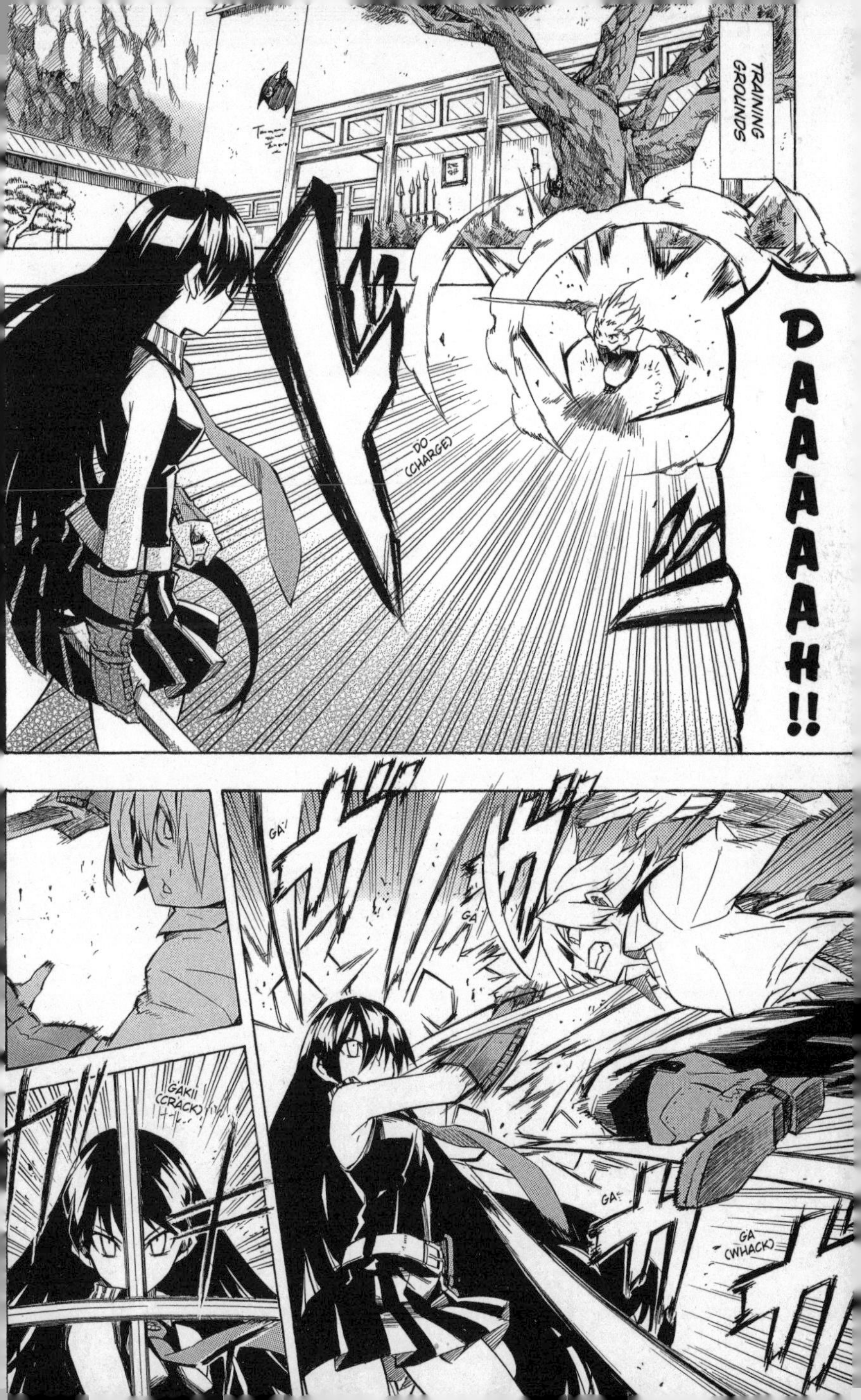
TRAINING GROUNDS
DAAAAAAH!!
DO (CHARGE)
GA
GA
GAKII (CRACK)
GA
GA (WHACK)

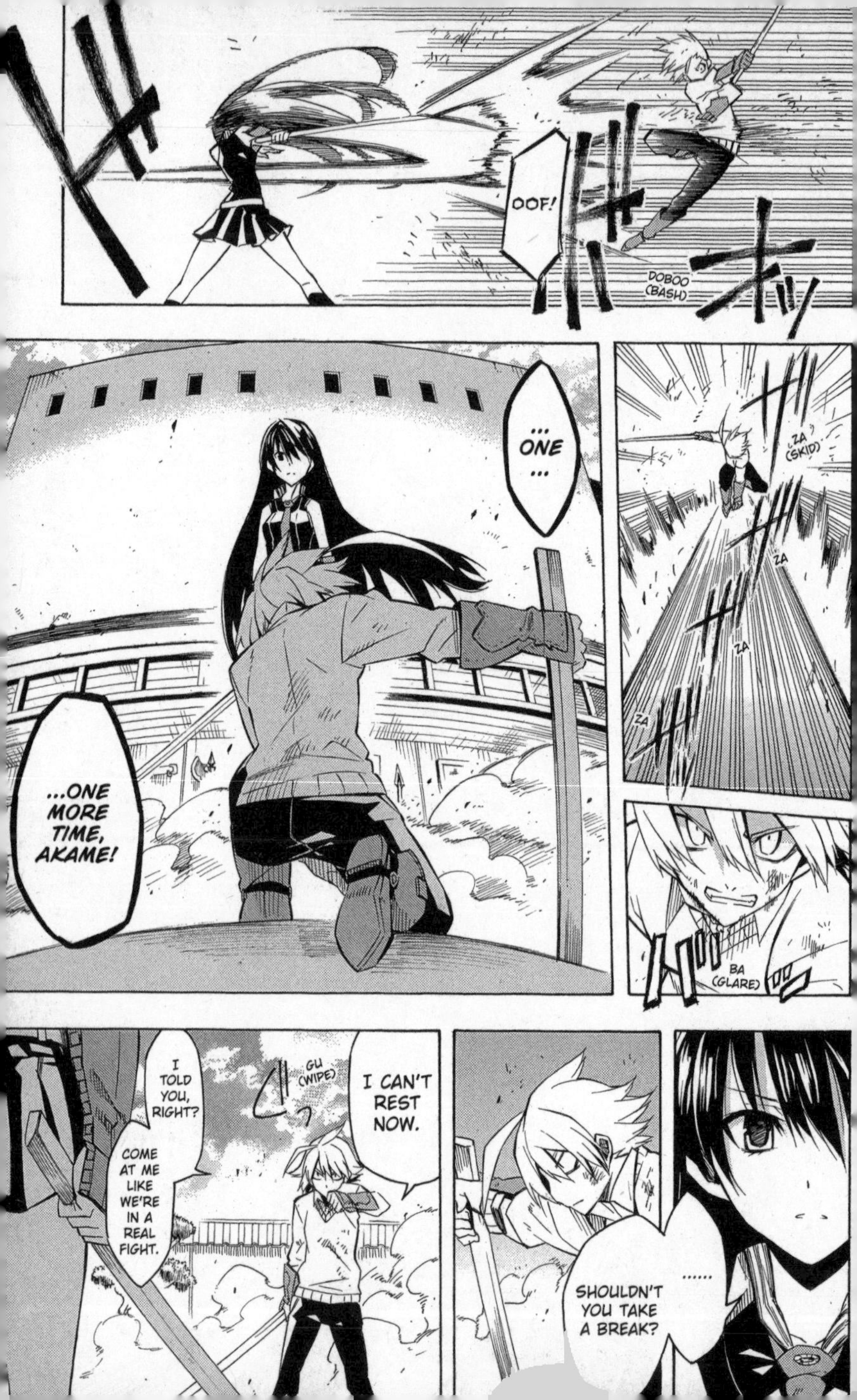
OOF!
DOBOO (BASH)
ZA (SKID)
ZA
ZA
ZA
BA (GLARE)
...ONE ...
...ONE MORE TIME, AKAME!
......
SHOULDN'T YOU TAKE A BREAK?
I CAN'T REST NOW.
GU (WIPE)
I TOLD YOU, RIGHT?
COME AT ME LIKE WE'RE IN A REAL FIGHT.

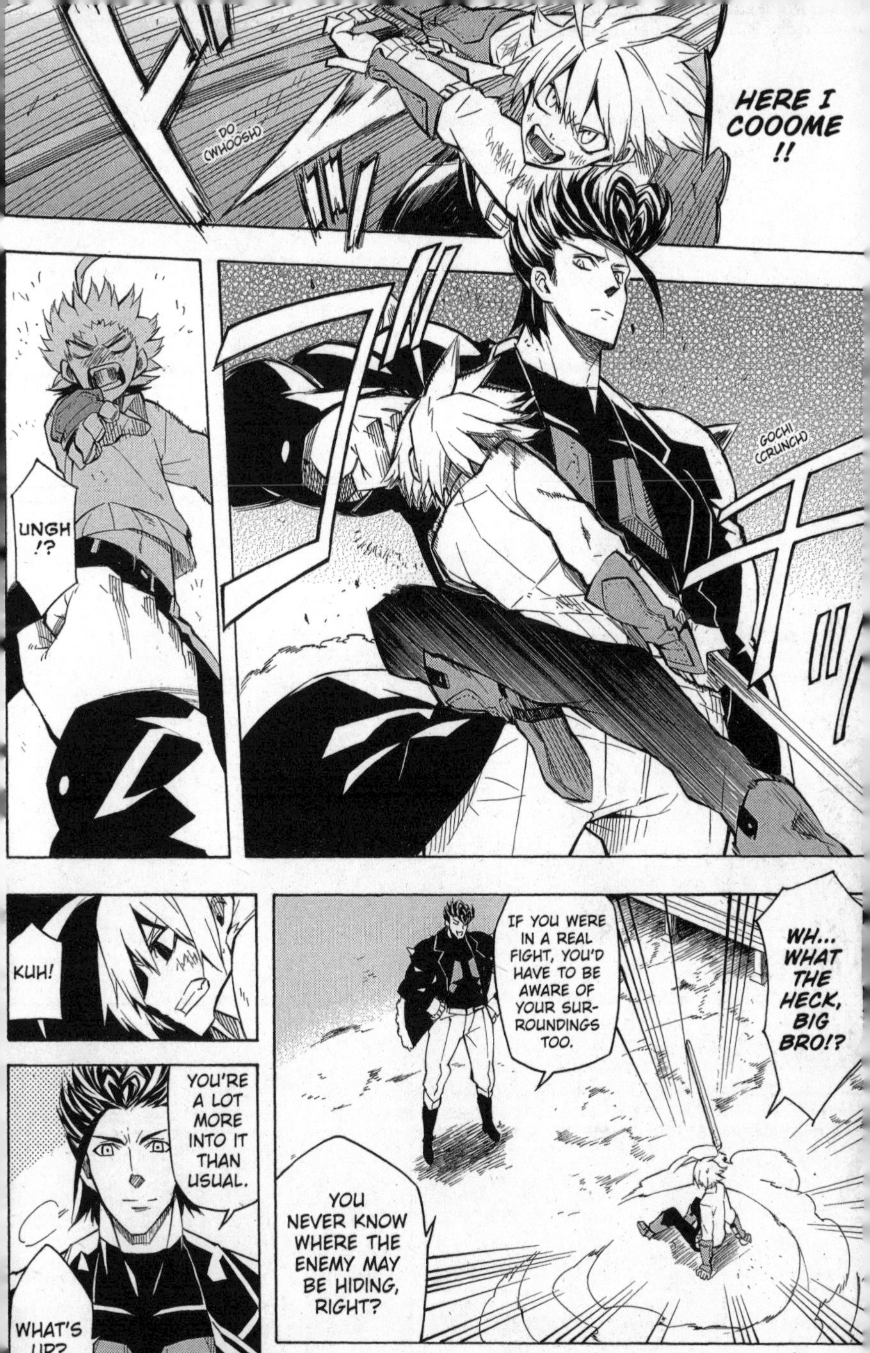
HERE I COOOME !!
DO (WHOOSH)
GOCHI (CRUNCH)
UNGH !?
WH... WHAT THE HECK, BIG BRO!?
IF YOU WERE IN A REAL FIGHT, YOU'D HAVE TO BE AWARE OF YOUR SUR-ROUNDINGS TOO.
YOU NEVER KNOW WHERE THE ENEMY MAY BE HIDING, RIGHT?
KUH!
YOU'RE A LOT MORE INTO IT THAN USUAL.
WHAT'S UP?

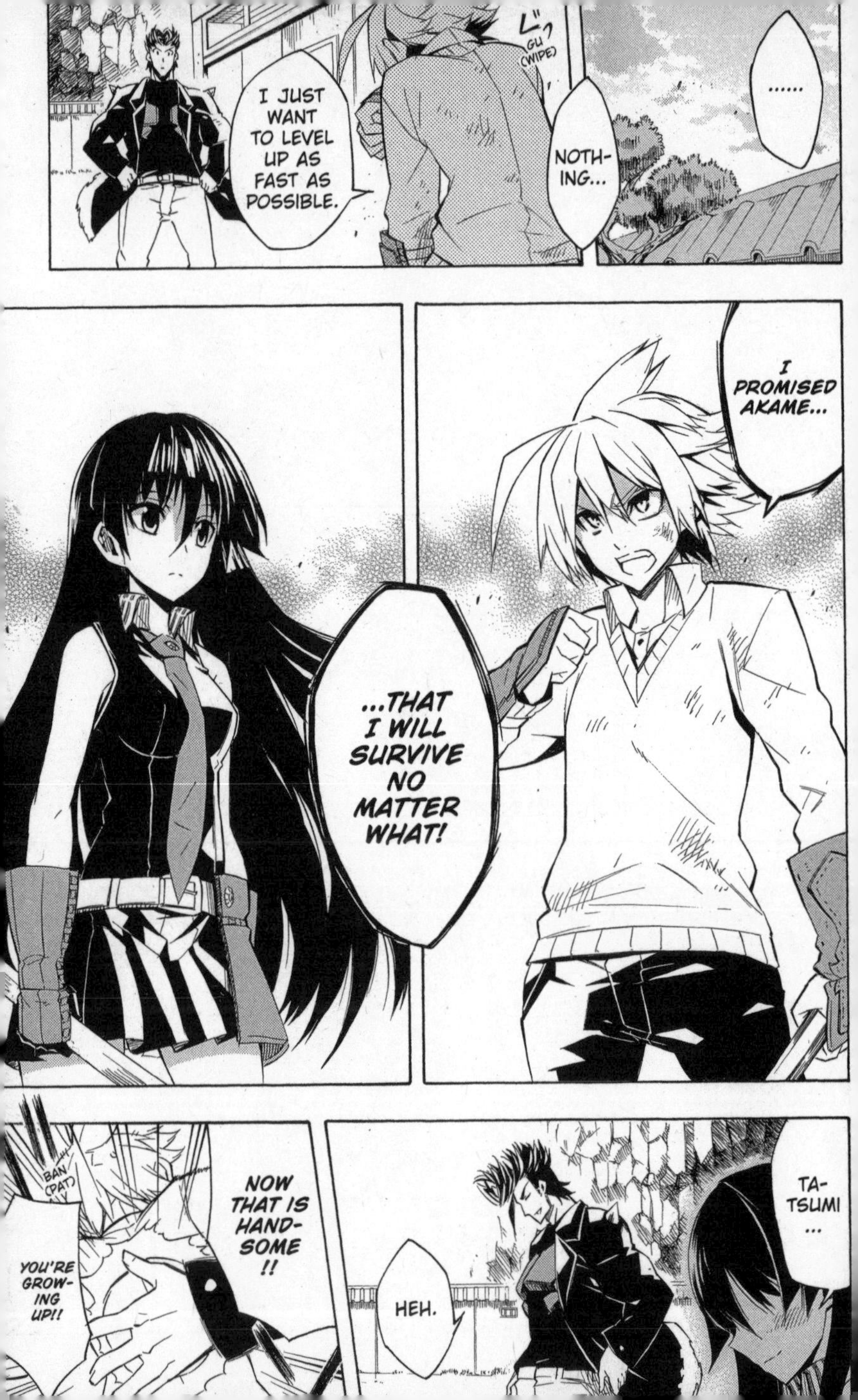
......
GU (WIPE)
NOTH-ING...
I JUST WANT TO LEVEL UP AS FAST AS POSSIBLE.
I PROMISED AKAME...
...THAT I WILL SURVIVE NO MATTER WHAT!
TA-TSUMI ...
HEH.
NOW THAT IS HAND-SOME !!
BAN (PAT)
YOU'RE GROW-ING UP!!

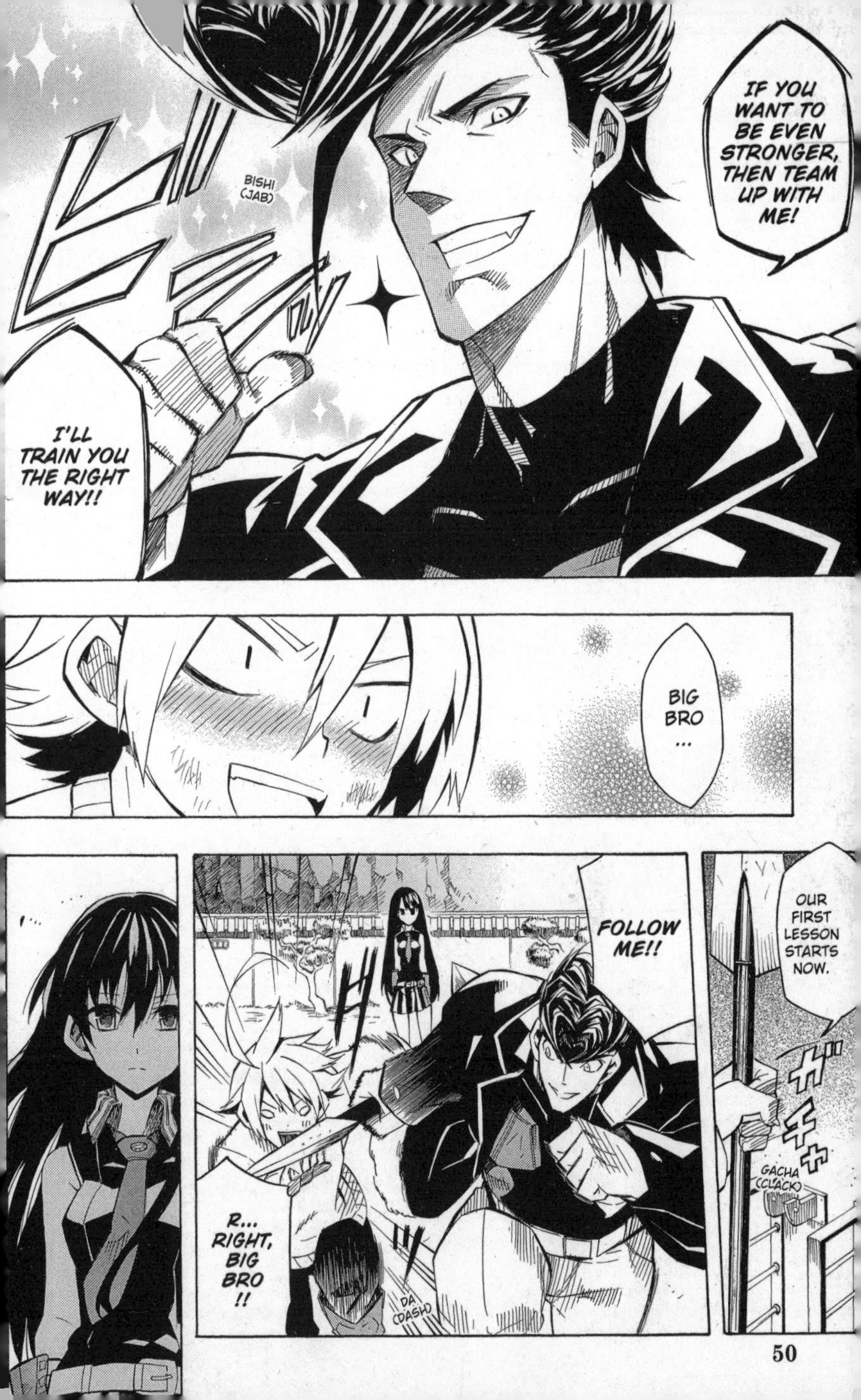
IF YOU WANT TO BE EVEN STRONGER, THEN TEAM UP WITH ME!
BISHI (JAB)
I'LL TRAIN YOU THE RIGHT WAY!!
BIG BRO ...
OUR FIRST LESSON STARTS NOW.
GACHA (CLACK)
FOLLOW ME!!
R... RIGHT, BIG BRO!!
DA (DASH)
...

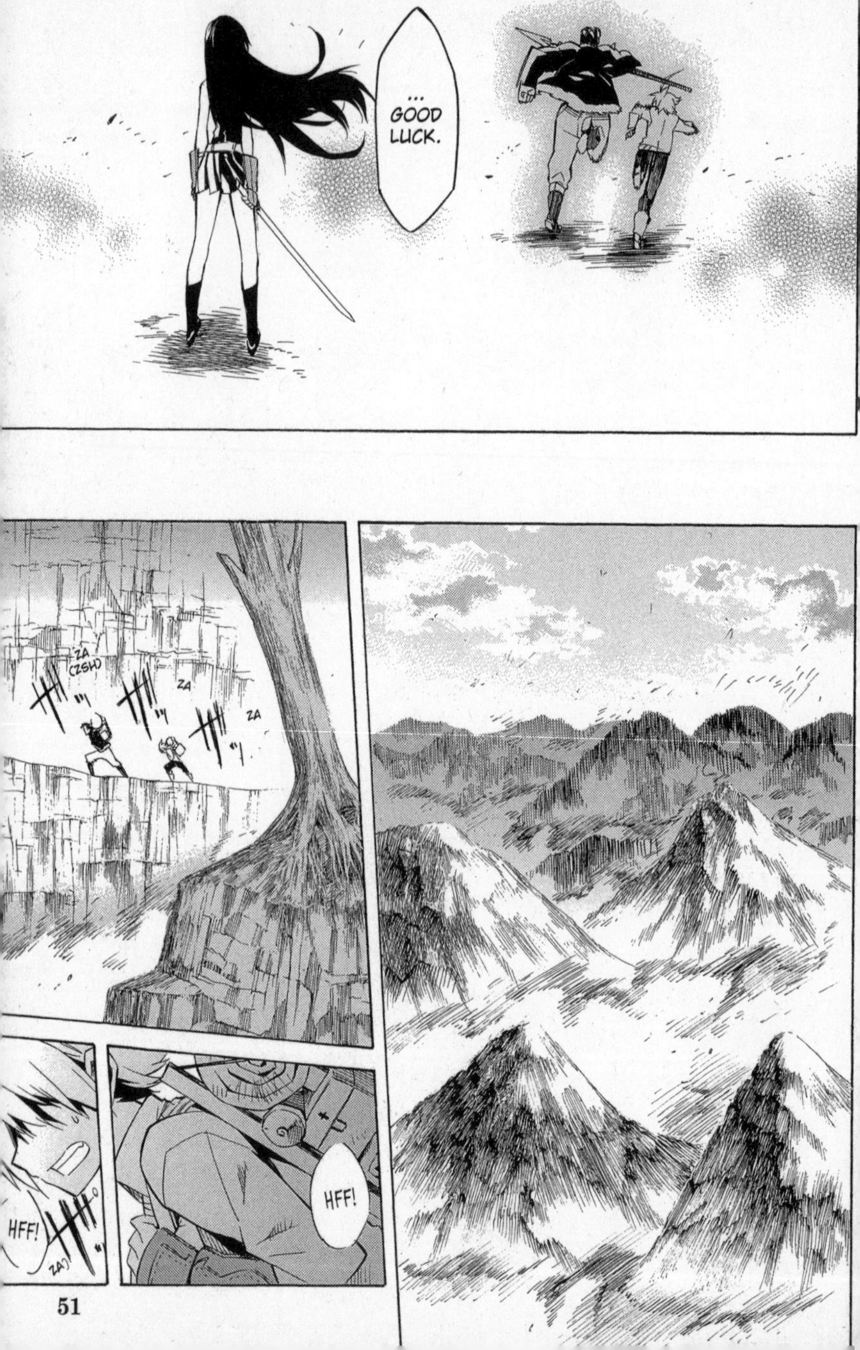
...GOOD LUCK.
ZA (ZSH)
ZA
ZA
HFF!
HFF!
ZA

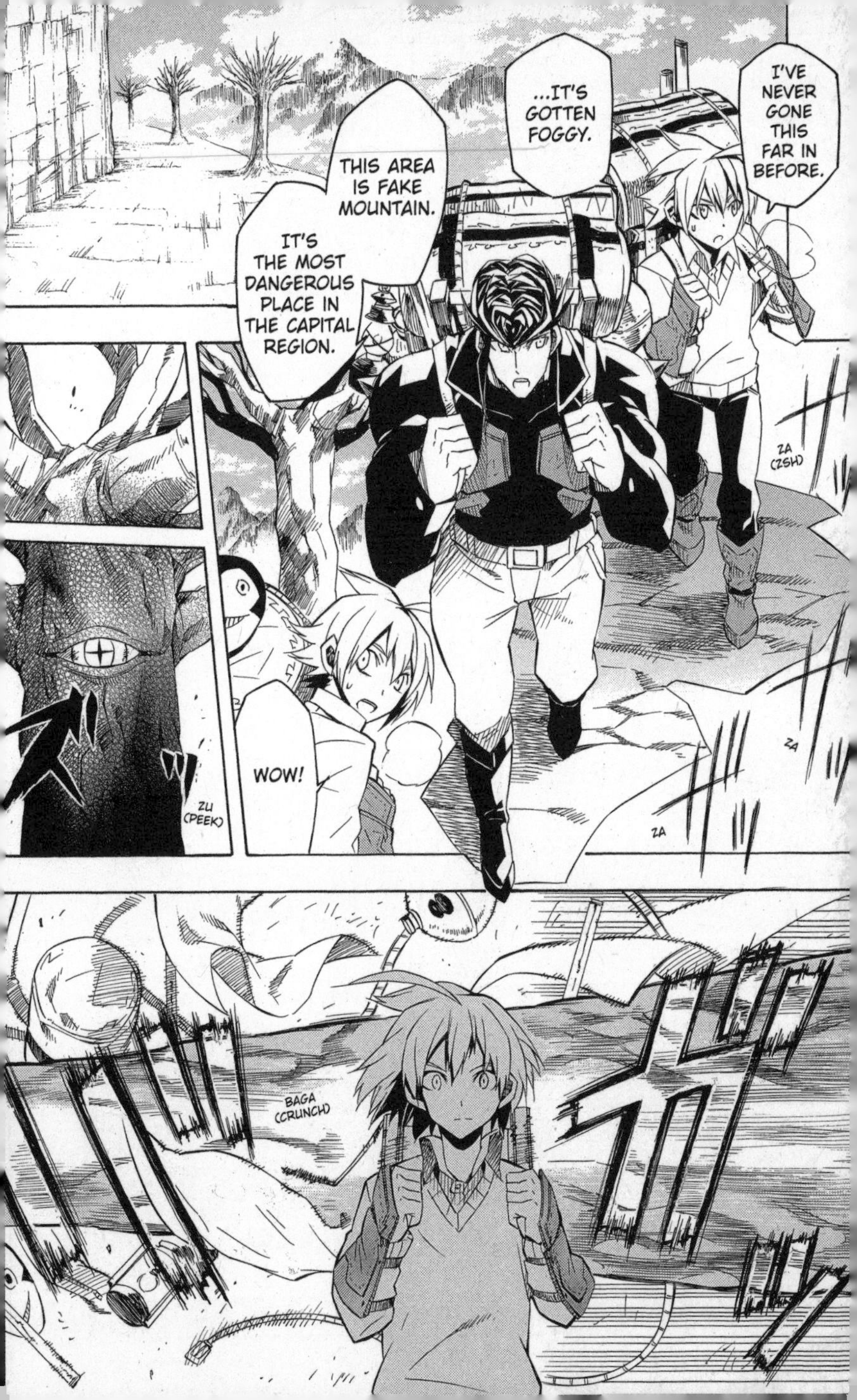
I'VE NEVER GONE THIS FAR IN BEFORE.
...IT'S GOTTEN FOGGY.
THIS AREA IS FAKE MOUNTAIN.
IT'S THE MOST DANGEROUS PLACE IN THE CAPITAL REGION.
ZA (ZSH)
ZA
ZA
WOW!
ZU (PEEK)
BAGA (CRUNCH)

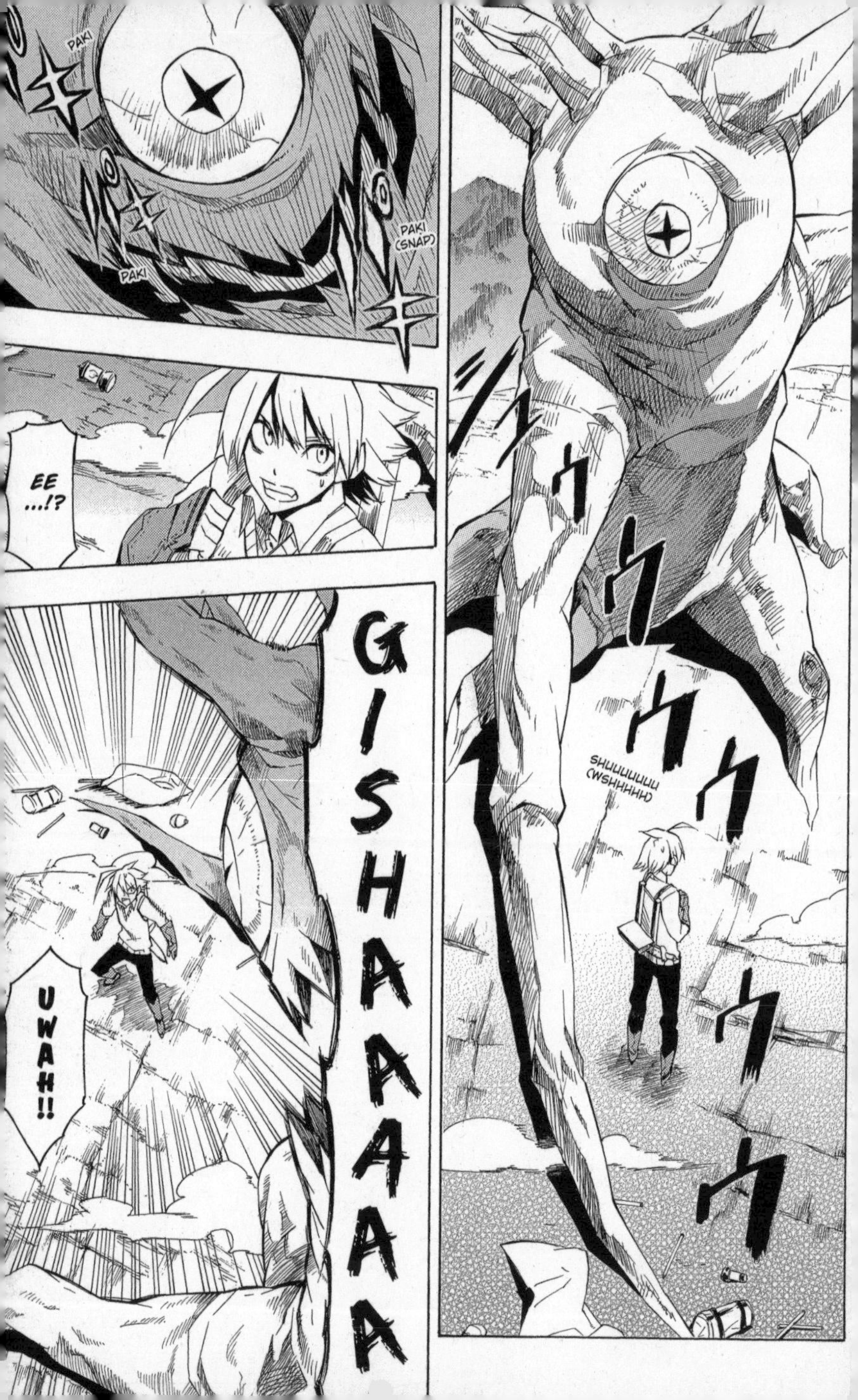
SHUUUUUUUU
(WSHHHHH)
PAKI
PAKI
(SNAP)
PAKI
EE ...!?
GISHAAAAA
UWAH!!

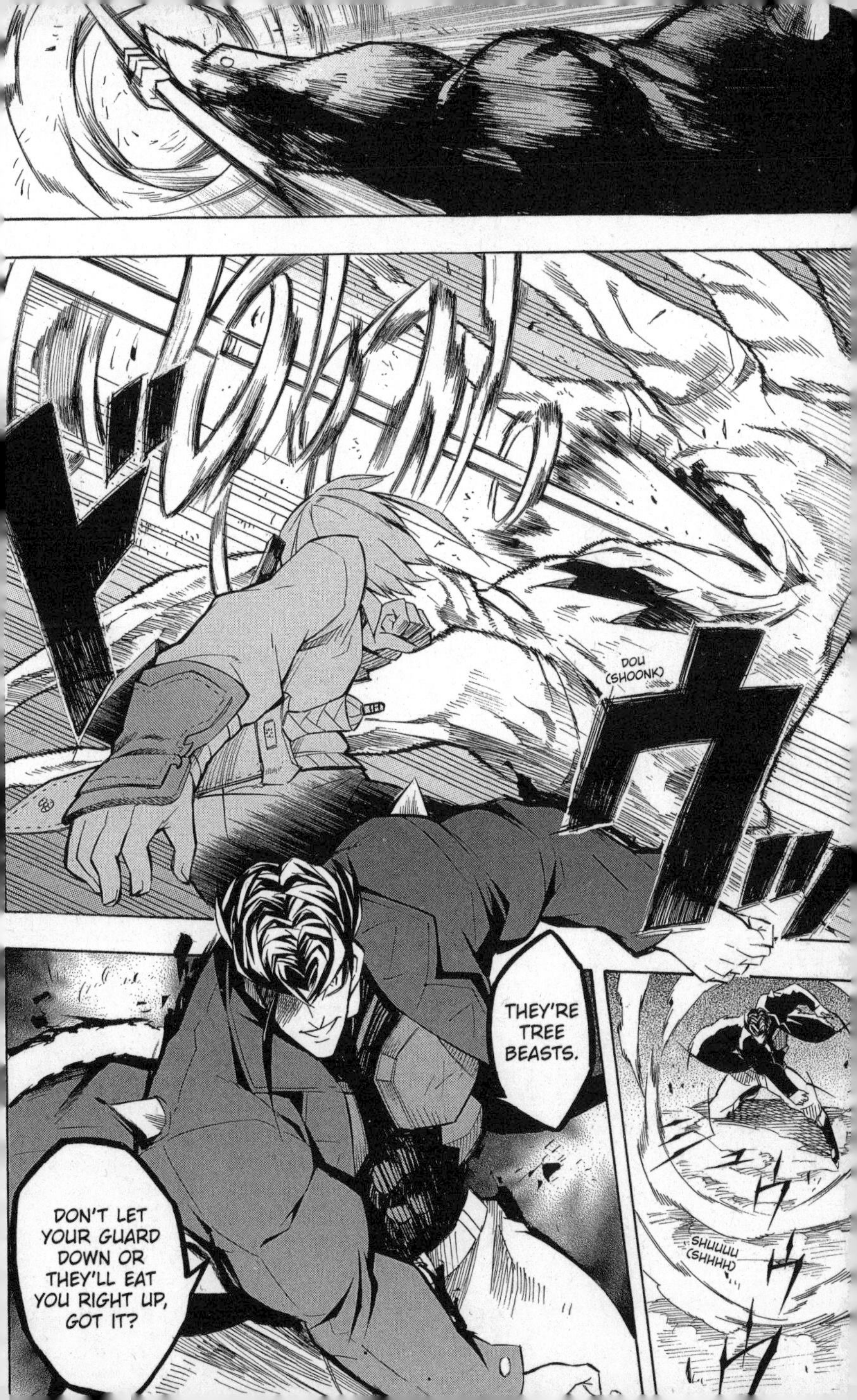
DOU (SHOONK)
SHUUUU (SHHHH)
THEY'RE TREE BEASTS.
DON'T LET YOUR GUARD DOWN OR THEY'LL EAT YOU RIGHT UP, GOT IT?

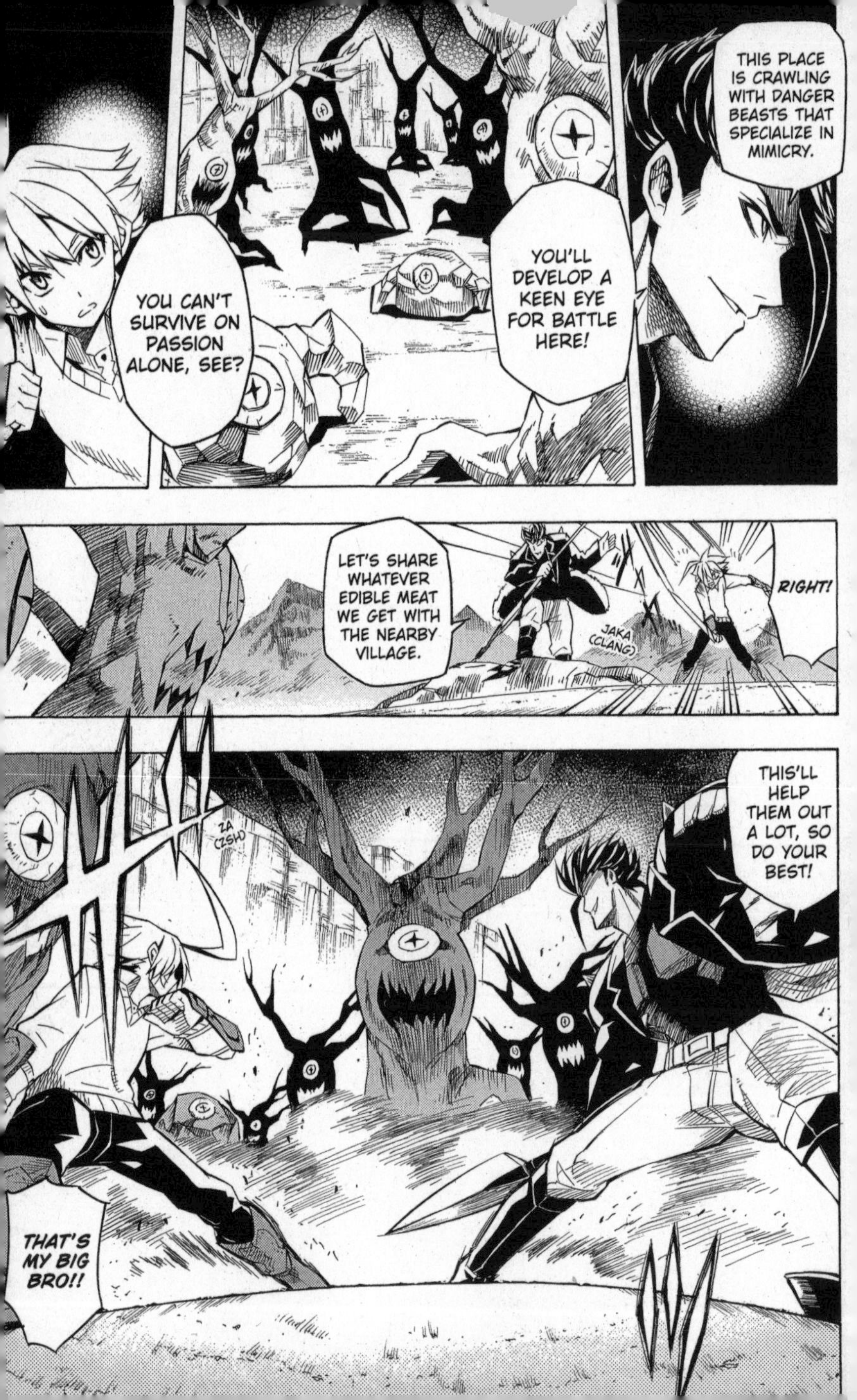
THIS PLACE IS CRAWLING WITH DANGER BEASTS THAT SPECIALIZE IN MIMICRY.
YOU'LL DEVELOP A KEEN EYE FOR BATTLE HERE!
YOU CAN'T SURVIVE ON PASSION ALONE, SEE?
RIGHT!
LET'S SHARE WHATEVER EDIBLE MEAT WE GET WITH THE NEARBY VILLAGE.
JAKA (CLANG)
THIS'LL HELP THEM OUT A LOT, SO DO YOUR BEST!
ZA (ZSH)
THAT'S MY BIG BRO!!

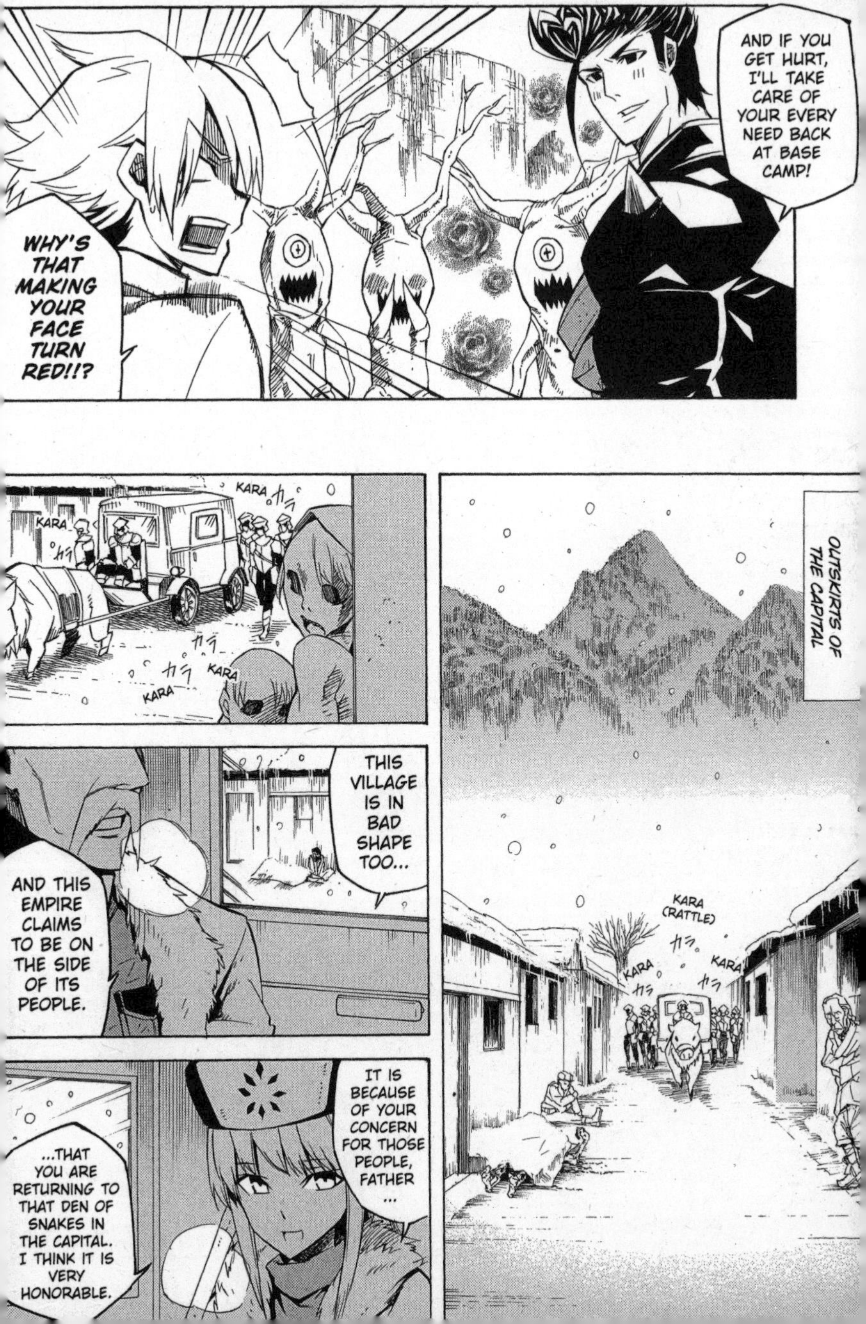
AND IF YOU GET HURT, I'LL TAKE CARE OF YOUR EVERY NEED BACK AT BASE CAMP!
WHY'S THAT MAKING YOUR FACE TURN RED!!?
OUTSKIRTS OF THE CAPITAL
KARA (RATTLE)
KARA
KARA
KARA
KARA
KARA
KARA
THIS VILLAGE IS IN BAD SHAPE TOO...
AND THIS EMPIRE CLAIMS TO BE ON THE SIDE OF ITS PEOPLE.
IT IS BECAUSE OF YOUR CONCERN FOR THOSE PEOPLE, FATHER...
...THAT YOU ARE RETURNING TO THAT DEN OF SNAKES IN THE CAPITAL. I THINK IT IS VERY HONORABLE.

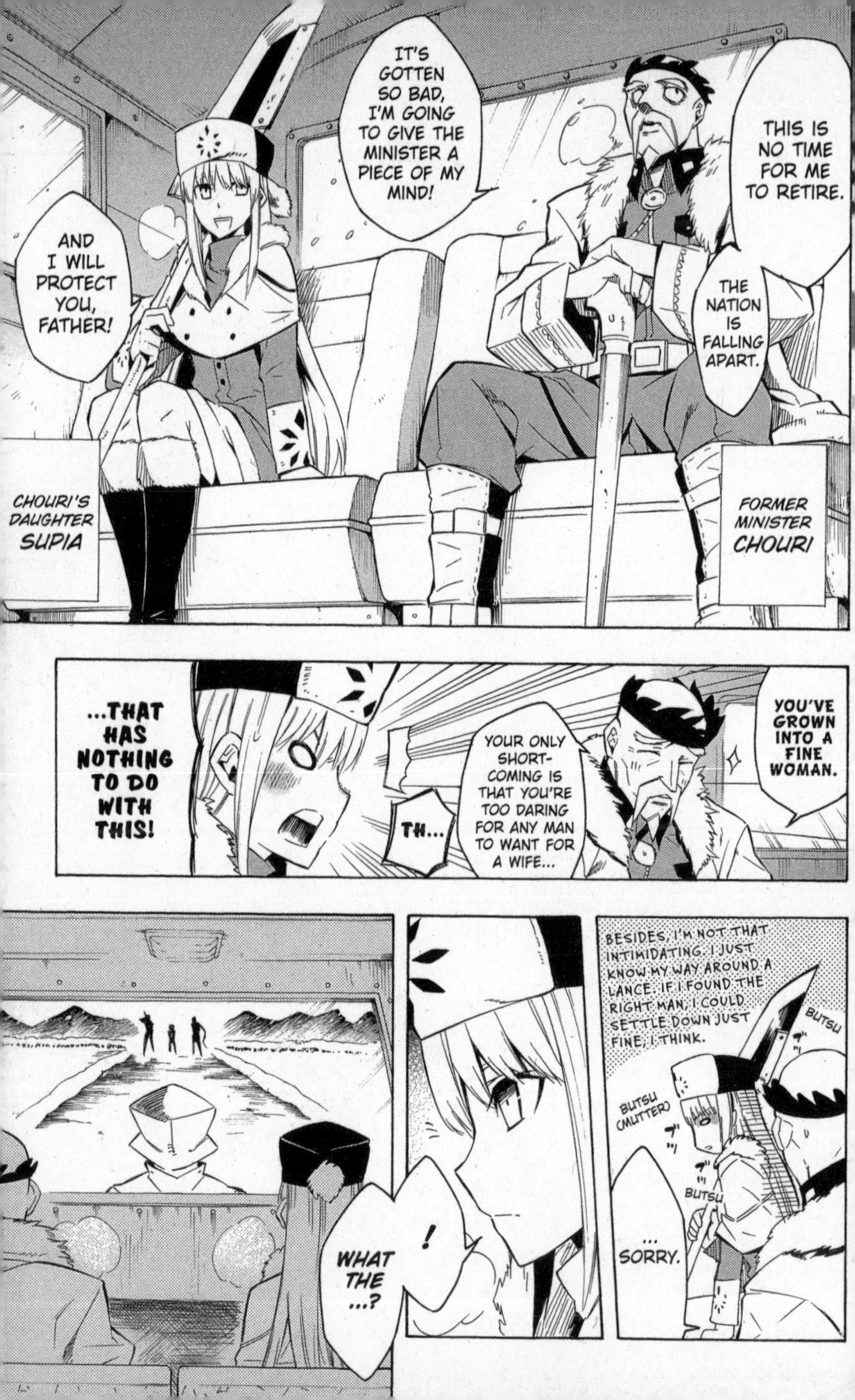
THIS IS NO TIME FOR ME TO RETIRE.
THE NATION IS FALLING APART.
IT'S GOTTEN SO BAD, I'M GOING TO GIVE THE MINISTER A PIECE OF MY MIND!
AND I WILL PROTECT YOU, FATHER!
FORMER MINISTER CHOURI
CHOURI'S DAUGHTER SUPIA
YOU'VE GROWN INTO A FINE WOMAN.
YOUR ONLY SHORT-COMING IS THAT YOU'RE TOO DARING FOR ANY MAN TO WANT FOR A WIFE...
TH...
...THAT HAS NOTHING TO DO WITH THIS!
BESIDES, I'M NOT THAT INTIMIDATING. I JUST KNOW MY WAY AROUND A LANCE. IF I FOUND THE RIGHT MAN, I COULD SETTLE DOWN JUST FINE, I THINK.
BUTSU
BUTSU (MUTTER)
BUTSU
...SORRY.
!
WHAT THE ...?

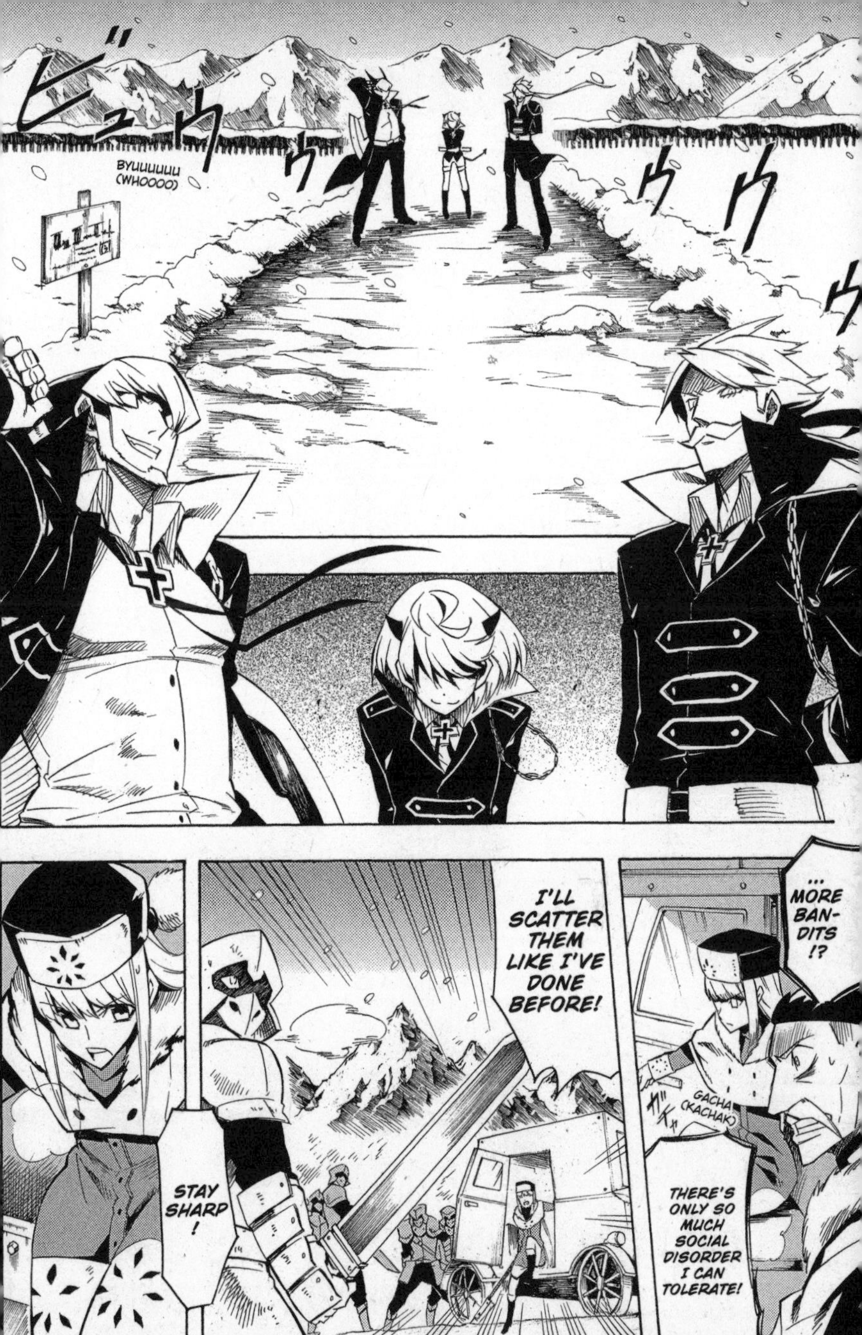
ビュウウウウ
BYUUUUUU (WHOOOO)
...MORE BAN-DITS!?
GACHA (KACHAK)
THERE'S ONLY SO MUCH SOCIAL DISORDER I CAN TOLERATE!
I'LL SCATTER THEM LIKE I'VE DONE BEFORE!
STAY SHARP!

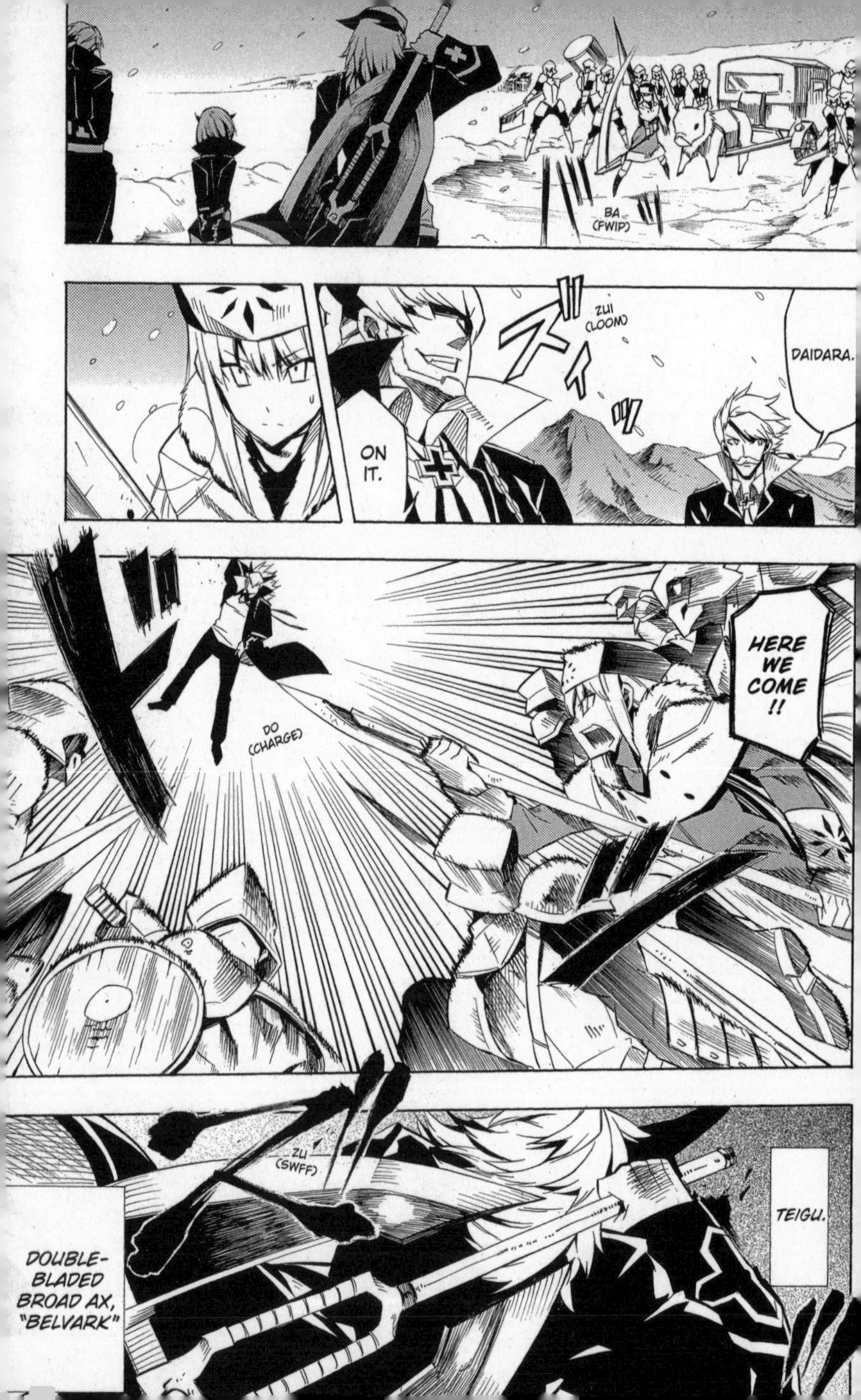
BA
(FWIP)
DAIDARA.
ZUI
(LOOM)
ON
IT.
HERE
WE
COME
!!
DO
(CHARGE)
TEIGU.
ZU
(SWFF)
DOUBLE-
BLADED
BROAD AX,
"BELVARK"

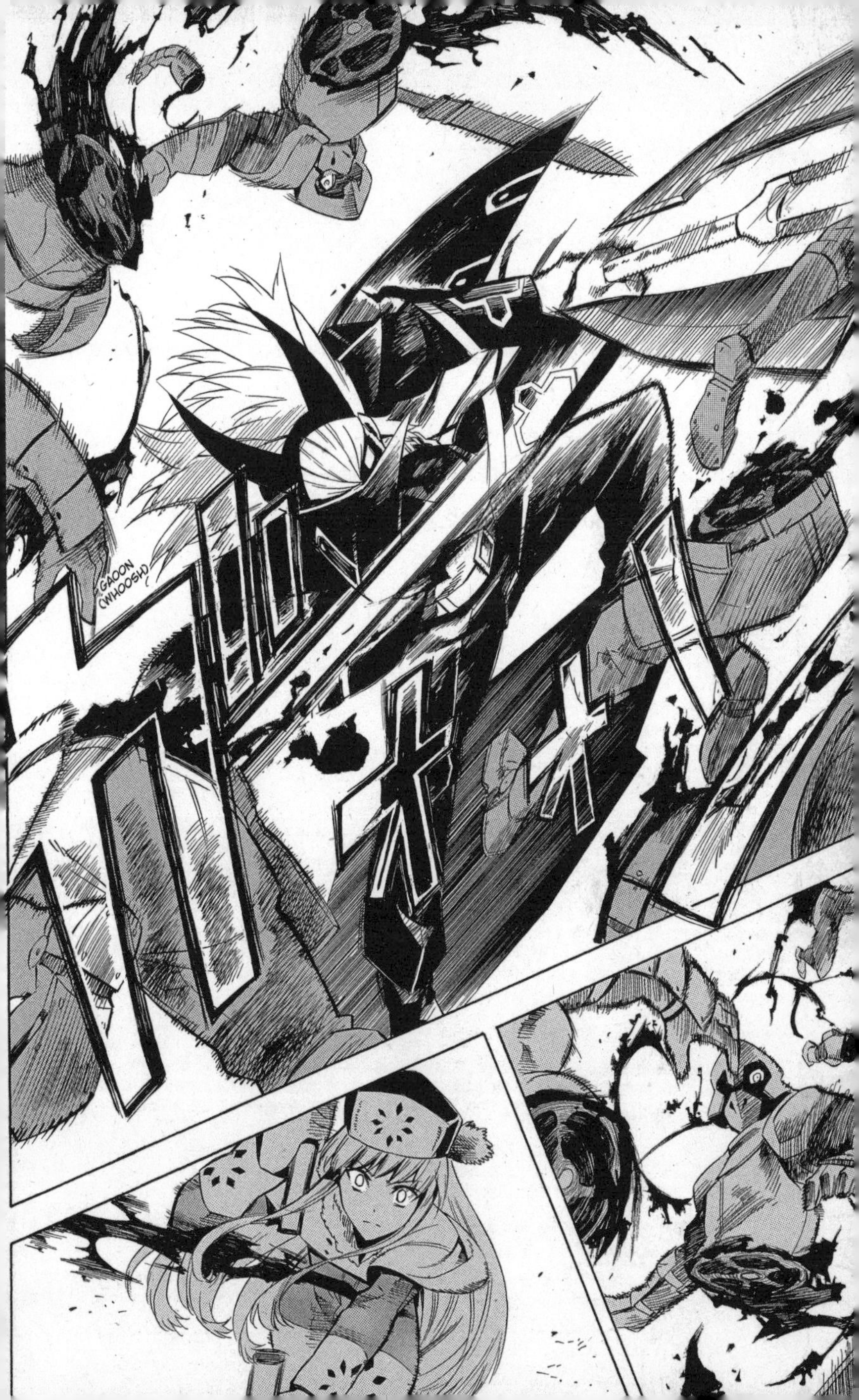
GAOON (WHOOSH)

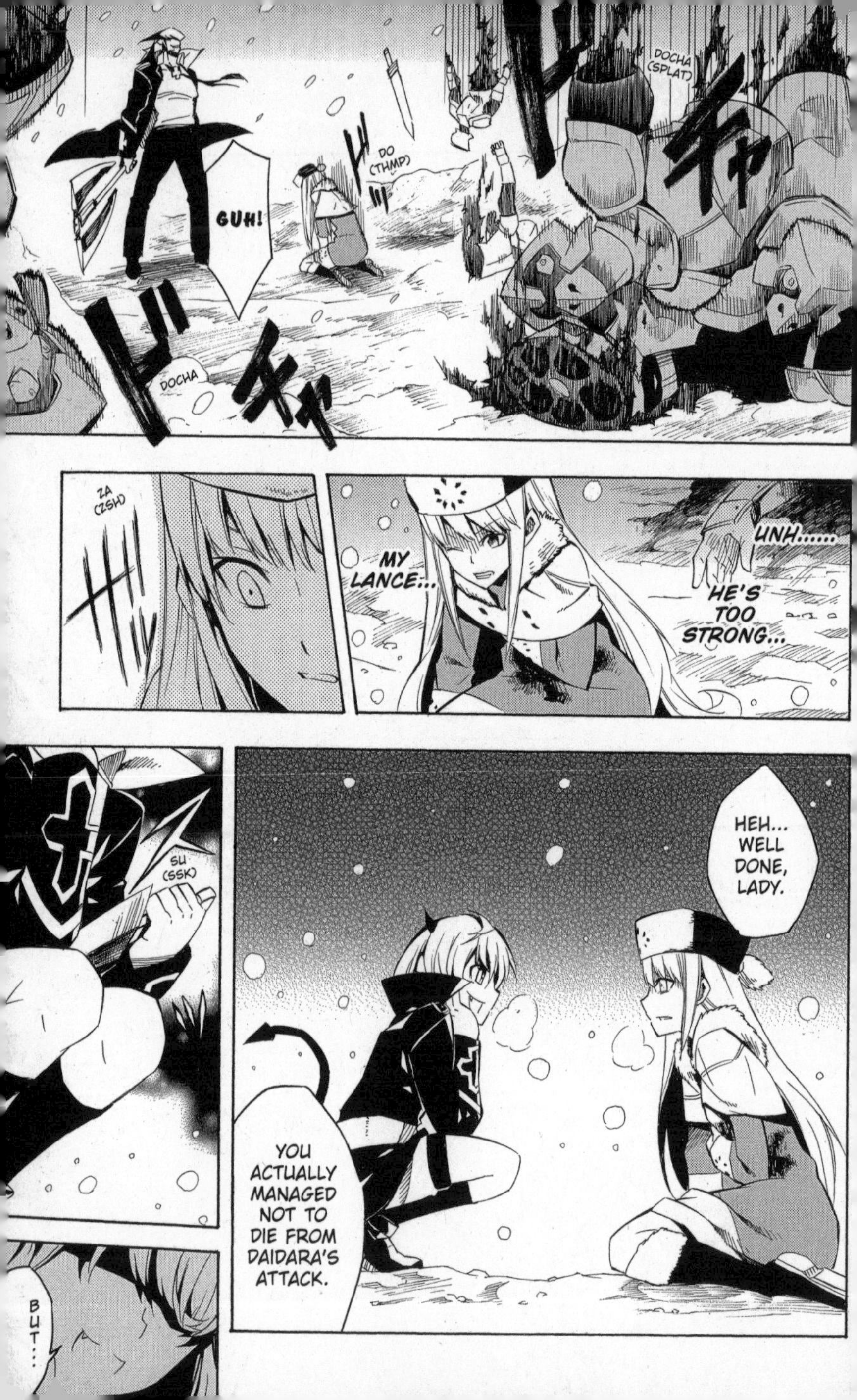
DOCHA (SPLAT)
DO (THMP)
GUH!
DOCHA
UNH......
HE'S TOO STRONG...
MY LANCE...
ZA (ZSH)
HEH... WELL DONE, LADY.
YOU ACTUALLY MANAGED NOT TO DIE FROM DAIDARA'S ATTACK.
SU (SSK)
BUT...

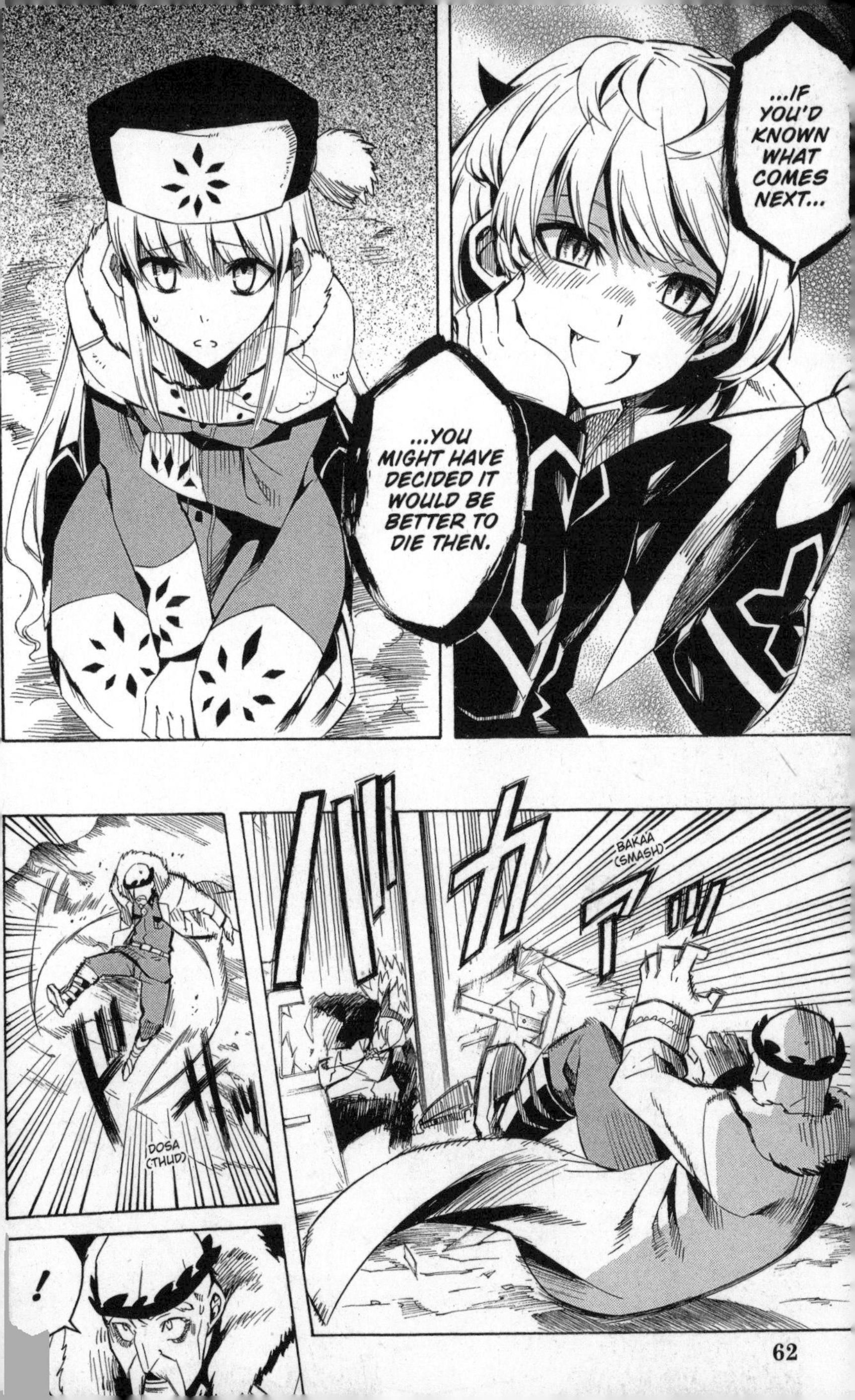

...IF YOU'D KNOWN WHAT COMES NEXT...
...YOU MIGHT HAVE DECIDED IT WOULD BE BETTER TO DIE THEN.
バカァッ
BAKAA (SMASH)
ドサッ
DOSA (THUD)
!

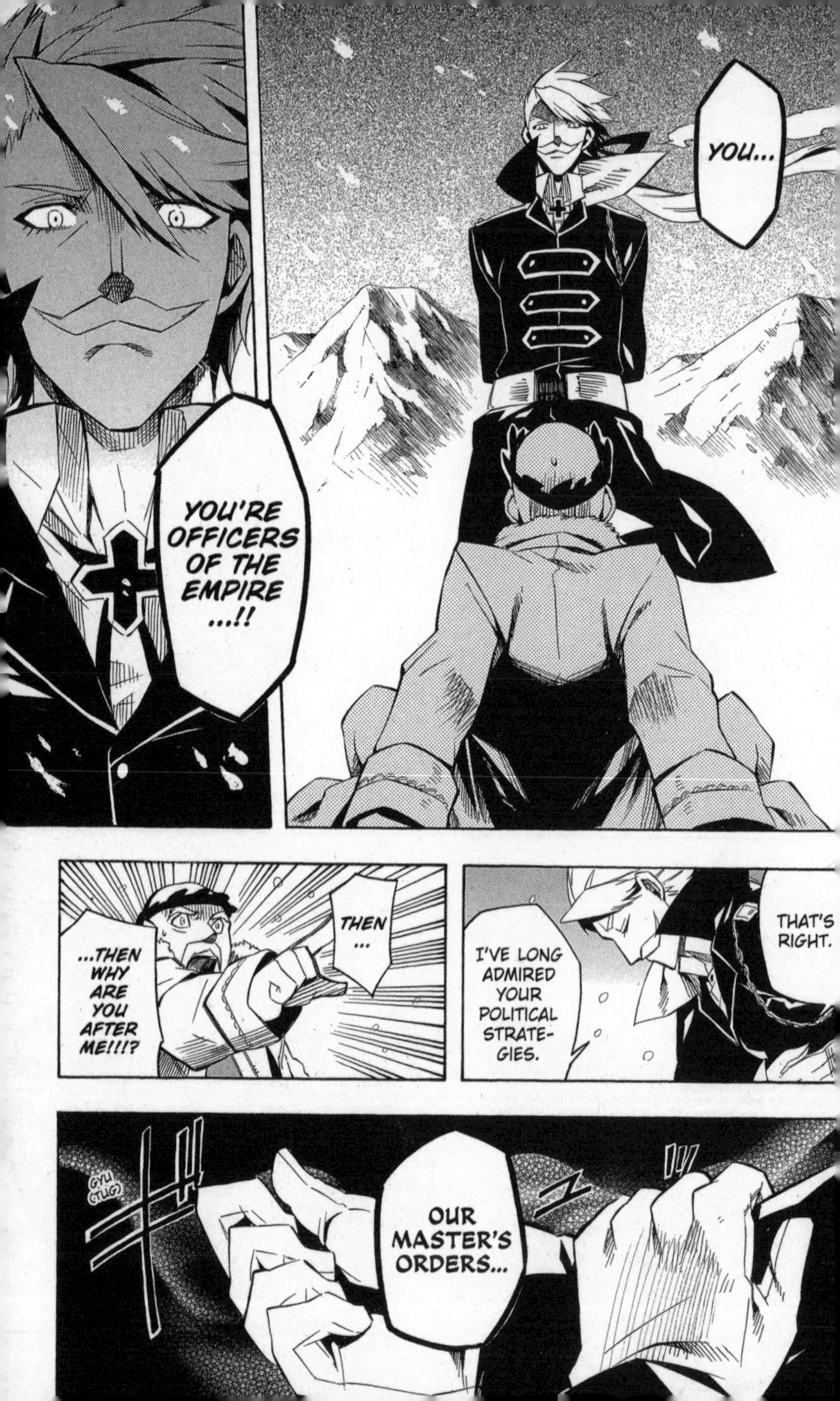
YOU...
YOU'RE OFFICERS OF THE EMPIRE ...!!
THAT'S RIGHT.
I'VE LONG ADMIRED YOUR POLITICAL STRATE-GIES.
THEN ...
...THEN WHY ARE YOU AFTER ME!!!?
GYU (TUG)
OUR MASTER'S ORDERS...

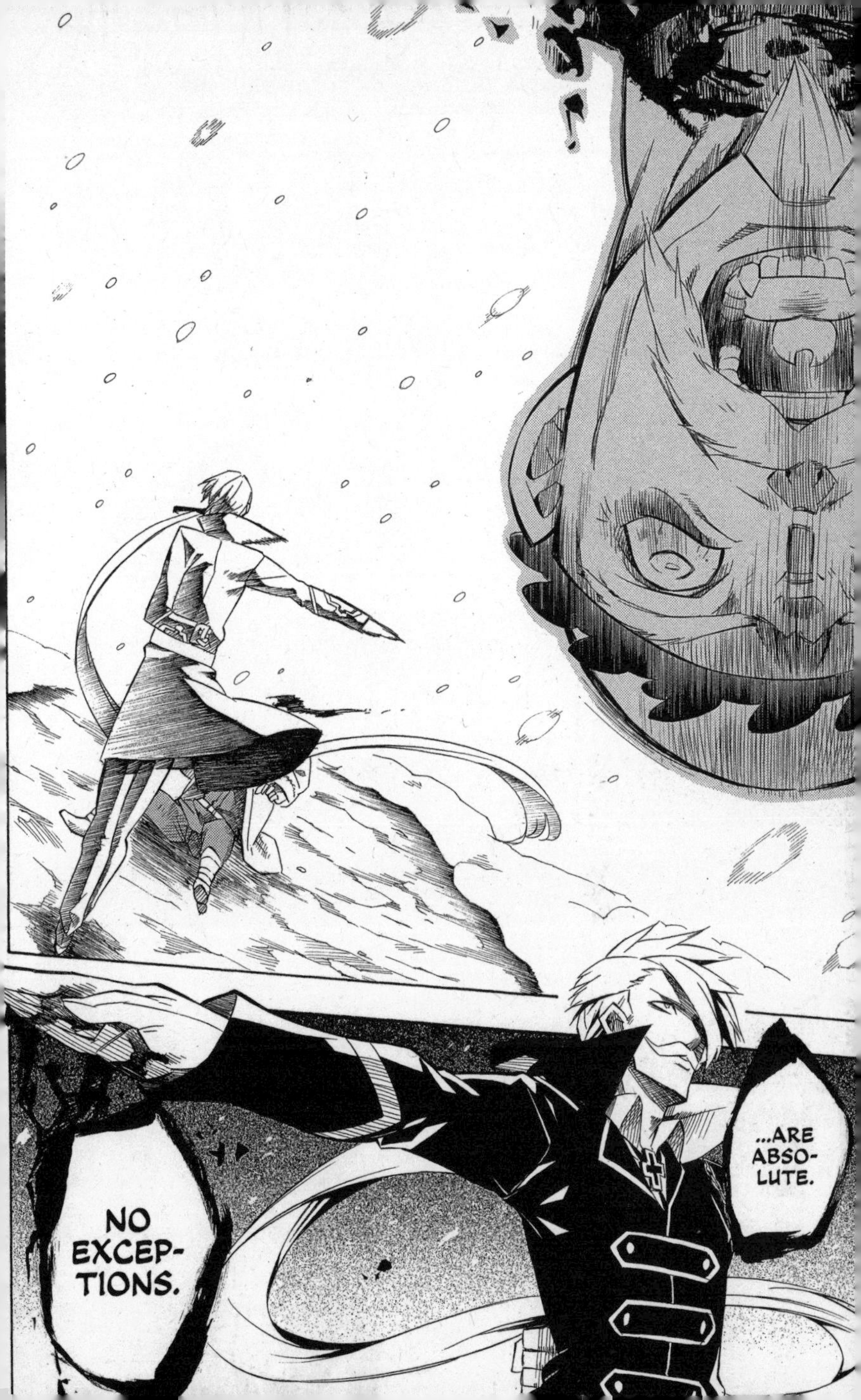
...ARE ABSOLUTE.
NO EXCEPTIONS.

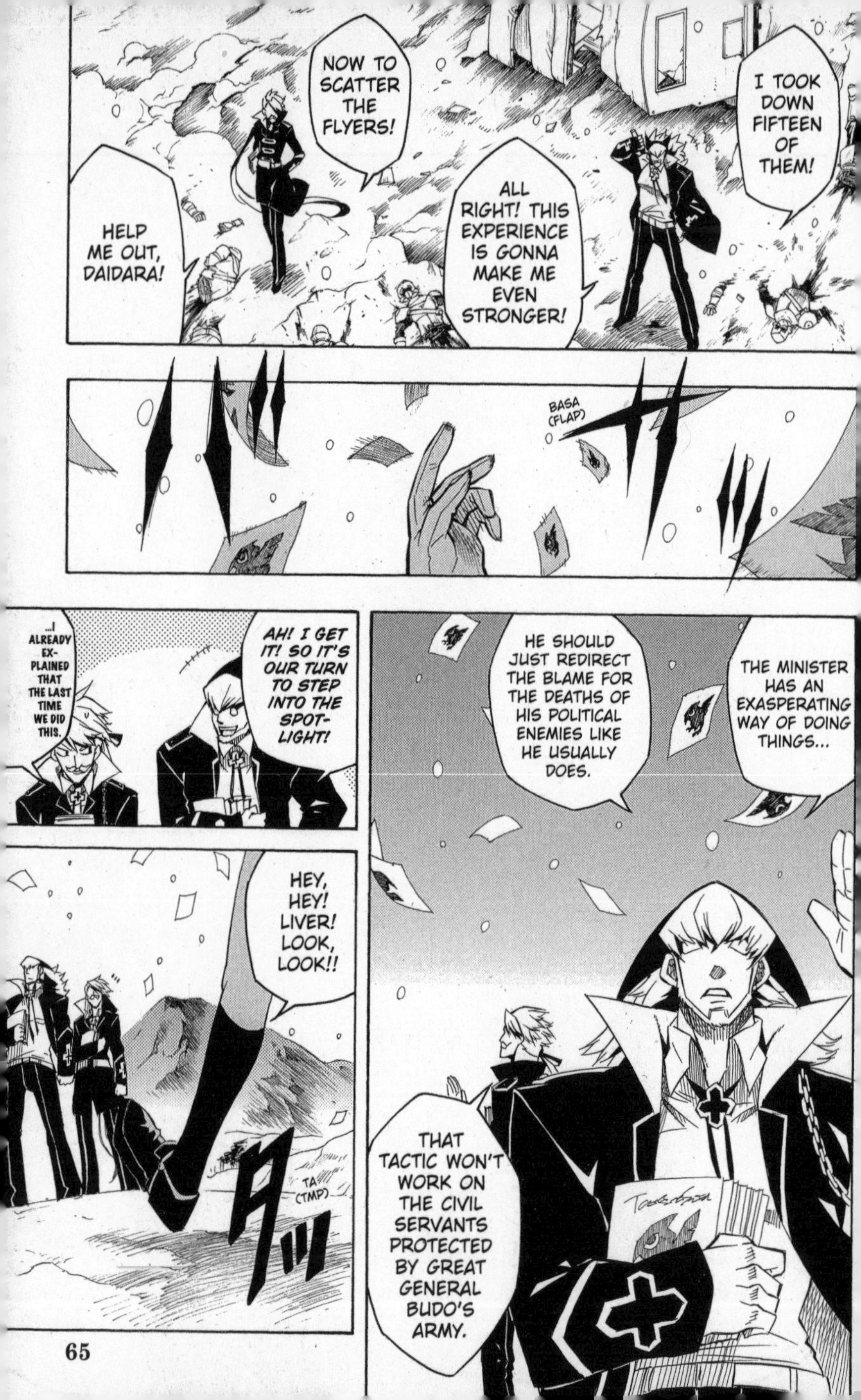
I TOOK DOWN FIFTEEN OF THEM!
ALL RIGHT! THIS EXPERIENCE IS GONNA MAKE ME EVEN STRONGER!
NOW TO SCATTER THE FLYERS!
HELP ME OUT, DAIDARA!
BASA (FLAP)
THE MINISTER HAS AN EXASPERATING WAY OF DOING THINGS...
HE SHOULD JUST REDIRECT THE BLAME FOR THE DEATHS OF HIS POLITICAL ENEMIES LIKE HE USUALLY DOES.
THAT TACTIC WON'T WORK ON THE CIVIL SERVANTS PROTECTED BY GREAT GENERAL BUDO'S ARMY.
AH! I GET IT! SO IT'S OUR TURN TO STEP INTO THE SPOT-LIGHT!
...I ALREADY EX-PLAINED THAT THE LAST TIME WE DID THIS.
HEY, HEY! LIVER! LOOK, LOOK!!
TA (TMP)

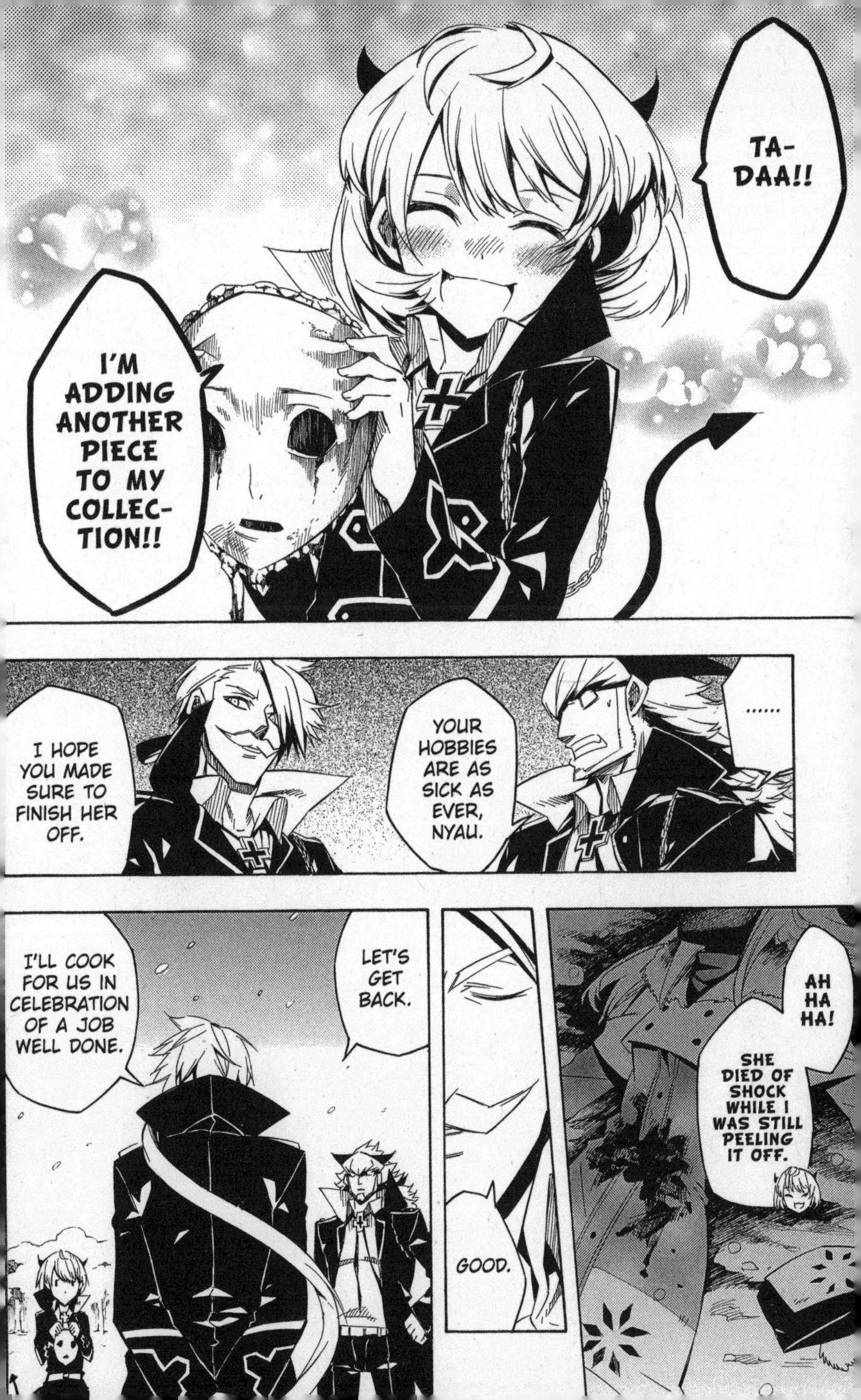
TA-DAA!!
I'M ADDING ANOTHER PIECE TO MY COLLECTION!!
......
YOUR HOBBIES ARE AS SICK AS EVER, NYAU.
I HOPE YOU MADE SURE TO FINISH HER OFF.
AH HA HA!
SHE DIED OF SHOCK WHILE I WAS STILL PEELING IT OFF.
GOOD.
LET'S GET BACK.
I'LL COOK FOR US IN CELEBRATION OF A JOB WELL DONE.

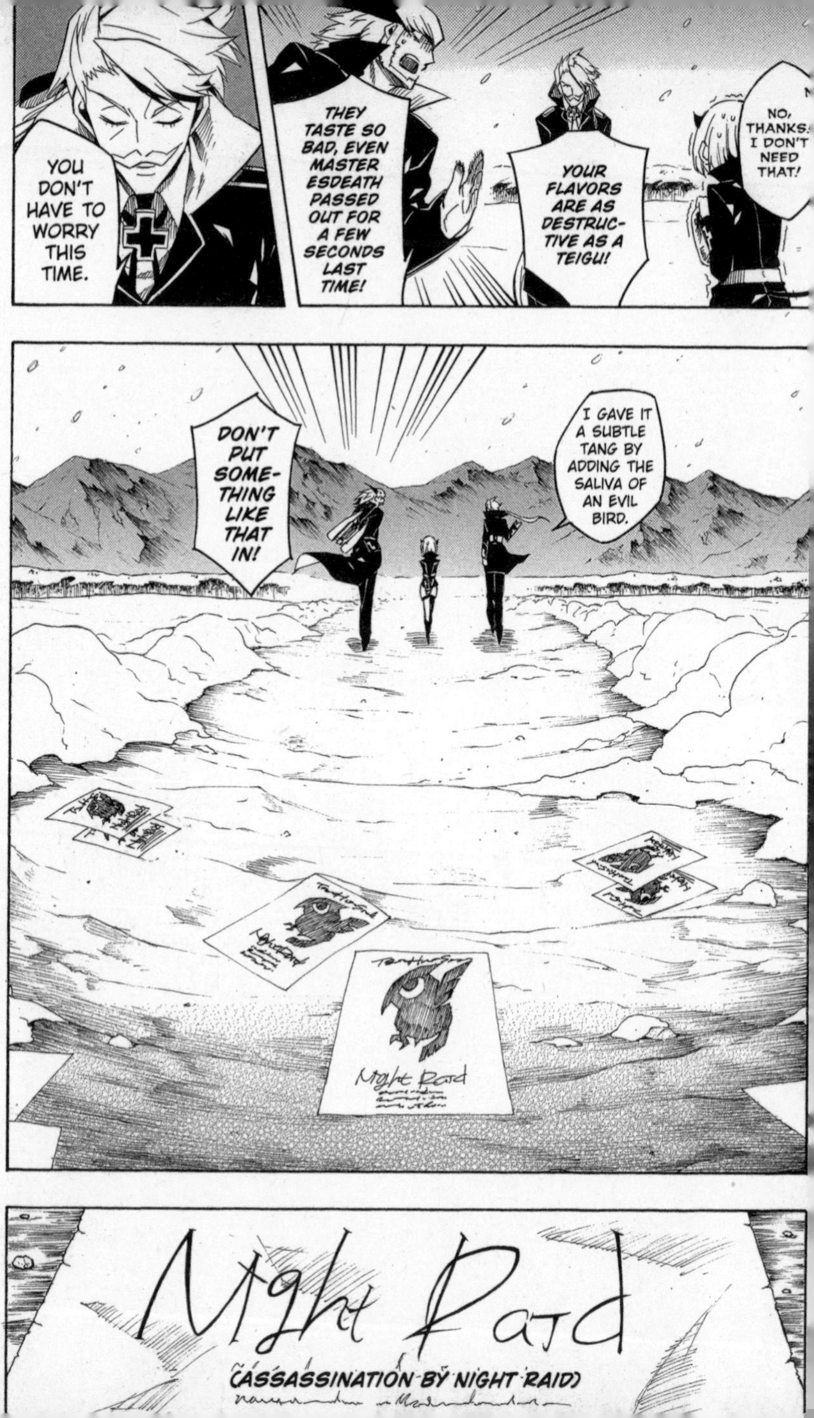
NO, THANKS! I DON'T NEED THAT!
YOUR FLAVORS ARE AS DESTRUCTIVE AS A TEIGU!
THEY TASTE SO BAD, EVEN MASTER ESDEATH PASSED OUT FOR A FEW SECONDS LAST TIME!
YOU DON'T HAVE TO WORRY THIS TIME.
I GAVE IT A SUBTLE TANG BY ADDING THE SALIVA OF AN EVIL BIRD.
DON'T PUT SOMETHING LIKE THAT IN!
Night Raid
(ASSASSINATION BY NIGHT RAID)

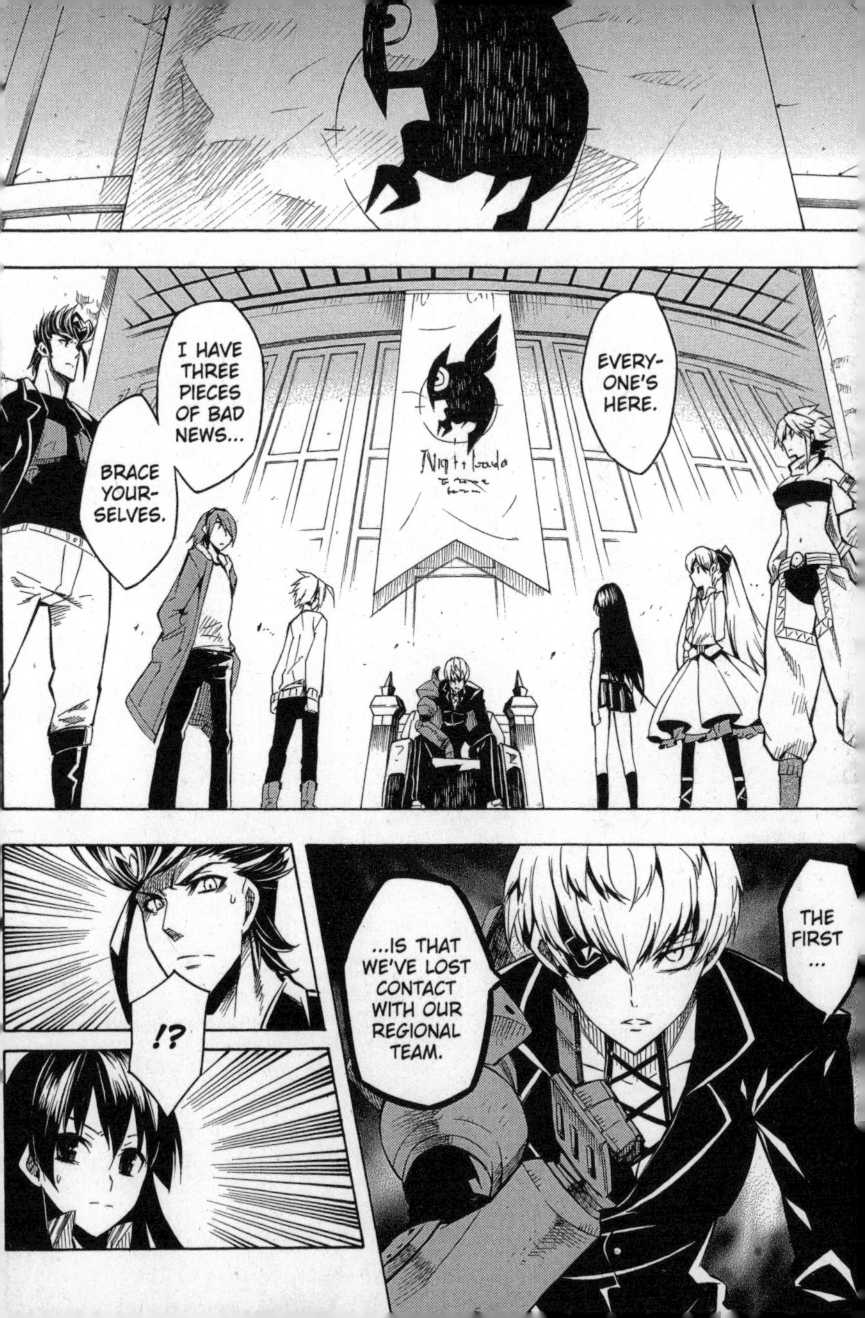
EVERY-ONE'S HERE.
I HAVE THREE PIECES OF BAD NEWS...
BRACE YOUR-SELVES.
THE FIRST ...
...IS THAT WE'VE LOST CONTACT WITH OUR REGIONAL TEAM.
!?

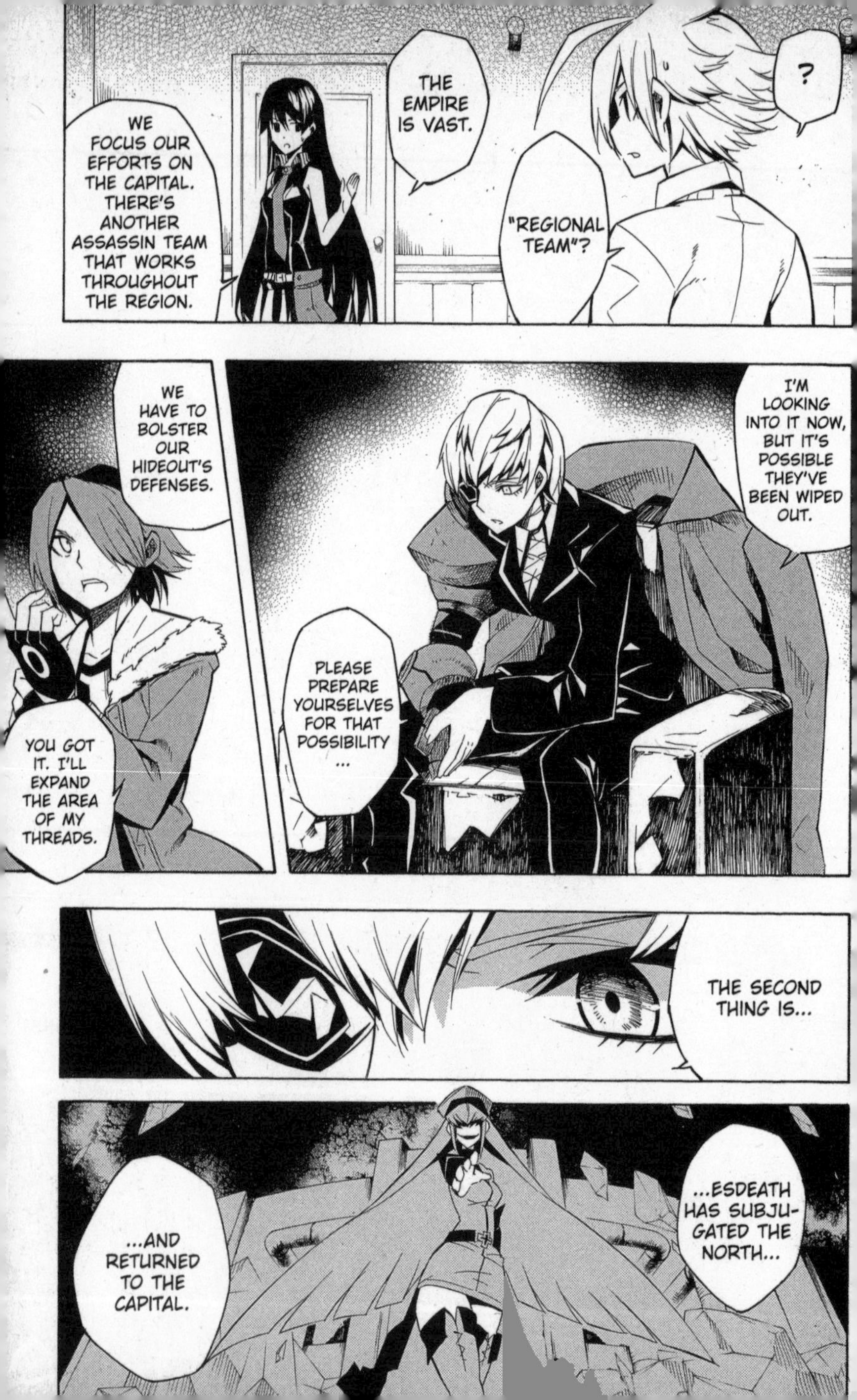
?
"REGIONAL TEAM"?
THE EMPIRE IS VAST.
WE FOCUS OUR EFFORTS ON THE CAPITAL. THERE'S ANOTHER ASSASSIN TEAM THAT WORKS THROUGHOUT THE REGION.
I'M LOOKING INTO IT NOW, BUT IT'S POSSIBLE THEY'VE BEEN WIPED OUT.
PLEASE PREPARE YOURSELVES FOR THAT POSSIBILITY...
WE HAVE TO BOLSTER OUR HIDEOUT'S DEFENSES.
YOU GOT IT. I'LL EXPAND THE AREA OF MY THREADS.
THE SECOND THING IS...
...ESDEATH HAS SUBJUGATED THE NORTH...
...AND RETURNED TO THE CAPITAL.

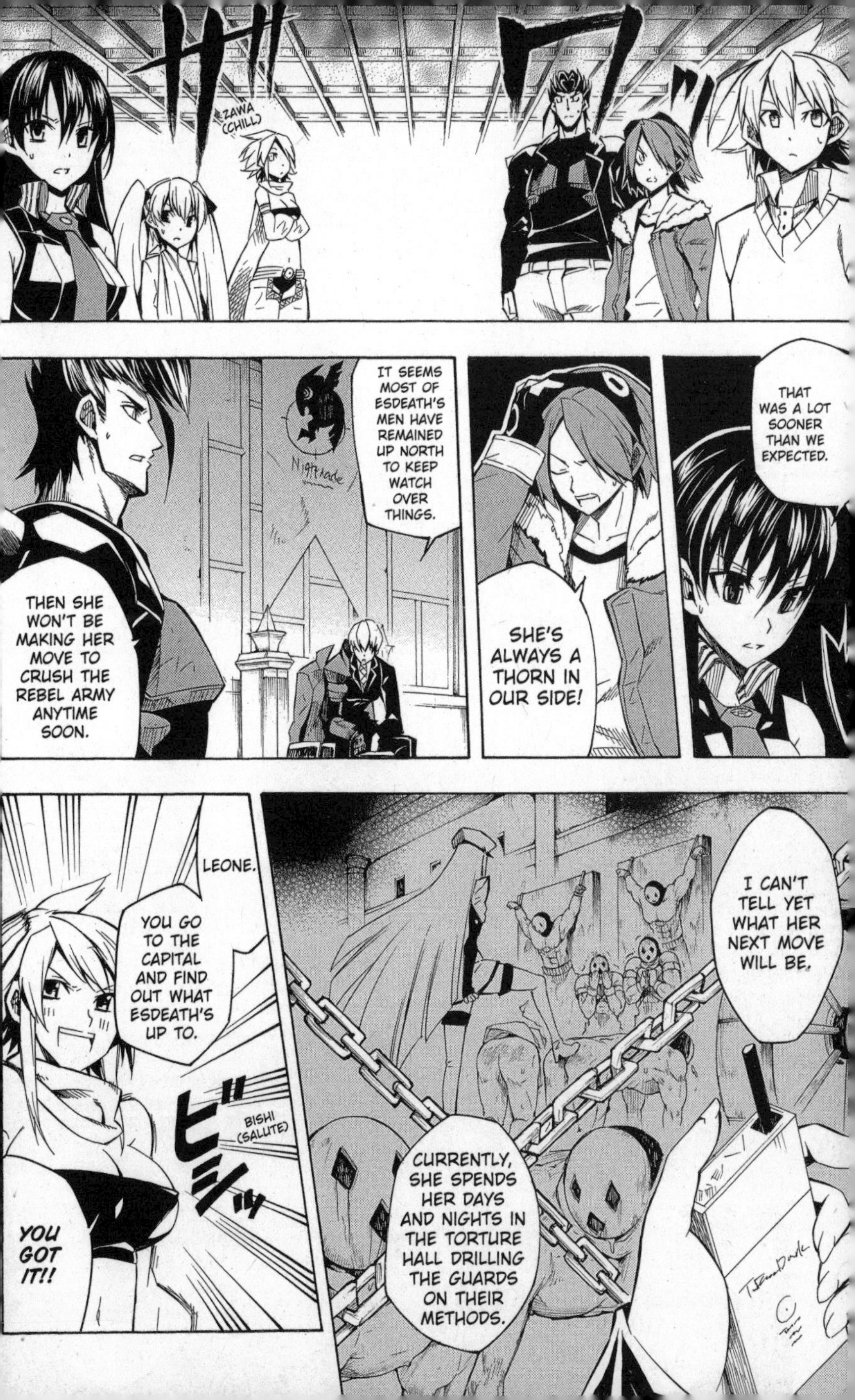
ZAWA (CHILL)
THAT WAS A LOT SOONER THAN WE EXPECTED.
SHE'S ALWAYS A THORN IN OUR SIDE!
IT SEEMS MOST OF ESDEATH'S MEN HAVE REMAINED UP NORTH TO KEEP WATCH OVER THINGS.
THEN SHE WON'T BE MAKING HER MOVE TO CRUSH THE REBEL ARMY ANYTIME SOON.
I CAN'T TELL YET WHAT HER NEXT MOVE WILL BE.
CURRENTLY, SHE SPENDS HER DAYS AND NIGHTS IN THE TORTURE HALL DRILLING THE GUARDS ON THEIR METHODS.
LEONE.
YOU GO TO THE CAPITAL AND FIND OUT WHAT ESDEATH'S UP TO.
BISHI (SALUTE)
YOU GOT IT!!

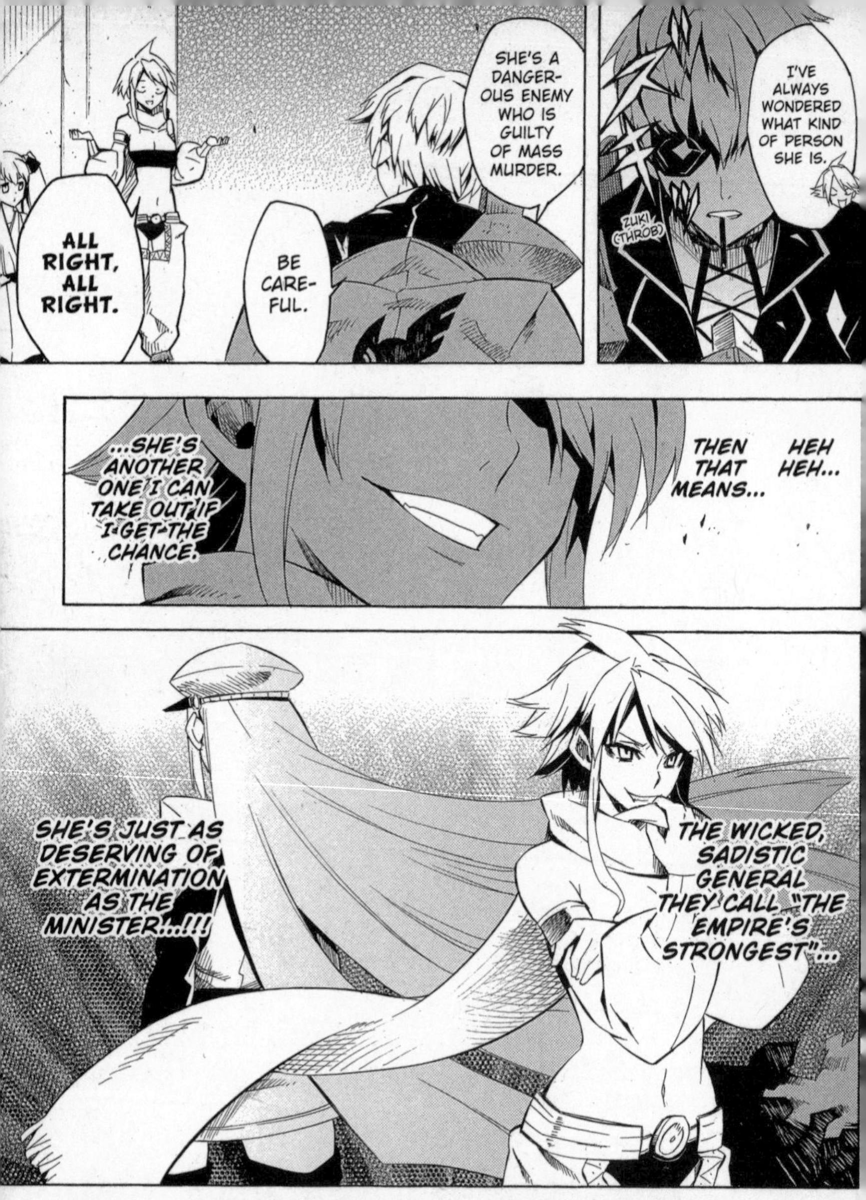
I'VE ALWAYS WONDERED WHAT KIND OF PERSON SHE IS.
ZUKI (THROB)
SHE'S A DANGER-OUS ENEMY WHO IS GUILTY OF MASS MURDER.
BE CARE-FUL.
ALL RIGHT, ALL RIGHT.
HEH HEH...
THEN THAT MEANS...
...SHE'S ANOTHER ONE I CAN TAKE OUT IF I GET THE CHANCE.
THE WICKED, SADISTIC GENERAL THEY CALL "THE EMPIRE'S STRONGEST"...
SHE'S JUST AS DESERVING OF EXTERMINATION AS THE MINISTER...!!!

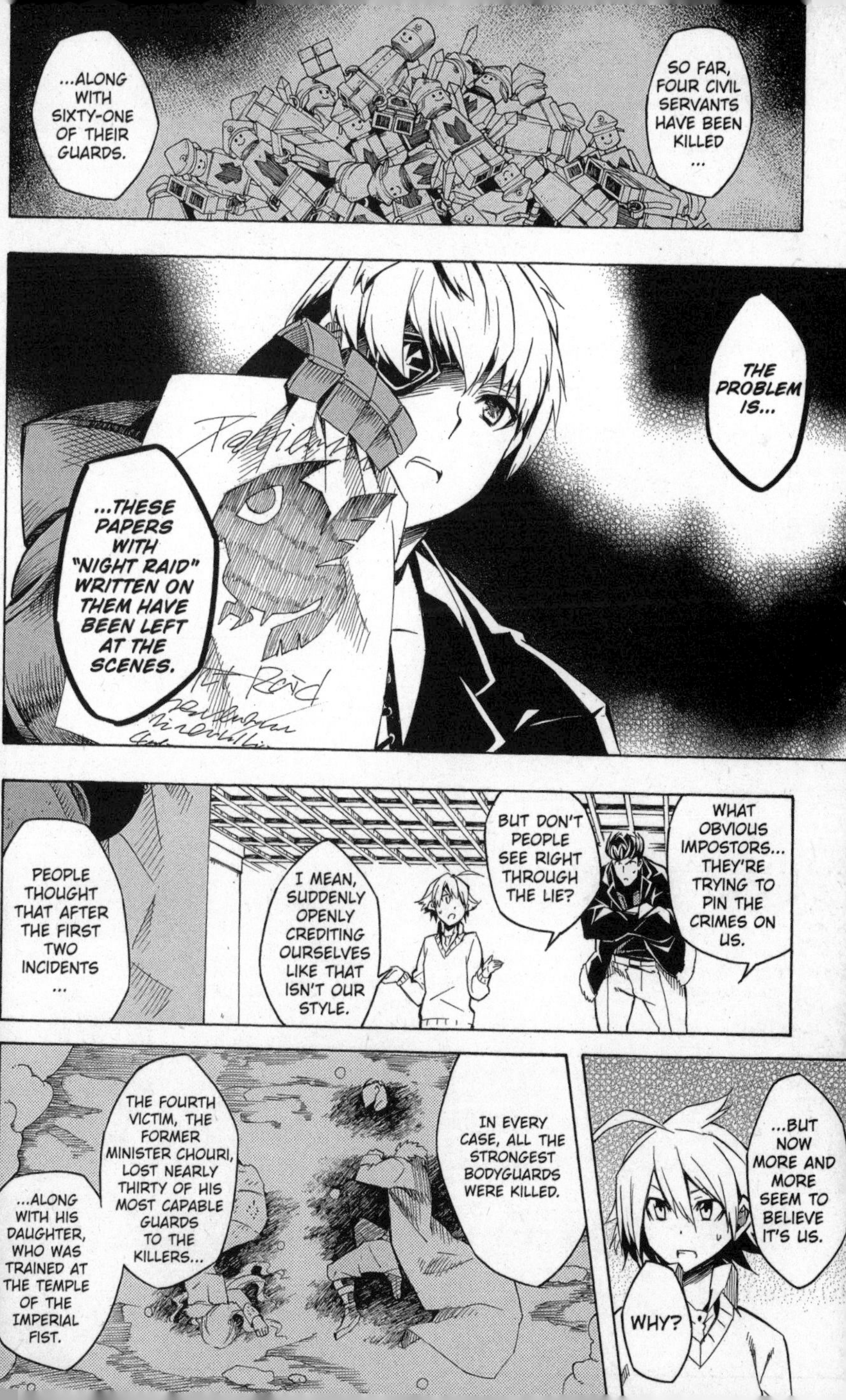
SO FAR, FOUR CIVIL SERVANTS HAVE BEEN KILLED ...
...ALONG WITH SIXTY-ONE OF THEIR GUARDS.
THE PROBLEM IS...
...THESE PAPERS WITH "NIGHT RAID" WRITTEN ON THEM HAVE BEEN LEFT AT THE SCENES.
WHAT OBVIOUS IMPOSTORS... THEY'RE TRYING TO PIN THE CRIMES ON US.
BUT DON'T PEOPLE SEE RIGHT THROUGH THE LIE?
I MEAN, SUDDENLY OPENLY CREDITING OURSELVES LIKE THAT ISN'T OUR STYLE.
PEOPLE THOUGHT THAT AFTER THE FIRST TWO INCIDENTS ...
...BUT NOW MORE AND MORE SEEM TO BELIEVE IT'S US.
WHY?
IN EVERY CASE, ALL THE STRONGEST BODYGUARDS WERE KILLED.
THE FOURTH VICTIM, THE FORMER MINISTER CHOURI, LOST NEARLY THIRTY OF HIS MOST CAPABLE GUARDS TO THE KILLERS...
...ALONG WITH HIS DAUGHTER, WHO WAS TRAINED AT THE TEMPLE OF THE IMPERIAL FIST.

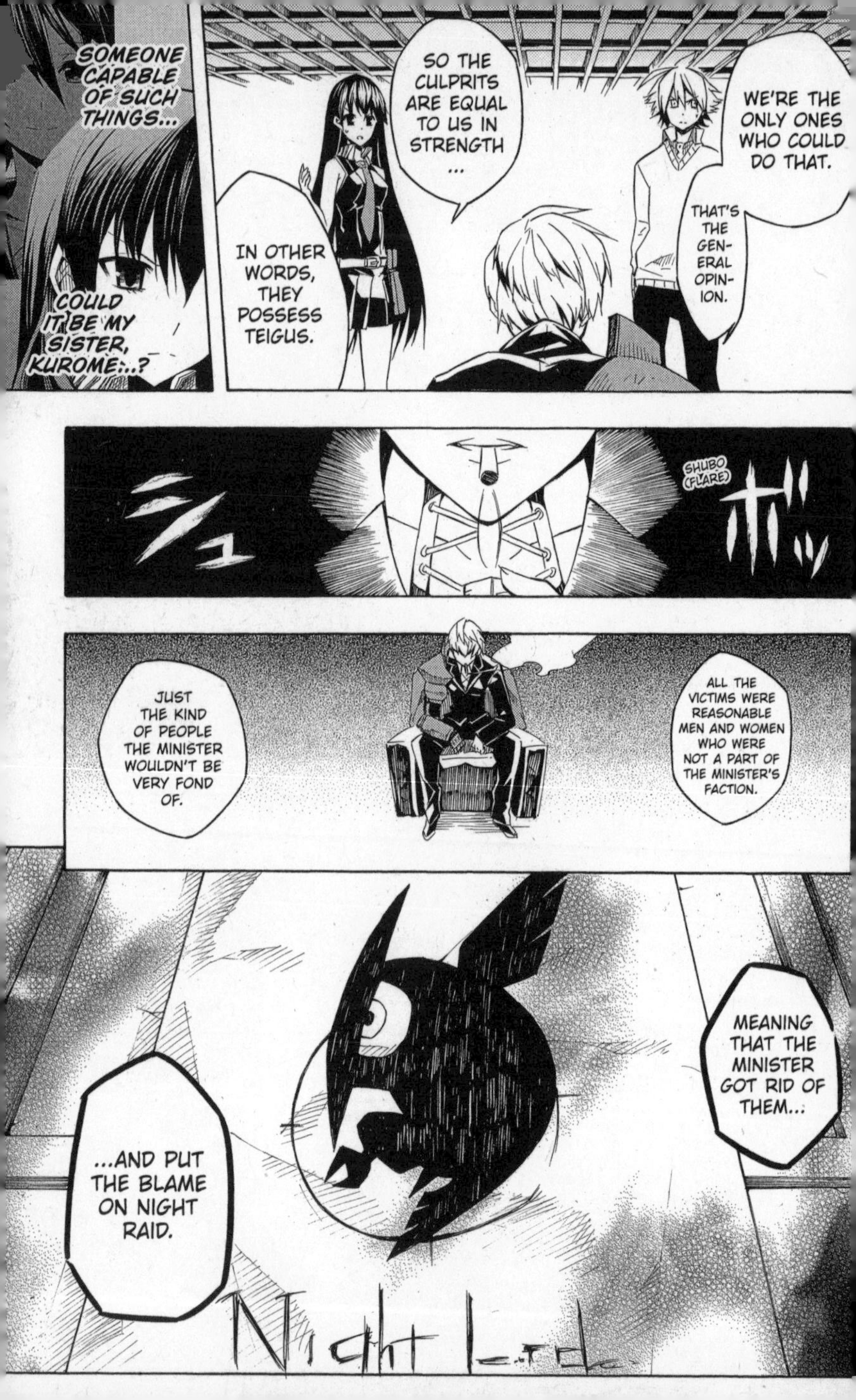

WE'RE THE ONLY ONES WHO COULD DO THAT.
THAT'S THE GEN-ERAL OPIN-ION.
SO THE CULPRITS ARE EQUAL TO US IN STRENGTH ...
IN OTHER WORDS, THEY POSSESS TEIGUS.
SOMEONE CAPABLE OF SUCH THINGS...
COULD IT BE MY SISTER, KUROME...?
SHUBO (FLARE)
ボッ
シュ
ALL THE VICTIMS WERE REASONABLE MEN AND WOMEN WHO WERE NOT A PART OF THE MINISTER'S FACTION.
JUST THE KIND OF PEOPLE THE MINISTER WOULDN'T BE VERY FOND OF.
MEANING THAT THE MINISTER GOT RID OF THEM...
...AND PUT THE BLAME ON NIGHT RAID.

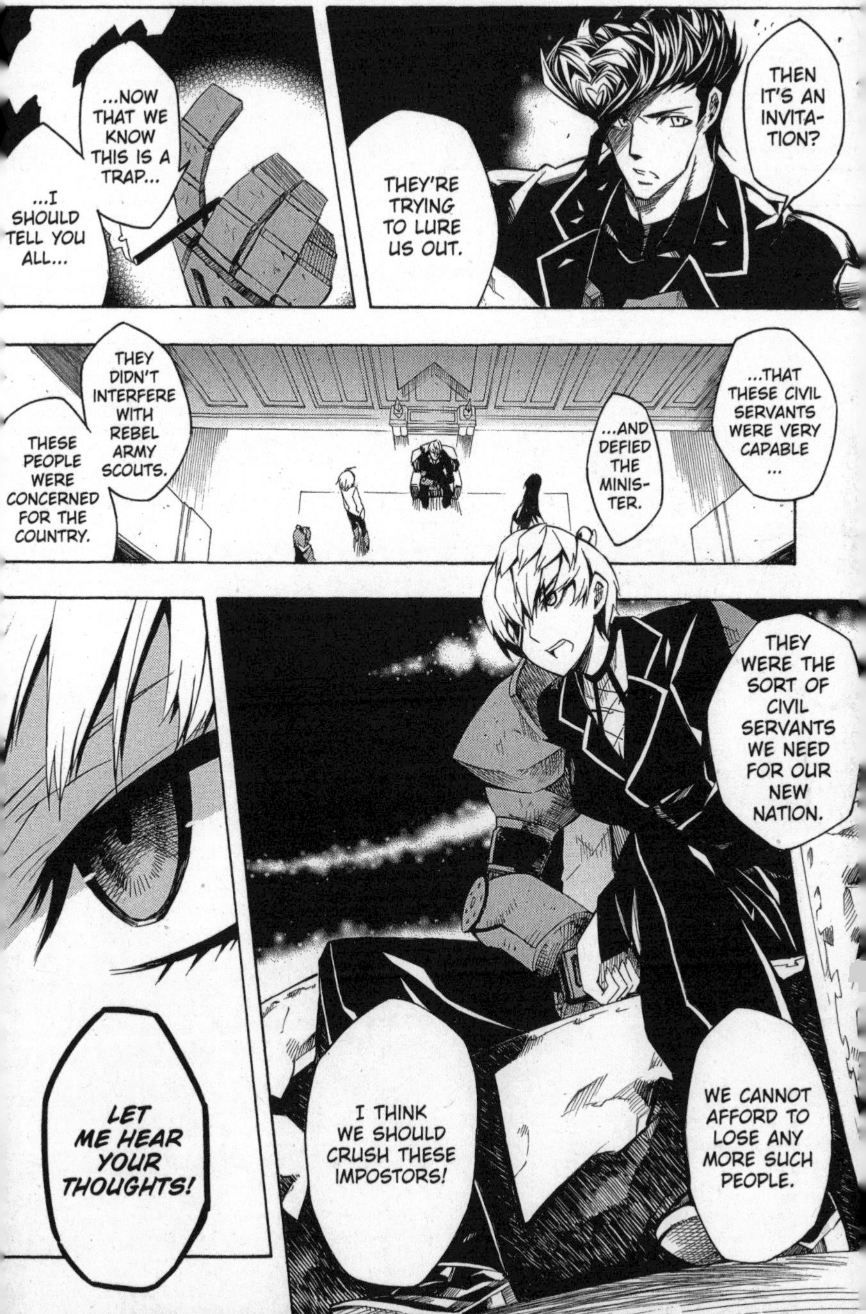
THEN IT'S AN INVITATION?
THEY'RE TRYING TO LURE US OUT.
...NOW THAT WE KNOW THIS IS A TRAP...
...I SHOULD TELL YOU ALL...
...THAT THESE CIVIL SERVANTS WERE VERY CAPABLE...
...AND DEFIED THE MINISTER.
THEY DIDN'T INTERFERE WITH REBEL ARMY SCOUTS.
THESE PEOPLE WERE CONCERNED FOR THE COUNTRY.
THEY WERE THE SORT OF CIVIL SERVANTS WE NEED FOR OUR NEW NATION.
WE CANNOT AFFORD TO LOSE ANY MORE SUCH PEOPLE.
I THINK WE SHOULD CRUSH THESE IMPOSTORS!
LET ME HEAR YOUR THOUGHTS!

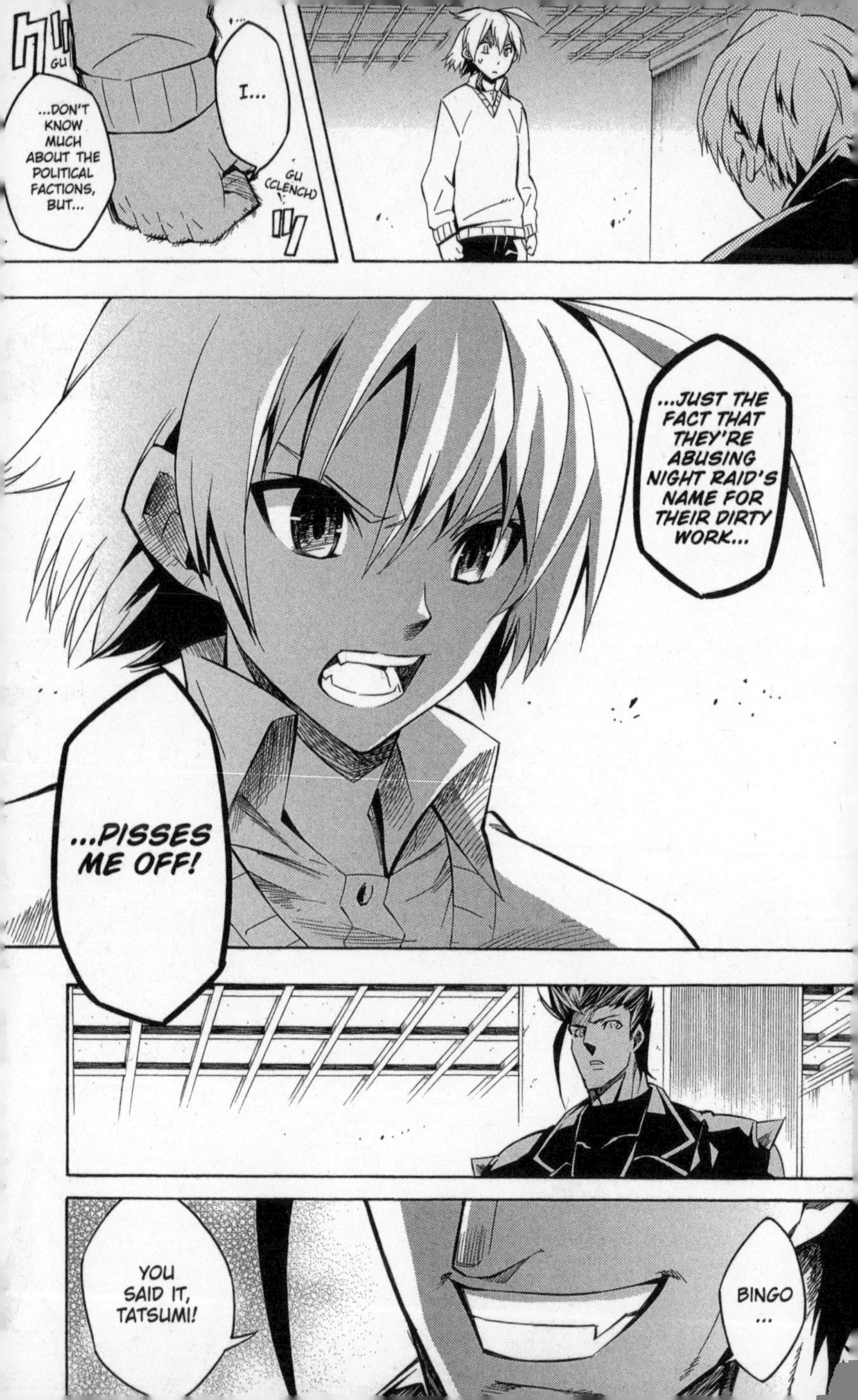
I...
GU
...DON'T KNOW MUCH ABOUT THE POLITICAL FACTIONS, BUT...
GU (CLENCH)
...JUST THE FACT THAT THEY'RE ABUSING NIGHT RAID'S NAME FOR THEIR DIRTY WORK...
...PISSES ME OFF!
BINGO ...
YOU SAID IT, TATSUMI!

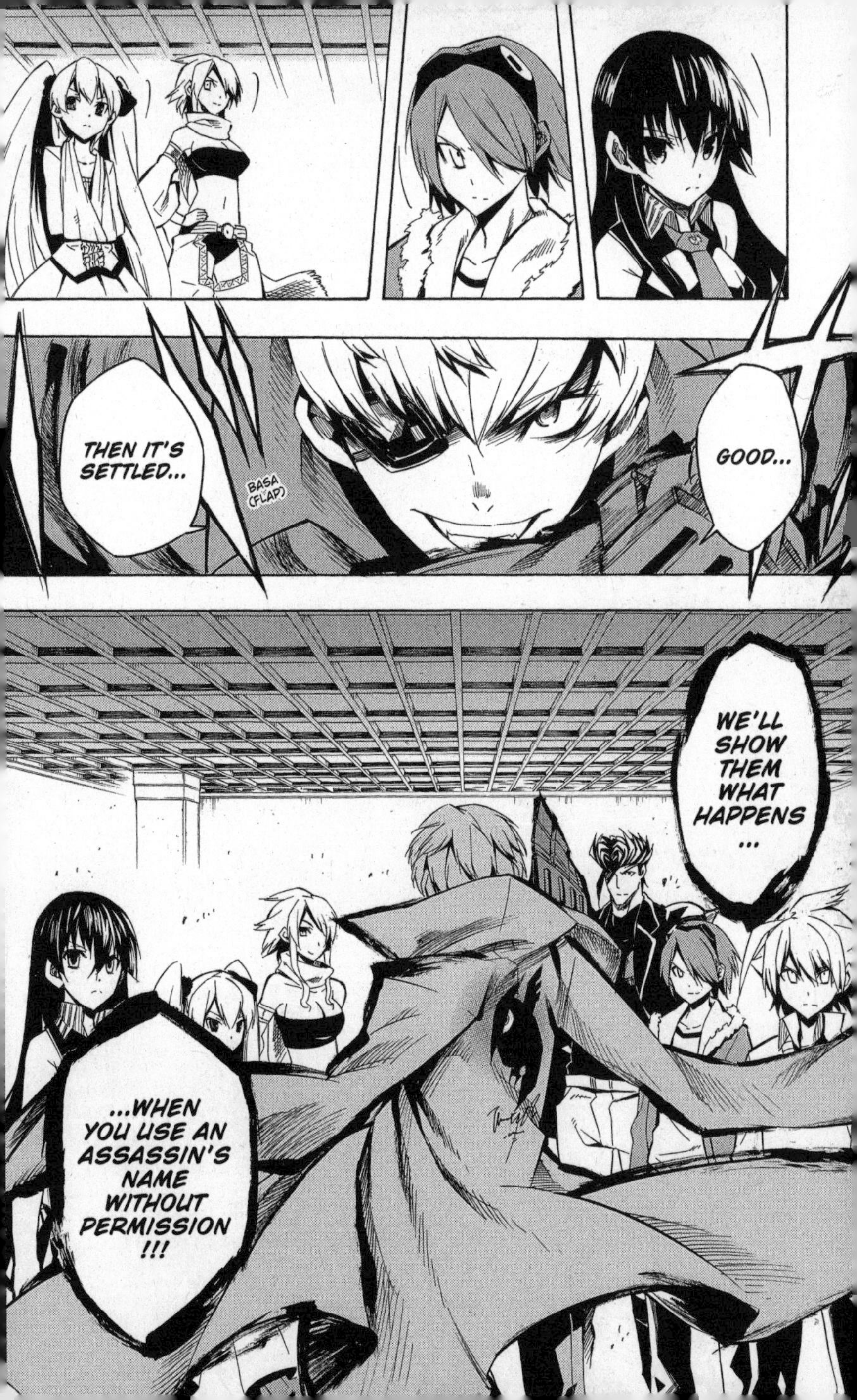
GOOD...
BASA (FLAP)
THEN IT'S SETTLED...
WE'LL SHOW THEM WHAT HAPPENS ...
...WHEN YOU USE AN ASSASSIN'S NAME WITHOUT PERMISSION !!!

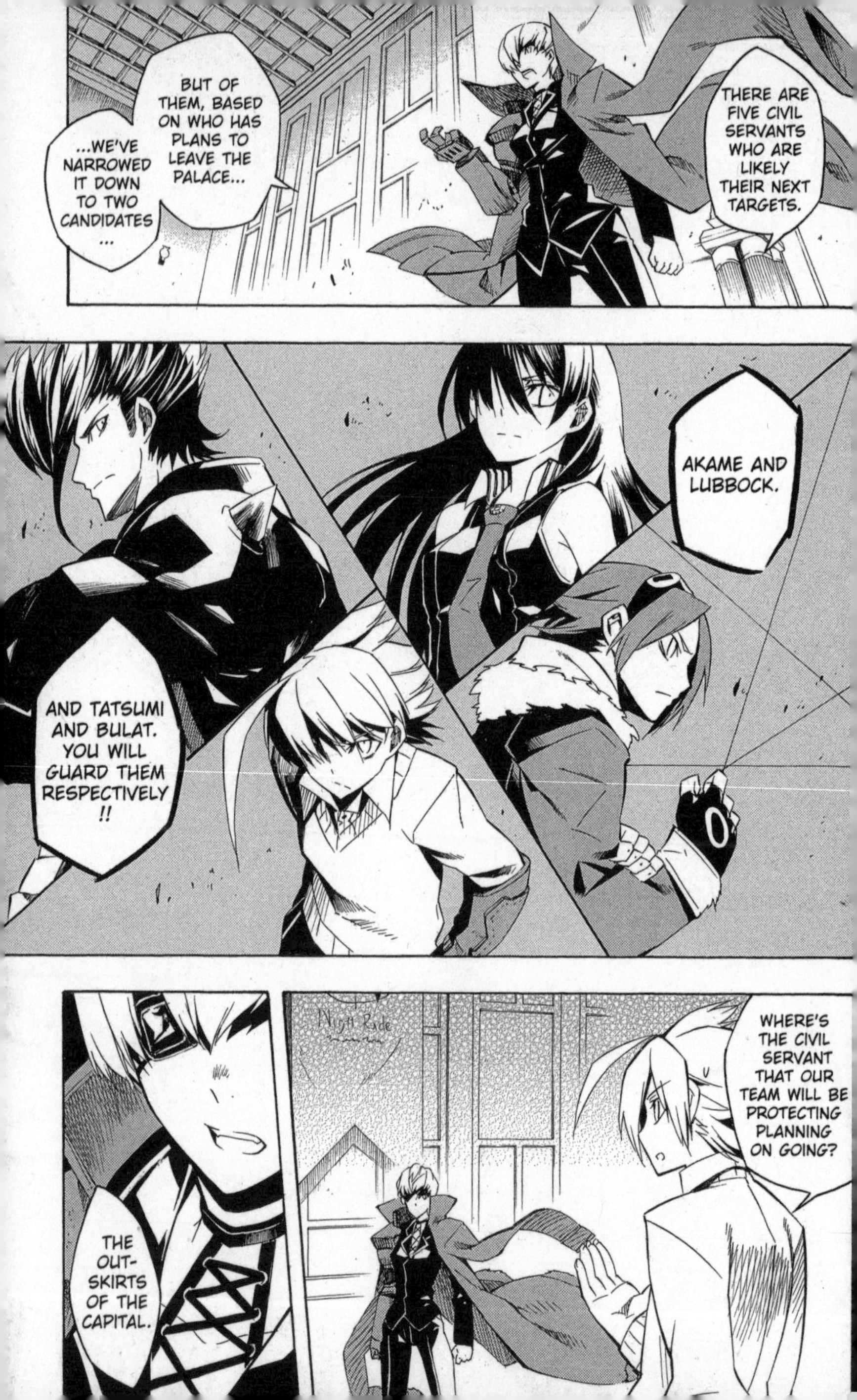
THERE ARE FIVE CIVIL SERVANTS WHO ARE LIKELY THEIR NEXT TARGETS.
BUT OF THEM, BASED ON WHO HAS PLANS TO LEAVE THE PALACE...
...WE'VE NARROWED IT DOWN TO TWO CANDIDATES ...
AKAME AND LUBBOCK.
AND TATSUMI AND BULAT. YOU WILL GUARD THEM RESPECTIVELY !!
WHERE'S THE CIVIL SERVANT THAT OUR TEAM WILL BE PROTECTING PLANNING ON GOING?
Night Raid
THE OUT-SKIRTS OF THE CAPITAL.

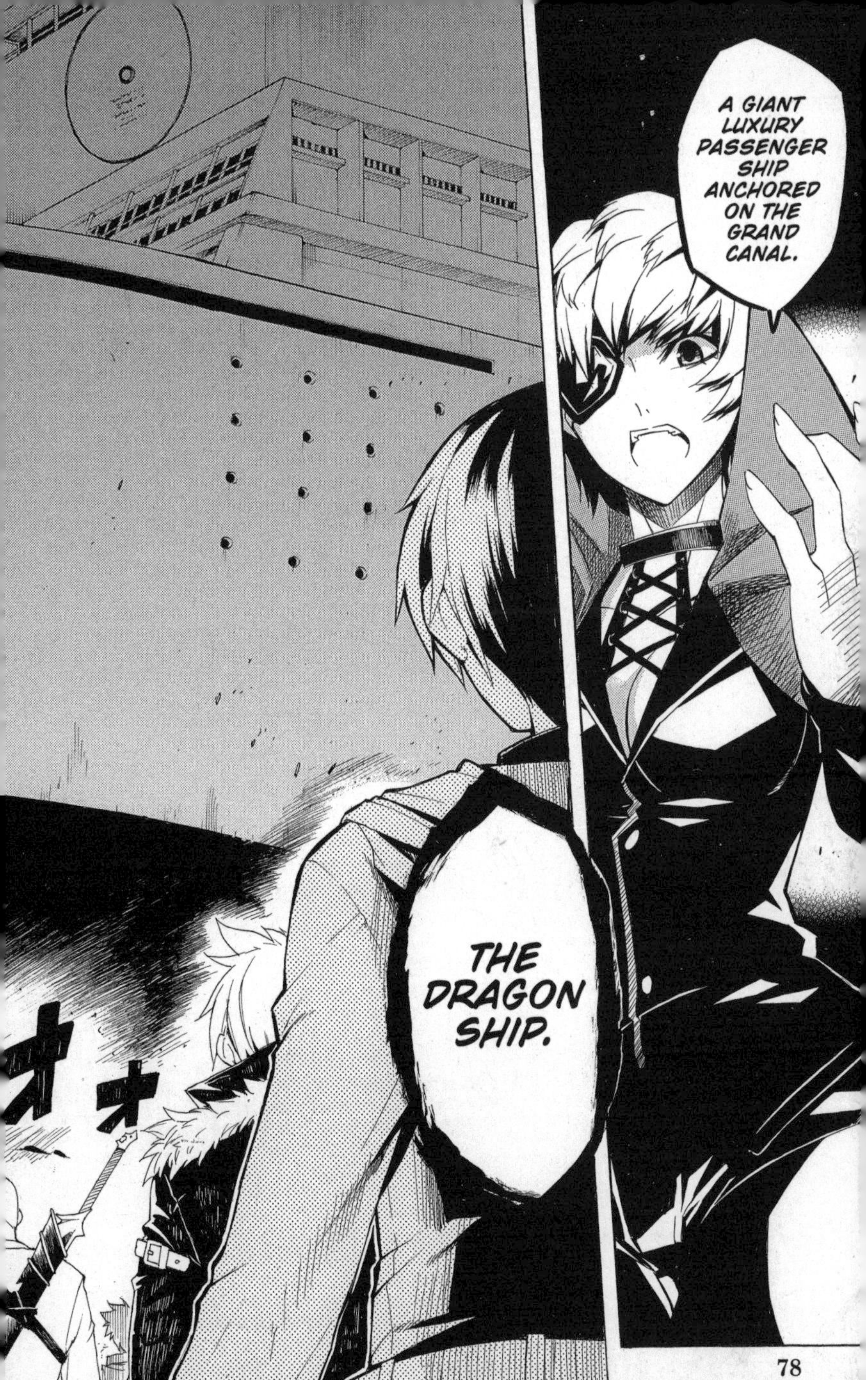
A GIANT LUXURY PASSENGER SHIP ANCHORED ON THE GRAND CANAL.
THE DRAGON SHIP.
オオ

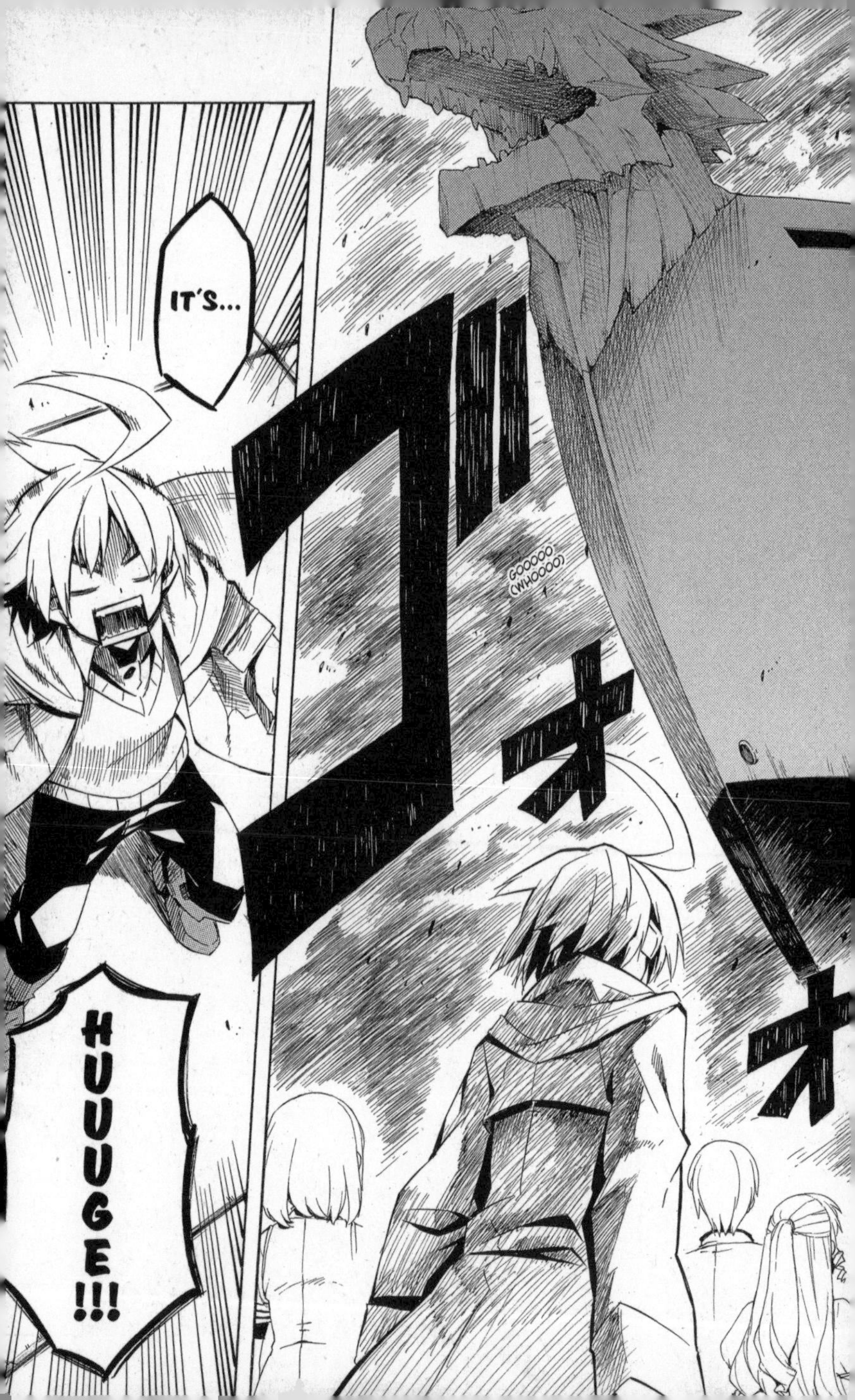
ゴォオ
GOOOOO
(WHOOOO)
IT'S...
HUUUGE!!!

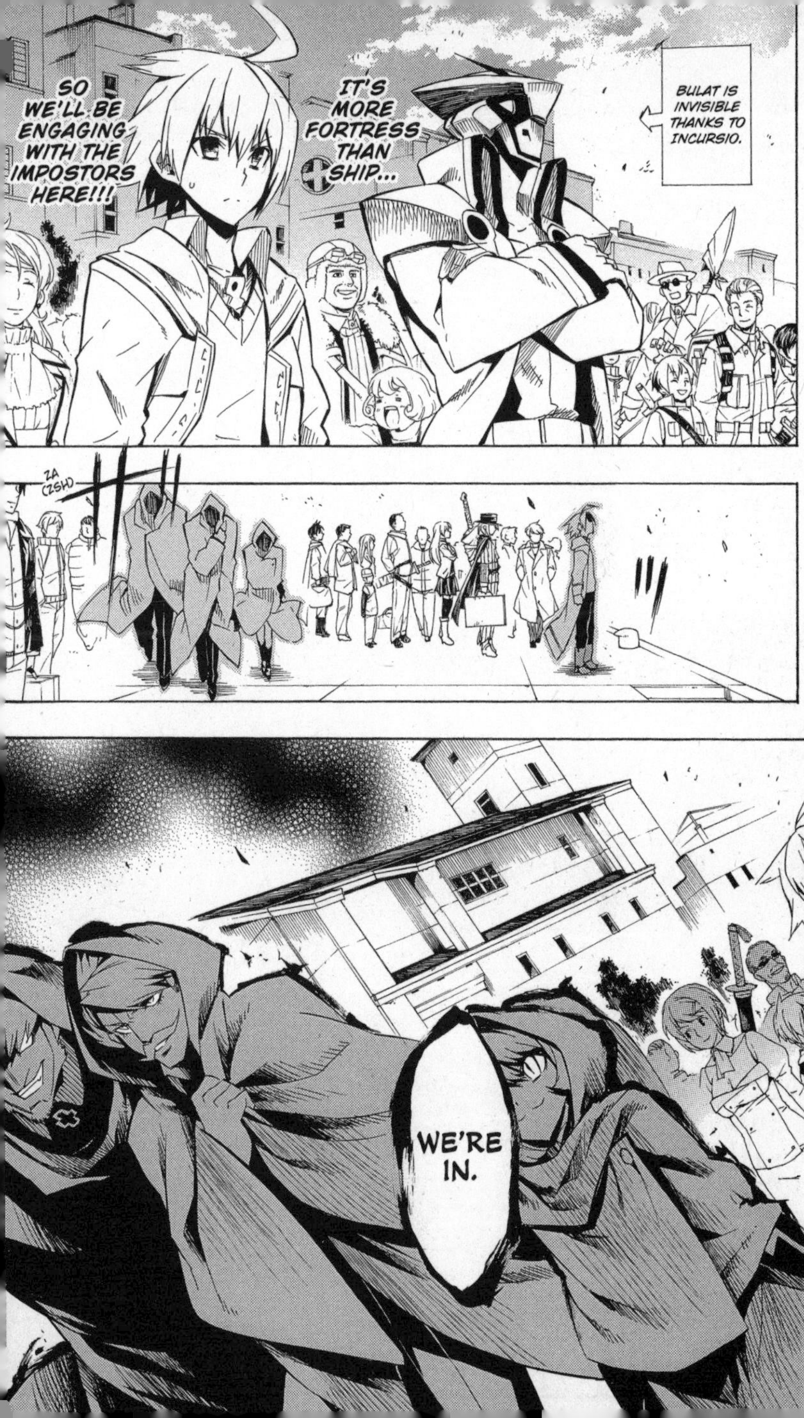
BULAT IS INVISIBLE THANKS TO INCURSIO.
IT'S MORE FORTRESS THAN SHIP...
SO WE'LL BE ENGAGING WITH THE IMPOSTORS HERE!!!
ZA (ZSH)
WE'RE IN.

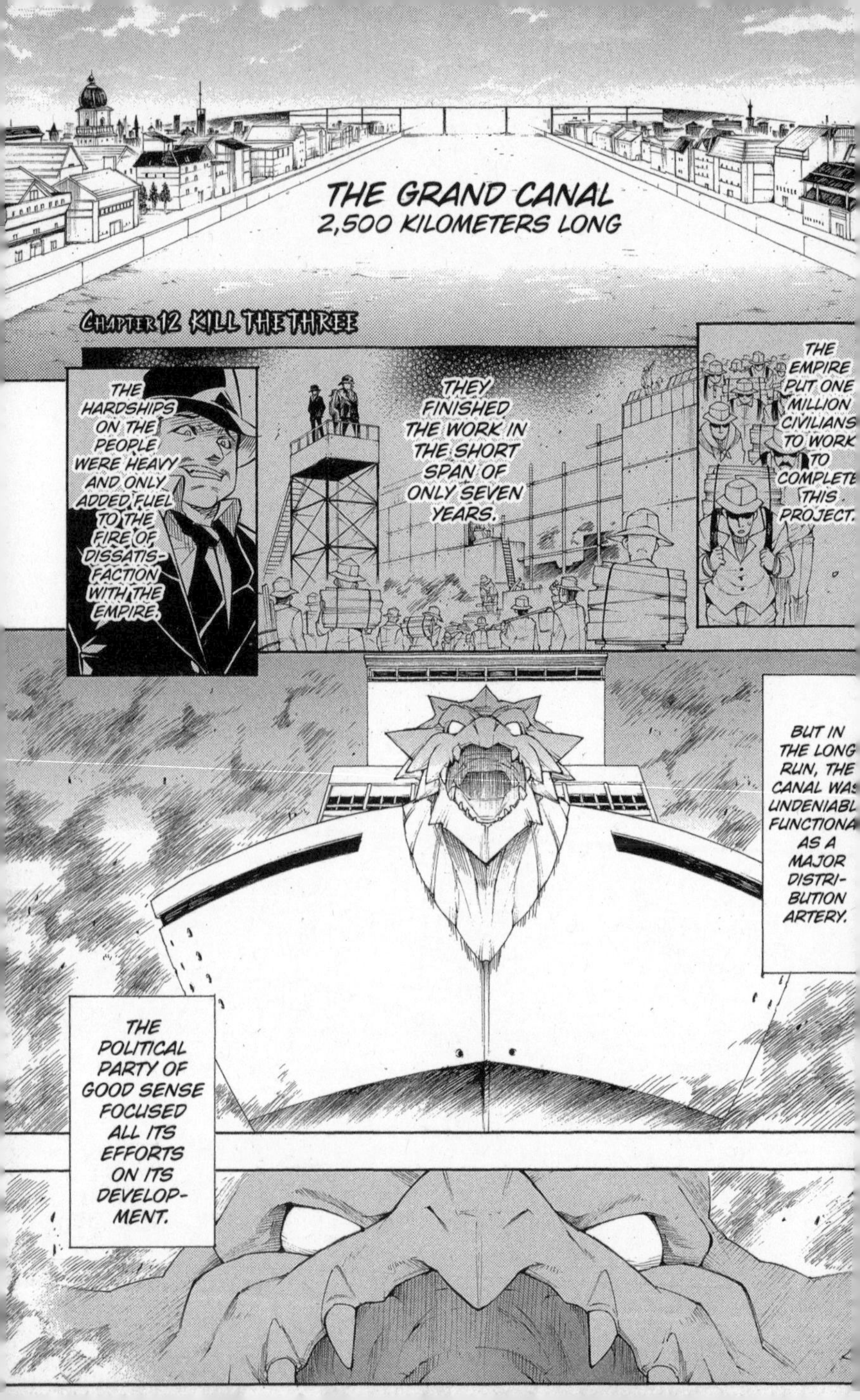
THE GRAND CANAL
2,500 KILOMETERS LONG
CHAPTER 12 KILL THE THREE
THE EMPIRE PUT ONE MILLION CIVILIANS TO WORK TO COMPLETE THIS PROJECT.
THEY FINISHED THE WORK IN THE SHORT SPAN OF ONLY SEVEN YEARS.
THE HARDSHIPS ON THE PEOPLE WERE HEAVY AND ONLY ADDED FUEL TO THE FIRE OF DISSATIS-FACTION WITH THE EMPIRE.
BUT IN THE LONG RUN, THE CANAL WAS UNDENIABL FUNCTIONA AS A MAJOR DISTRI-BUTION ARTERY.
THE POLITICAL PARTY OF GOOD SENSE FOCUSED ALL ITS EFFORTS ON ITS DEVELOP-MENT.

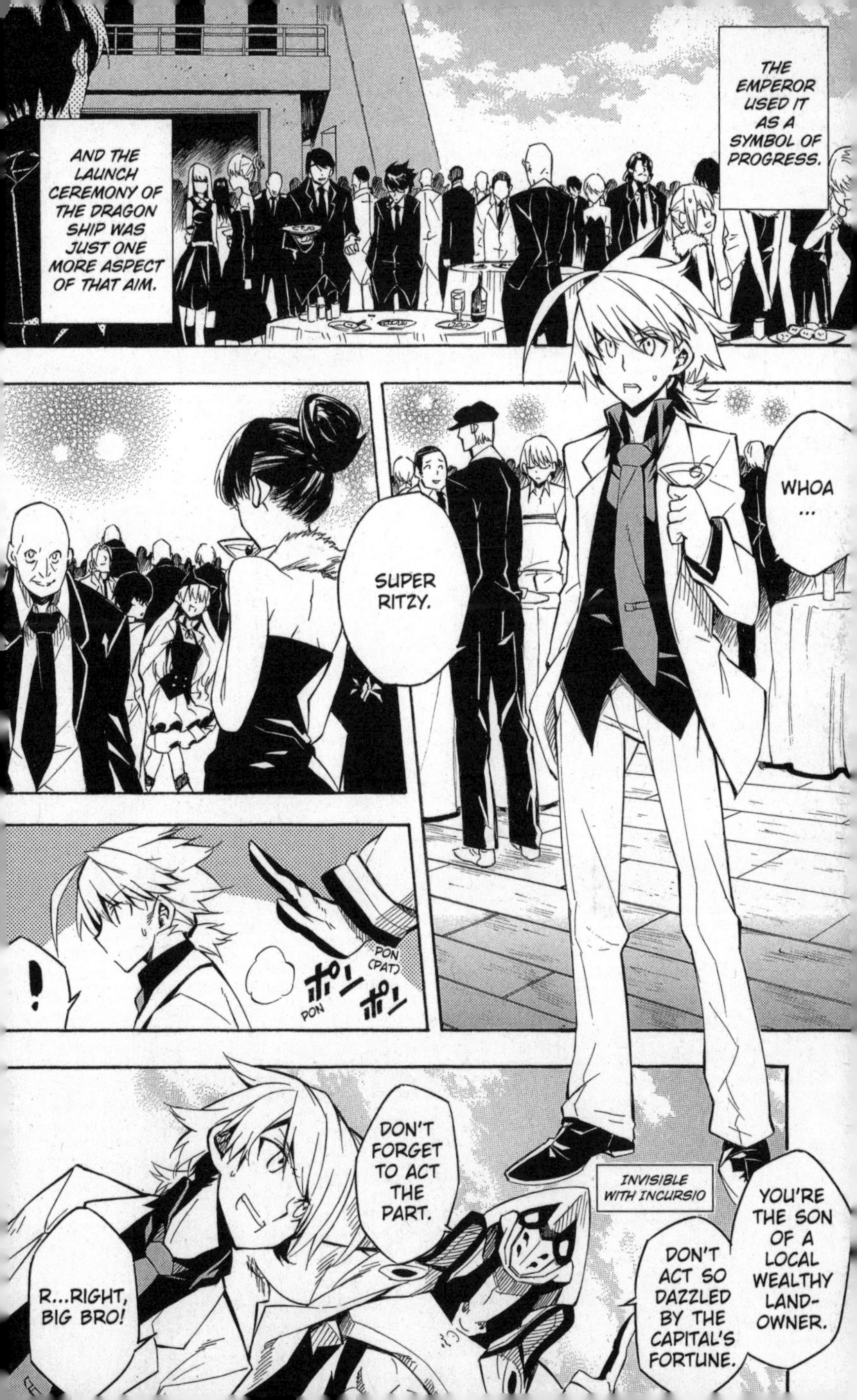
THE EMPEROR USED IT AS A SYMBOL OF PROGRESS.
AND THE LAUNCH CEREMONY OF THE DRAGON SHIP WAS JUST ONE MORE ASPECT OF THAT AIM.
WHOA ...
SUPER RITZY.
ポン ポン
PON (PAT)
PON
!
INVISIBLE WITH INCURSIO
YOU'RE THE SON OF A LOCAL WEALTHY LAND-OWNER.
DON'T ACT SO DAZZLED BY THE CAPITAL'S FORTUNE.
DON'T FORGET TO ACT THE PART.
R...RIGHT, BIG BRO!

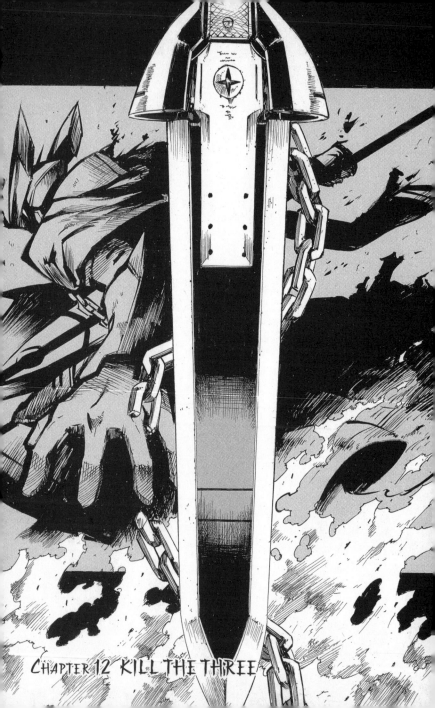

CHAPTER 12 KILL THE THREE

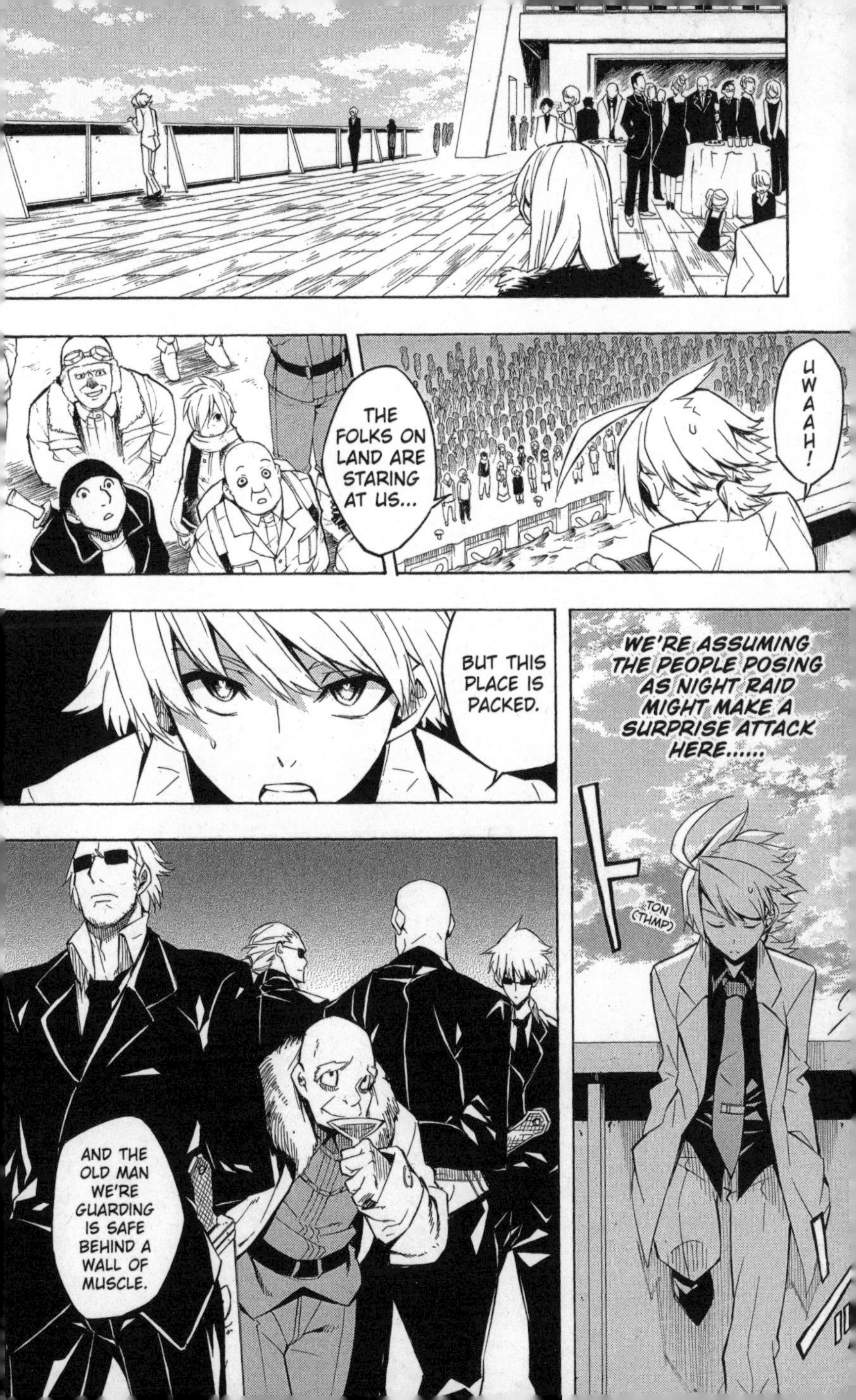
UWAAH!
THE FOLKS ON LAND ARE STARING AT US...
WE'RE ASSUMING THE PEOPLE POSING AS NIGHT RAID MIGHT MAKE A SURPRISE ATTACK HERE......
TON (THMP)
BUT THIS PLACE IS PACKED.
AND THE OLD MAN WE'RE GUARDING IS SAFE BEHIND A WALL OF MUSCLE.

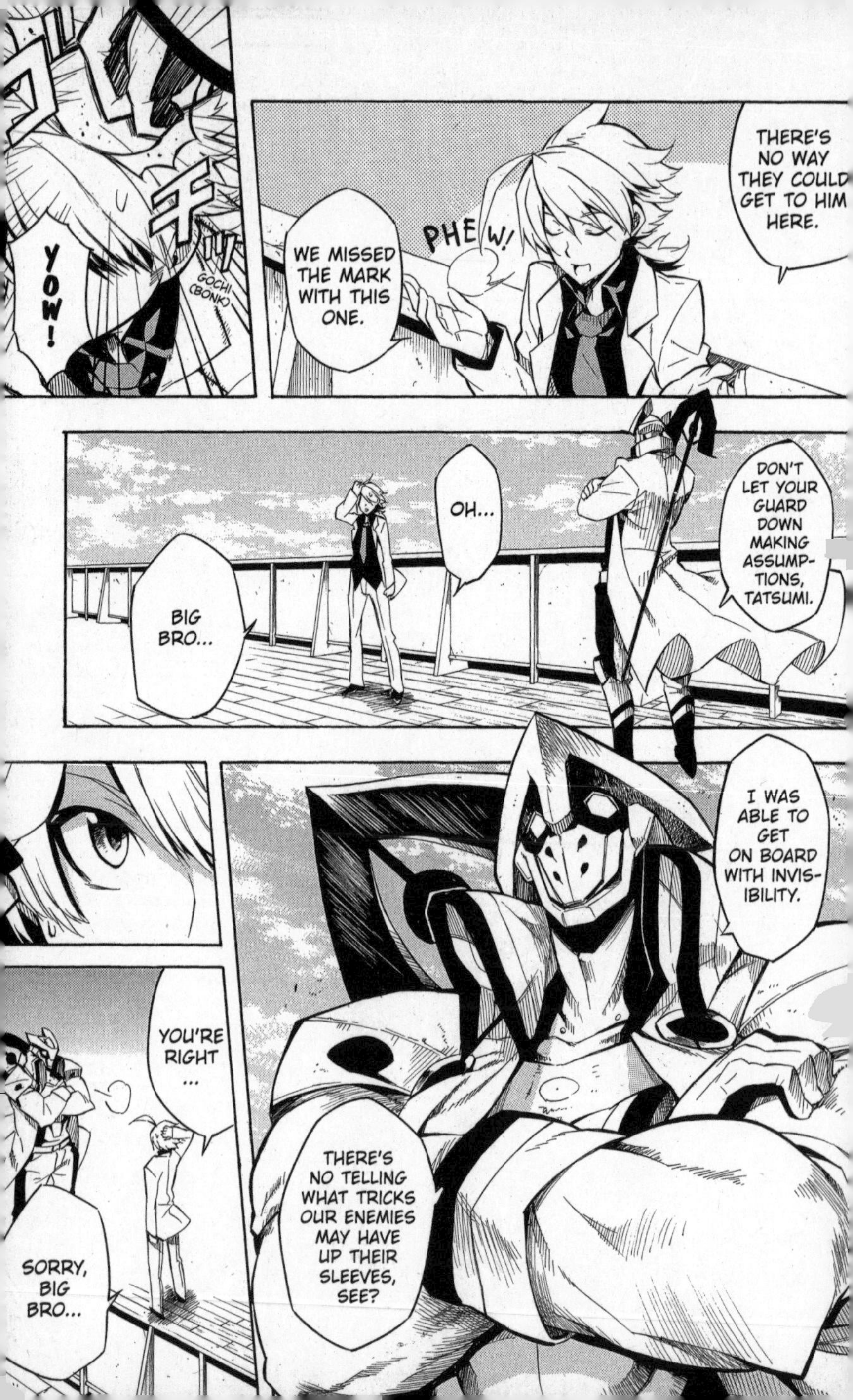
THERE'S NO WAY THEY COULD GET TO HIM HERE.
PHEW!
WE MISSED THE MARK WITH THIS ONE.
GOCHI (BONK)
YOW!
DON'T LET YOUR GUARD DOWN MAKING ASSUMPTIONS, TATSUMI.
OH...
BIG BRO...
I WAS ABLE TO GET ON BOARD WITH INVISIBILITY.
THERE'S NO TELLING WHAT TRICKS OUR ENEMIES MAY HAVE UP THEIR SLEEVES, SEE?
YOU'RE RIGHT ...
SORRY, BIG BRO...

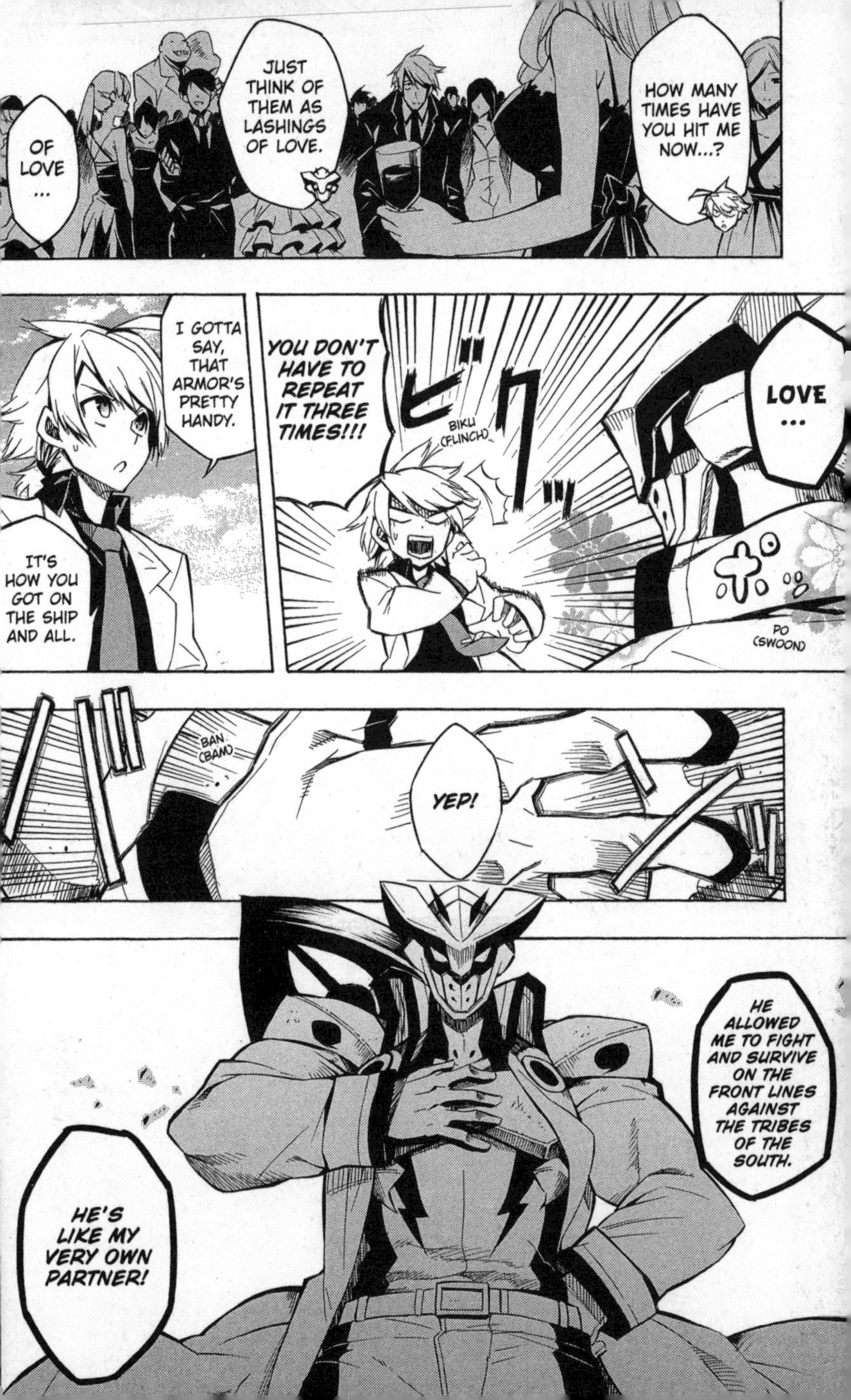
HOW MANY TIMES HAVE YOU HIT ME NOW...?
JUST THINK OF THEM AS LASHINGS OF LOVE.
OF LOVE ...
LOVE ...
PO (SWOON)
YOU DON'T HAVE TO REPEAT IT THREE TIMES!!!
BIKU (FLINCH)
I GOTTA SAY, THAT ARMOR'S PRETTY HANDY.
IT'S HOW YOU GOT ON THE SHIP AND ALL.
BAN (BAM)
YEP!
HE ALLOWED ME TO FIGHT AND SURVIVE ON THE FRONT LINES AGAINST THE TRIBES OF THE SOUTH.
HE'S LIKE MY VERY OWN PARTNER!

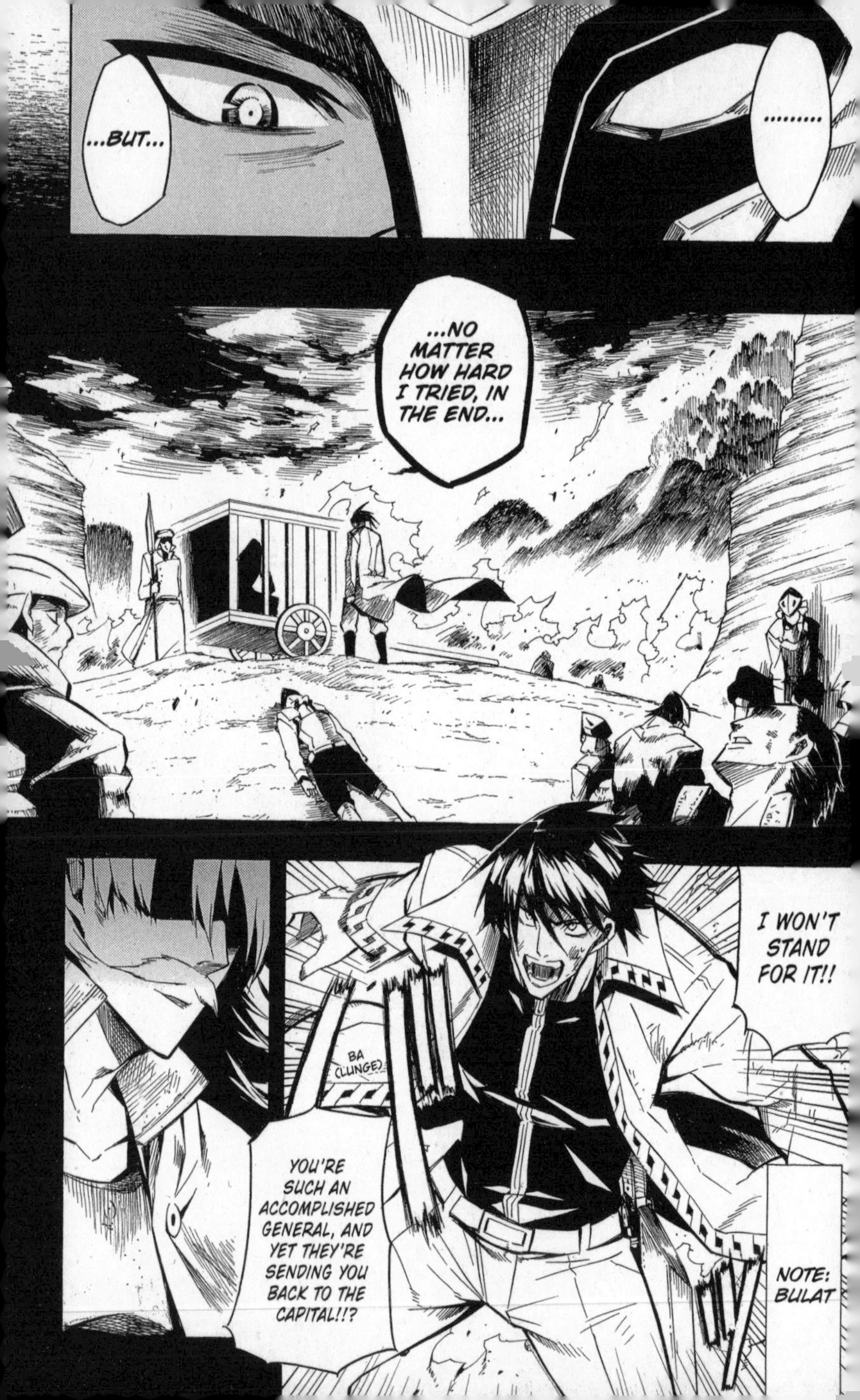
....
...BUT...
...NO MATTER HOW HARD I TRIED, IN THE END...
I WON'T STAND FOR IT!!
BA (LUNGE)
YOU'RE SUCH AN ACCOMPLISHED GENERAL, AND YET THEY'RE SENDING YOU BACK TO THE CAPITAL!!?
NOTE: BULAT

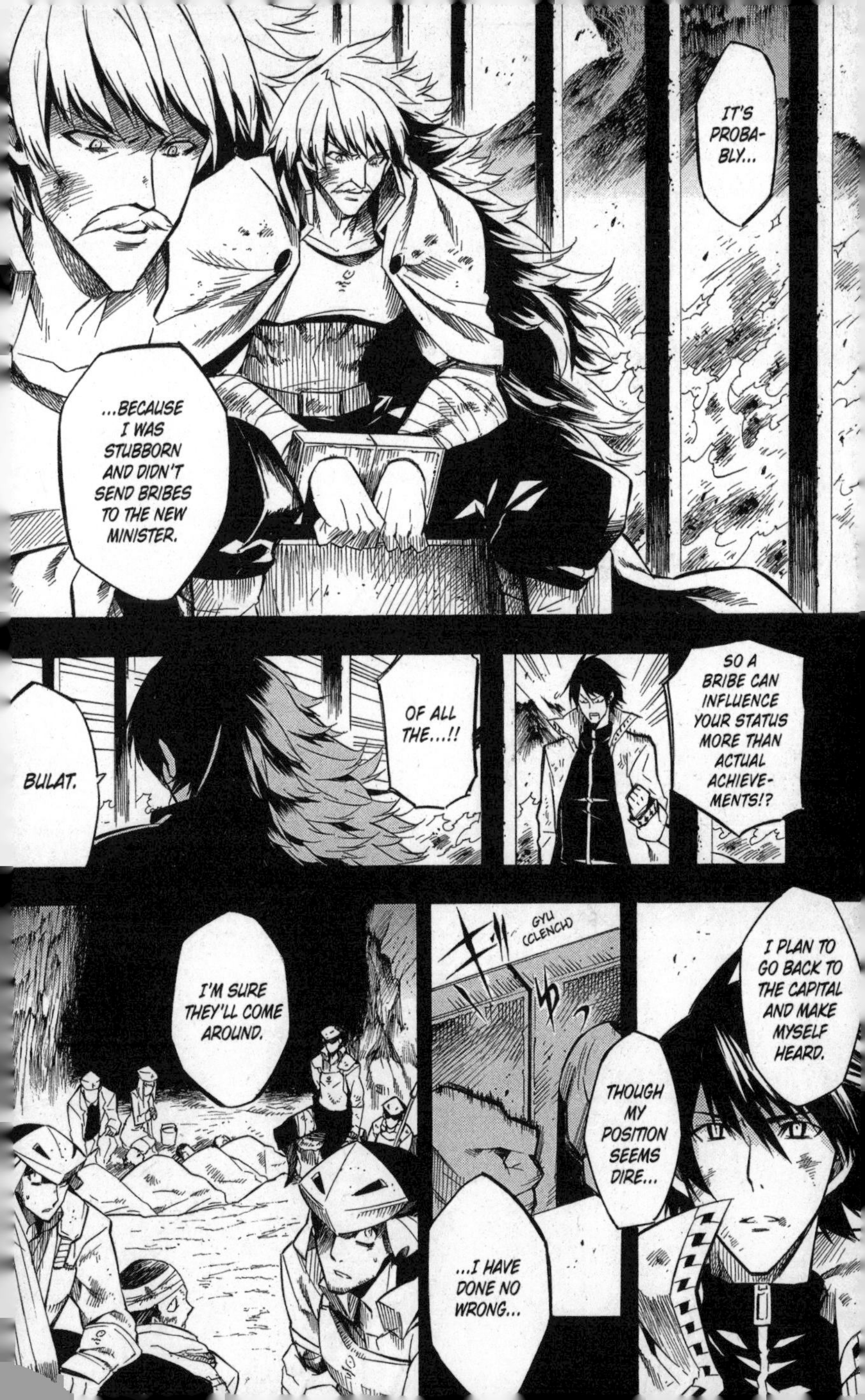

IT'S PROBA-BLY...
...BECAUSE I WAS STUBBORN AND DIDN'T SEND BRIBES TO THE NEW MINISTER.
SO A BRIBE CAN INFLUENCE YOUR STATUS MORE THAN ACTUAL ACHIEVE-MENTS!?
OF ALL THE...!!
BULAT.
I PLAN TO GO BACK TO THE CAPITAL AND MAKE MYSELF HEARD.
GYU (CLENCH)
THOUGH MY POSITION SEEMS DIRE...
...I HAVE DONE NO WRONG...
I'M SURE THEY'LL COME AROUND.

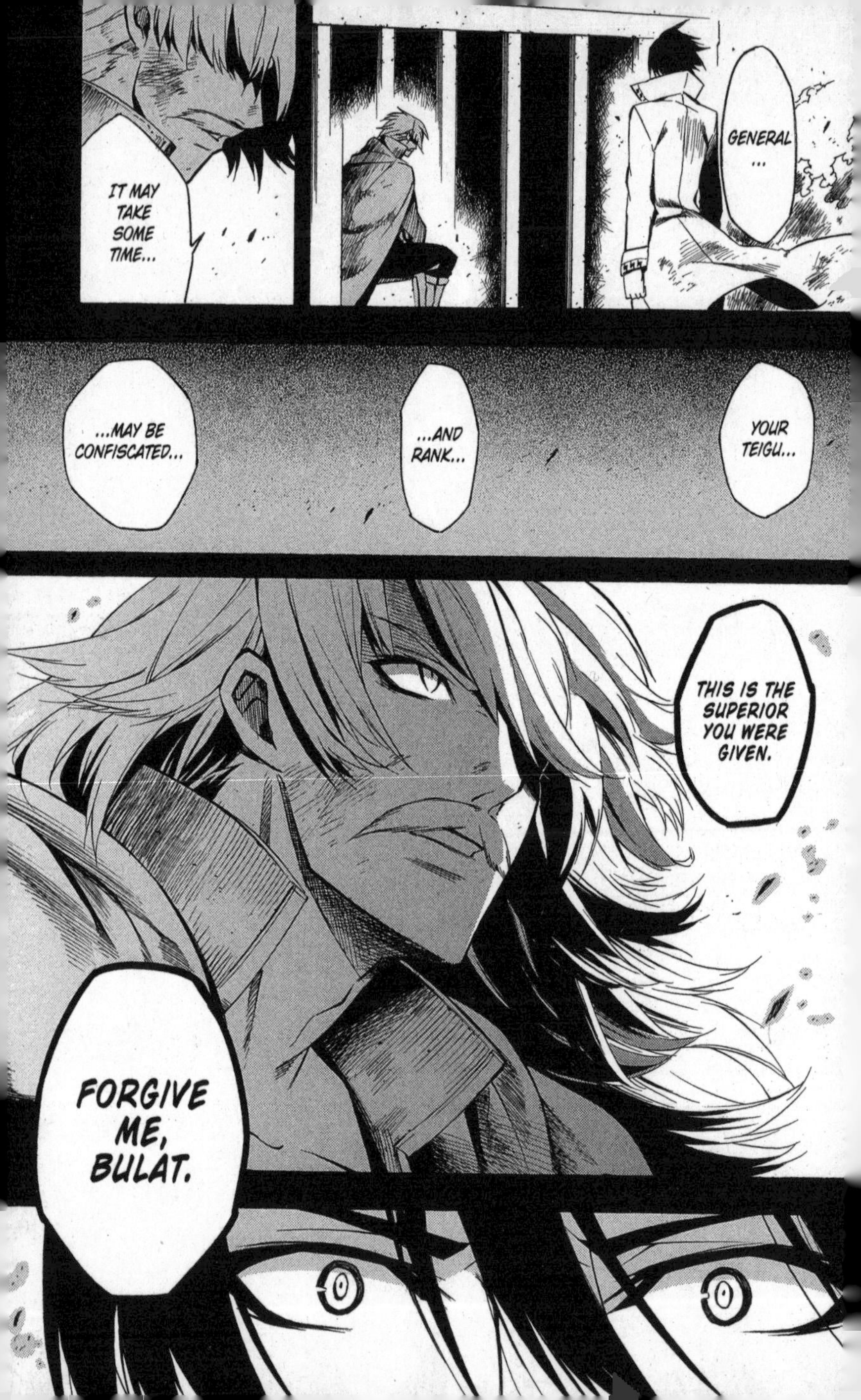
GENERAL ...
IT MAY TAKE SOME TIME...
YOUR TEIGU...
...AND RANK...
...MAY BE CONFISCATED...
THIS IS THE SUPERIOR YOU WERE GIVEN.
FORGIVE ME, BULAT.

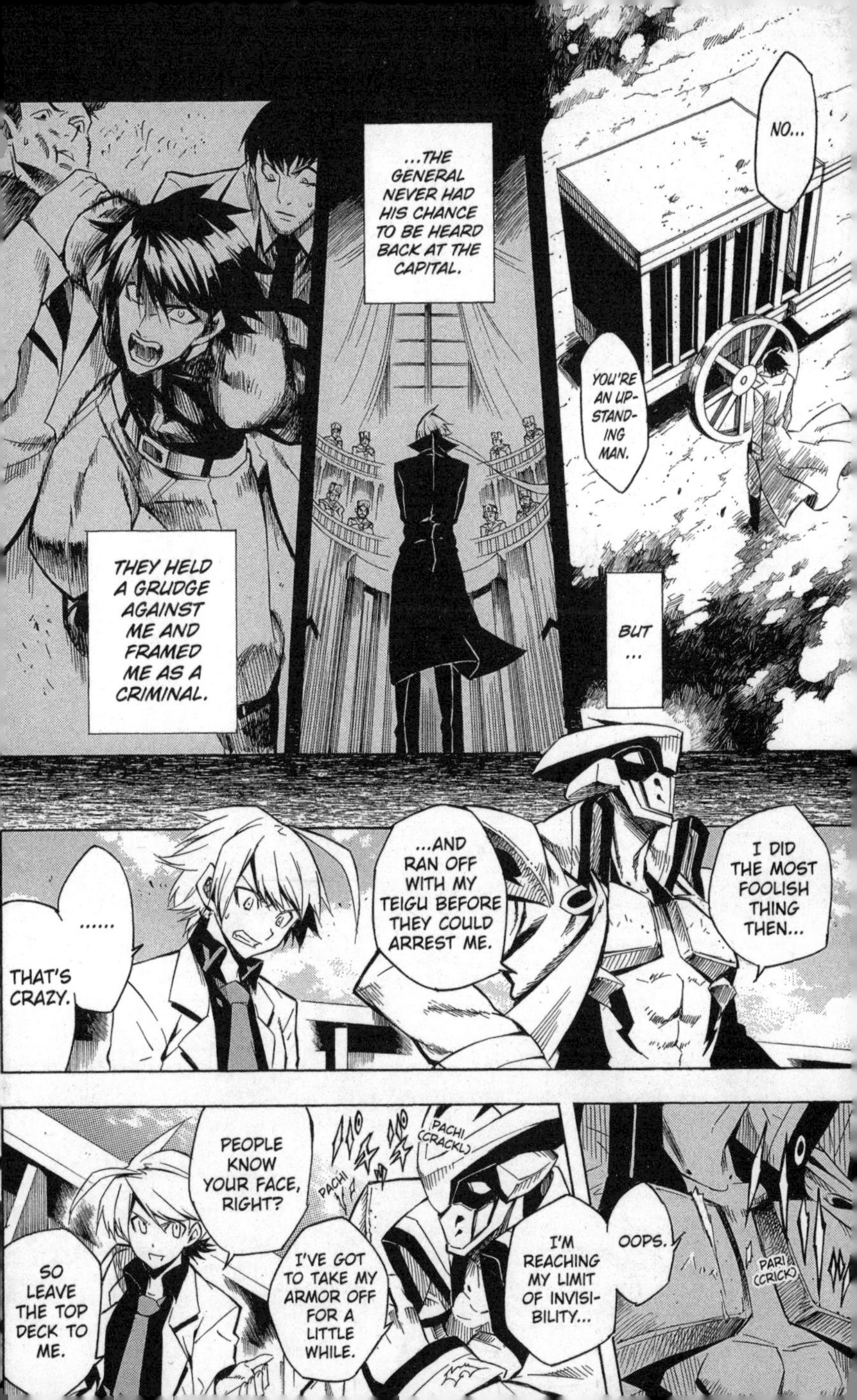
NO...
YOU'RE AN UP-STANDING MAN.
BUT ...
...THE GENERAL NEVER HAD HIS CHANCE TO BE HEARD BACK AT THE CAPITAL.
THEY HELD A GRUDGE AGAINST ME AND FRAMED ME AS A CRIMINAL.
I DID THE MOST FOOLISH THING THEN...
...AND RAN OFF WITH MY TEIGU BEFORE THEY COULD ARREST ME.
......
THAT'S CRAZY.
PARI (CRICK)
OOPS.
I'M REACHING MY LIMIT OF INVISI-BILITY...
PACHI (CRACKL)
PACHI
I'VE GOT TO TAKE MY ARMOR OFF FOR A LITTLE WHILE.
PEOPLE KNOW YOUR FACE, RIGHT?
SO LEAVE THE TOP DECK TO ME.

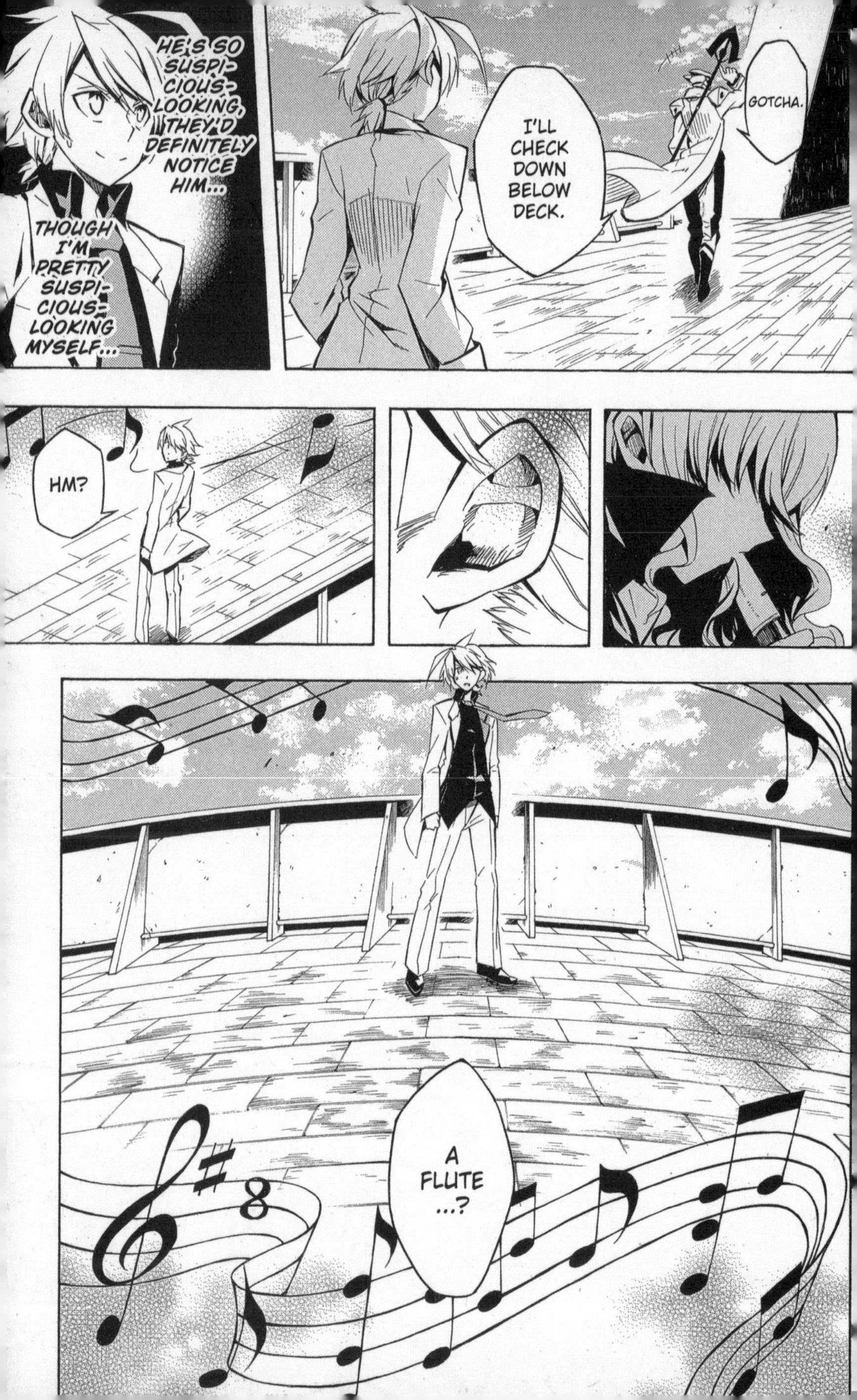
GOTCHA.
I'LL CHECK DOWN BELOW DECK.
HE'S SO SUSPICIOUS-LOOKING, THEY'D DEFINITELY NOTICE HIM...
THOUGH I'M PRETTY SUSPICIOUS-LOOKING MYSELF...
HM?
A FLUTE ...?

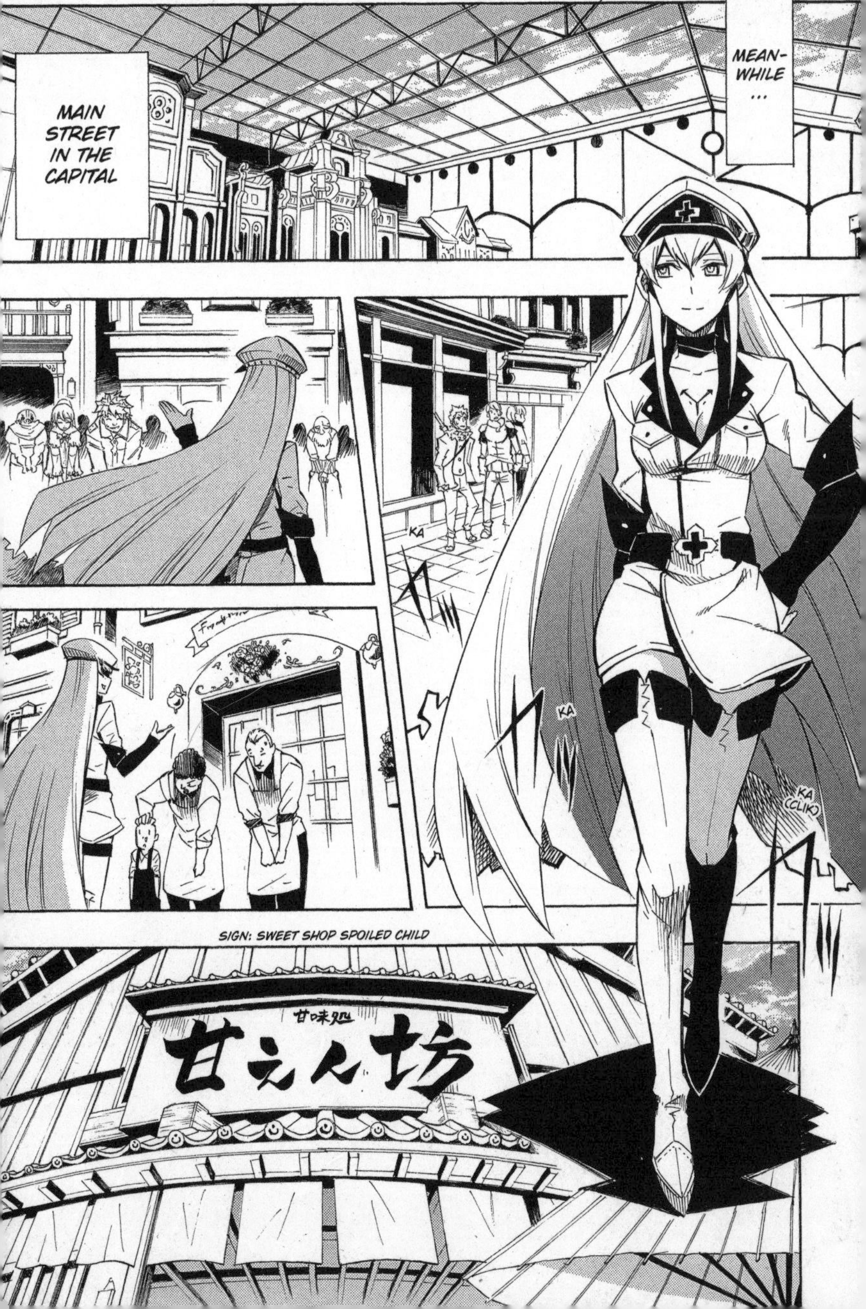
MEAN-WHILE...
MAIN STREET IN THE CAPITAL
KA
KA (CLIK)
KA
SIGN: SWEET SHOP SPOILED CHILD
甘味処
甘えん坊

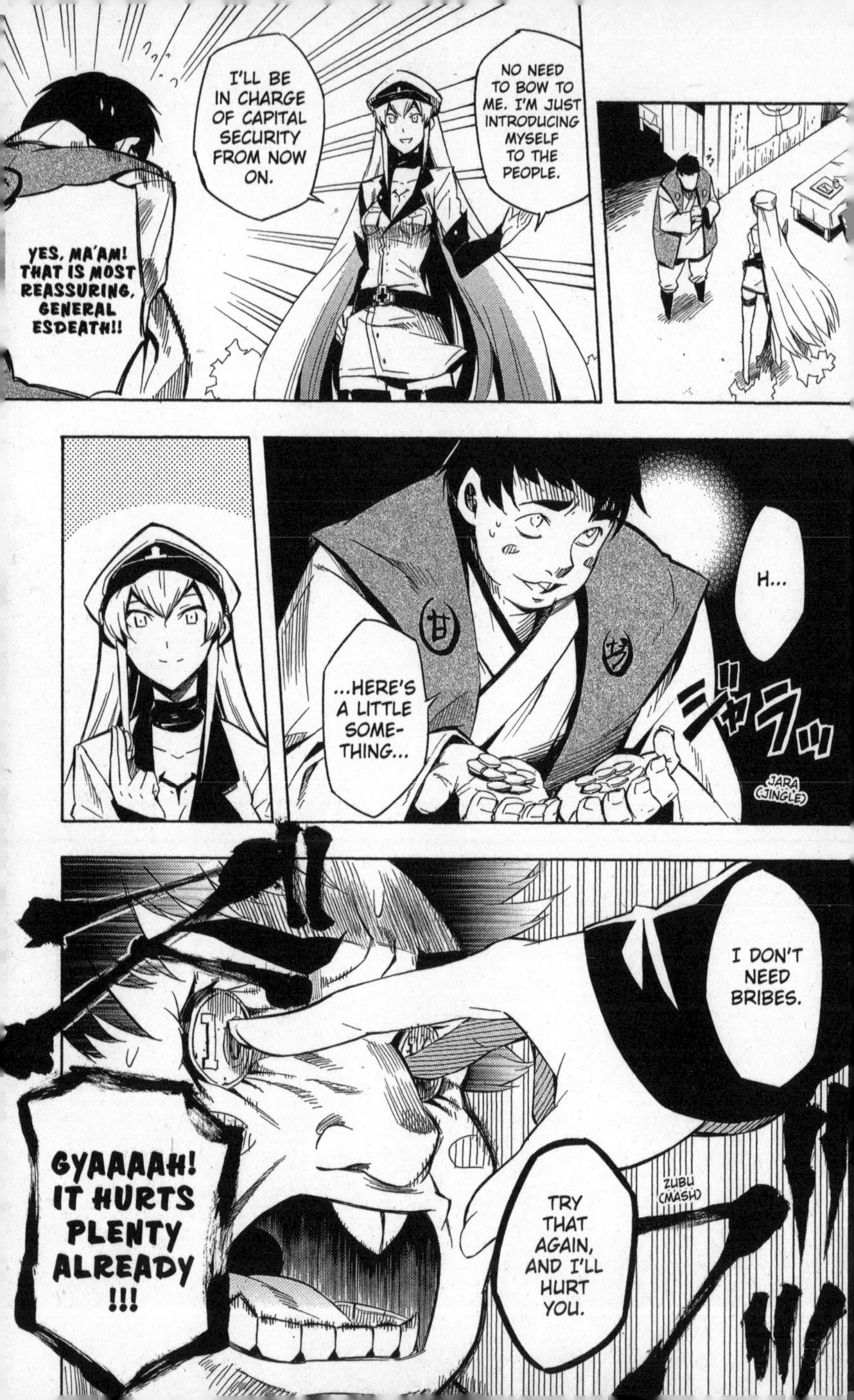
NO NEED TO BOW TO ME. I'M JUST INTRODUCING MYSELF TO THE PEOPLE.
I'LL BE IN CHARGE OF CAPITAL SECURITY FROM NOW ON.
YES, MA'AM! THAT IS MOST REASSURING, GENERAL ESDEATH!!
H...
ジャラッ
JARA (JINGLE)
...HERE'S A LITTLE SOME-THING...
I DON'T NEED BRIBES.
TRY THAT AGAIN, AND I'LL HURT YOU.
ZUBU (MASH)
GYAAAAH! IT HURTS PLENTY ALREADY !!!

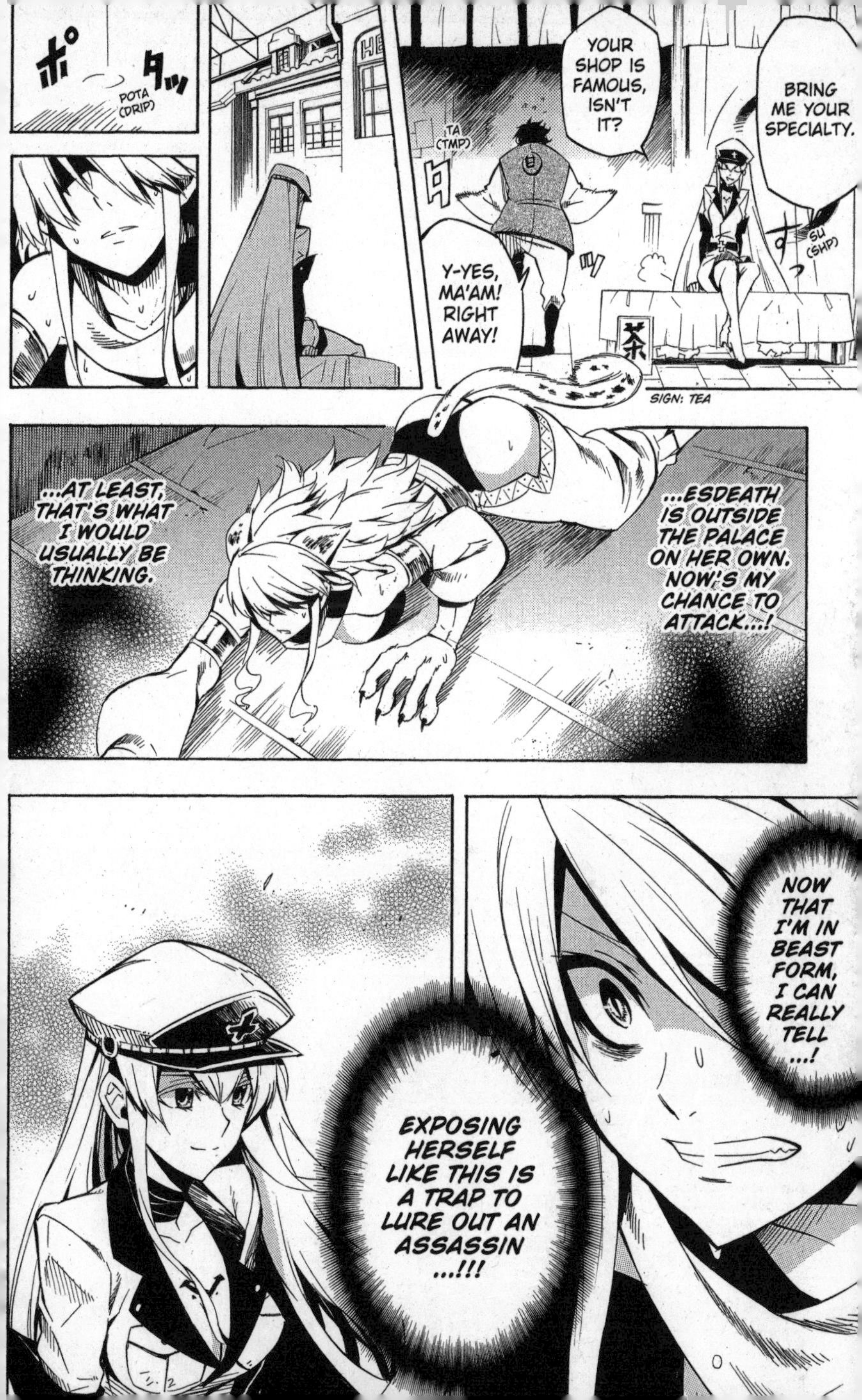
BRING ME YOUR SPECIALTY.
SU (SHP)
YOUR SHOP IS FAMOUS, ISN'T IT?
TA (TMP)
Y-YES, MA'AM! RIGHT AWAY!
SIGN: TEA
POTA (DRIP)
...ESDEATH IS OUTSIDE THE PALACE ON HER OWN. NOW'S MY CHANCE TO ATTACK...!
...AT LEAST, THAT'S WHAT I WOULD USUALLY BE THINKING.
NOW THAT I'M IN BEAST FORM, I CAN REALLY TELL ...!
...
EXPOSING HERSELF LIKE THIS IS A TRAP TO LURE OUT AN ASSASSIN ...!!!

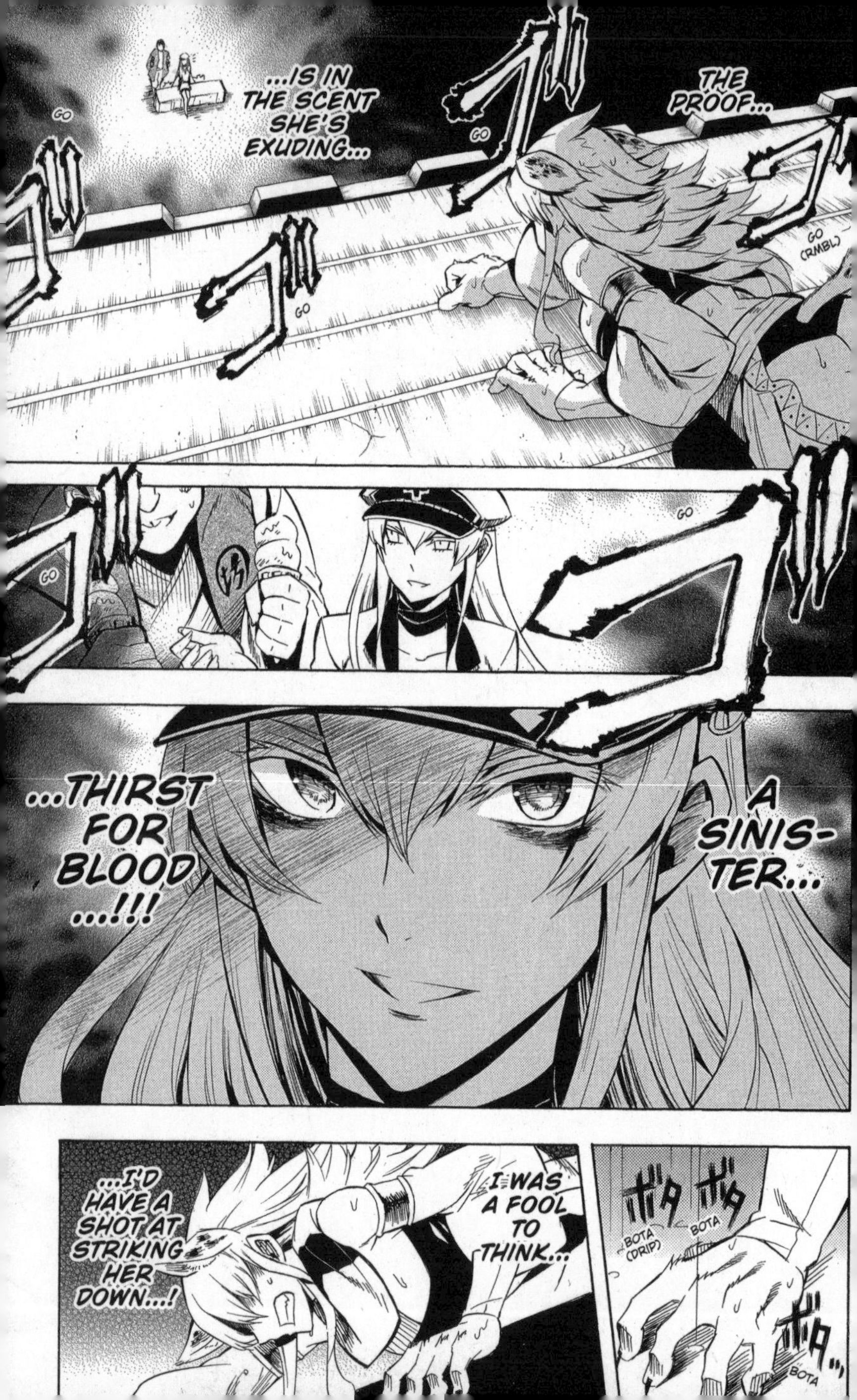
THE PROOF...
GO (RMBL)
GO
...IS IN THE SCENT SHE'S EXUDING...
GO
GO
GO
GO
A SINIS-TER...
...THIRST FOR BLOOD ...!!!
BOTA (DRIP)
BOTA
BOTA
I WAS A FOOL TO THINK...
...I'D HAVE A SHOT AT STRIKING HER DOWN...!

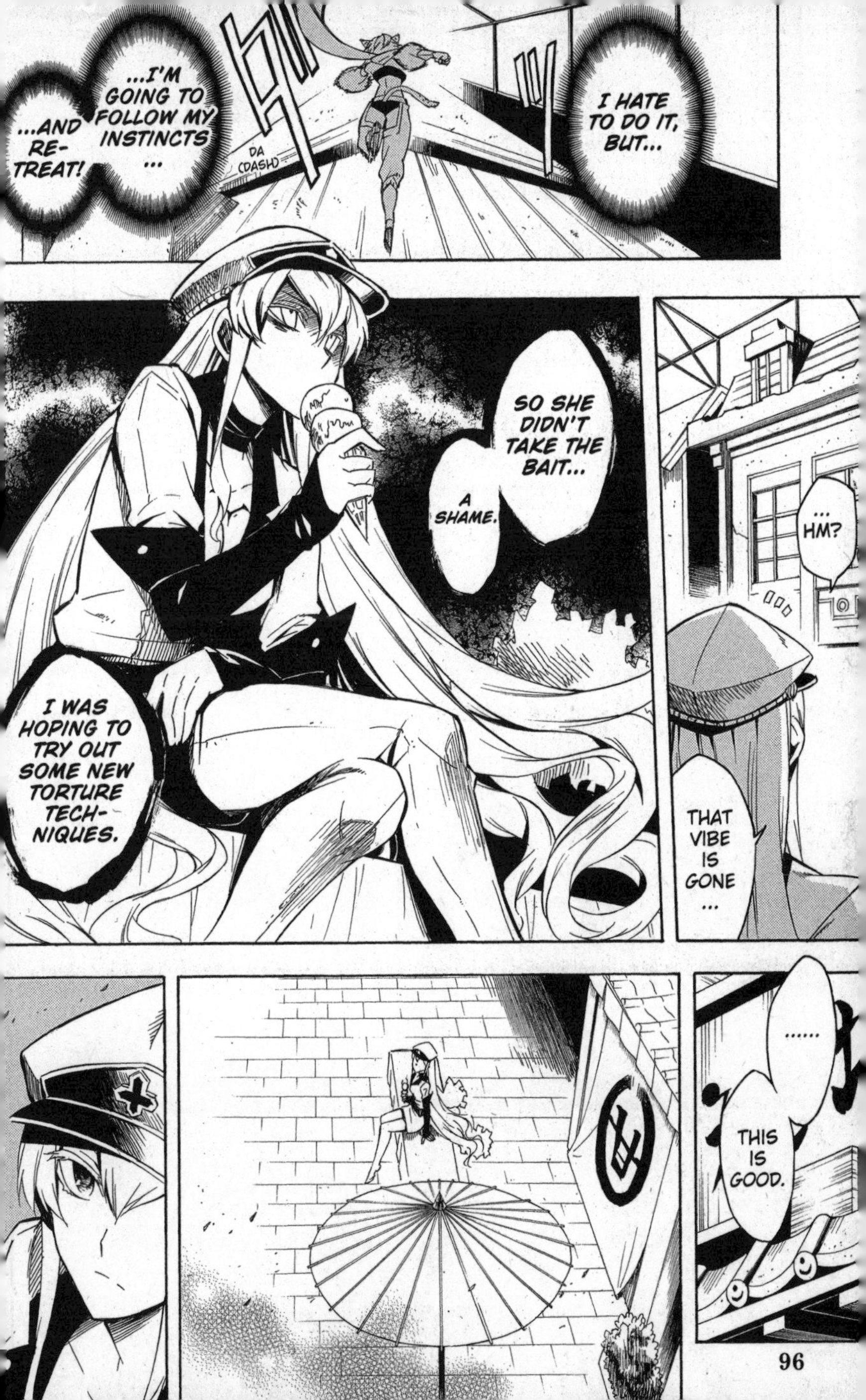
I HATE TO DO IT, BUT...
...I'M GOING TO FOLLOW MY INSTINCTS ...
DA (DASH)
...AND RE-TREAT!
... HM?
THAT VIBE IS GONE ...
SO SHE DIDN'T TAKE THE BAIT...
A SHAME.
I WAS HOPING TO TRY OUT SOME NEW TORTURE TECH-NIQUES.
......
THIS IS GOOD.

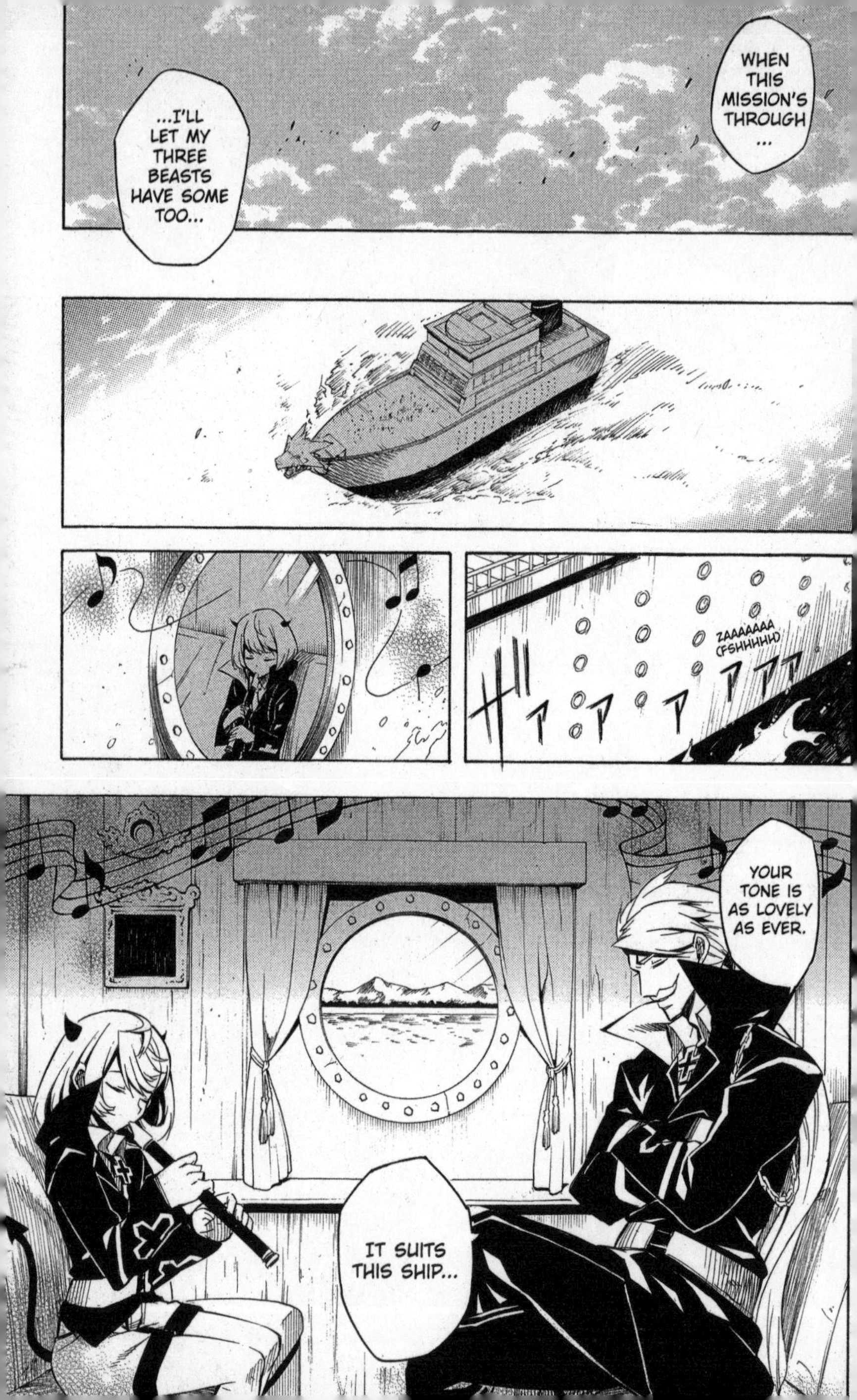
WHEN THIS MISSION'S THROUGH...
...I'LL LET MY THREE BEASTS HAVE SOME TOO...
ZAAAAAAA (FSHHHHH)
YOUR TONE IS AS LOVELY AS EVER.
IT SUITS THIS SHIP...

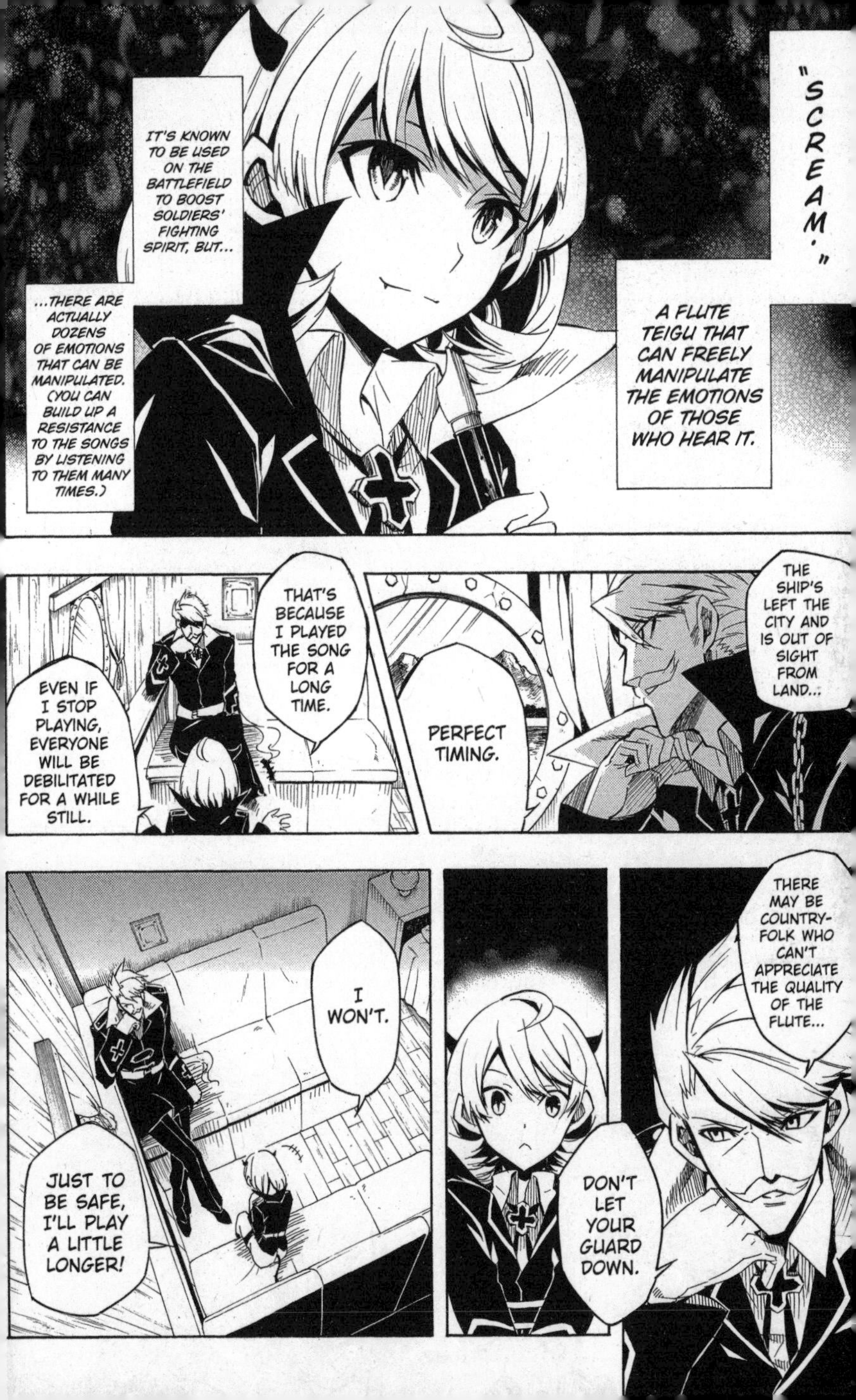
"SCREAM."
A FLUTE TEIGU THAT CAN FREELY MANIPULATE THE EMOTIONS OF THOSE WHO HEAR IT.
IT'S KNOWN TO BE USED ON THE BATTLEFIELD TO BOOST SOLDIERS' FIGHTING SPIRIT, BUT...
...THERE ARE ACTUALLY DOZENS OF EMOTIONS THAT CAN BE MANIPULATED. (YOU CAN BUILD UP A RESISTANCE TO THE SONGS BY LISTENING TO THEM MANY TIMES.)
THE SHIP'S LEFT THE CITY AND IS OUT OF SIGHT FROM LAND...
PERFECT TIMING.
THAT'S BECAUSE I PLAYED THE SONG FOR A LONG TIME.
EVEN IF I STOP PLAYING, EVERYONE WILL BE DEBILITATED FOR A WHILE STILL.
THERE MAY BE COUNTRY-FOLK WHO CAN'T APPRECIATE THE QUALITY OF THE FLUTE...
DON'T LET YOUR GUARD DOWN.
I WON'T.
JUST TO BE SAFE, I'LL PLAY A LITTLE LONGER!

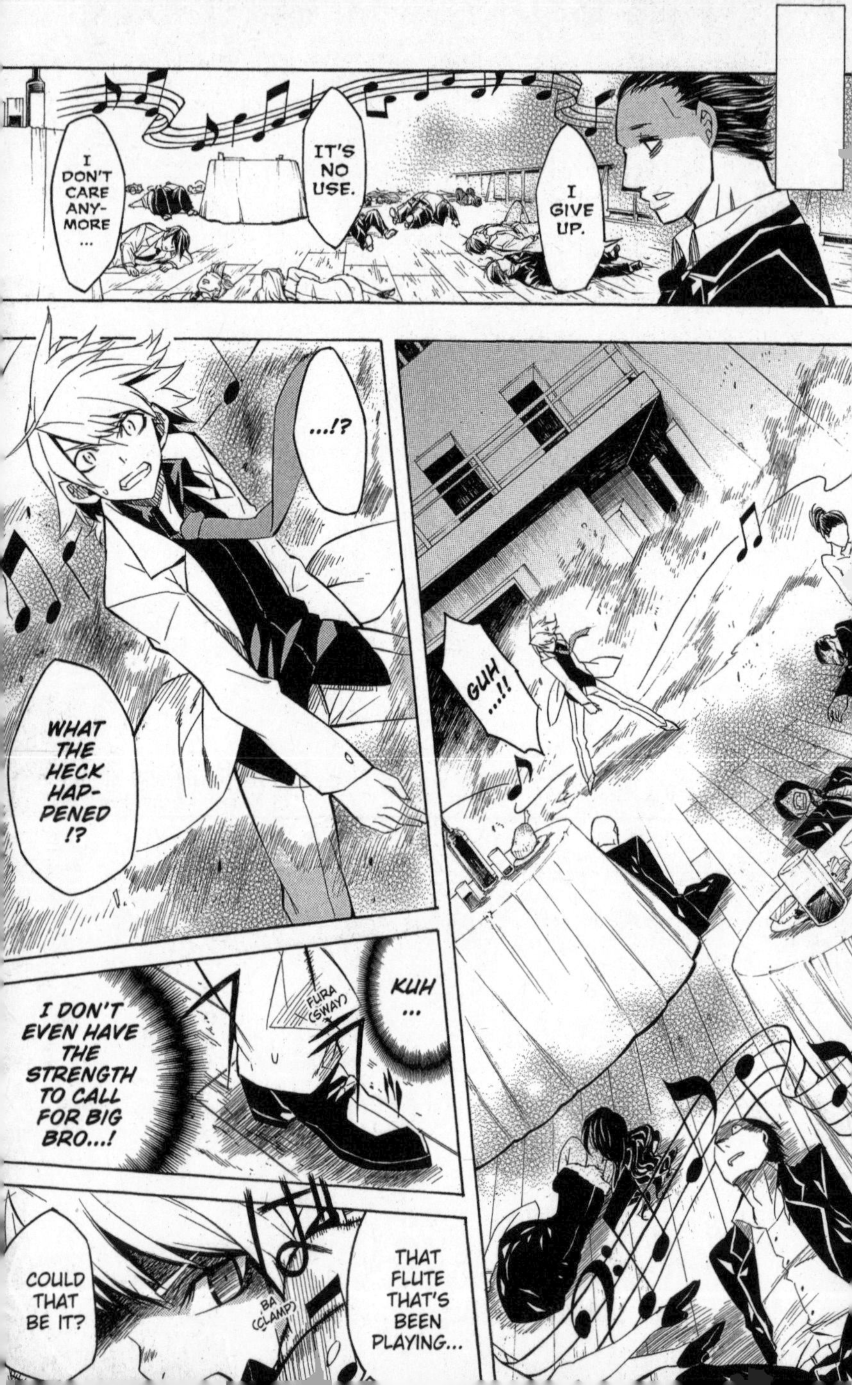
I GIVE UP.
IT'S NO USE.
I DON'T CARE ANY-MORE...
GUH...!!
...!?
WHAT THE HECK HAP-PENED!?
KUH...
FURA (SWAY)
I DON'T EVEN HAVE THE STRENGTH TO CALL FOR BIG BRO...!
THAT FLUTE THAT'S BEEN PLAYING...
BA (CLAMP)
COULD THAT BE IT?

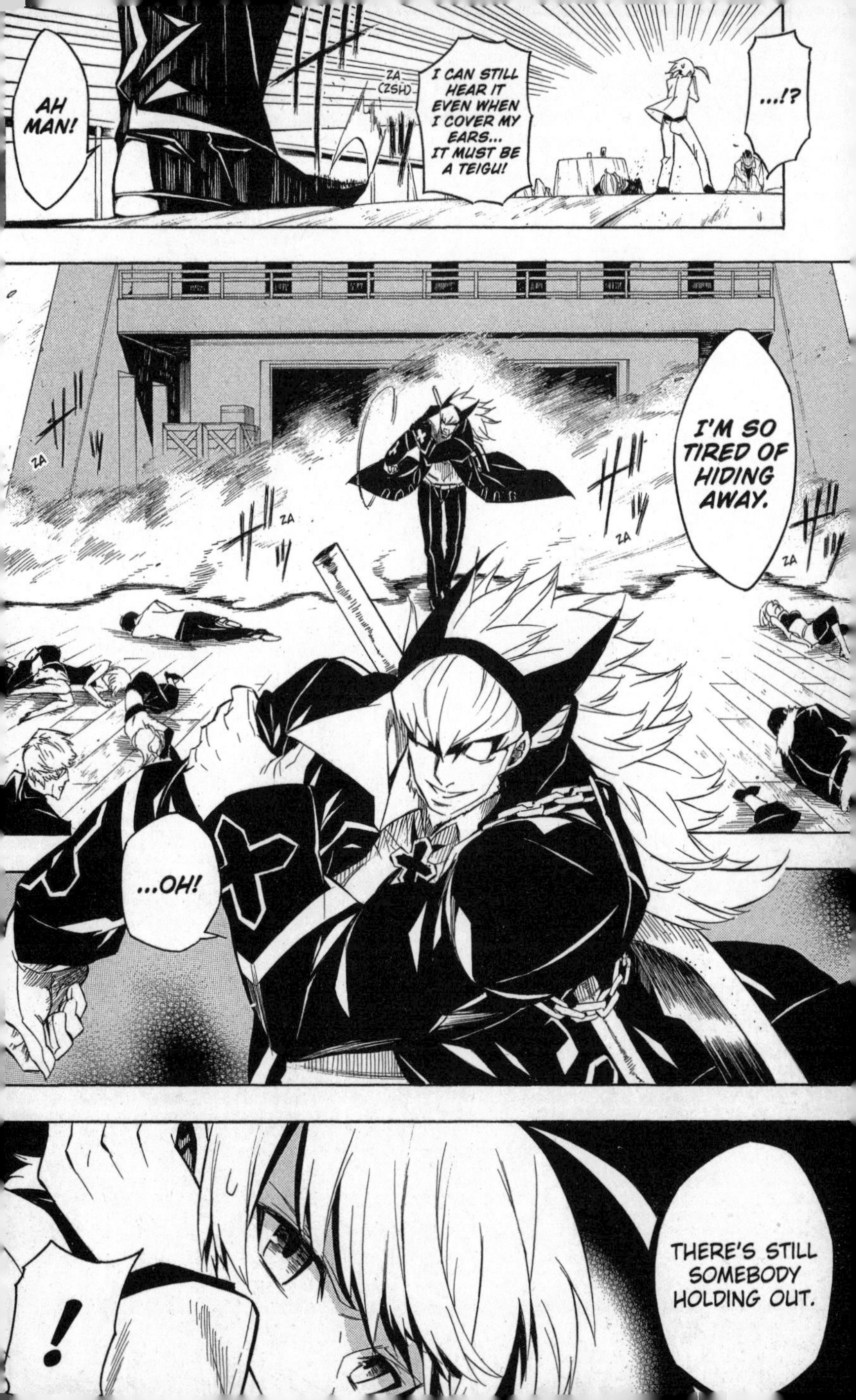
...!?
I CAN STILL HEAR IT EVEN WHEN I COVER MY EARS... IT MUST BE A TEIGU!
ZA (ZSH)
AH MAN!
I'M SO TIRED OF HIDING AWAY.
ZA
ZA
ZA
ZA
...OH!
THERE'S STILL SOMEBODY HOLDING OUT.
!

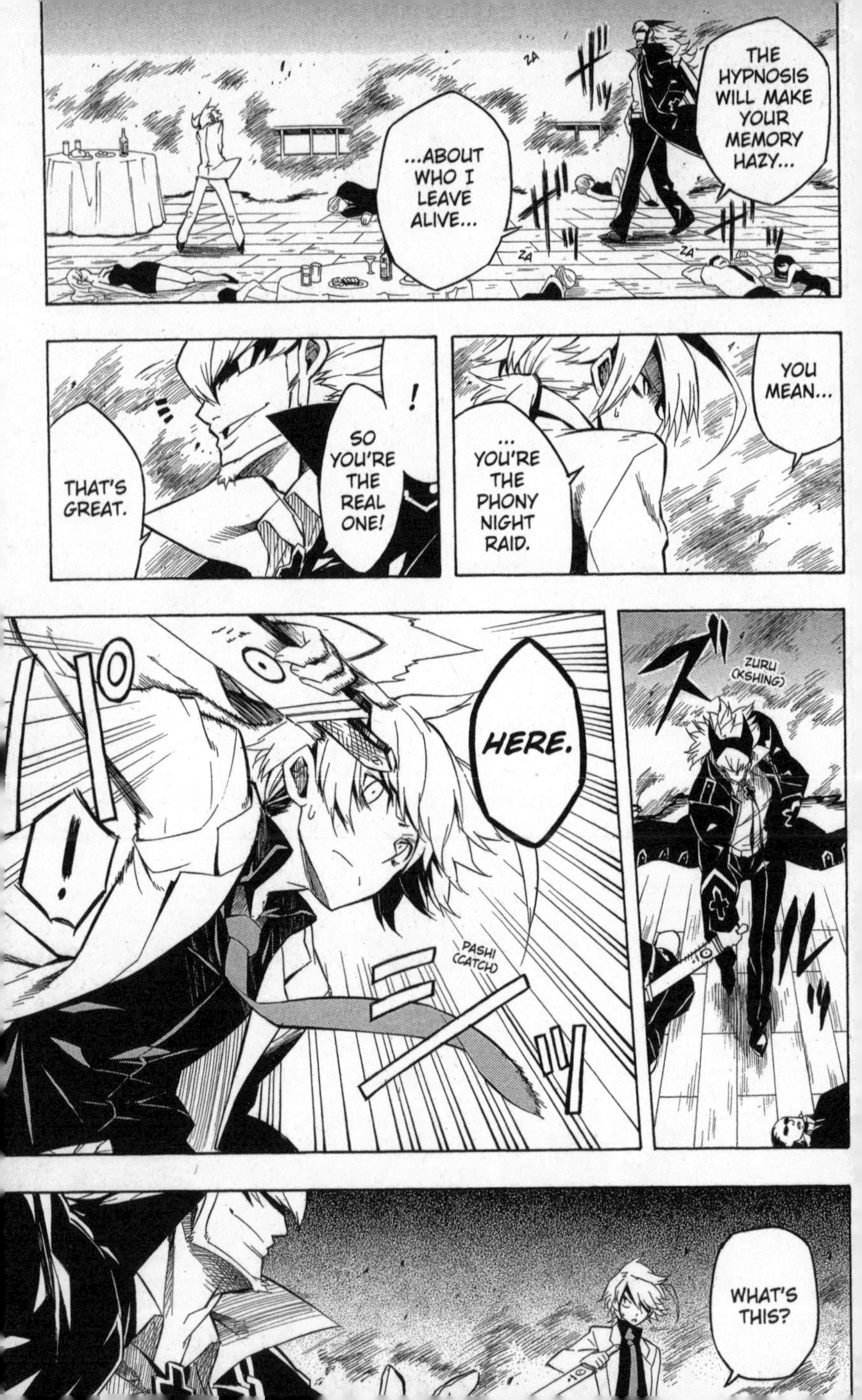
THE HYPNOSIS WILL MAKE YOUR MEMORY HAZY...
ZA
...ABOUT WHO I LEAVE ALIVE...
ZA
ZA
YOU MEAN...
...YOU'RE THE PHONY NIGHT RAID.
!
SO YOU'RE THE REAL ONE!
THAT'S GREAT.
ZURU (KSHING)
HERE.
PASHI (CATCH)
!
WHAT'S THIS?

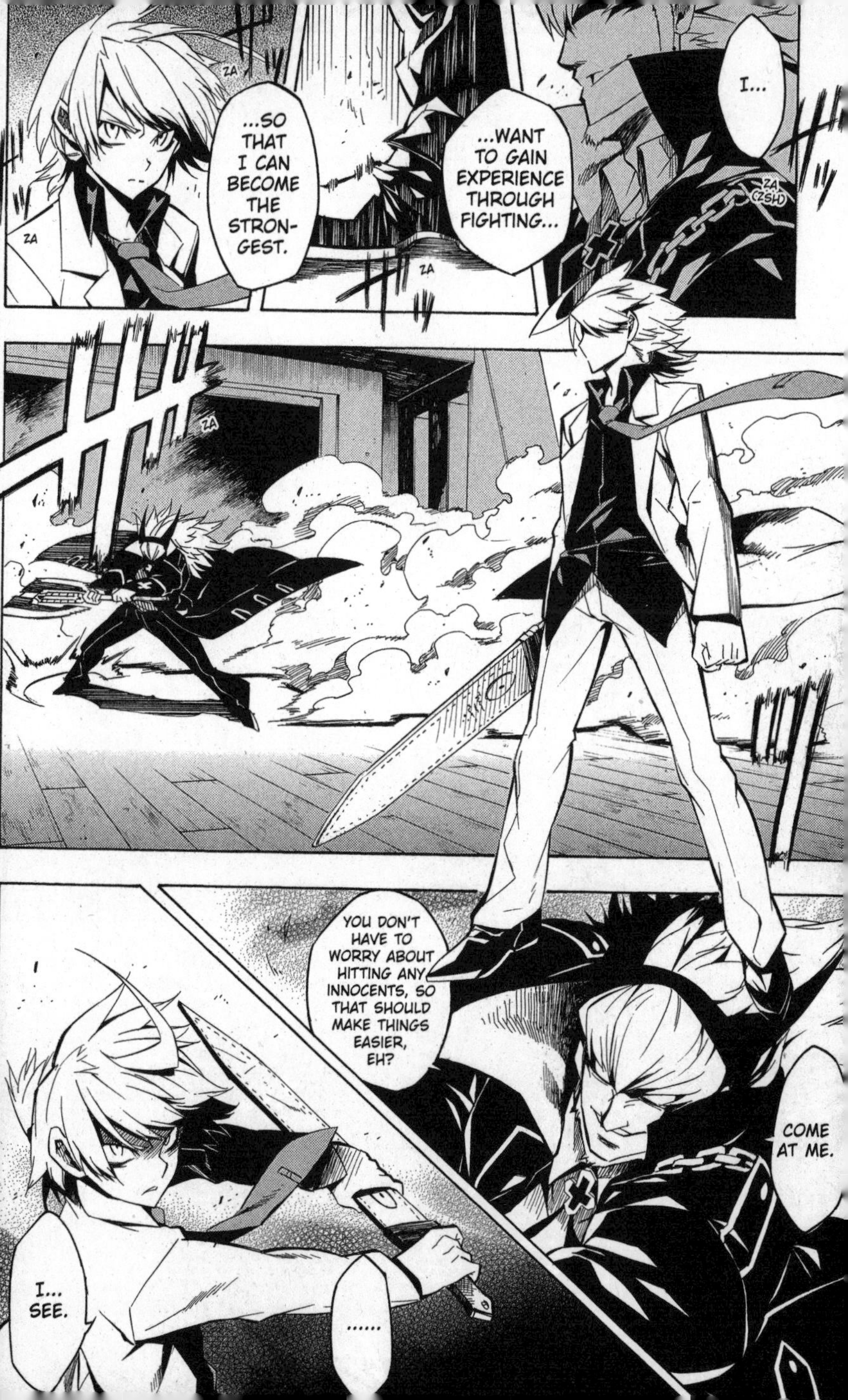
I...
ZA (ZSH)
...WANT TO GAIN EXPERIENCE THROUGH FIGHTING...
ZA
...SO THAT I CAN BECOME THE STRONG-GEST.
ZA
ZA
ZA
YOU DON'T HAVE TO WORRY ABOUT HITTING ANY INNOCENTS, SO THAT SHOULD MAKE THINGS EASIER, EH?
COME AT ME.
......
I... SEE.

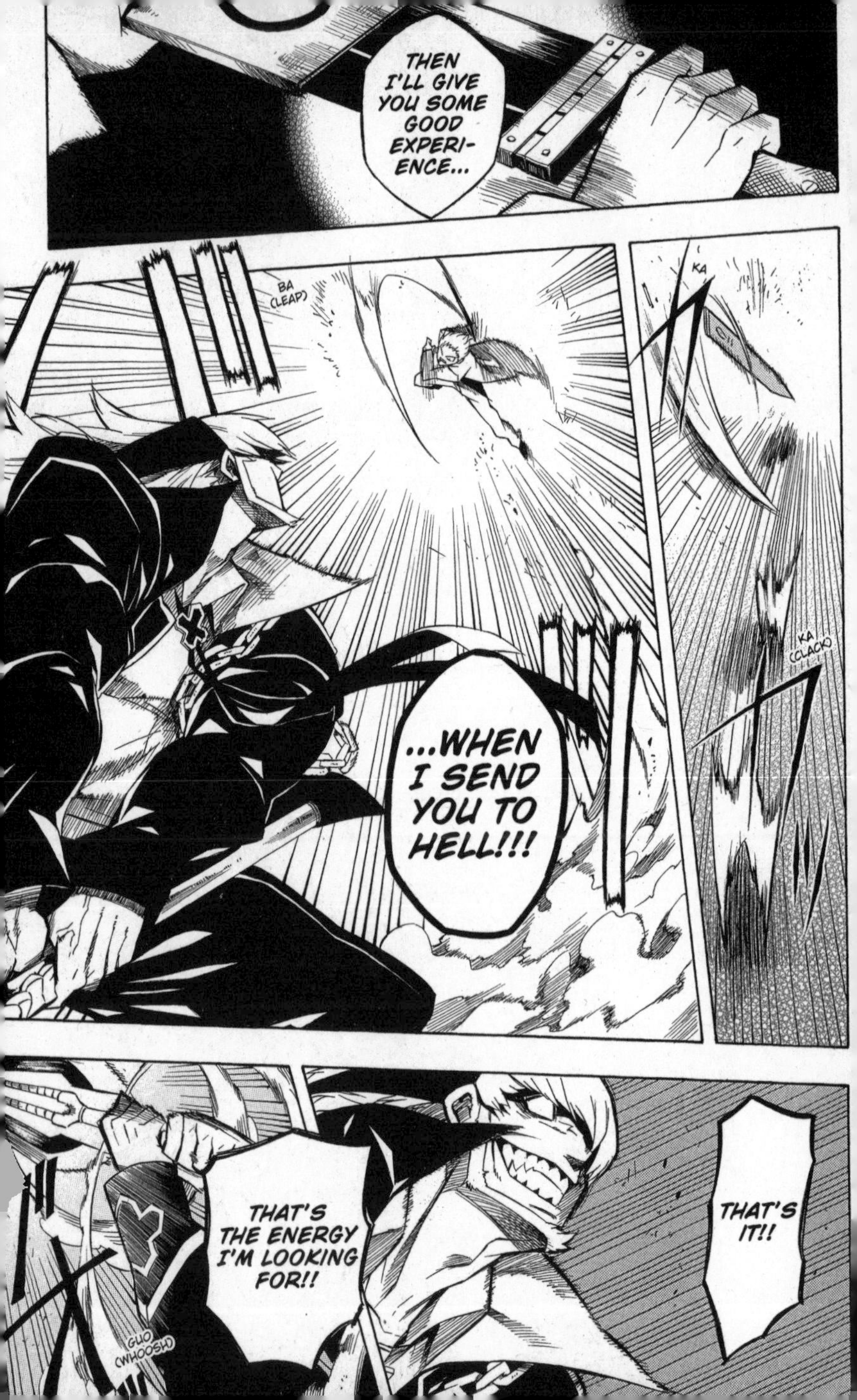
THEN I'LL GIVE YOU SOME GOOD EXPERIENCE...
KA
KA (CLACK)
BA (LEAP)
...WHEN I SEND YOU TO HELL!!!
THAT'S IT!!
THAT'S THE ENERGY I'M LOOKING FOR!!
GUO (WHOOSH)

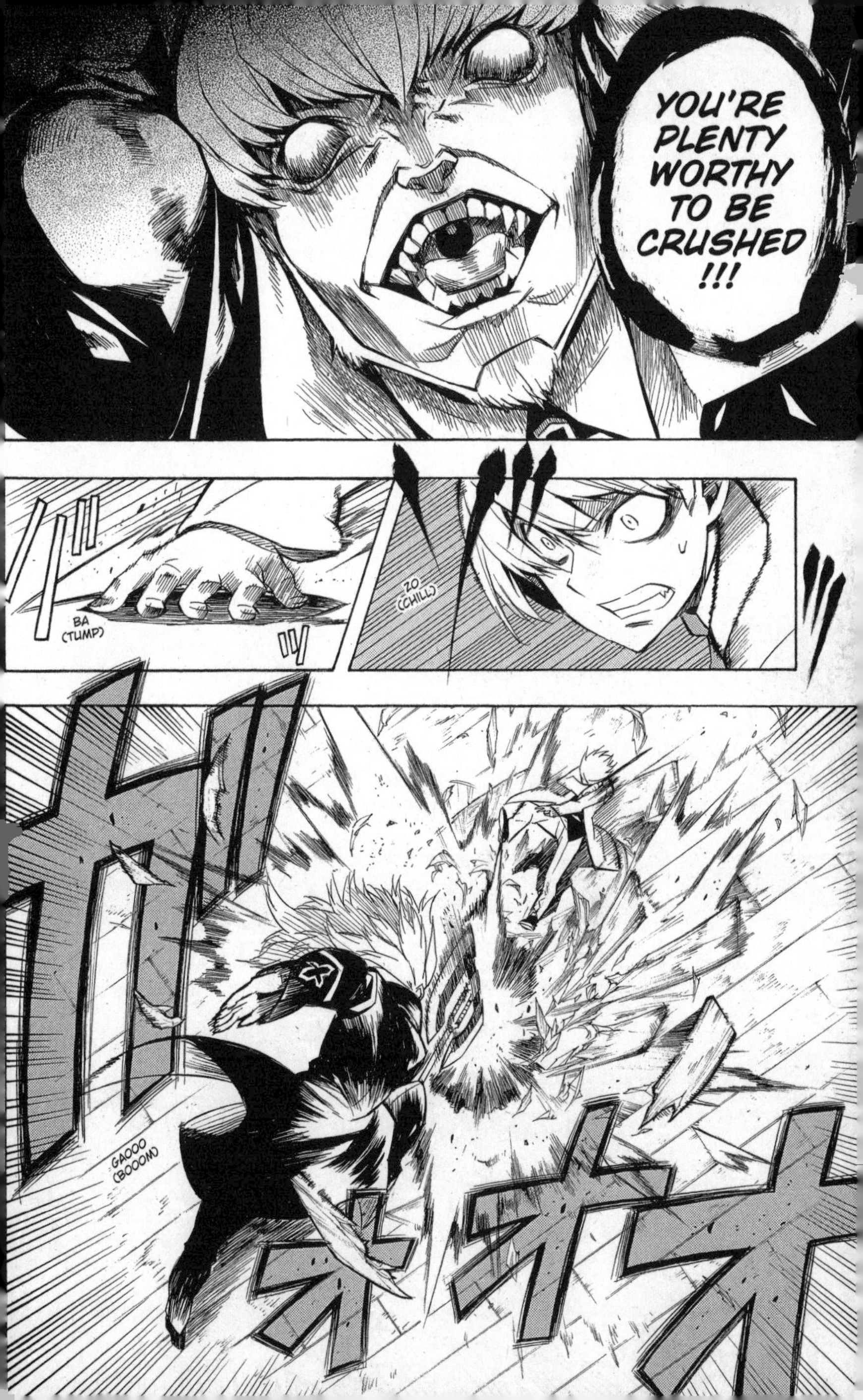
YOU'RE PLENTY WORTHY TO BE CRUSHED !!!
ZO (CHILL)
BA (TUMP)
GAOOO (BOOOM)

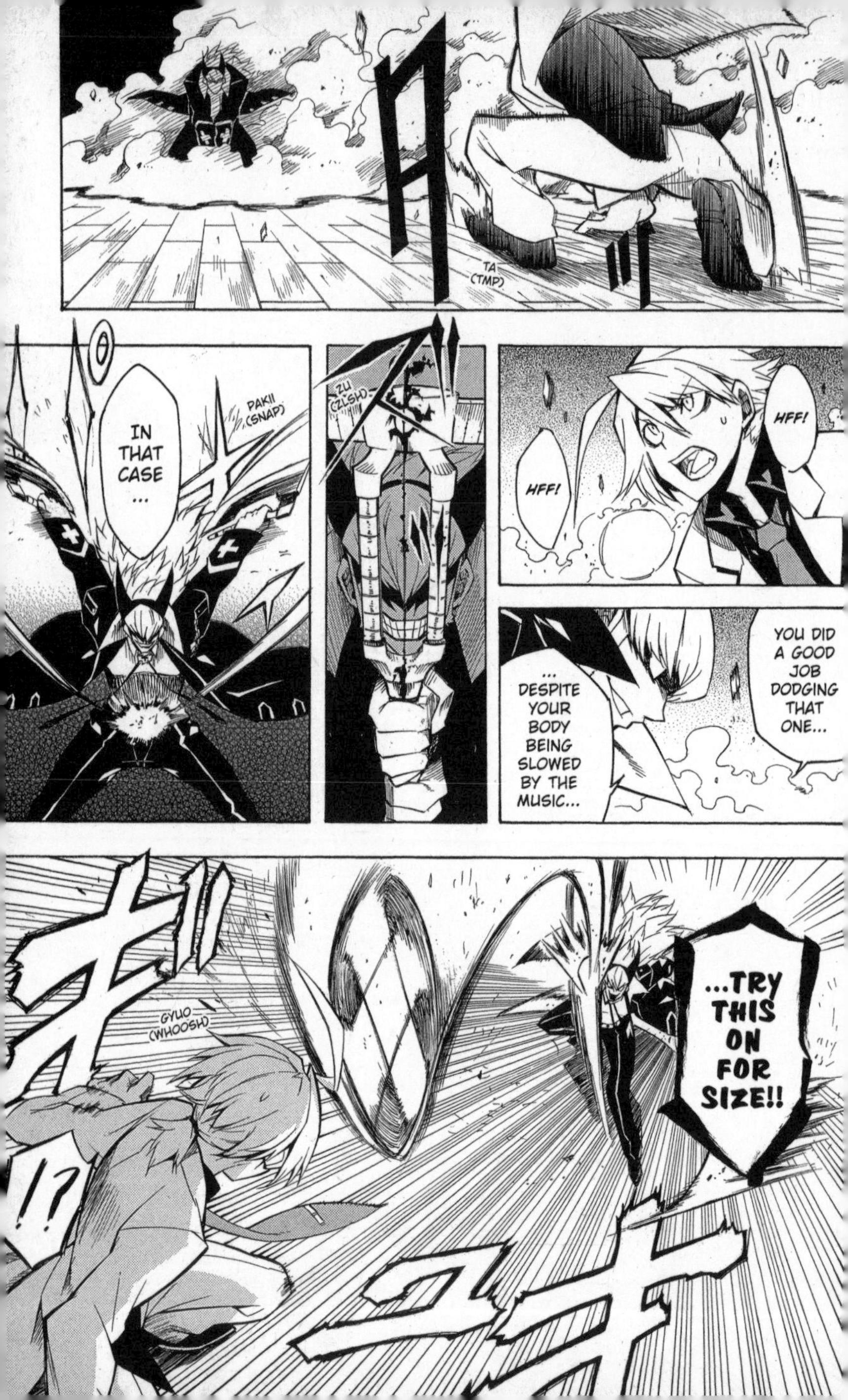
TA
(TMP)
HFF!
HFF!
YOU DID A GOOD JOB DODGING THAT ONE...
... DESPITE YOUR BODY BEING SLOWED BY THE MUSIC...
ZU
(ZLSH)
PAKII
(SNAP)
IN THAT CASE ...
...TRY THIS ON FOR SIZE!!
GYUO
(WHOOSH)
!?

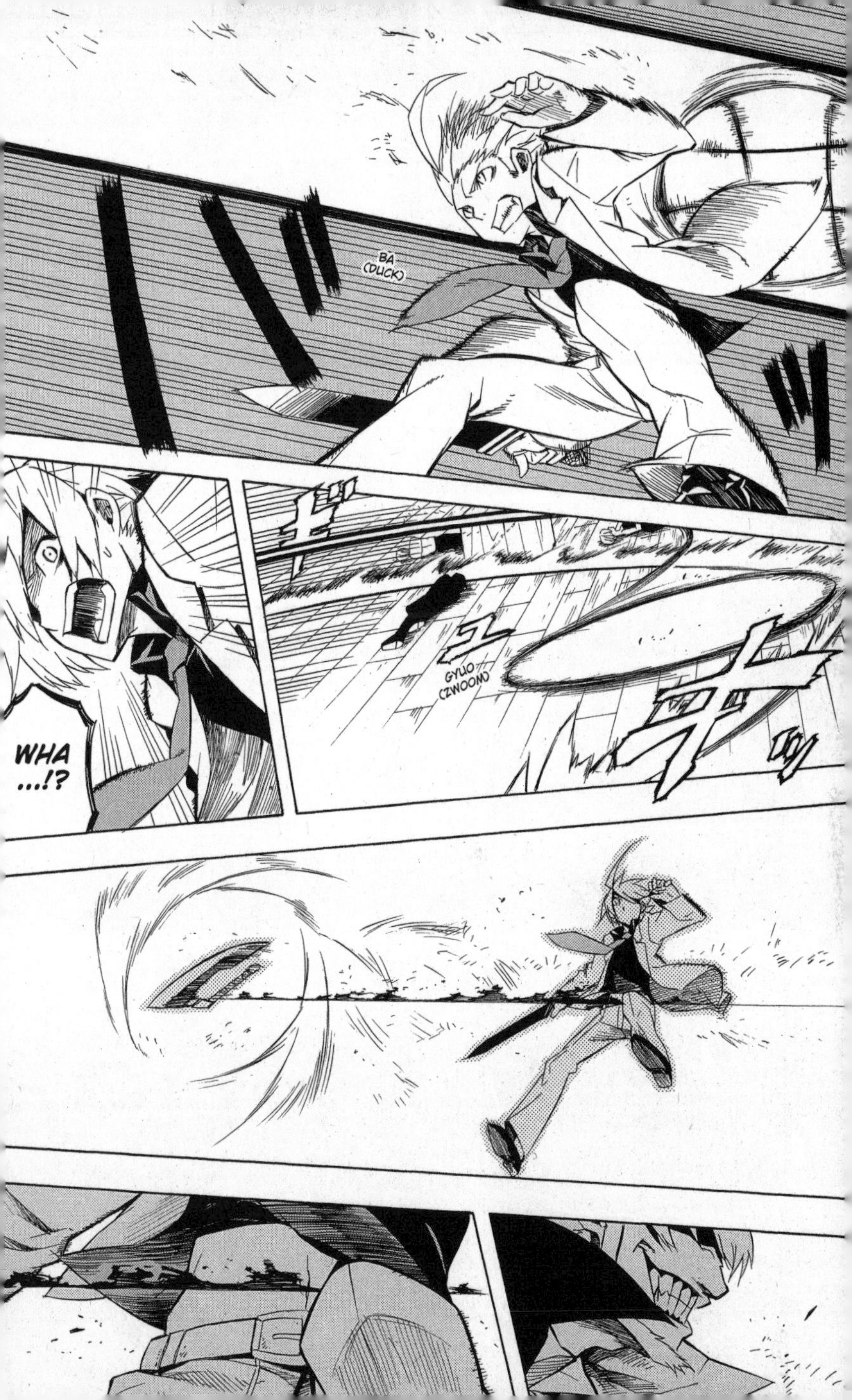
BA
(DUCK)
GYUO
(ZWOOM)
WHA
...!?

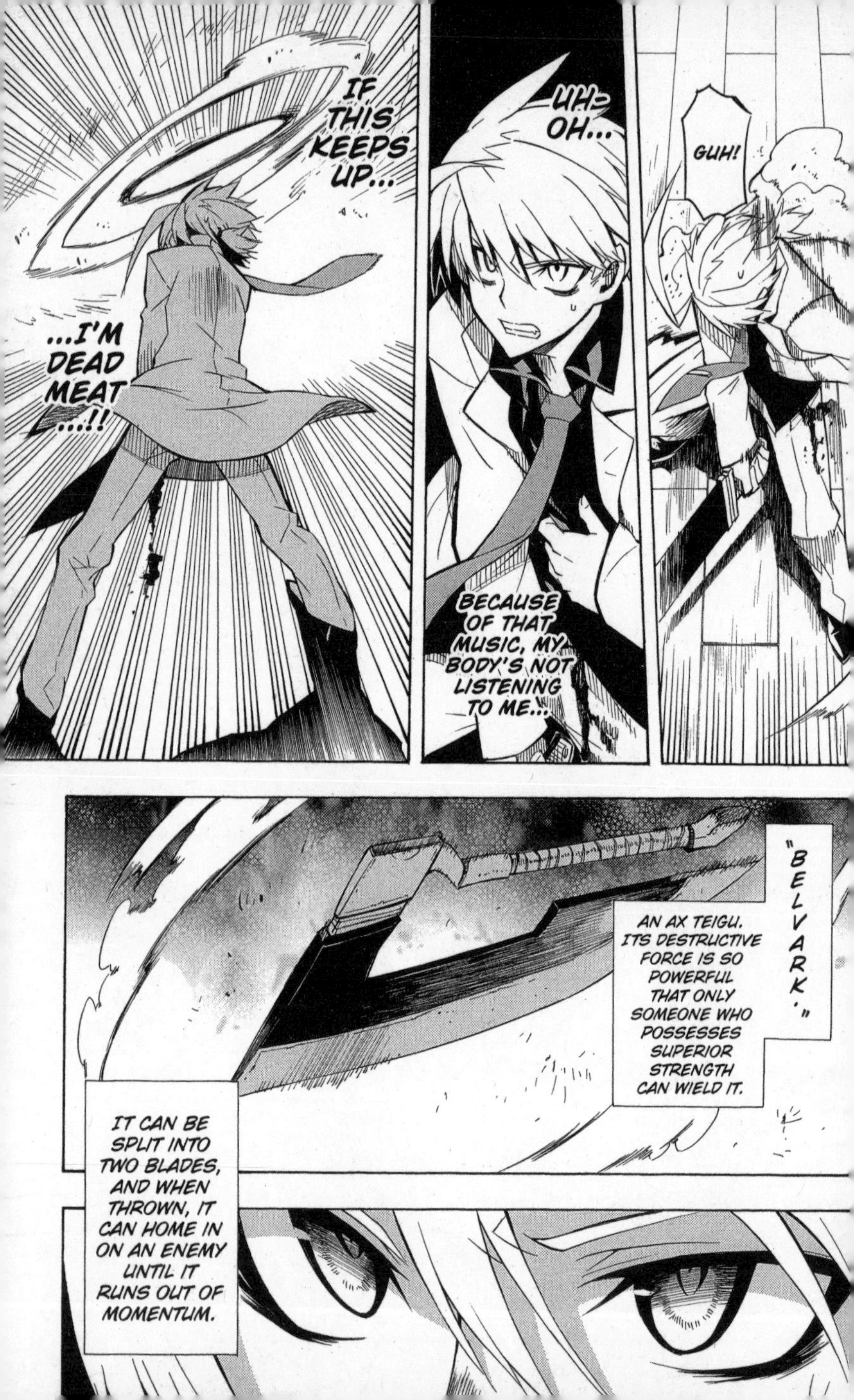
GUH!
UH-OH...
BECAUSE OF THAT MUSIC, MY BODY'S NOT LISTENING TO ME...
IF THIS KEEPS UP...
...I'M DEAD MEAT...!!
"BELVARK."
AN AX TEIGU. ITS DESTRUCTIVE FORCE IS SO POWERFUL THAT ONLY SOMEONE WHO POSSESSES SUPERIOR STRENGTH CAN WIELD IT.
IT CAN BE SPLIT INTO TWO BLADES, AND WHEN THROWN, IT CAN HOME IN ON AN ENEMY UNTIL IT RUNS OUT OF MOMENTUM.

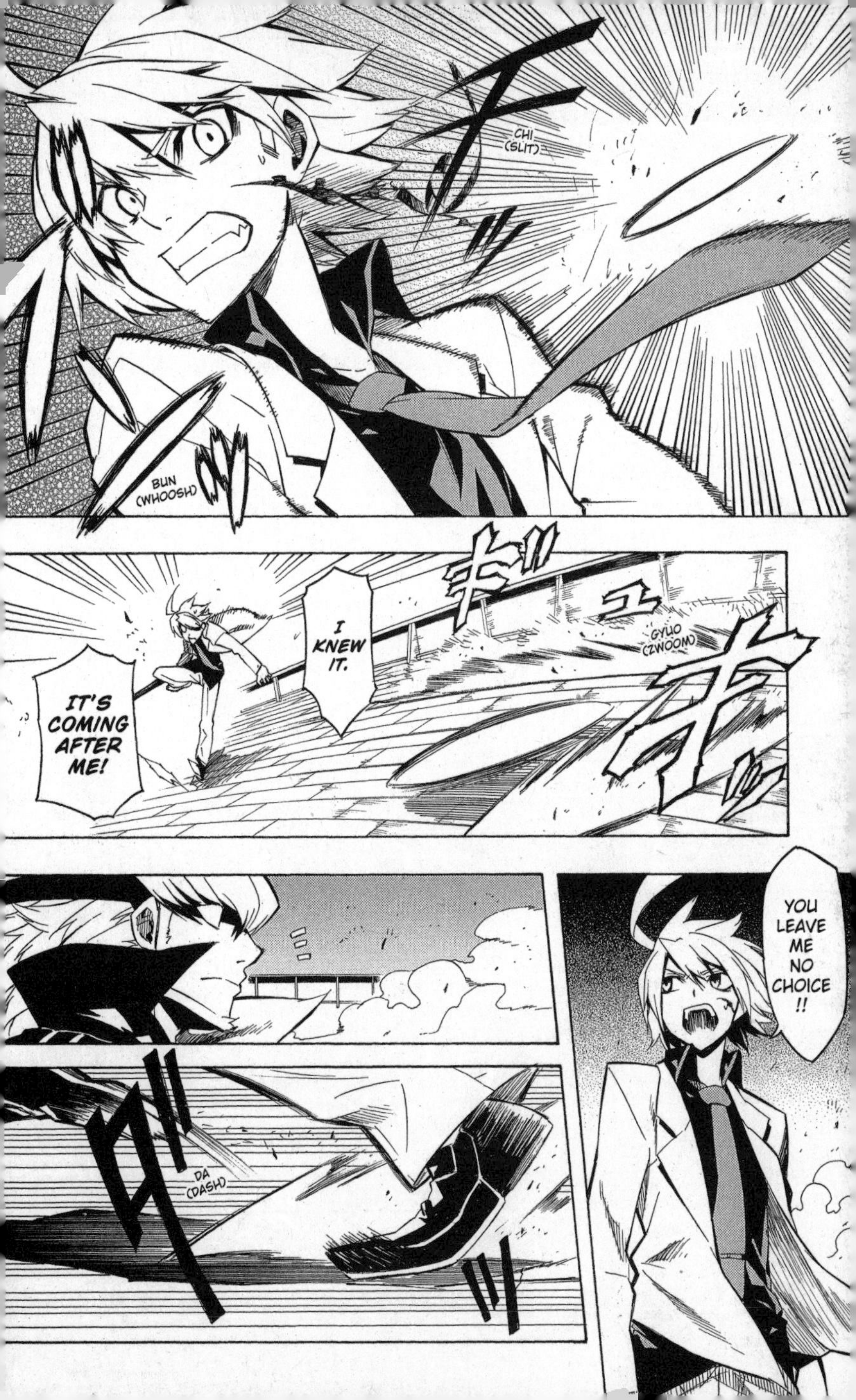
CHI (SLIT)
BUN (WHOOSH)
GYUO (ZWOOM)
I KNEW IT.
IT'S COMING AFTER ME!
YOU LEAVE ME NO CHOICE !!
DA (DASH)

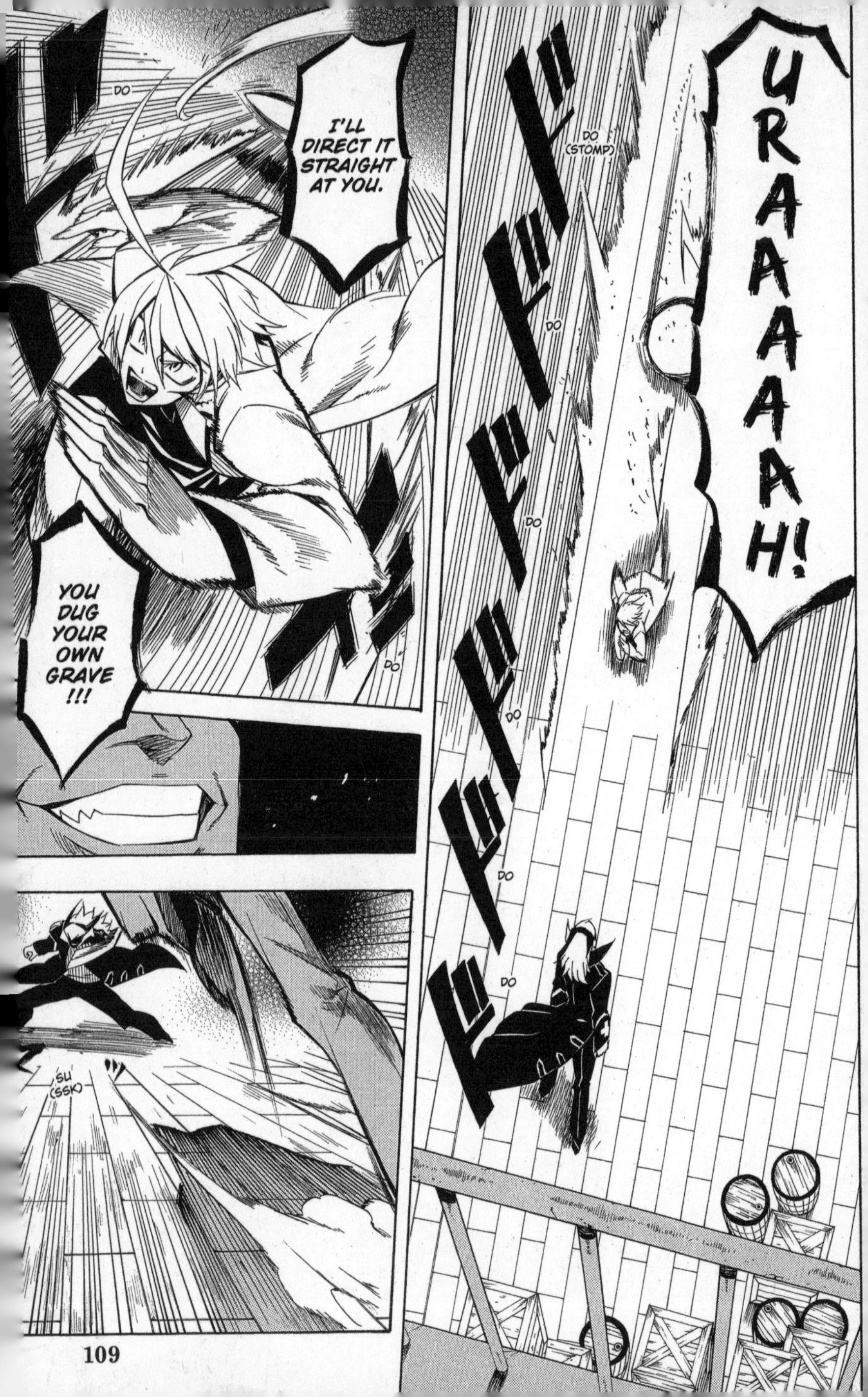
URAAAAAH!
DO (STOMP)
DO
DO
DO
DO
DO
DO
I'LL DIRECT IT STRAIGHT AT YOU.
YOU DUG YOUR OWN GRAVE!!!
DO
SU (SSK)

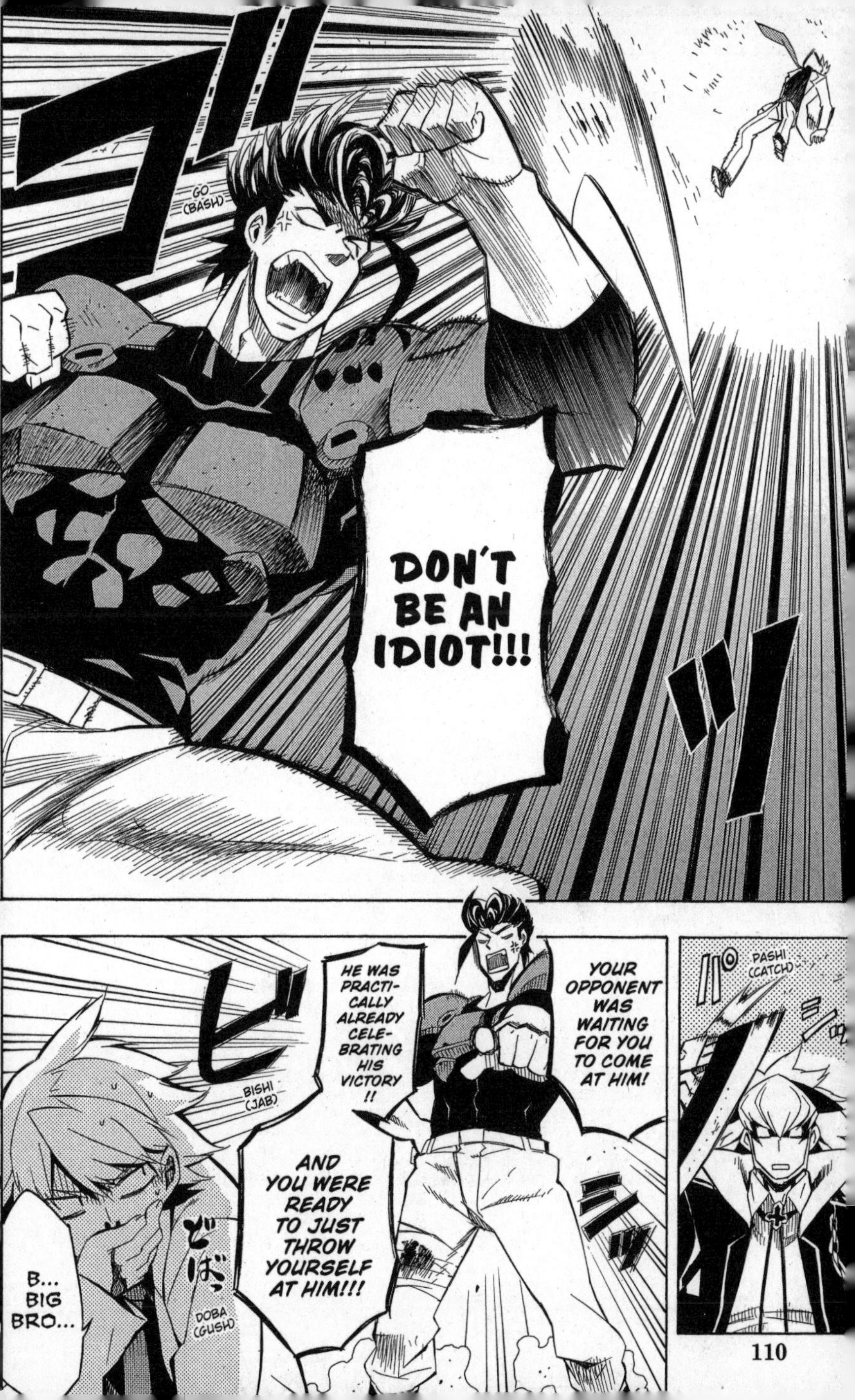
GO
(BASH)
DON'T BE AN IDIOT!!!
PASHI
(CATCH)
YOUR OPPONENT WAS WAITING FOR YOU TO COME AT HIM!
HE WAS PRACTICALLY ALREADY CELEBRATING HIS VICTORY!!
AND YOU WERE READY TO JUST THROW YOURSELF AT HIM!!!
BISHI
(JAB)
DOBA
(GUSH)
B... BIG BRO...

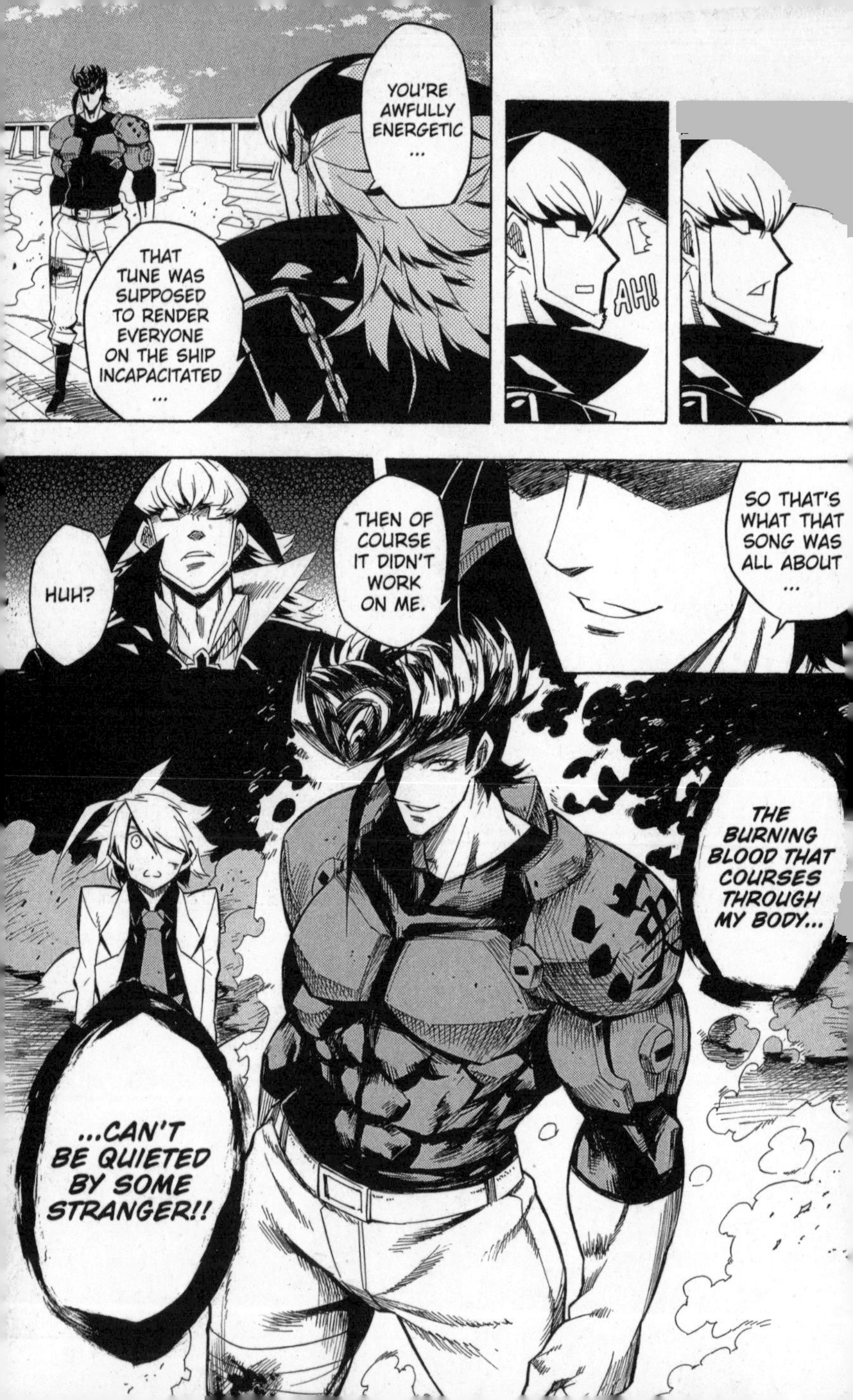
YOU'RE AWFULLY ENERGETIC ...
THAT TUNE WAS SUPPOSED TO RENDER EVERYONE ON THE SHIP INCAPACITATED ...
AH!
SO THAT'S WHAT THAT SONG WAS ALL ABOUT ...
THEN OF COURSE IT DIDN'T WORK ON ME.
HUH?
THE BURNING BLOOD THAT COURSES THROUGH MY BODY...
...CAN'T BE QUIETED BY SOME STRANGER!!

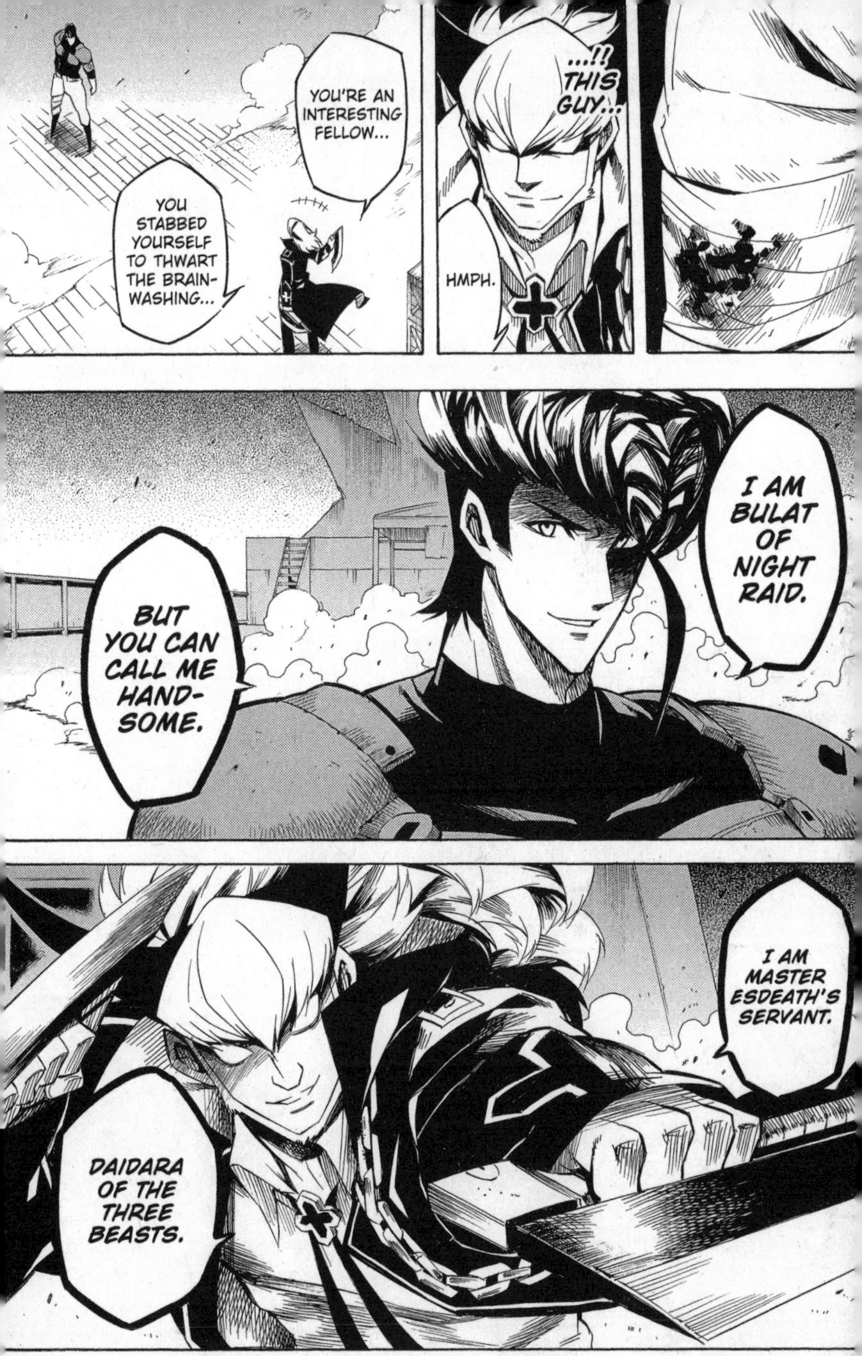
...!! THIS GUY...
HMPH.
YOU'RE AN INTERESTING FELLOW...
YOU STABBED YOURSELF TO THWART THE BRAIN-WASHING...
I AM BULAT OF NIGHT RAID.
BUT YOU CAN CALL ME HAND-SOME.
I AM MASTER ESDEATH'S SERVANT.
DAIDARA OF THE THREE BEASTS.

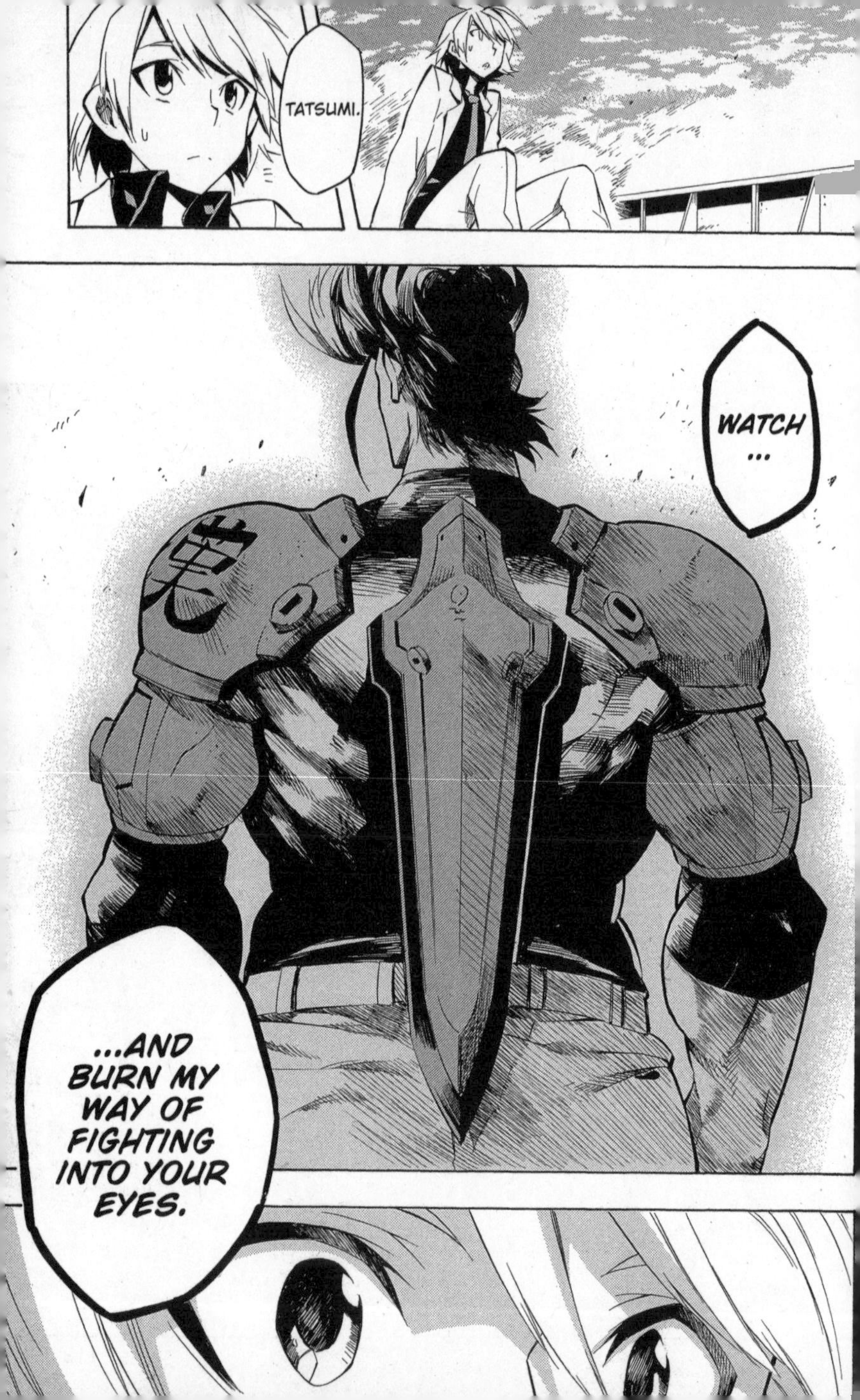
TATSUMI.
WATCH ...
...AND BURN MY WAY OF FIGHTING INTO YOUR EYES.

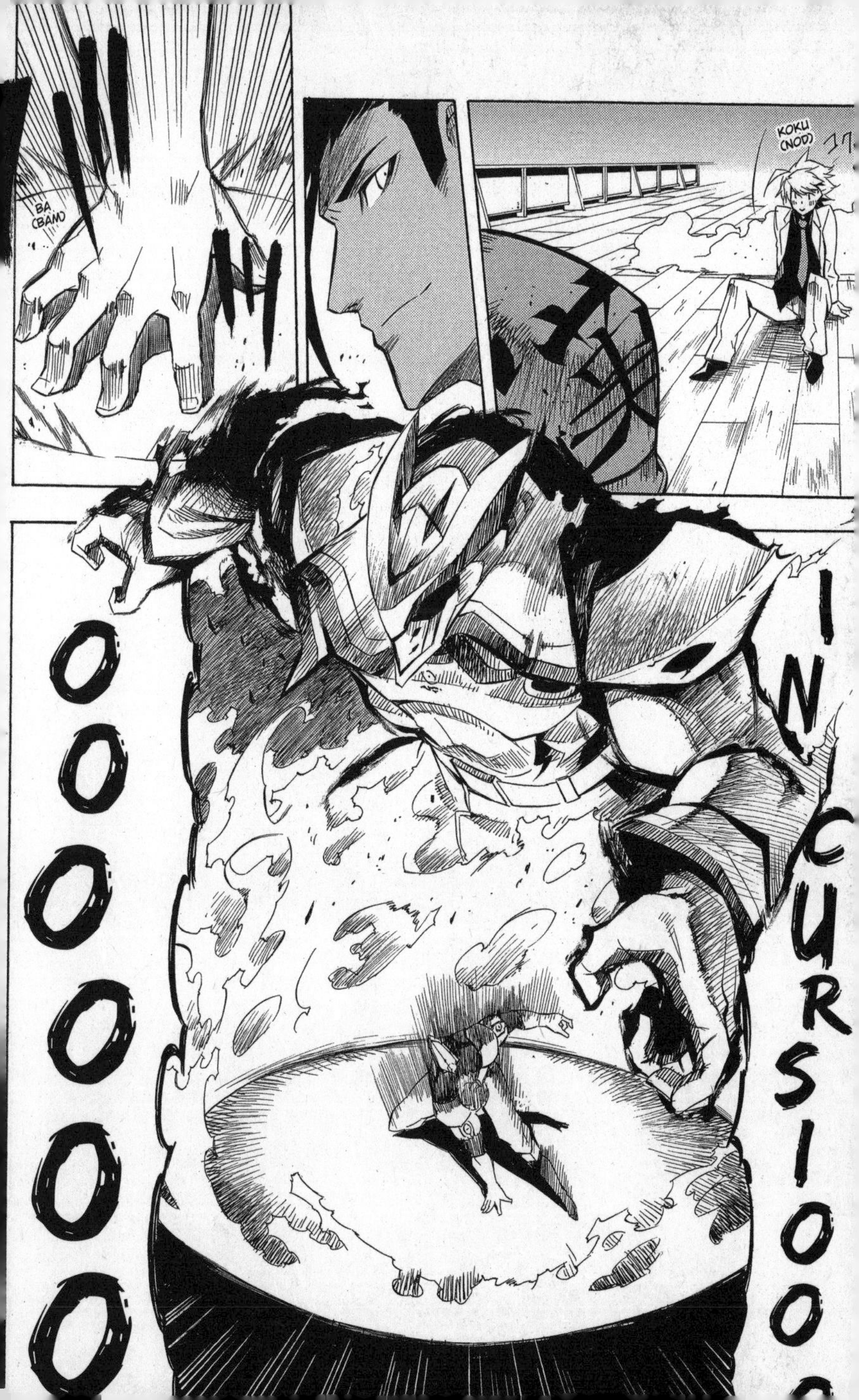
KOKU (NOD)
コク
BA (BAM)
INCURSIOO
OOOOOO

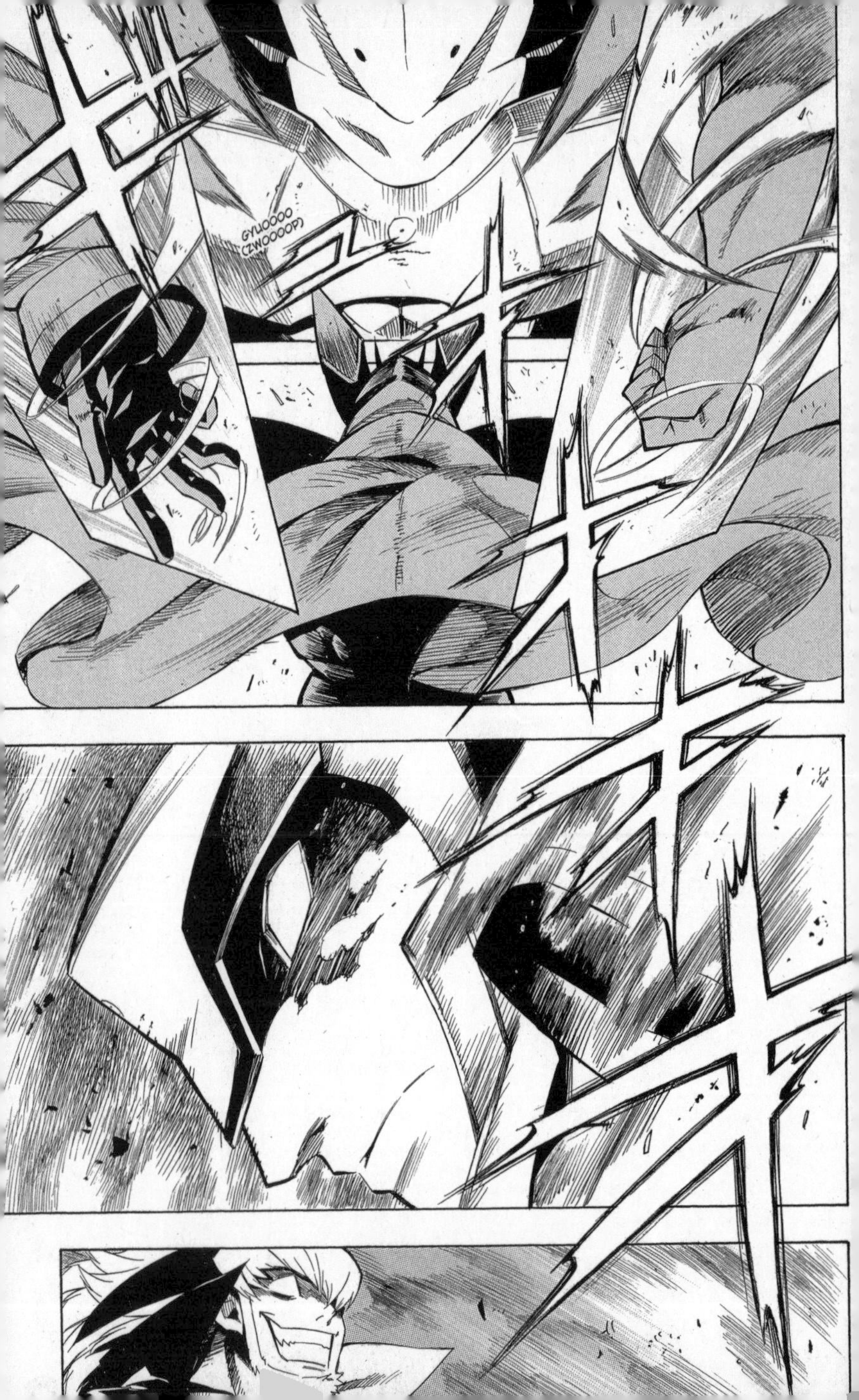
GYUOOOO (ZWOOOOOP)

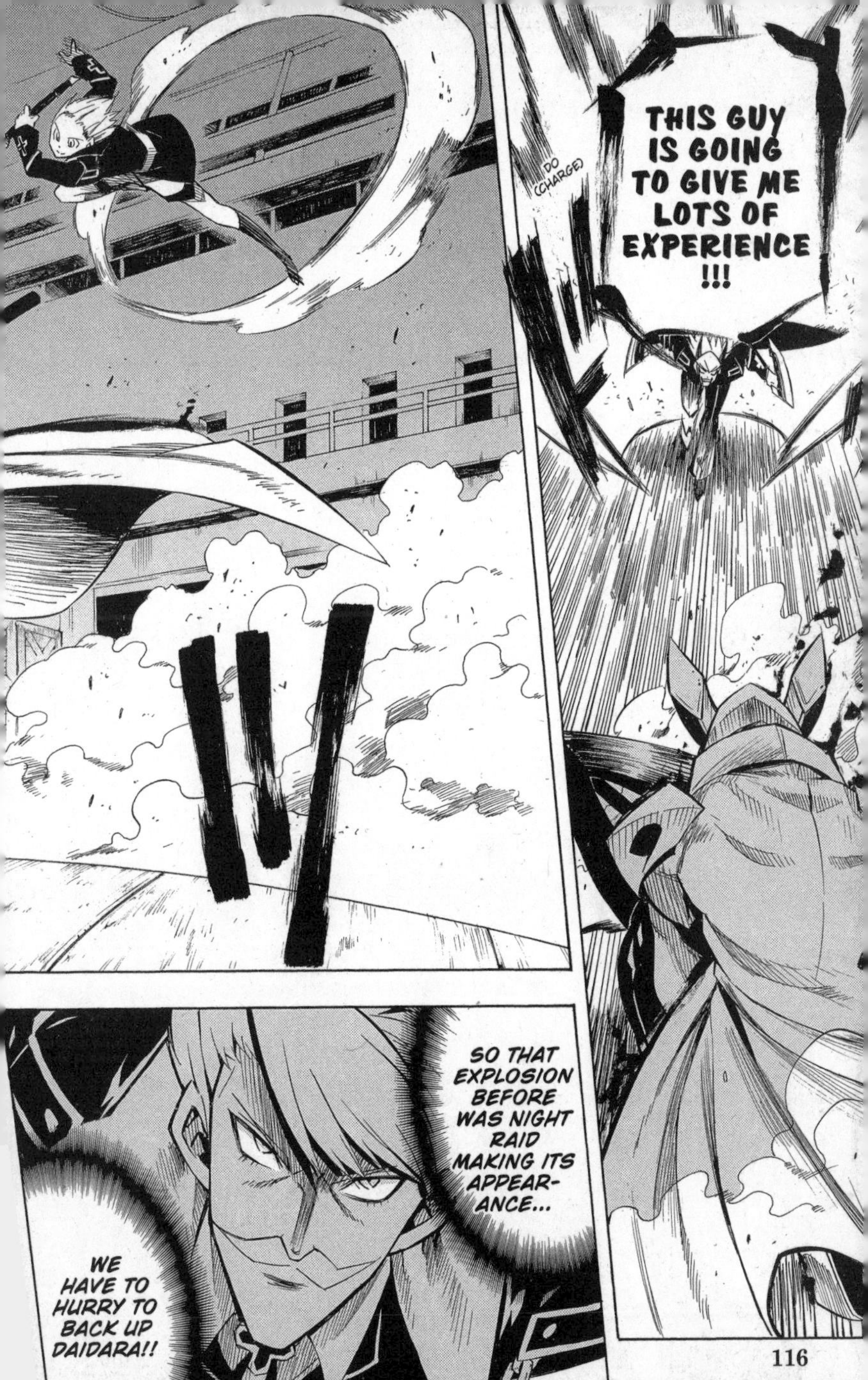
THIS GUY IS GOING TO GIVE ME LOTS OF EXPERIENCE!!!
DO (CHARGE)
SO THAT EXPLOSION BEFORE WAS NIGHT RAID MAKING ITS APPEAR-ANCE...
WE HAVE TO HURRY TO BACK UP DAIDARA!!

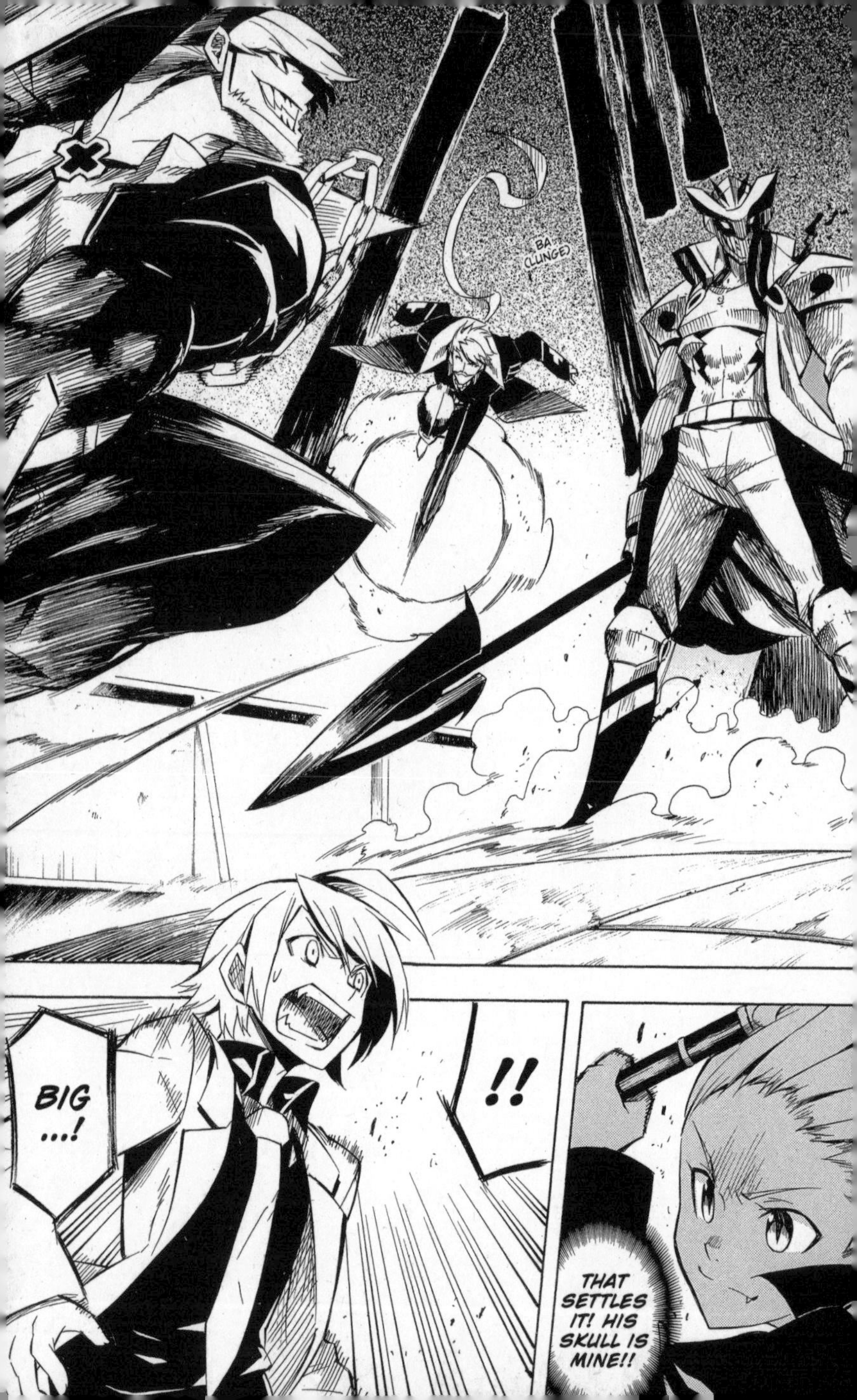
BA (LUNGE)
THAT SETTLES IT! HIS SKULL IS MINE!!
!!
BIG ...!

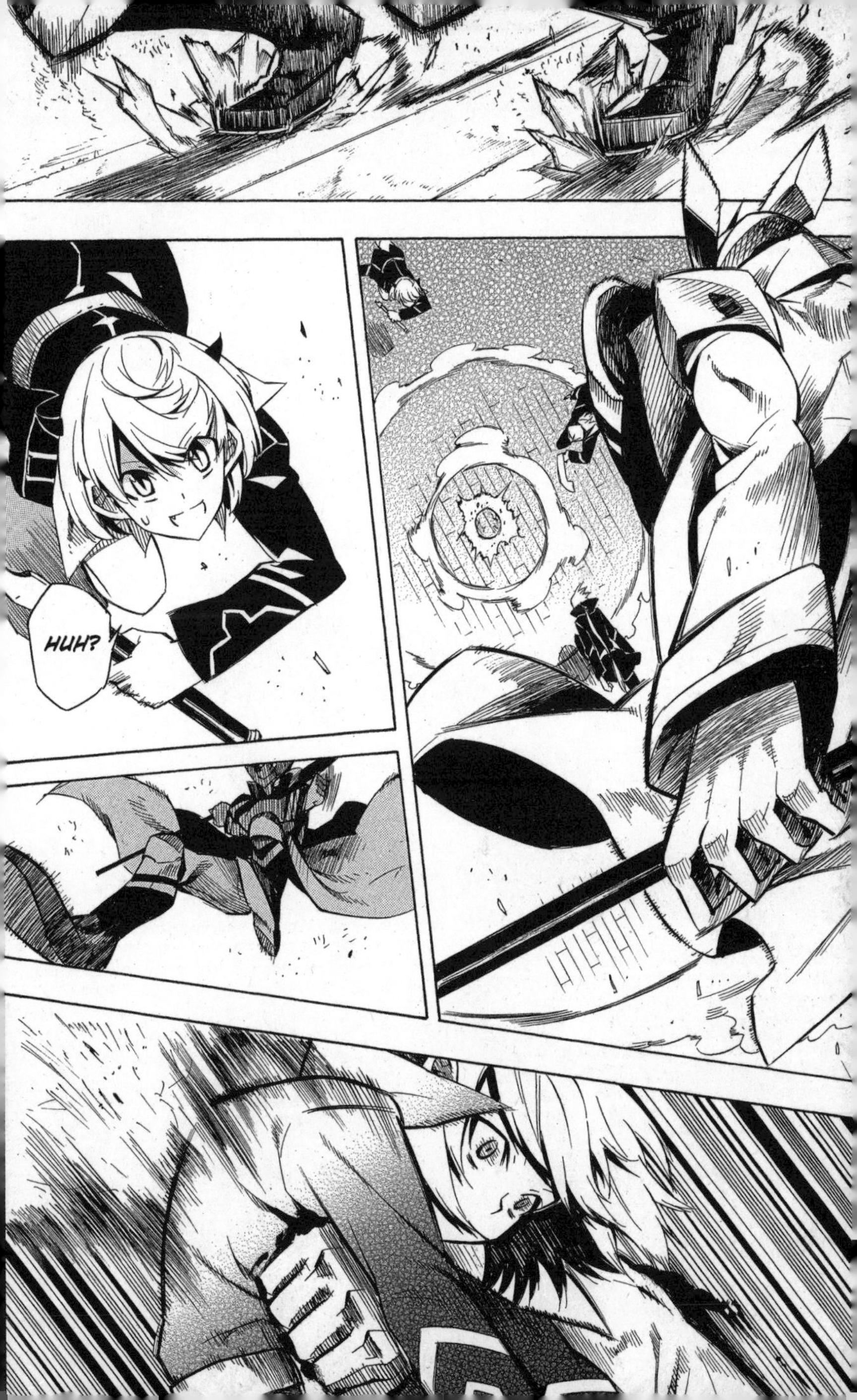
HUH?

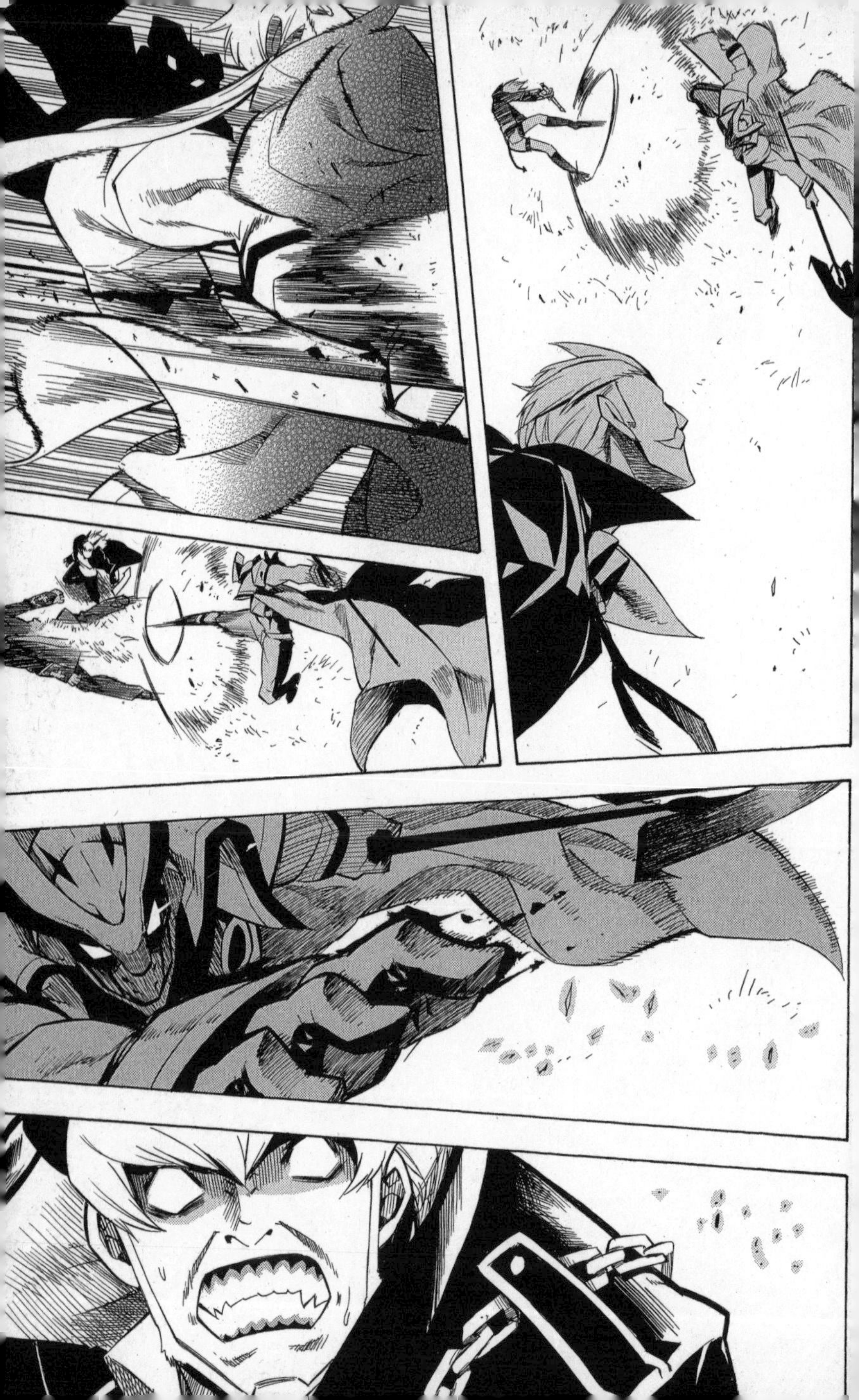

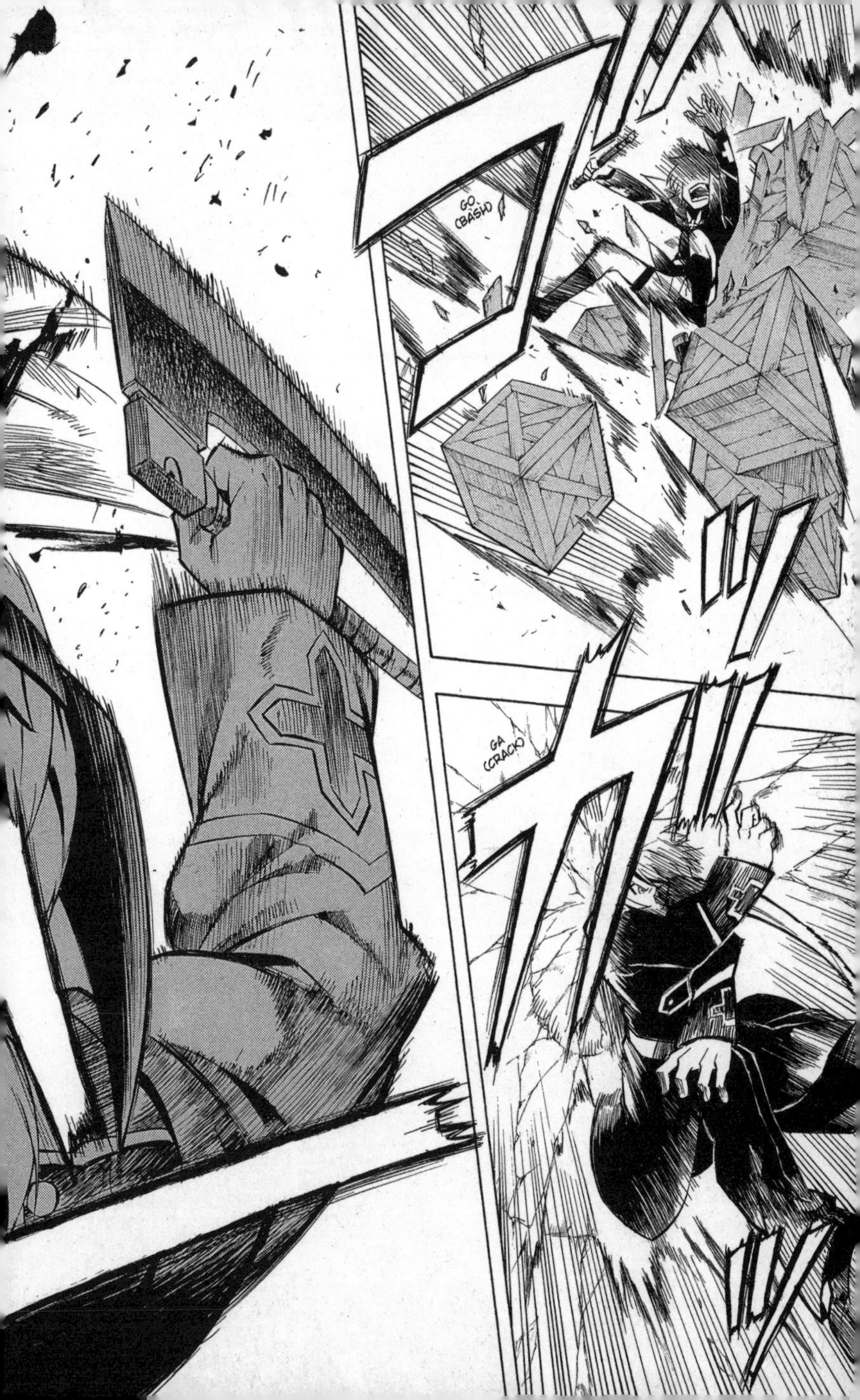
GO (BASH)
GA (CRACK)

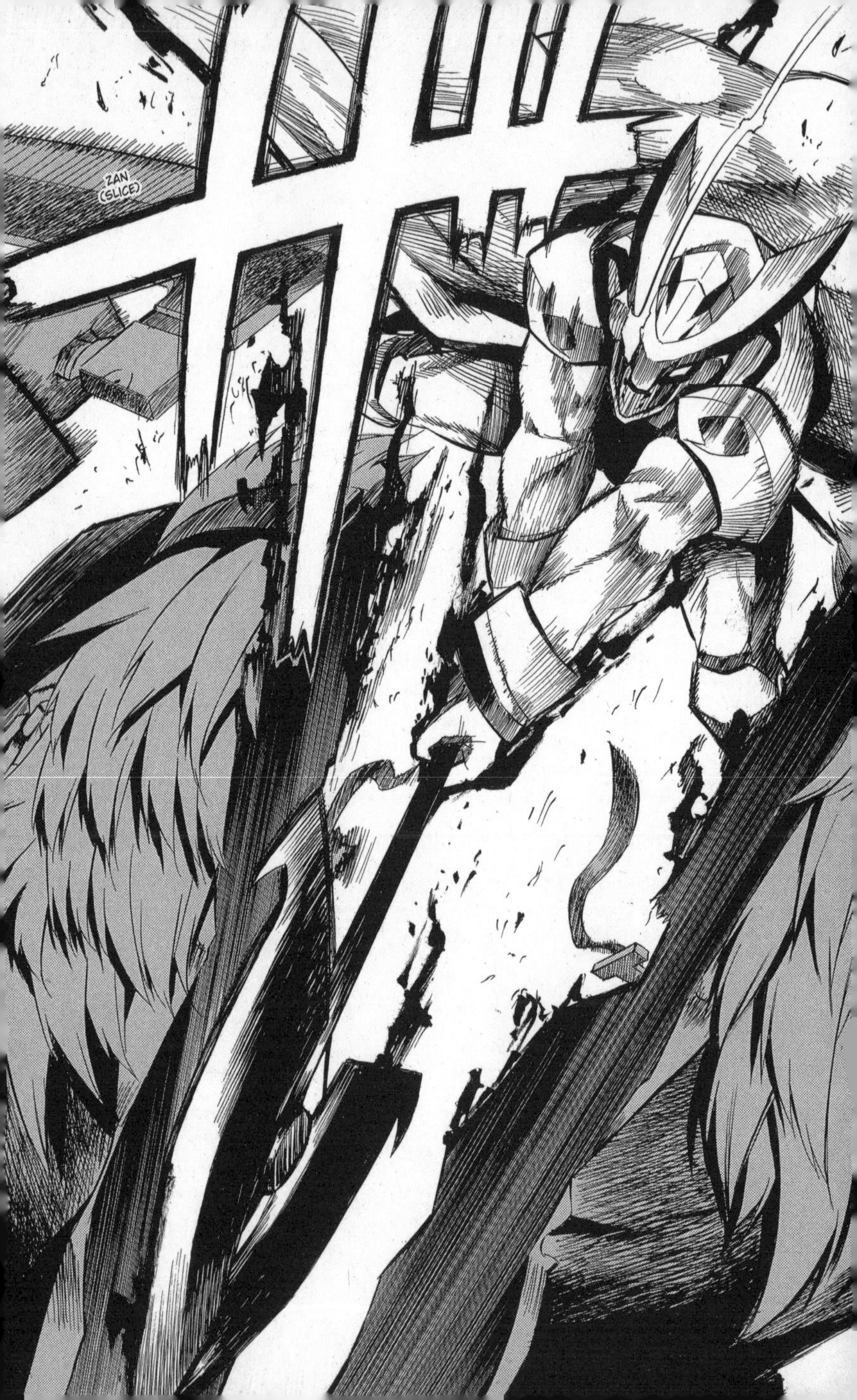
ZAN
(SLICE)

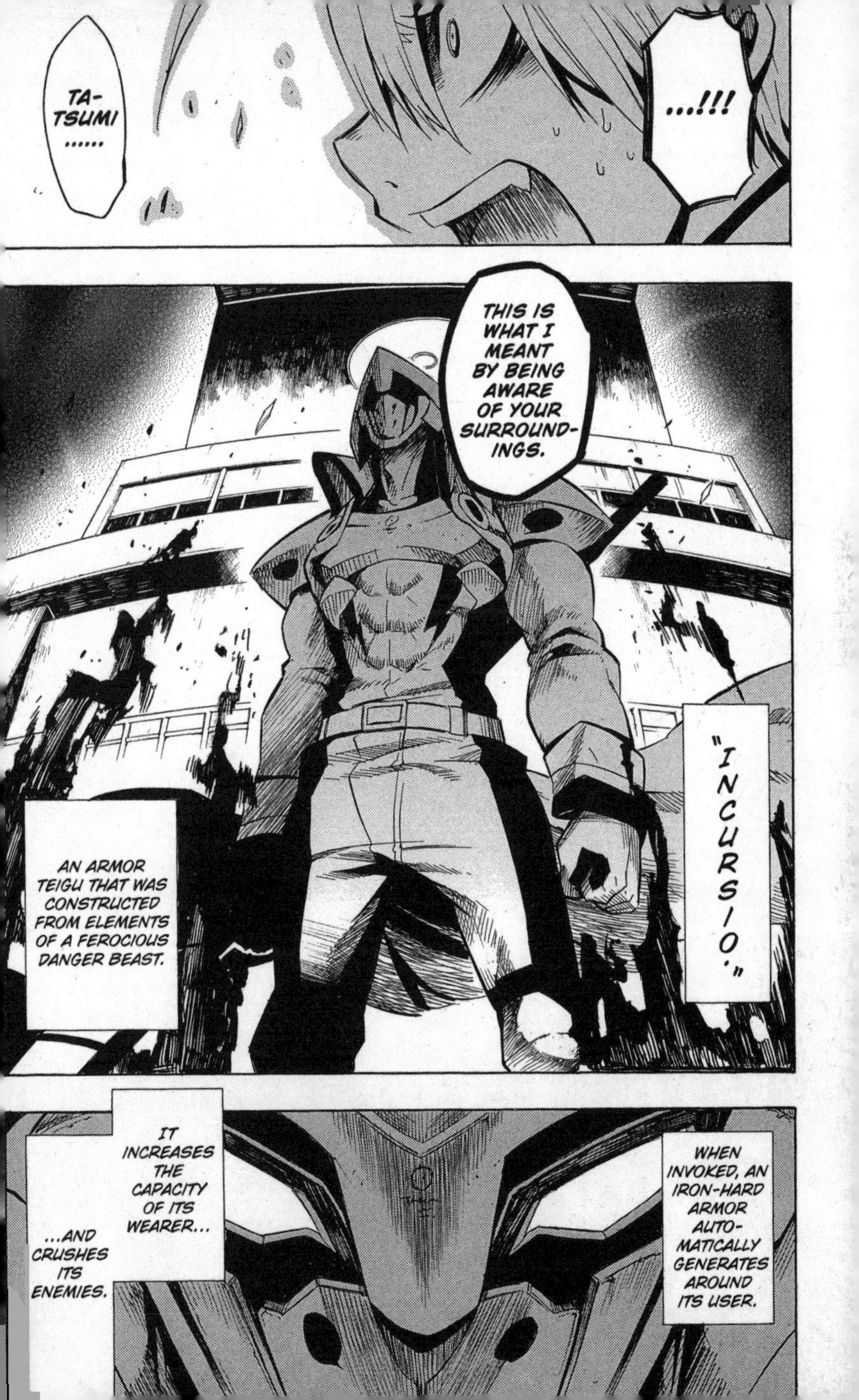
...!!!
TA-TSUMI ......
THIS IS WHAT I MEANT BY BEING AWARE OF YOUR SURROUND-INGS.
"INCURSIO."
AN ARMOR TEIGU THAT WAS CONSTRUCTED FROM ELEMENTS OF A FEROCIOUS DANGER BEAST.
WHEN INVOKED, AN IRON-HARD ARMOR AUTO-MATICALLY GENERATES AROUND ITS USER.
IT INCREASES THE CAPACITY OF ITS WEARER...
...AND CRUSHES ITS ENEMIES.

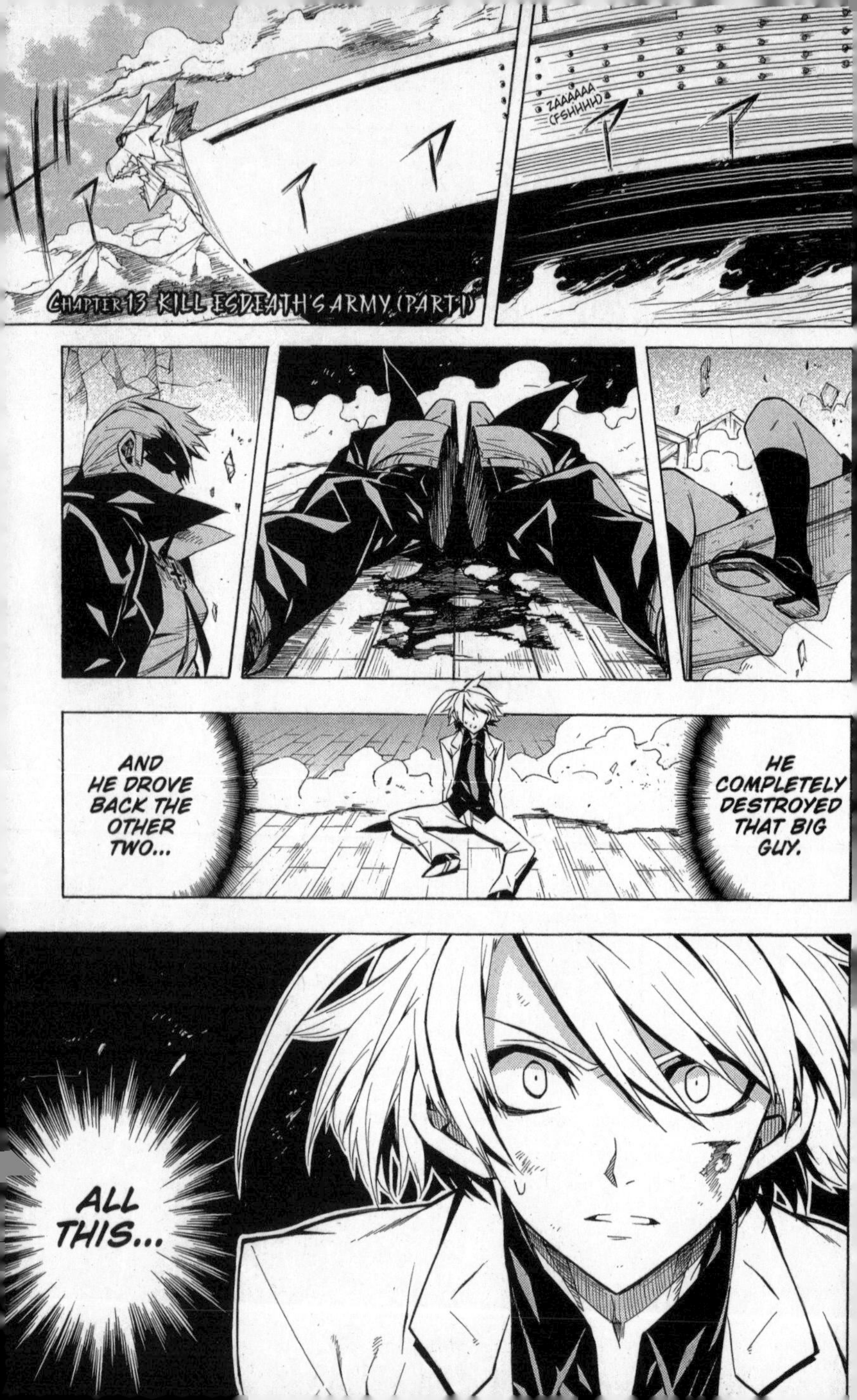
ZAAAAAA (FSHHHH)
CHAPTER 13 KILL ESDEATH'S ARMY (PART 1)
HE COMPLETELY DESTROYED THAT BIG GUY.
AND HE DROVE BACK THE OTHER TWO...
ALL THIS...

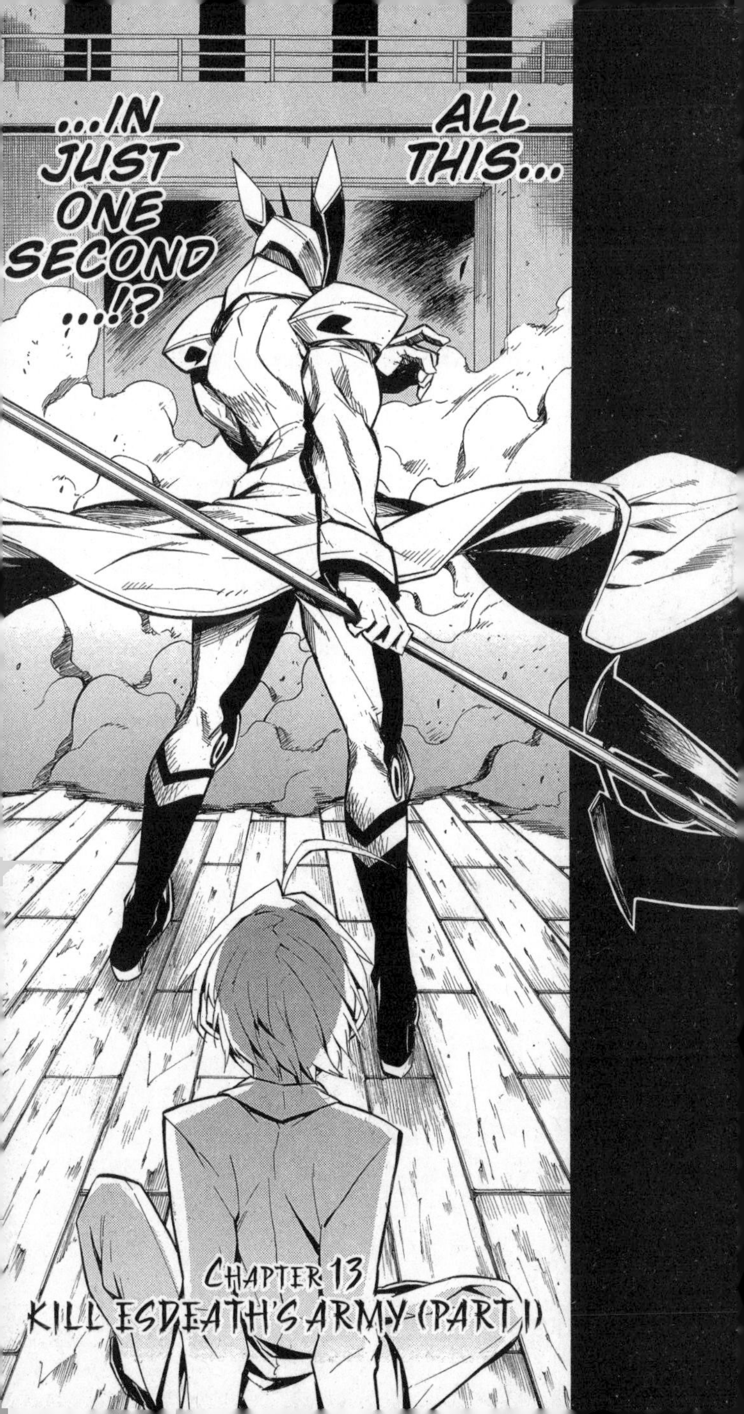
ALL THIS...
...IN JUST ONE SECOND ...!?
CHAPTER 13
KILL ESDEATH'S ARMY (PART 1)

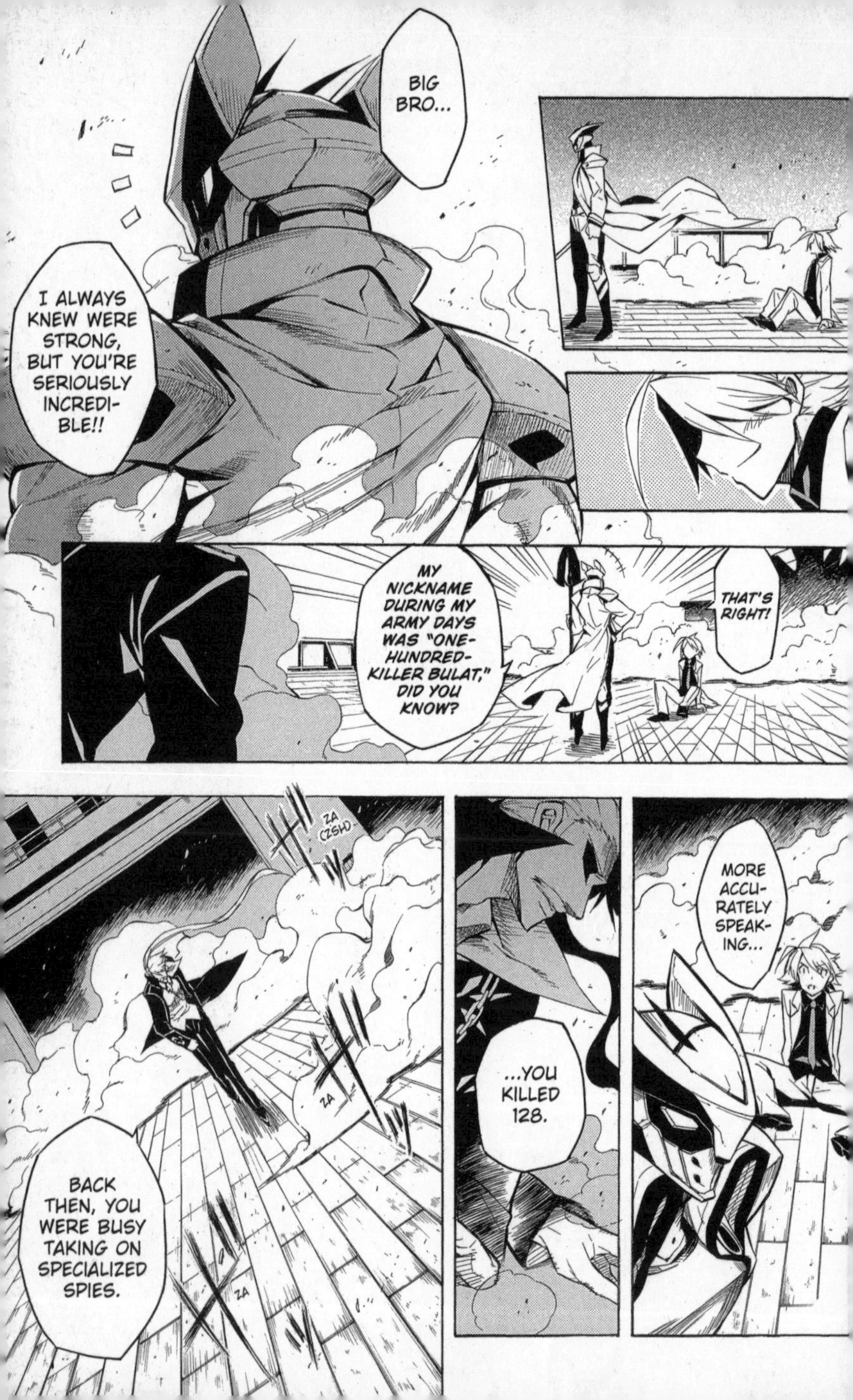
BIG BRO...
I ALWAYS KNEW WERE STRONG, BUT YOU'RE SERIOUSLY INCREDIBLE!!
THAT'S RIGHT!
MY NICKNAME DURING MY ARMY DAYS WAS "ONE-HUNDRED-KILLER BULAT," DID YOU KNOW?
MORE ACCURATELY SPEAKING...
...YOU KILLED 128.
ZA (ZSH)
ZA
ZA
BACK THEN, YOU WERE BUSY TAKING ON SPECIALIZED SPIES.

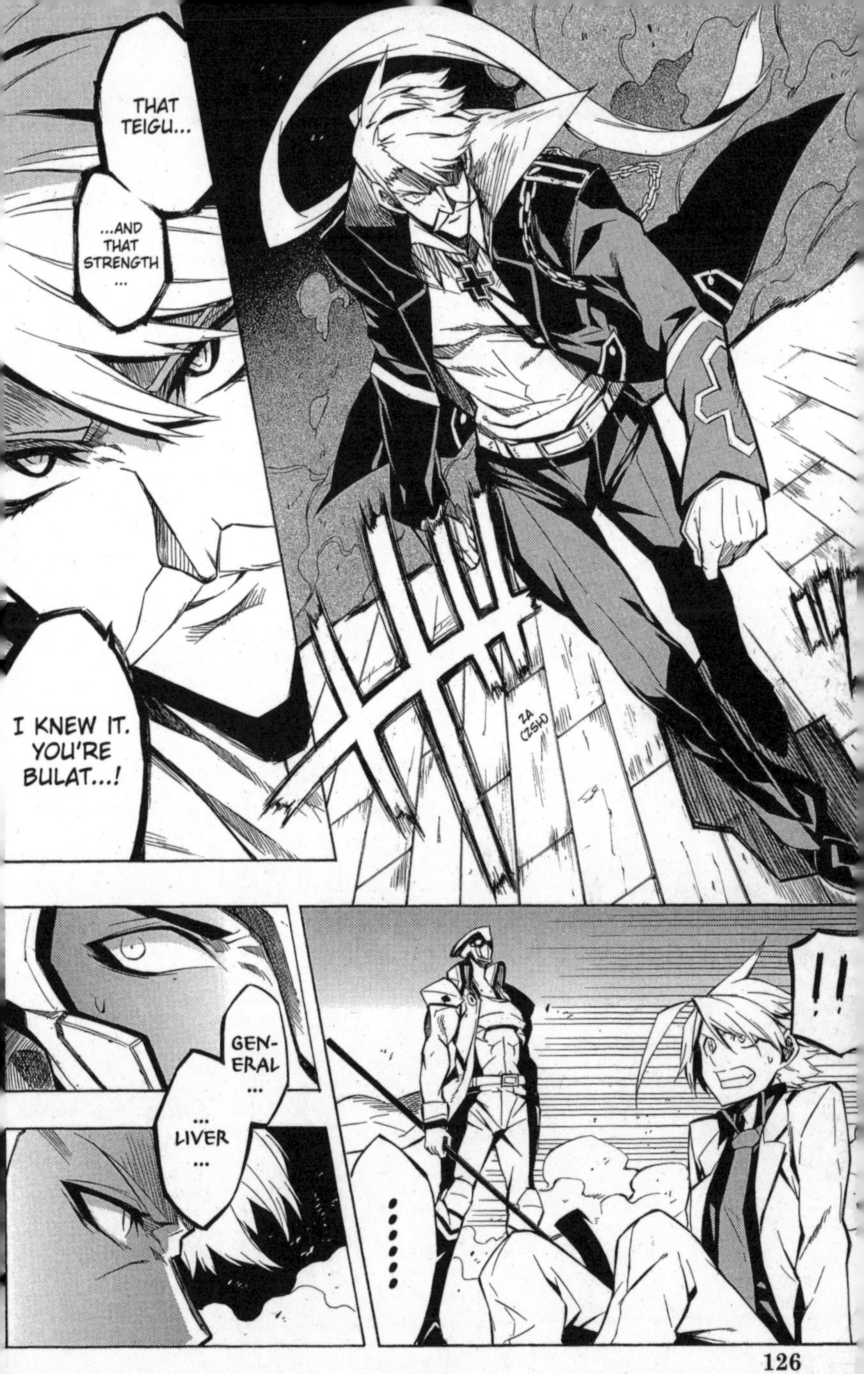
ZA (ZSH)
THAT TEIGU...
...AND THAT STRENGTH...
I KNEW IT. YOU'RE BULAT...!
!!
......
GEN-ERAL...
...LIVER...

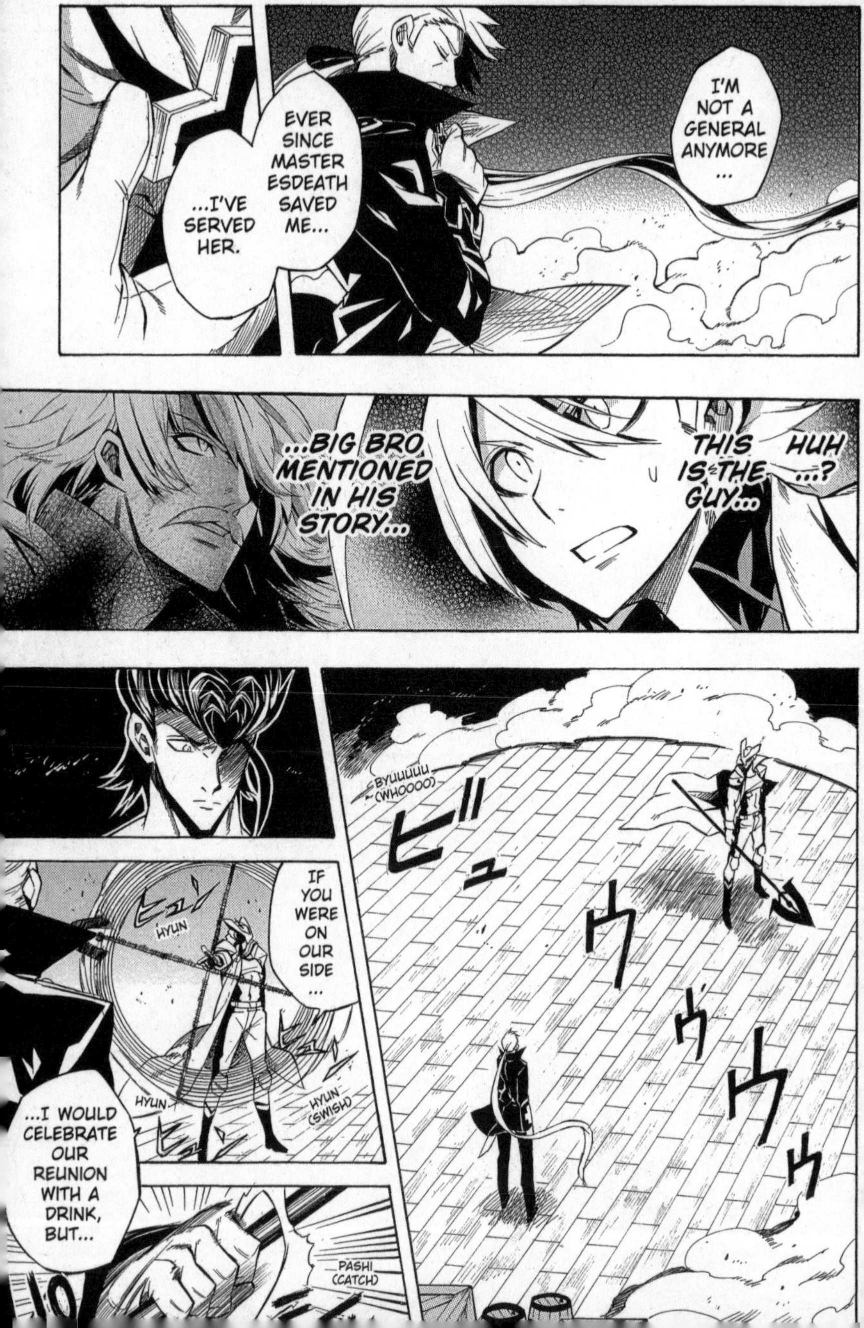

I'M NOT A GENERAL ANYMORE...
EVER SINCE MASTER ESDEATH SAVED ME...
...I'VE SERVED HER.
HUH...?
THIS IS THE GUY...
...BIG BRO MENTIONED IN HIS STORY...
BYUUUUU (WHOOOO)
...
IF YOU WERE ON OUR SIDE...
HYUN
HYUN
HYUN (SWISH)
...I WOULD CELEBRATE OUR REUNION WITH A DRINK, BUT...
PASHI (CATCH)

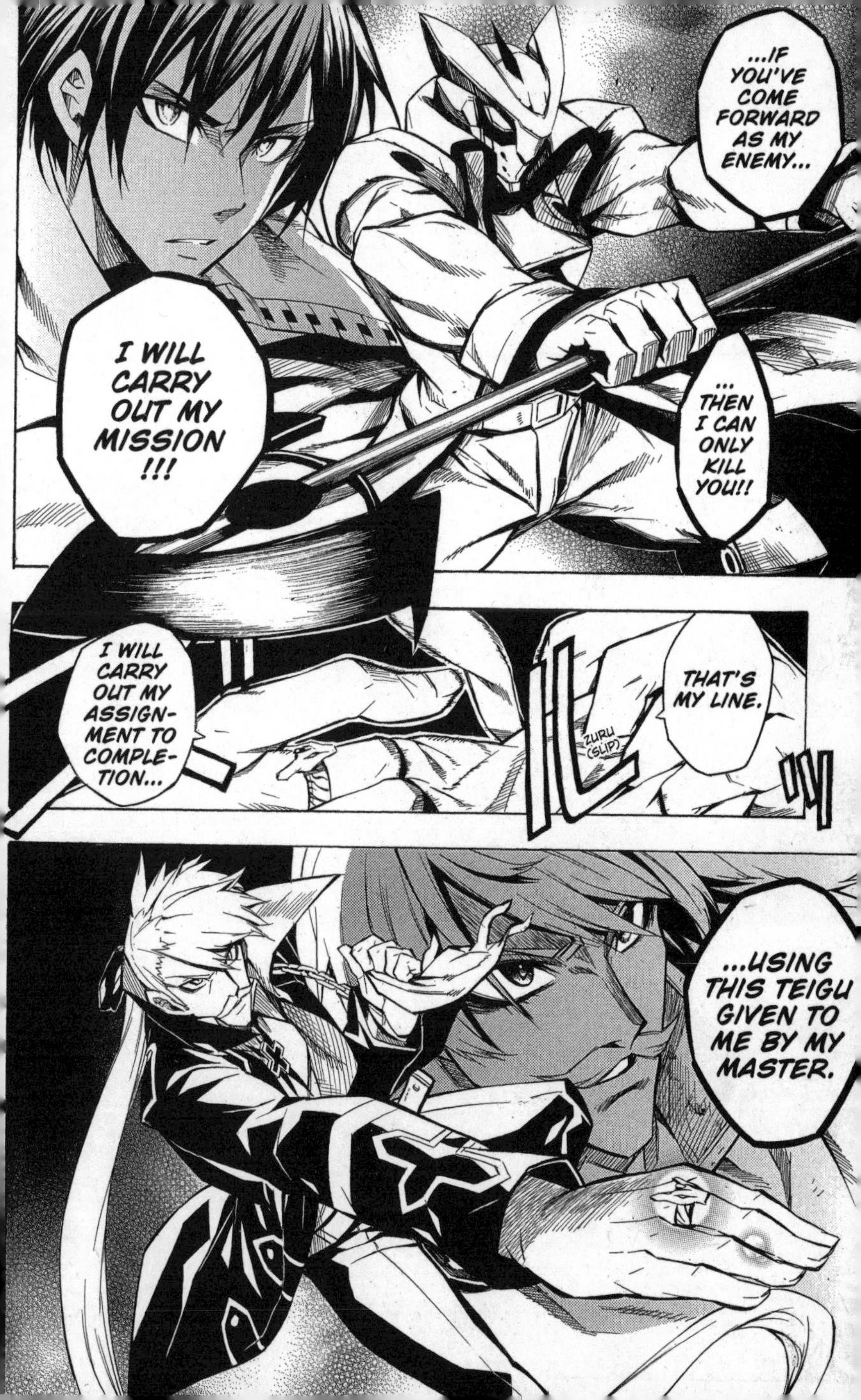
...IF YOU'VE COME FORWARD AS MY ENEMY...
... THEN I CAN ONLY KILL YOU!!
I WILL CARRY OUT MY MISSION !!!
THAT'S MY LINE.
ZURU (SLIP)
I WILL CARRY OUT MY ASSIGNMENT TO COMPLETION...
...USING THIS TEIGU GIVEN TO ME BY MY MASTER.

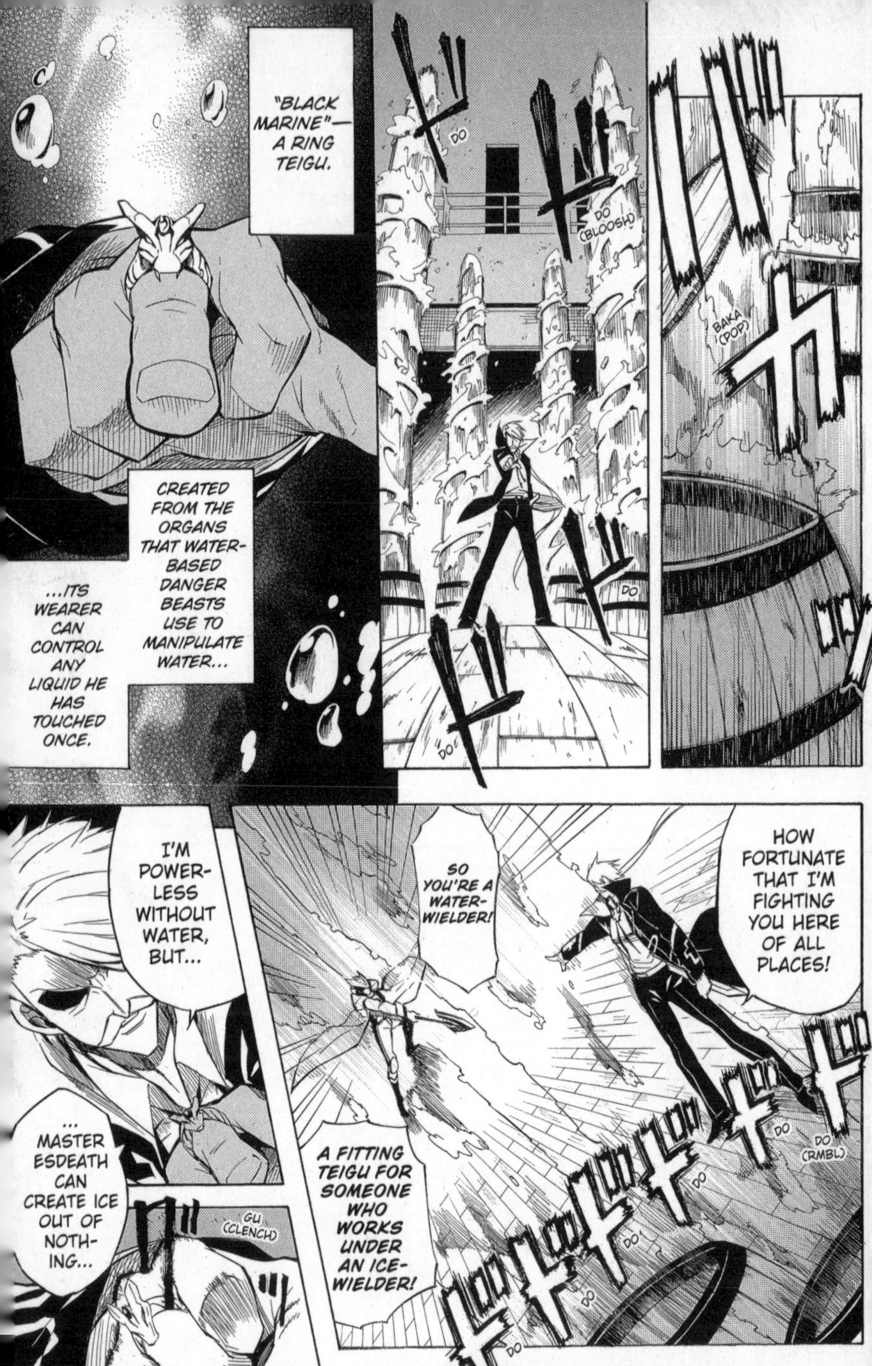
BAKA (POP)
DO
DO (BLOOSH)
DO
DO
"BLACK MARINE"— A RING TEIGU.
CREATED FROM THE ORGANS THAT WATER-BASED DANGER BEASTS USE TO MANIPULATE WATER...
...ITS WEARER CAN CONTROL ANY LIQUID HE HAS TOUCHED ONCE.
HOW FORTUNATE THAT I'M FIGHTING YOU HERE OF ALL PLACES!
SO YOU'RE A WATER-WIELDER!
A FITTING TEIGU FOR SOMEONE WHO WORKS UNDER AN ICE-WIELDER!
DO
DO (RMBL)
DO
DO
DO
DO
I'M POWERLESS WITHOUT WATER, BUT...
...MASTER ESDEATH CAN CREATE ICE OUT OF NOTHING...
GU (CLENCH)

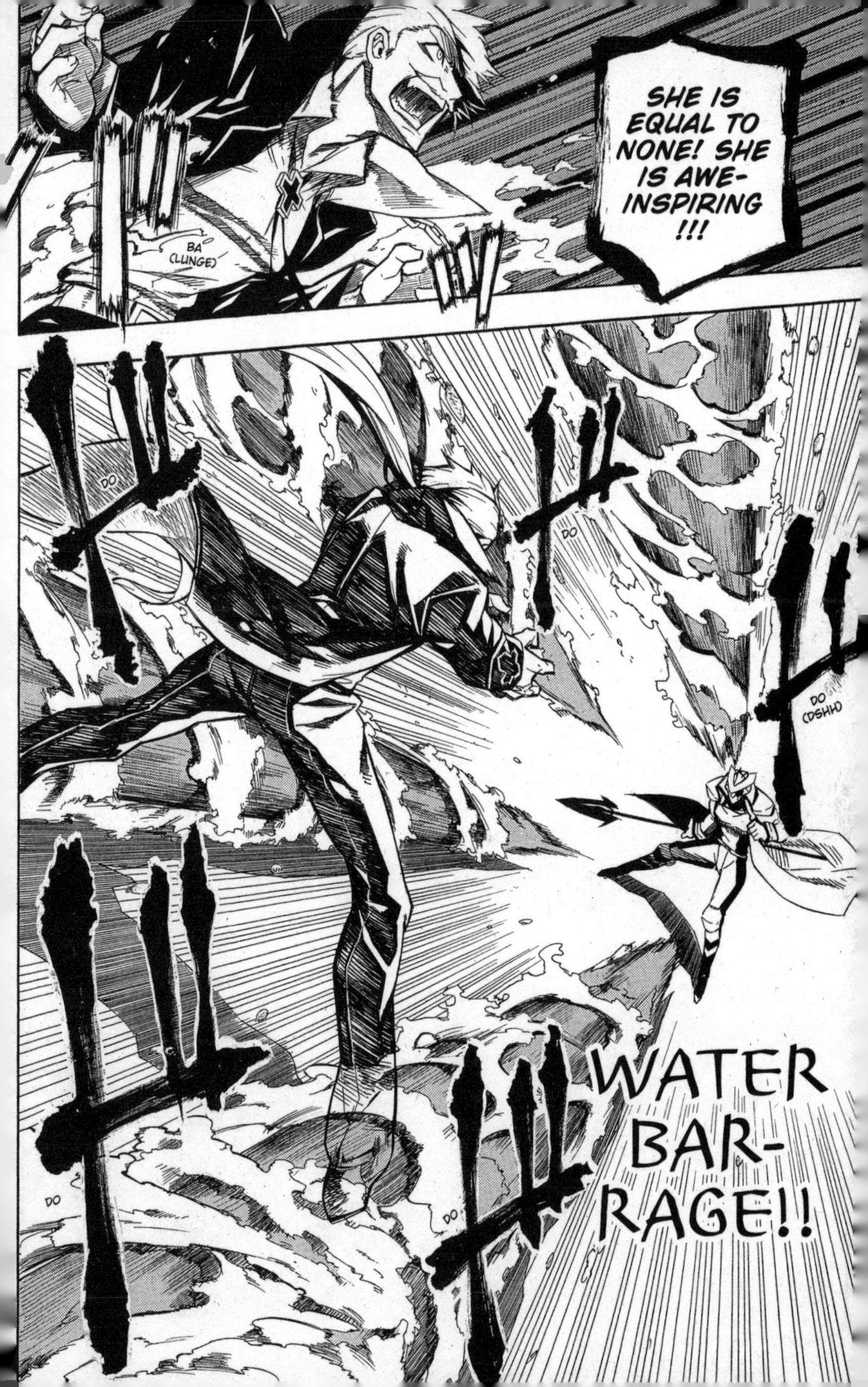
SHE IS EQUAL TO NONE! SHE IS AWE-INSPIRING!!!
BA (LUNGE)
DO (DSHH)
DO
DO
WATER BAR-RAGE!!
DO
DO

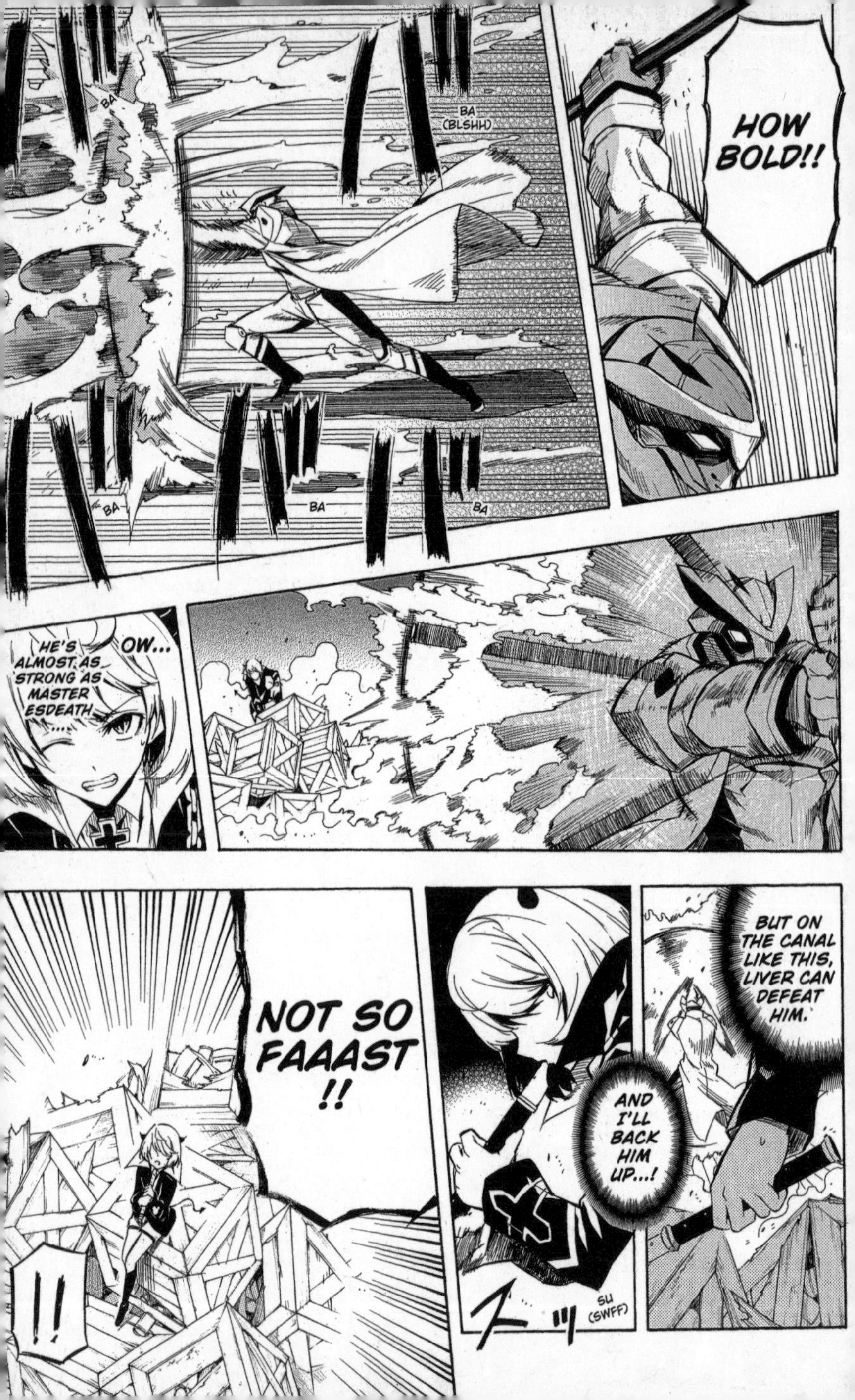
HOW BOLD!!
BA
BA (BLSHH)
BA
BA
BA
OW...
HE'S ALMOST AS STRONG AS MASTER ESDEATH...
BUT ON THE CANAL LIKE THIS, LIVER CAN DEFEAT HIM.
AND I'LL BACK HIM UP...!
SU (SWFF)
NOT SO FAAAST!!
!!

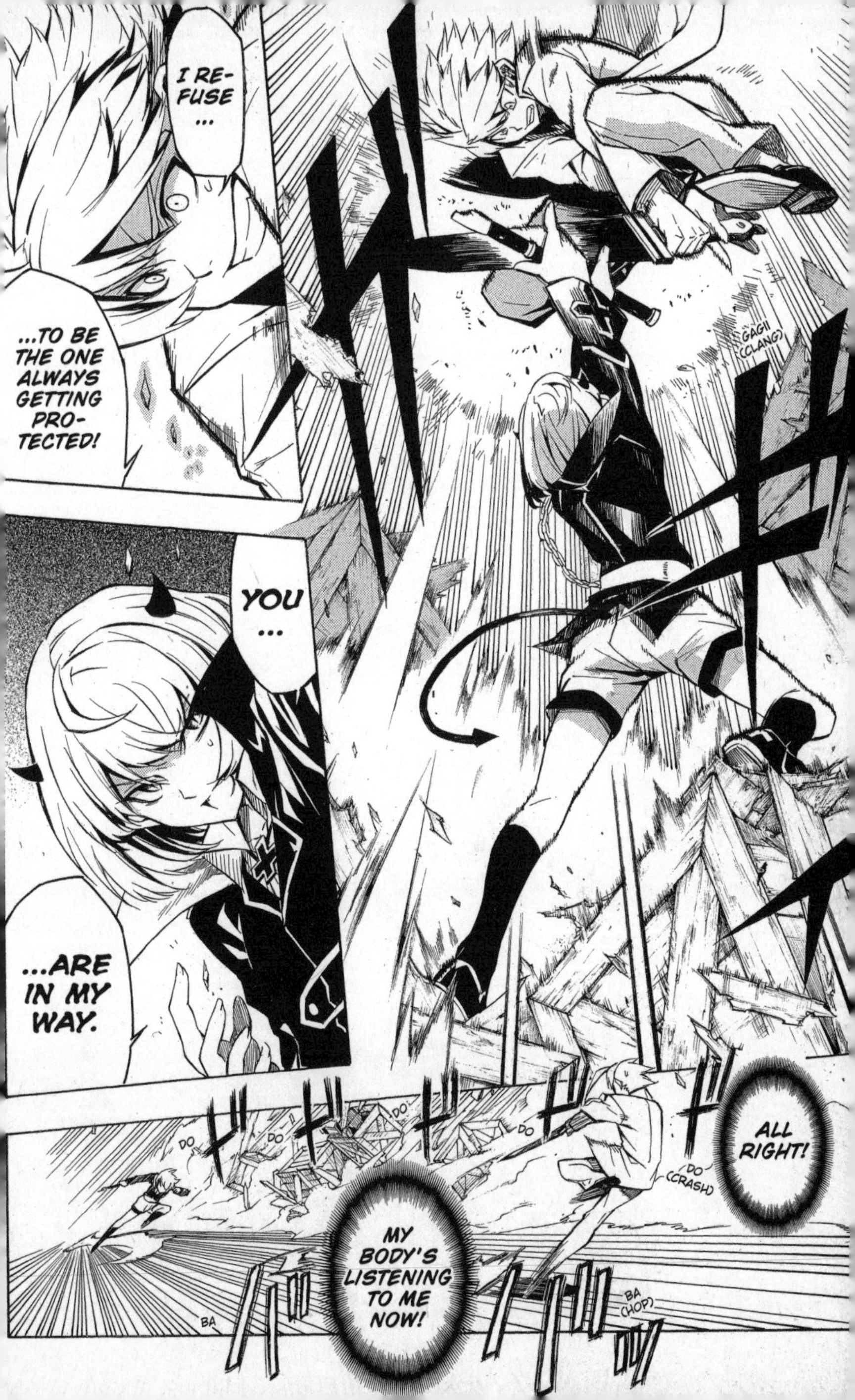
GAGII (CLANG)
I RE-FUSE ...
...TO BE THE ONE ALWAYS GETTING PRO-TECTED!
YOU ...
...ARE IN MY WAY.
ALL RIGHT!
DO (CRASH)
DO
DO
DO
DO
MY BODY'S LISTENING TO ME NOW!
BA (HOP)
BA

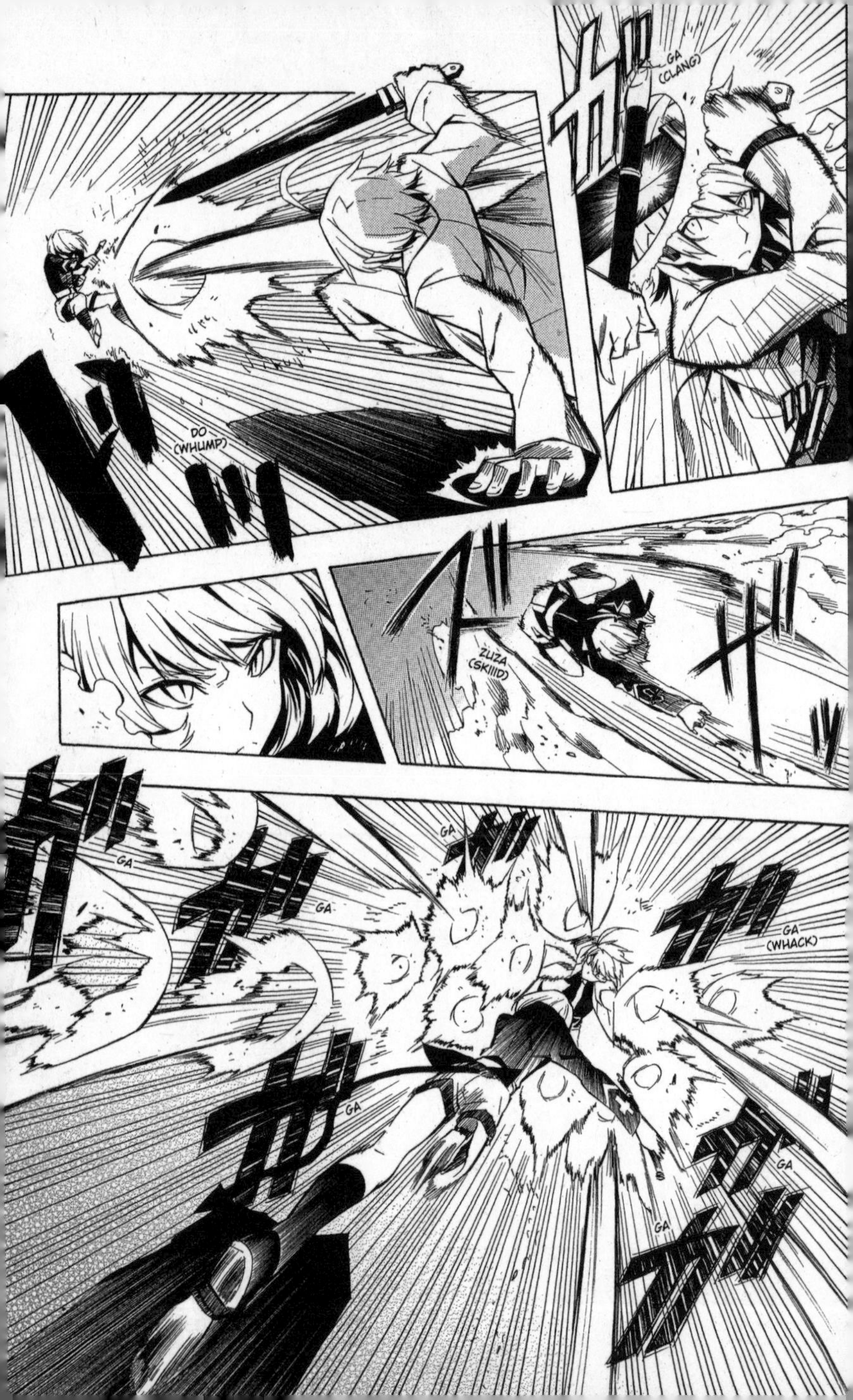
GA
(CLANG)
DO
(WHUMP)
ZUZA
(SKIIID)
GA
GA
(WHACK)
GA
GA
GA
GA
GA

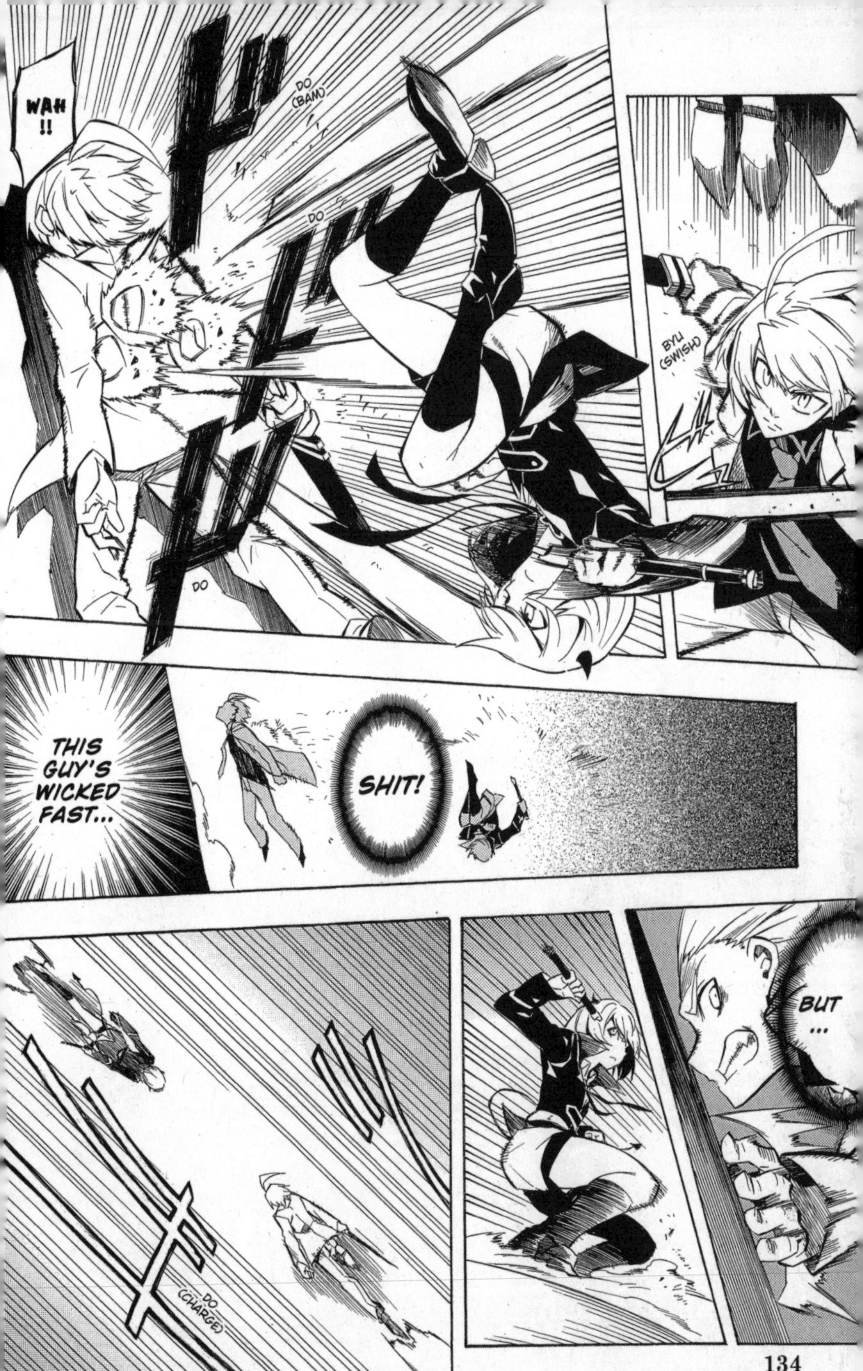
BYU (SWISH)
WAH !!
DO (BAM)
DO
DO
SHIT!
THIS GUY'S WICKED FAST...
BUT ...
DO (CHARGE)

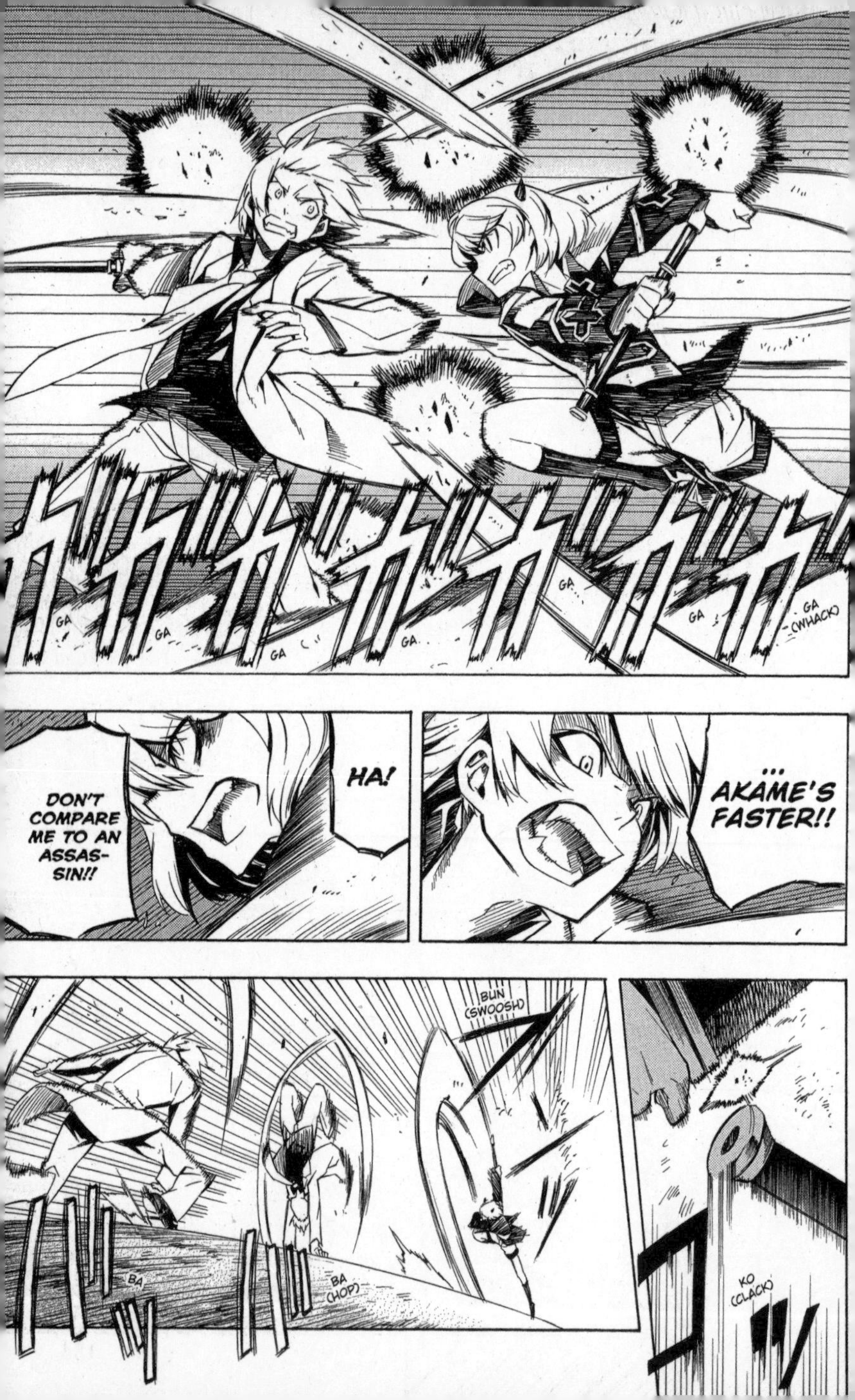
GA (WHACK)
GA
GA...
GA
GA
GA
GA
GA
...AKAME'S FASTER!!
HA!
DON'T COMPARE ME TO AN ASSAS-SIN!!
KO (CLACK)
BUN (SWOOSH)
BA (HOP)
BA

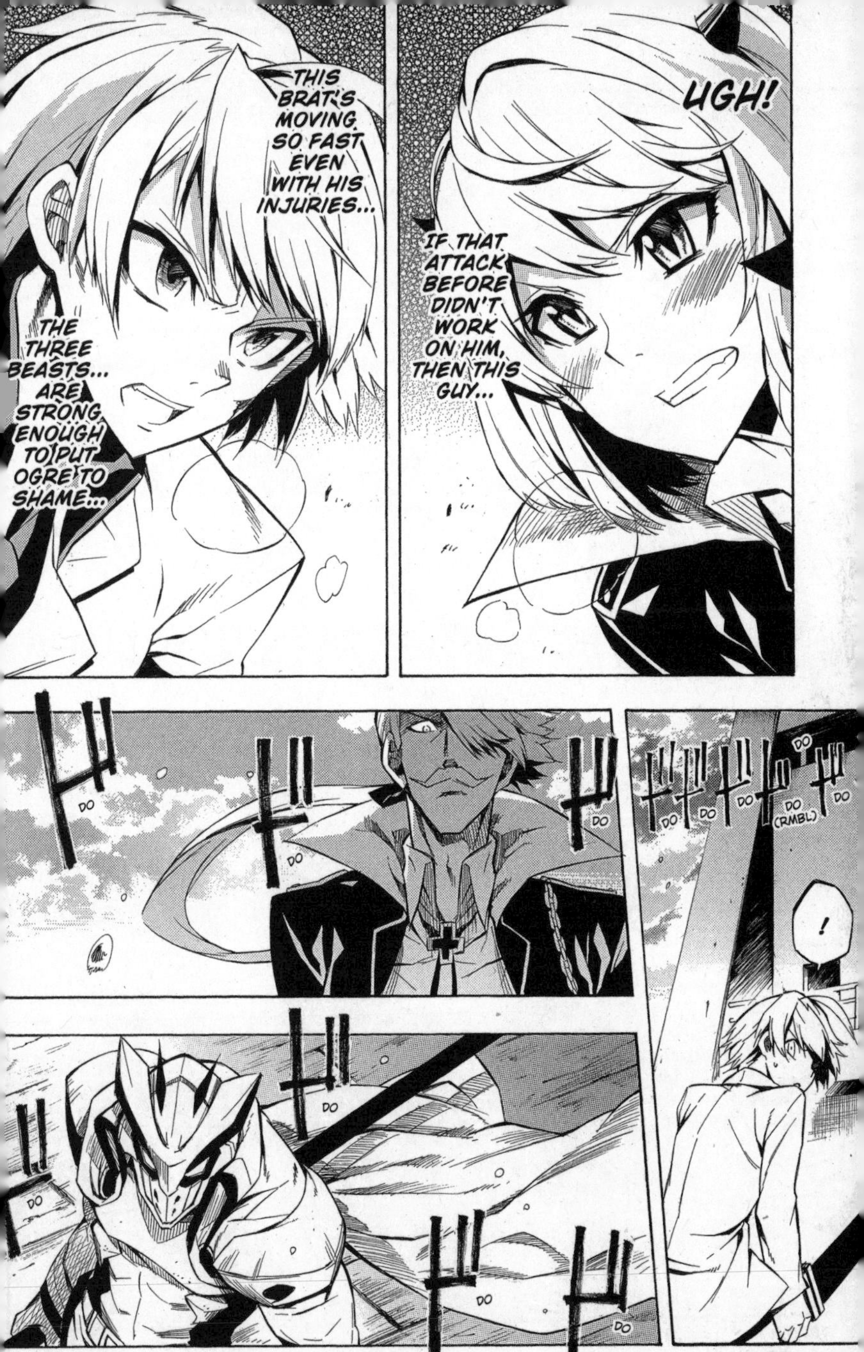
UGH!
IF THAT ATTACK BEFORE DIDN'T WORK ON HIM, THEN THIS GUY...
THIS BRAT'S MOVING SO FAST EVEN WITH HIS INJURIES...
THE THREE BEASTS... ARE STRONG ENOUGH TO PUT OGRE TO SHAME...
DO DO DO DO DO DO DO (RMBL)
!
DO DO DO
DO DO DO DO

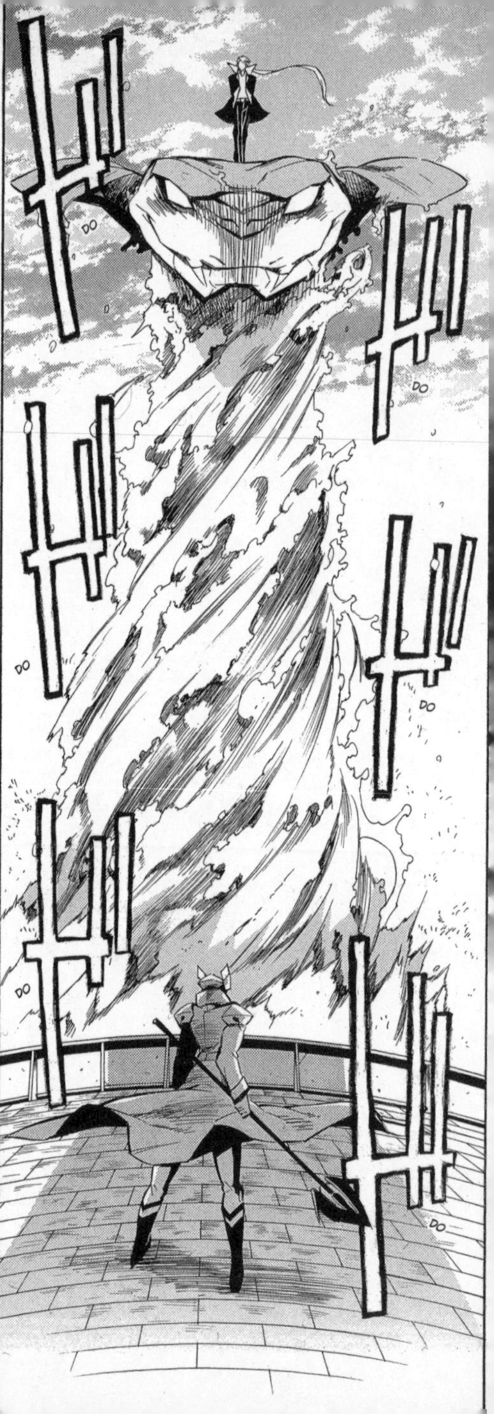
DO
DO
DO
DO
DO
DO

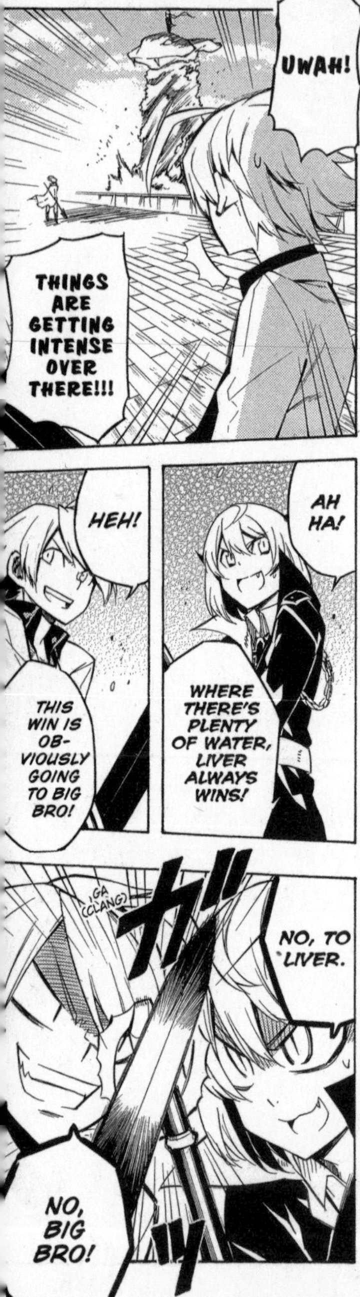
UWAH!
THINGS ARE GETTING INTENSE OVER THERE!!!
AH HA!
WHERE THERE'S PLENTY OF WATER, LIVER ALWAYS WINS!
HEH!
THIS WIN IS OB-VIOUSLY GOING TO BIG BRO!
GA (CLANG)
NO, TO LIVER.
NO, BIG BRO!

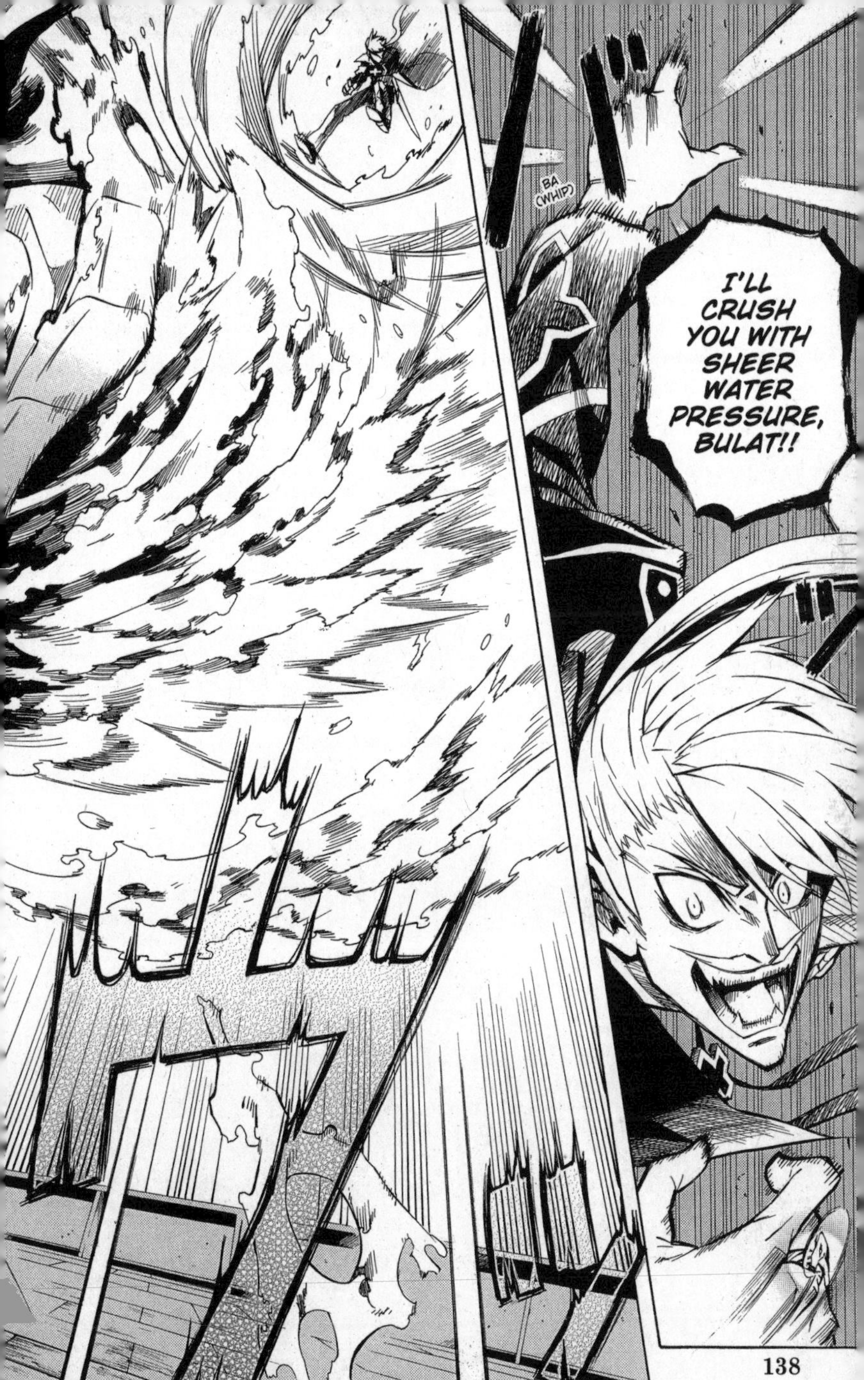
BA (WHIP)
I'LL CRUSH YOU WITH SHEER WATER PRESSURE, BULAT!!

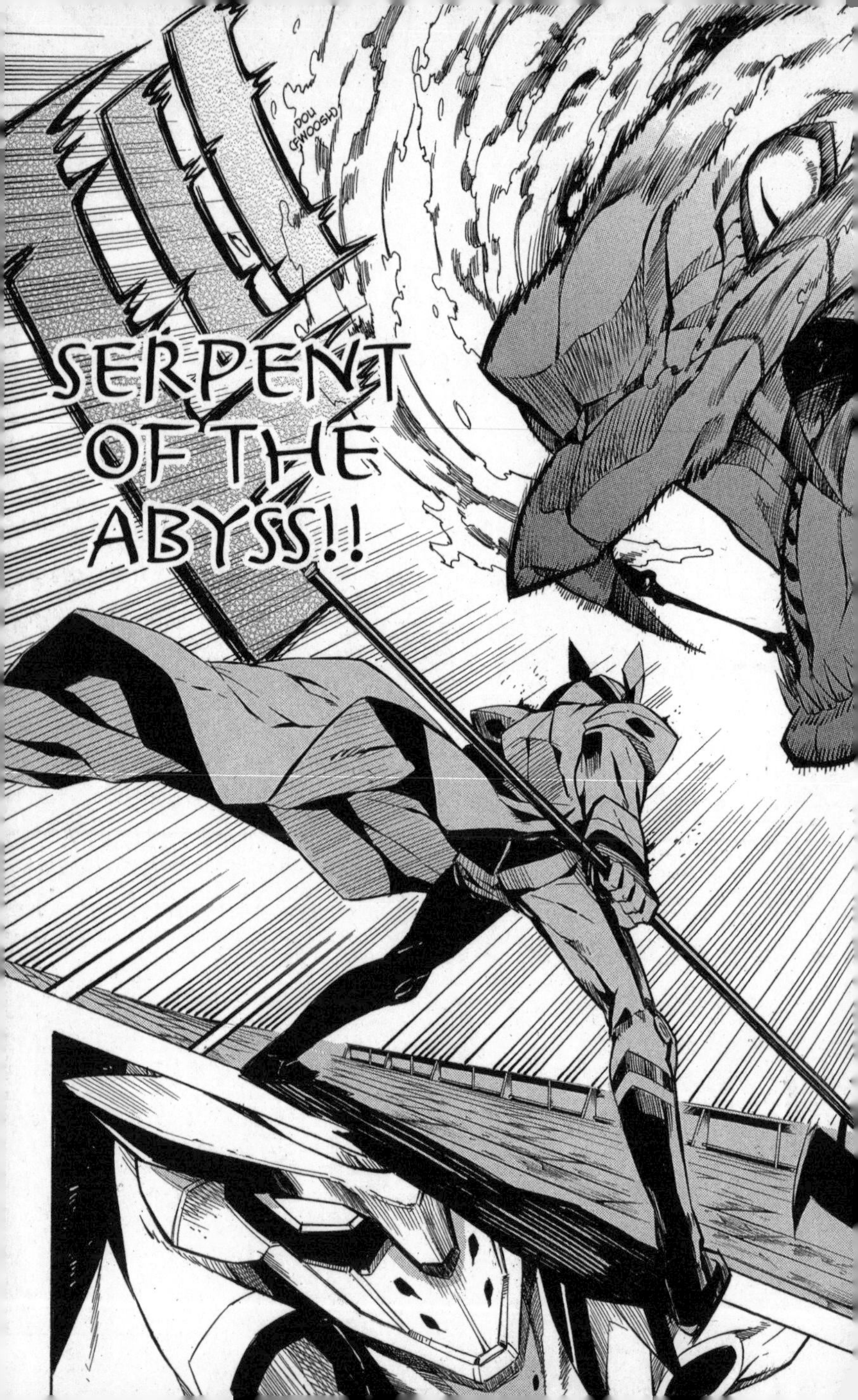
DOU (FWOOSH)
SERPENT OF THE ABYSS!!

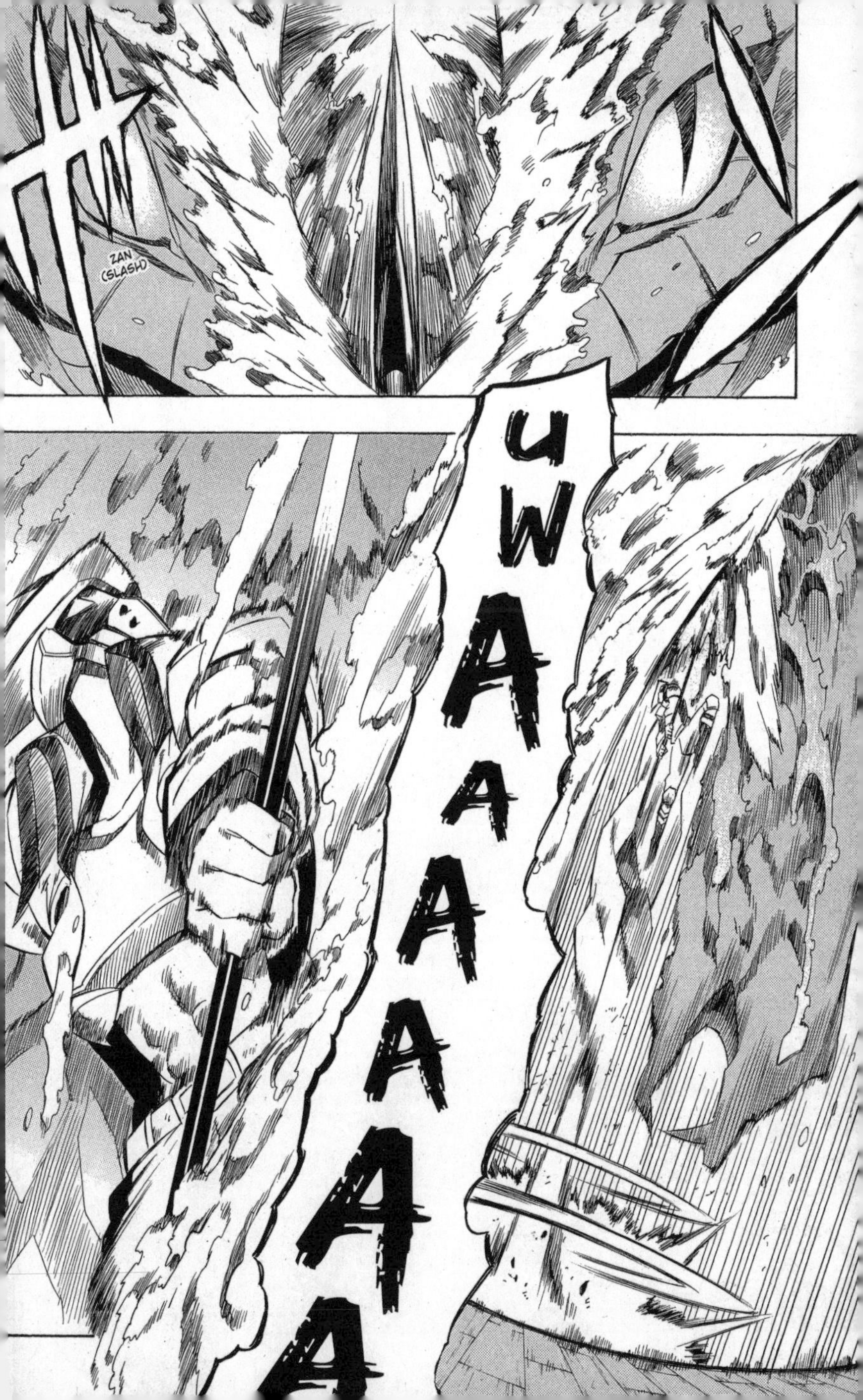
ZAN (SLASH)
UWAAAAAAA

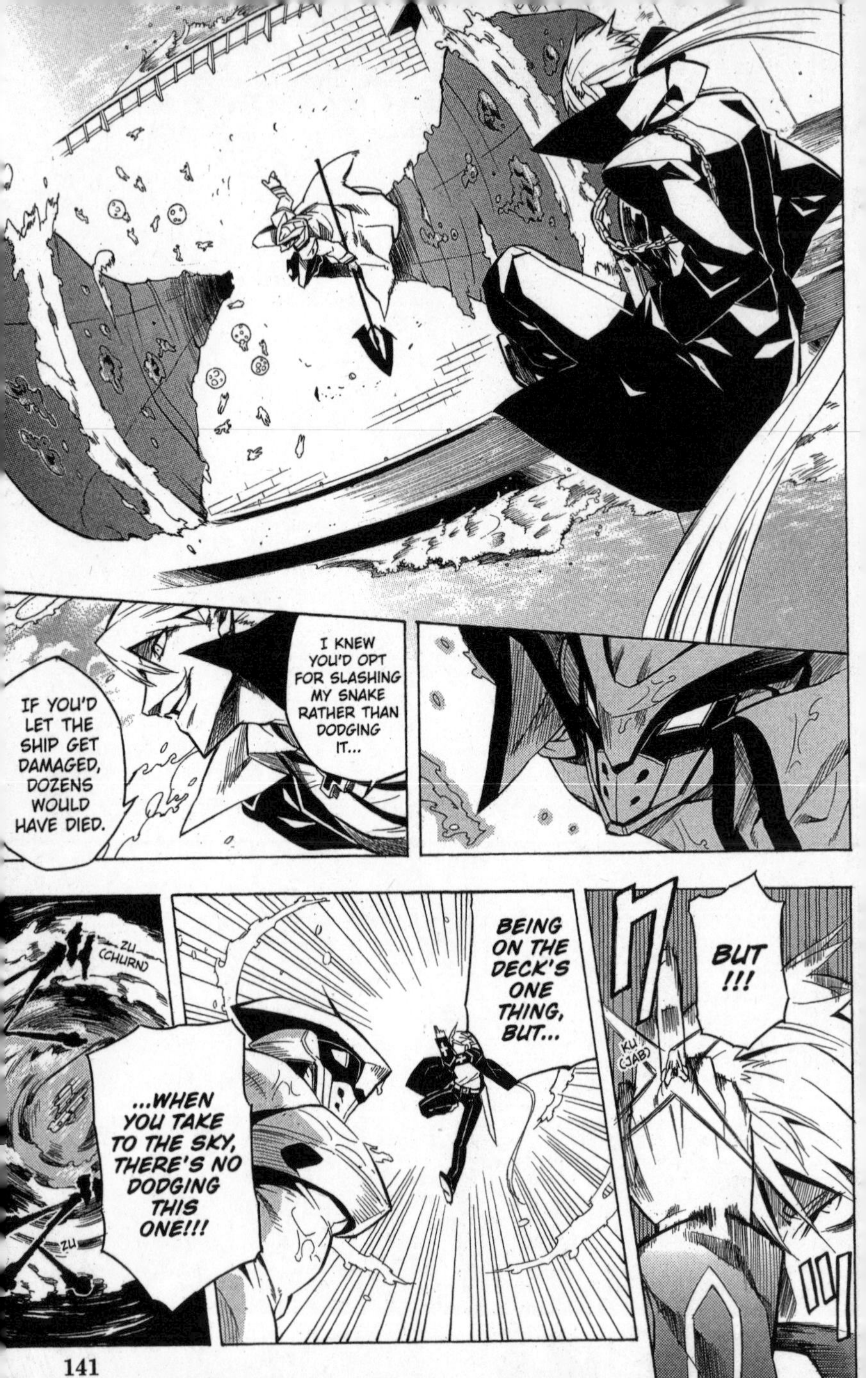
I KNEW YOU'D OPT FOR SLASHING MY SNAKE RATHER THAN DODGING IT...
IF YOU'D LET THE SHIP GET DAMAGED, DOZENS WOULD HAVE DIED.
BUT !!!
KU (JAB)
BEING ON THE DECK'S ONE THING, BUT...
...WHEN YOU TAKE TO THE SKY, THERE'S NO DODGING THIS ONE!!!
ZU (CHURN)
ZU

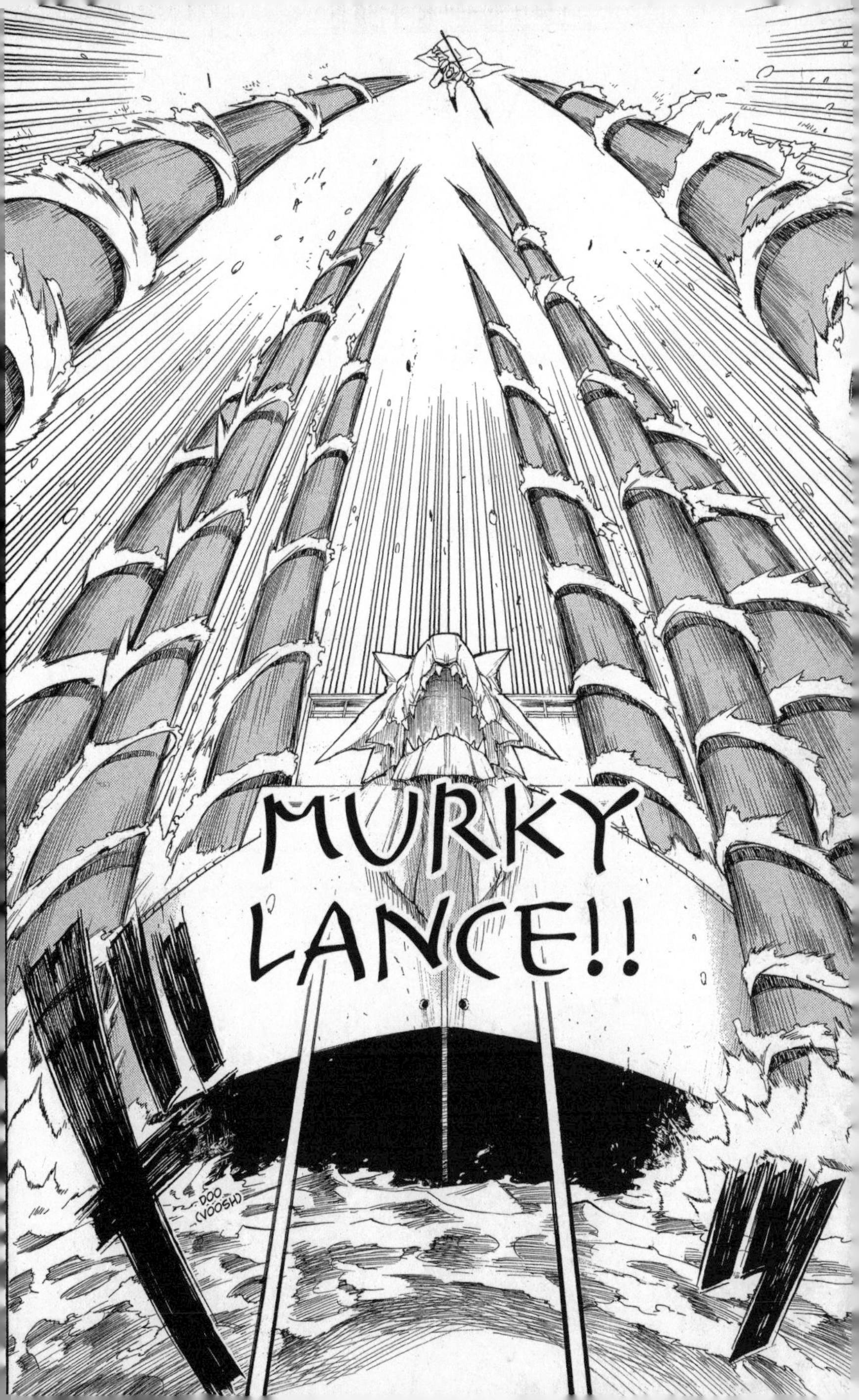
MURKY LANCE!!
DOO (VOOSH)

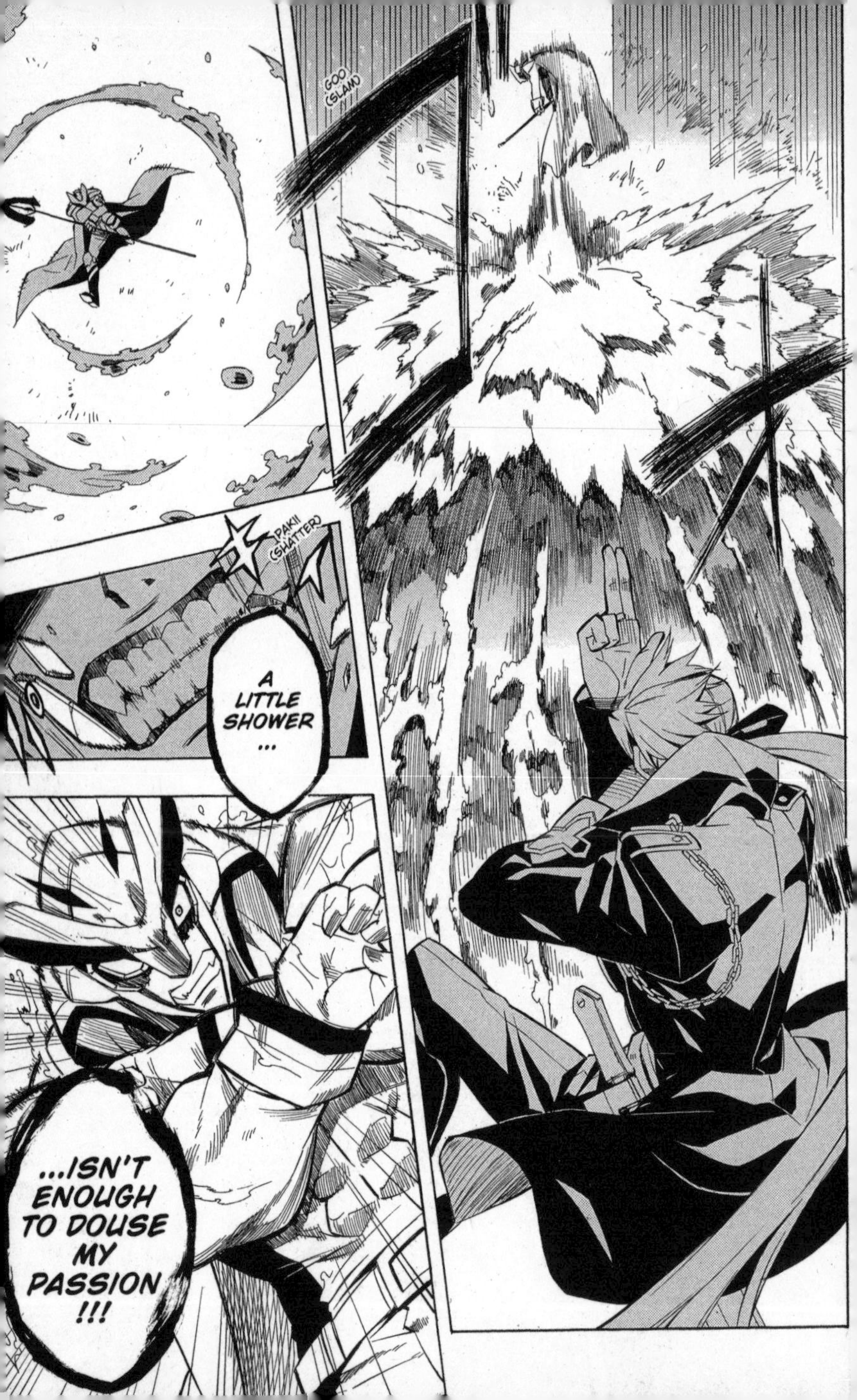
GOO (SLAM)
PAKI! (SHATTER)
A LITTLE SHOWER...
...ISN'T ENOUGH TO DOUSE MY PASSION!!!

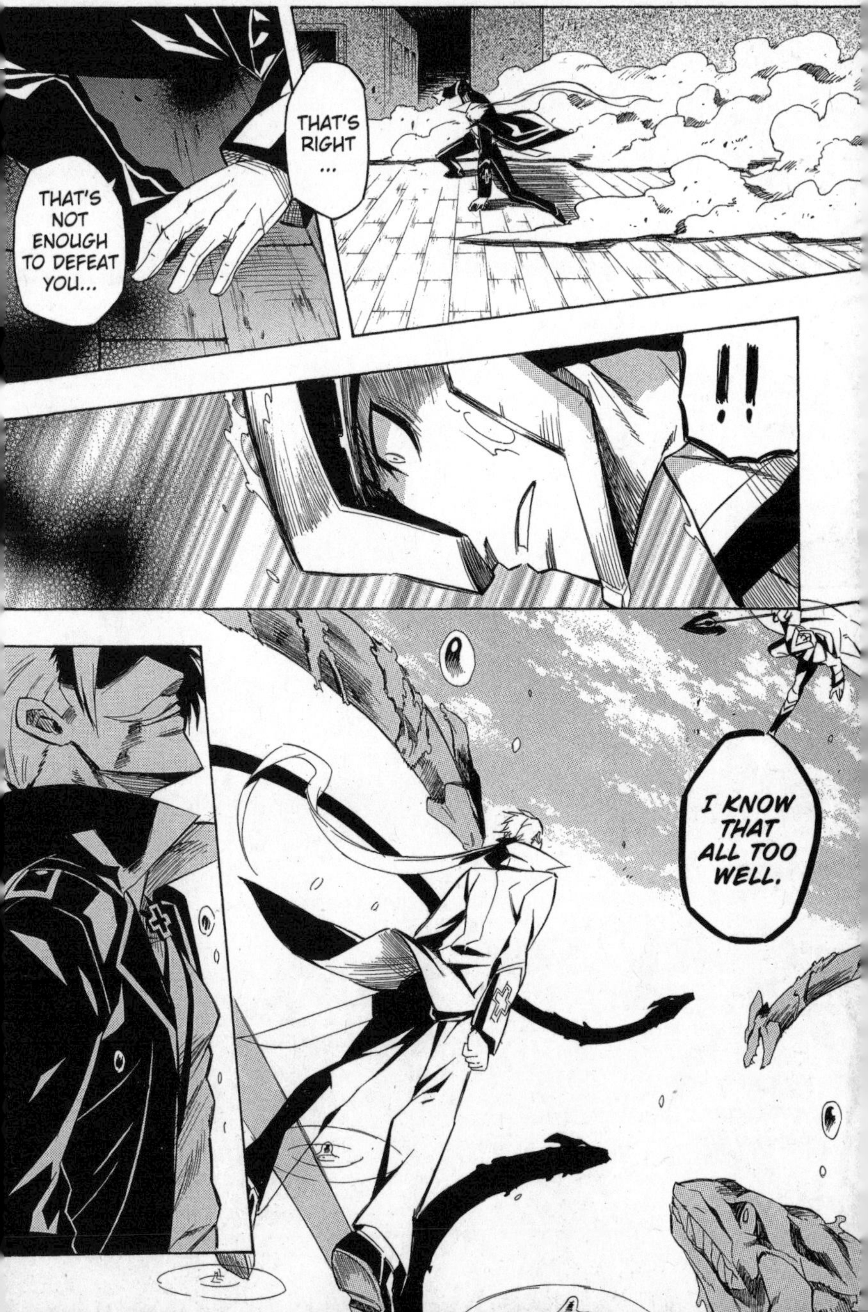
THAT'S RIGHT ...
THAT'S NOT ENOUGH TO DEFEAT YOU...
!!
I KNOW THAT ALL TOO WELL.

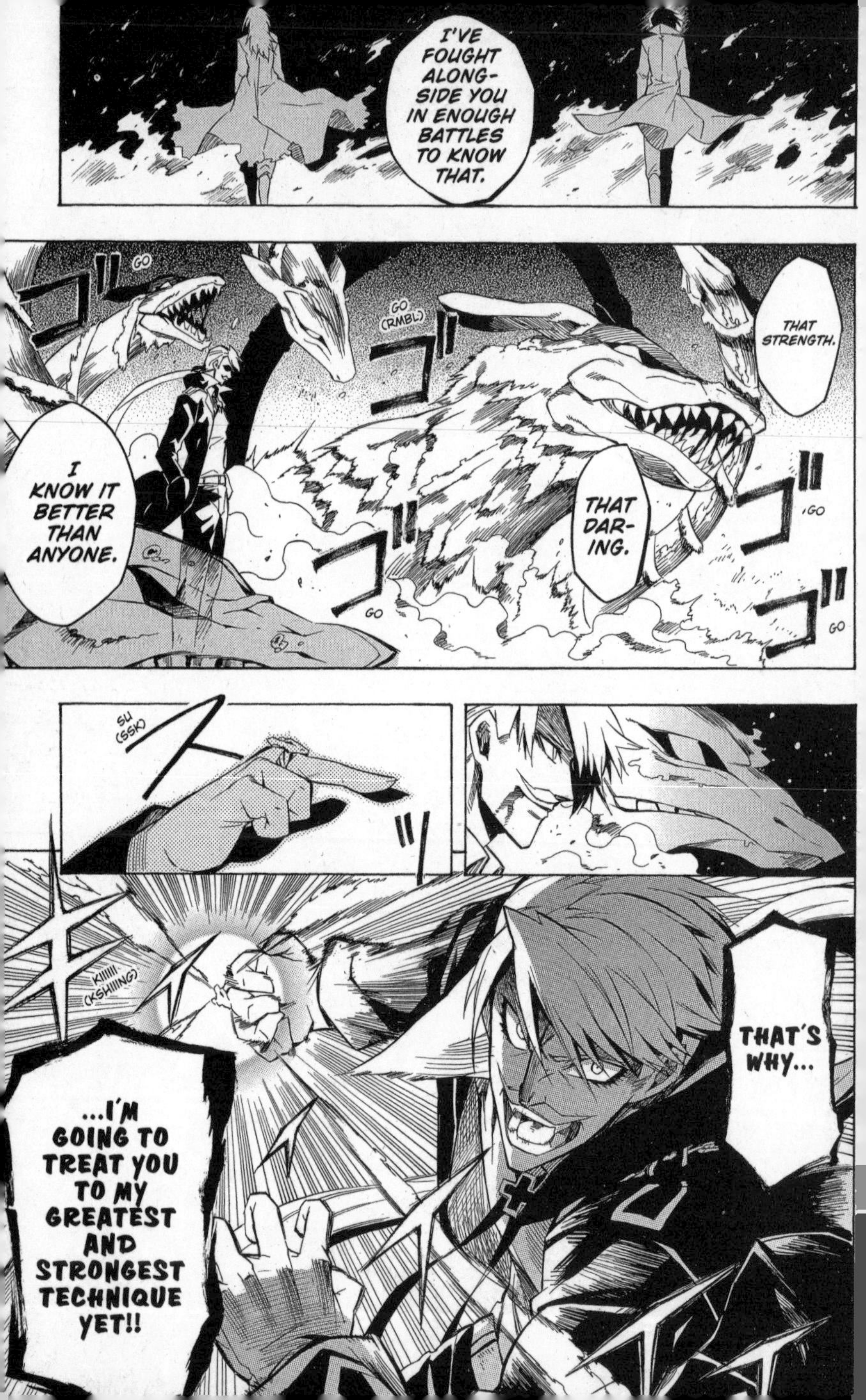
I'VE FOUGHT ALONG-SIDE YOU IN ENOUGH BATTLES TO KNOW THAT.
THAT STRENGTH.
GO
GO
THAT DAR-ING.
GO (RMBL)
GO
GO
I KNOW IT BETTER THAN ANYONE.
SU (SSK)
THAT'S WHY...
KIIIIII (KSHIIING)
...I'M GOING TO TREAT YOU TO MY GREATEST AND STRONGEST TECHNIQUE YET!!

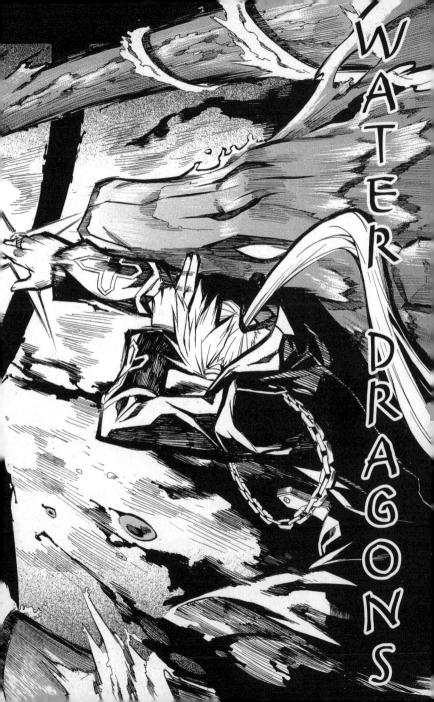

WATER DRAGONS

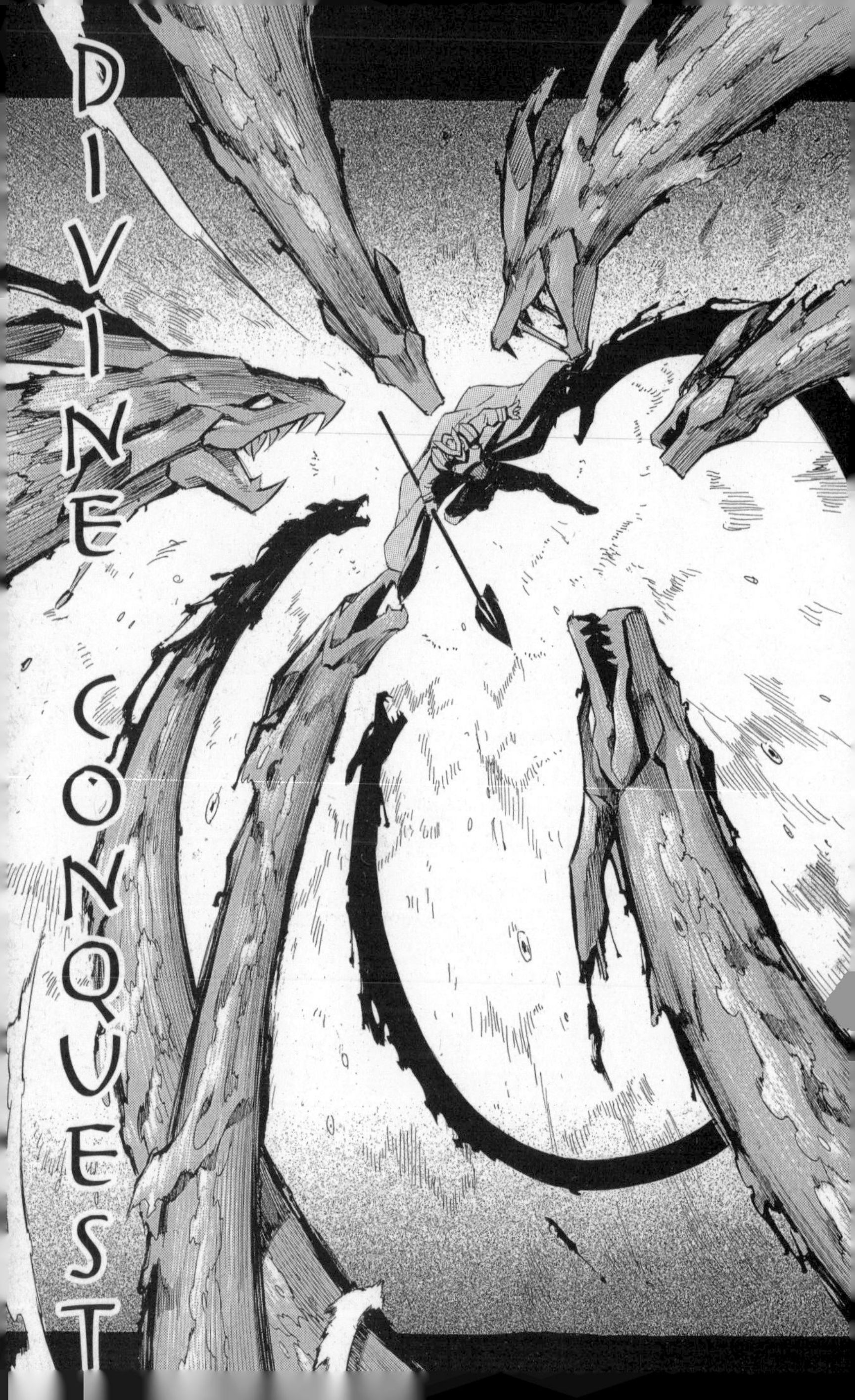
DIVINE CONQUEST

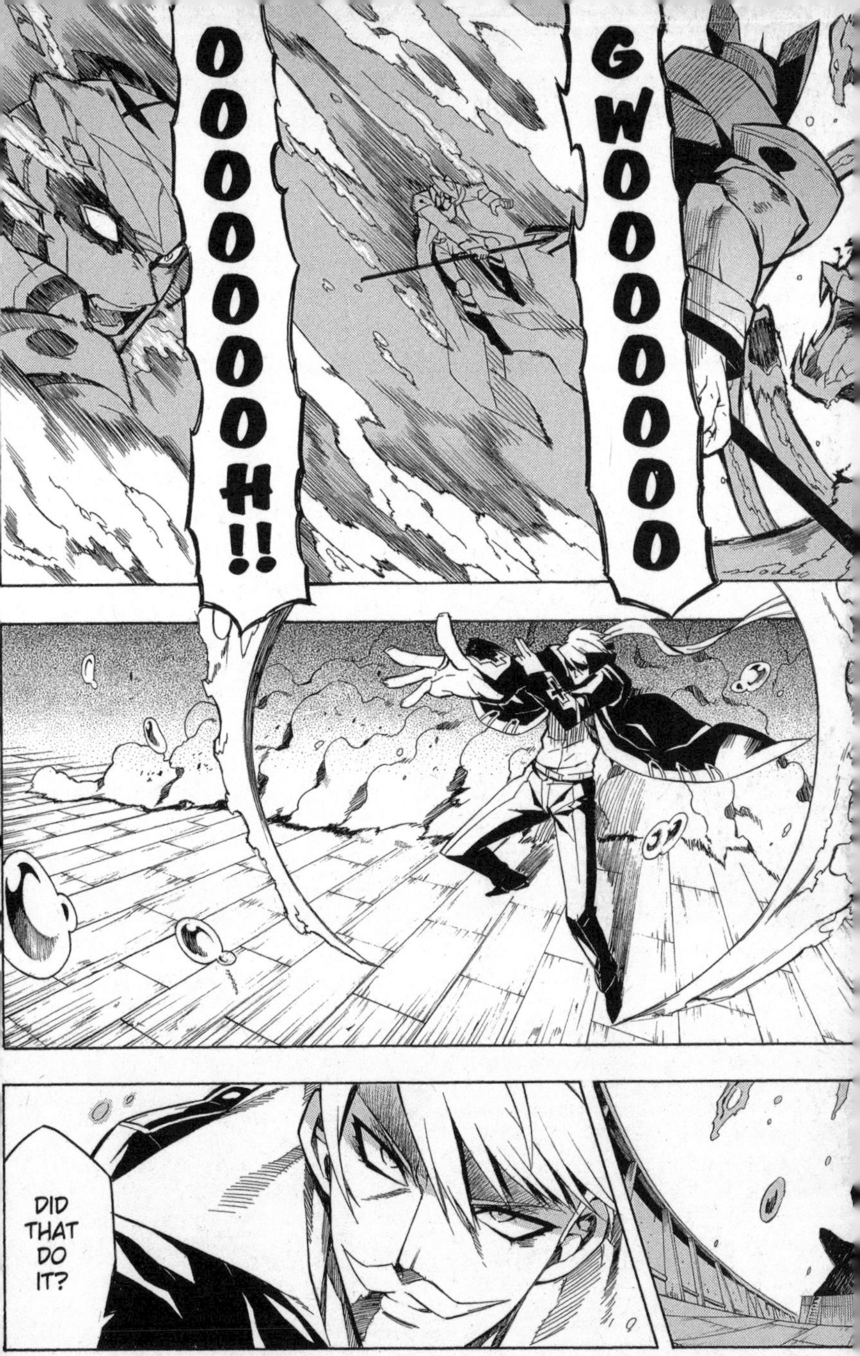
GWOOOOOOO
OOOOOOOH!!
DID THAT DO IT?

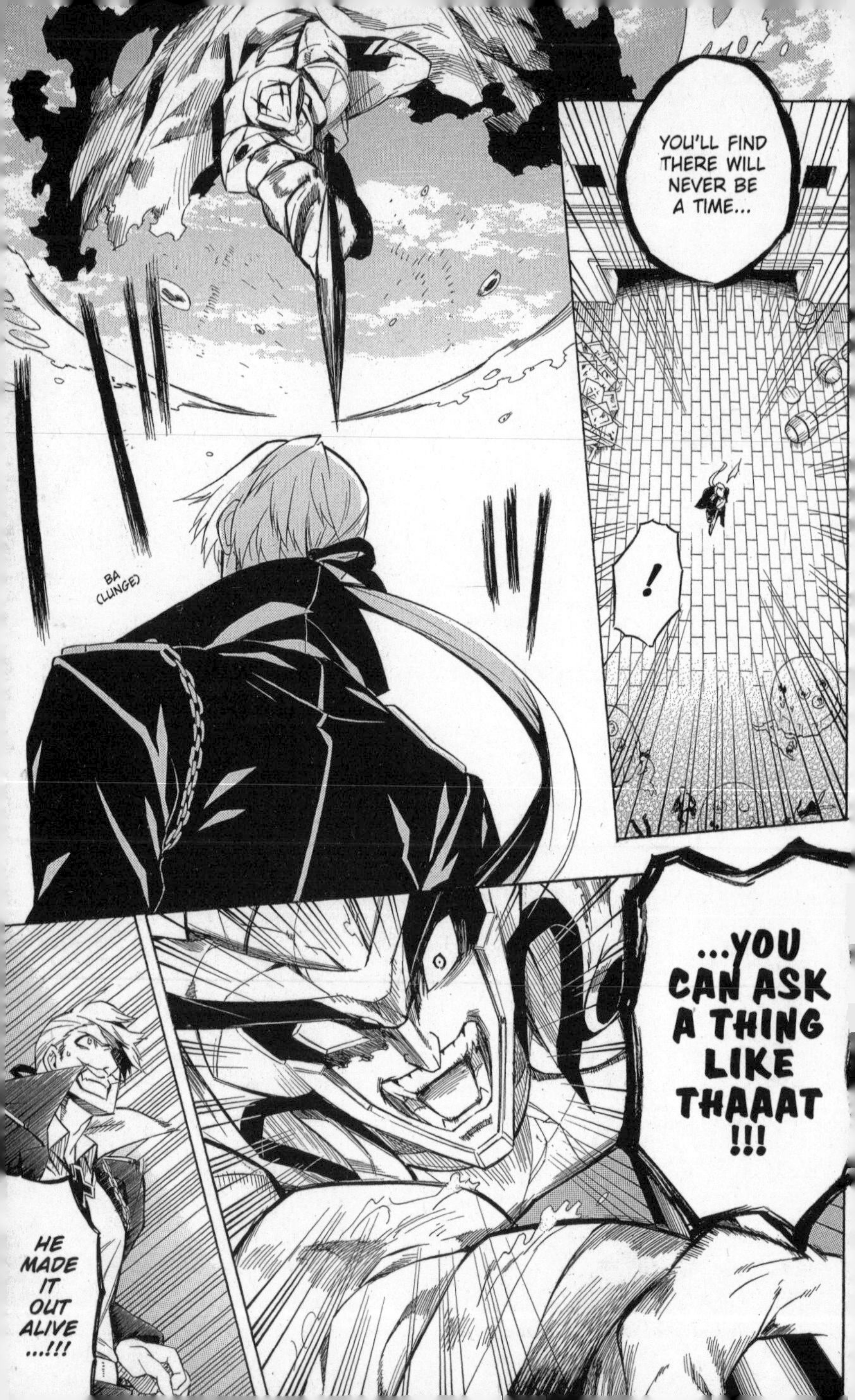
YOU'LL FIND THERE WILL NEVER BE A TIME...
!
BA (LUNGE)
...YOU CAN ASK A THING LIKE THAAAT!!!
HE MADE IT OUT ALIVE...!!!

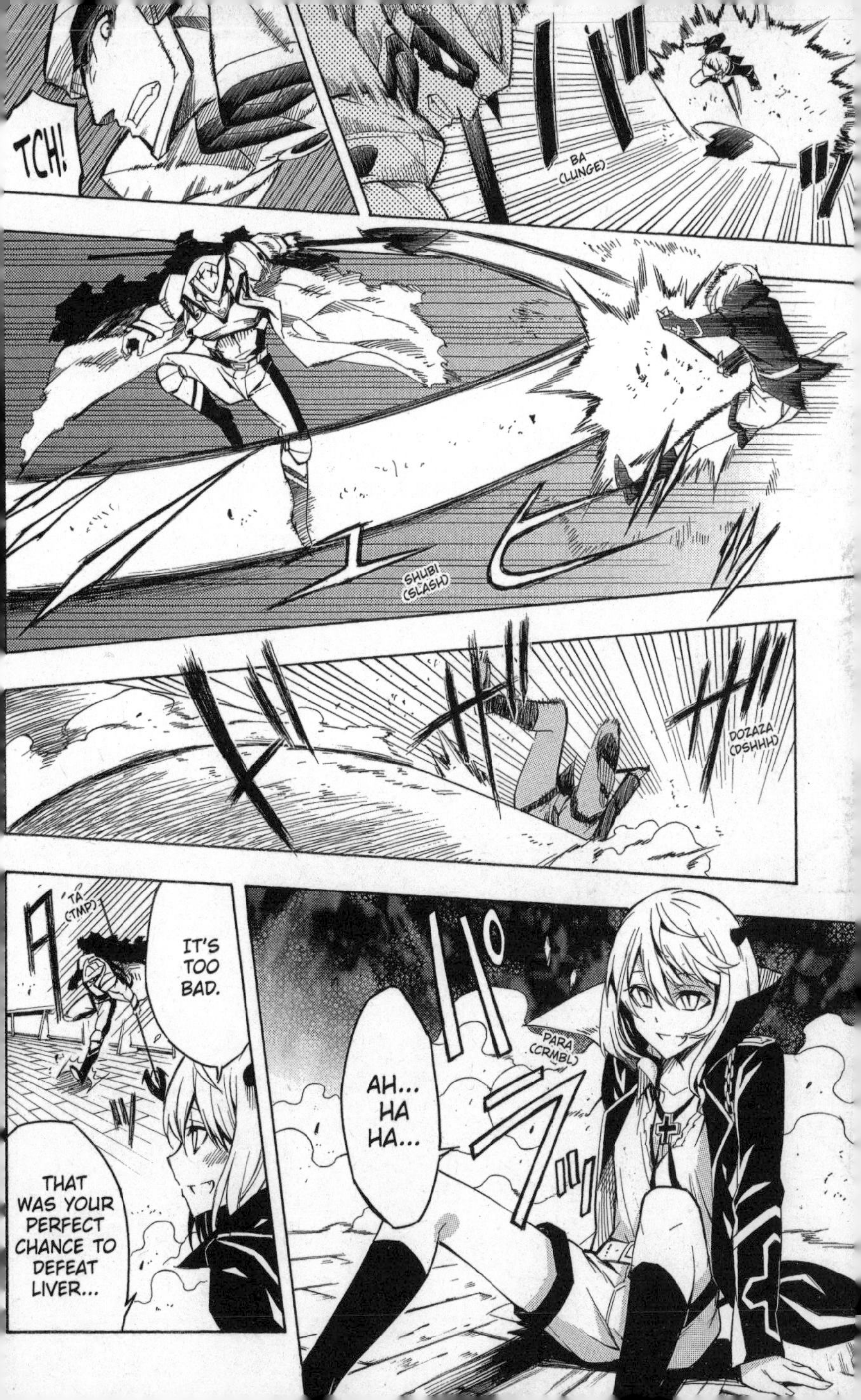
BA
(LUNGE)
TCH!
SHUBI
(SLASH)
DOZAZA
(DSHHH)
PARA
(CRMBL)
AH... HA HA...
TA
(TMP)
IT'S TOO BAD.
THAT WAS YOUR PERFECT CHANCE TO DEFEAT LIVER...

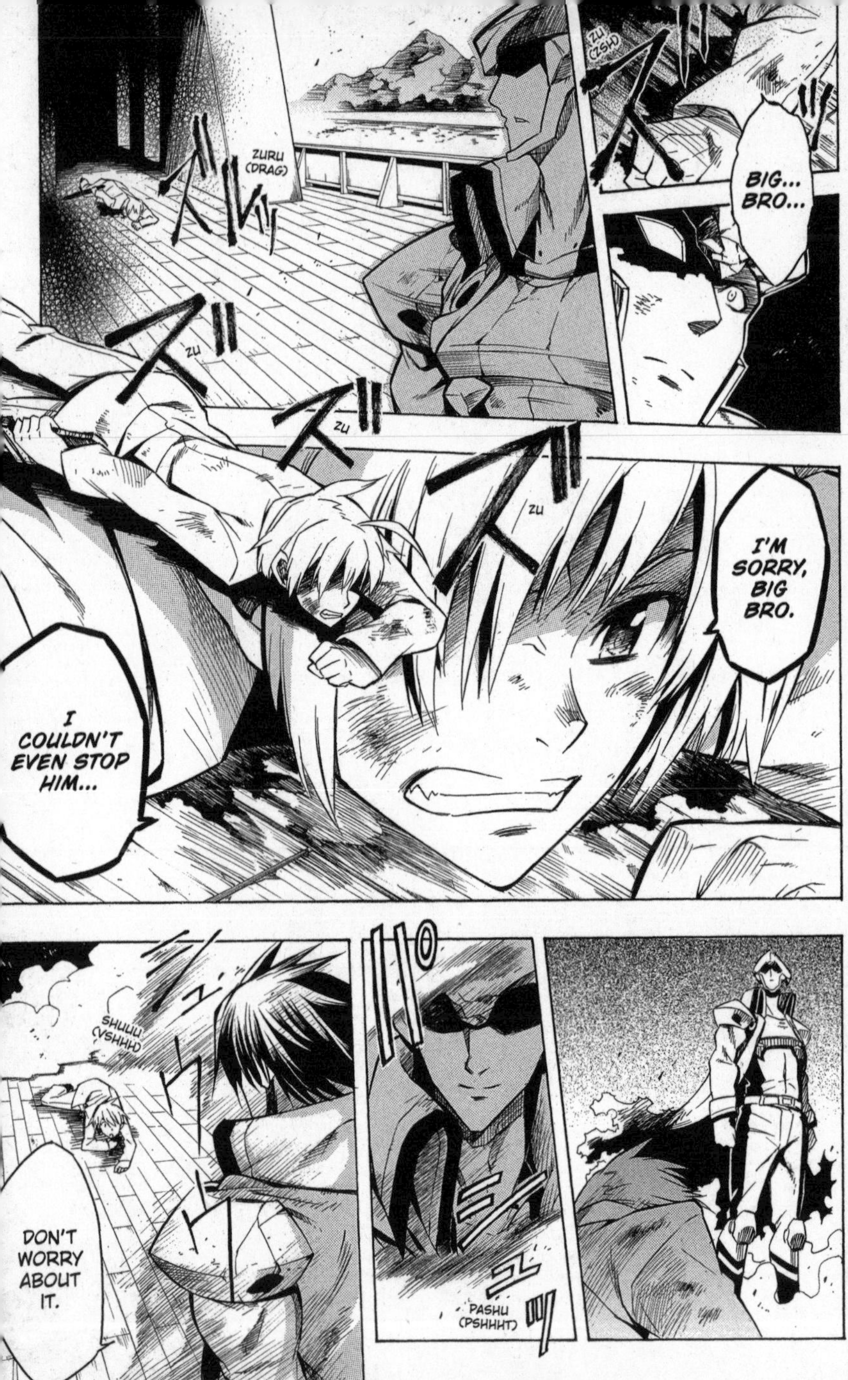
ZU (ZSH)
BIG... BRO...
ZURU (DRAG)
ZU
ZU
ZU
I'M SORRY, BIG BRO.
I COULDN'T EVEN STOP HIM...
PASHU (PSHHHT)
SHUUU (VSHHH)
DON'T WORRY ABOUT IT.

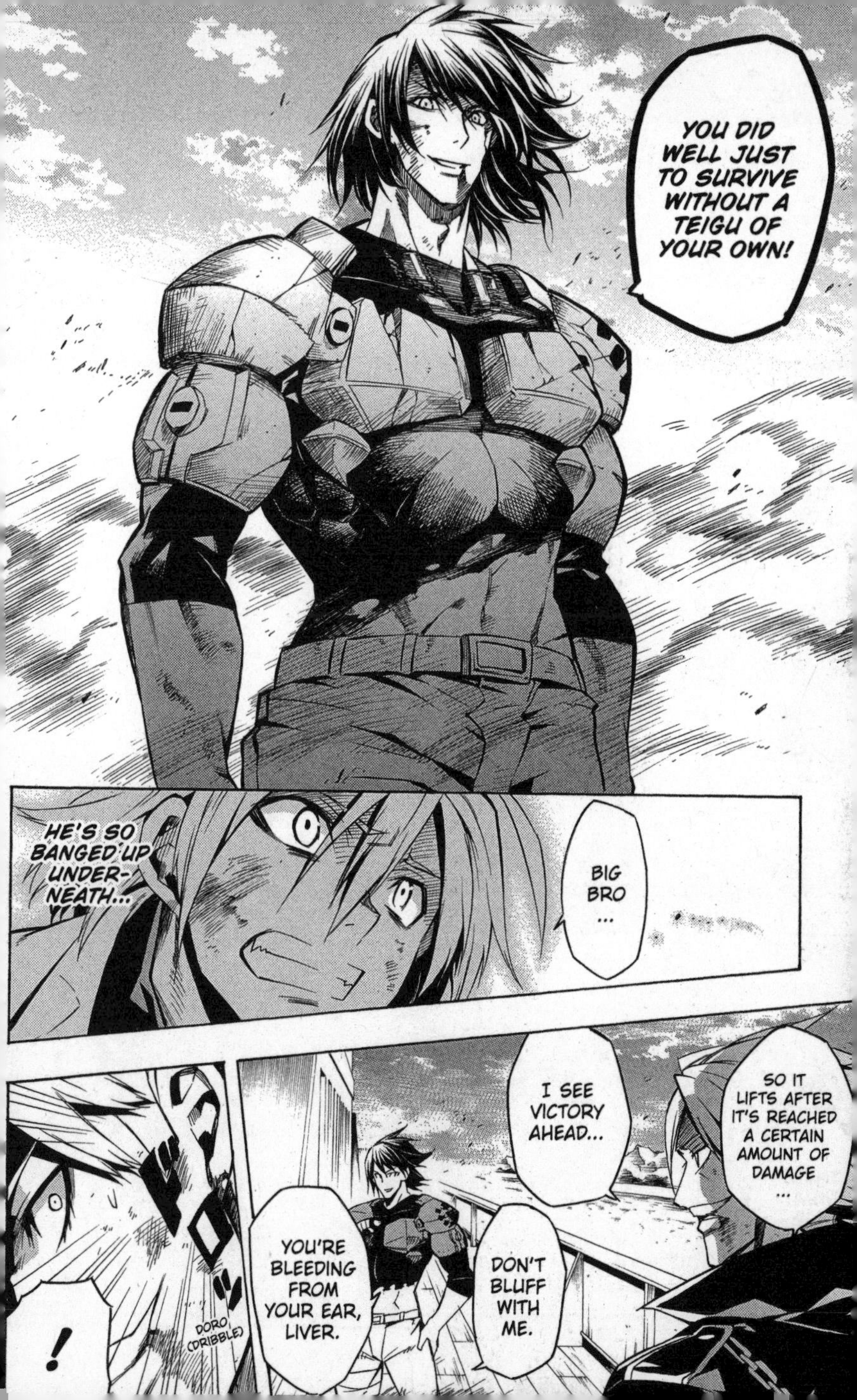
YOU DID WELL JUST TO SURVIVE WITHOUT A TEIGU OF YOUR OWN!
BIG BRO ...
HE'S SO BANGED UP UNDER-NEATH...
SO IT LIFTS AFTER IT'S REACHED A CERTAIN AMOUNT OF DAMAGE ...
I SEE VICTORY AHEAD...
DON'T BLUFF WITH ME.
YOU'RE BLEEDING FROM YOUR EAR, LIVER.
DORO (DRIBBLE)
!

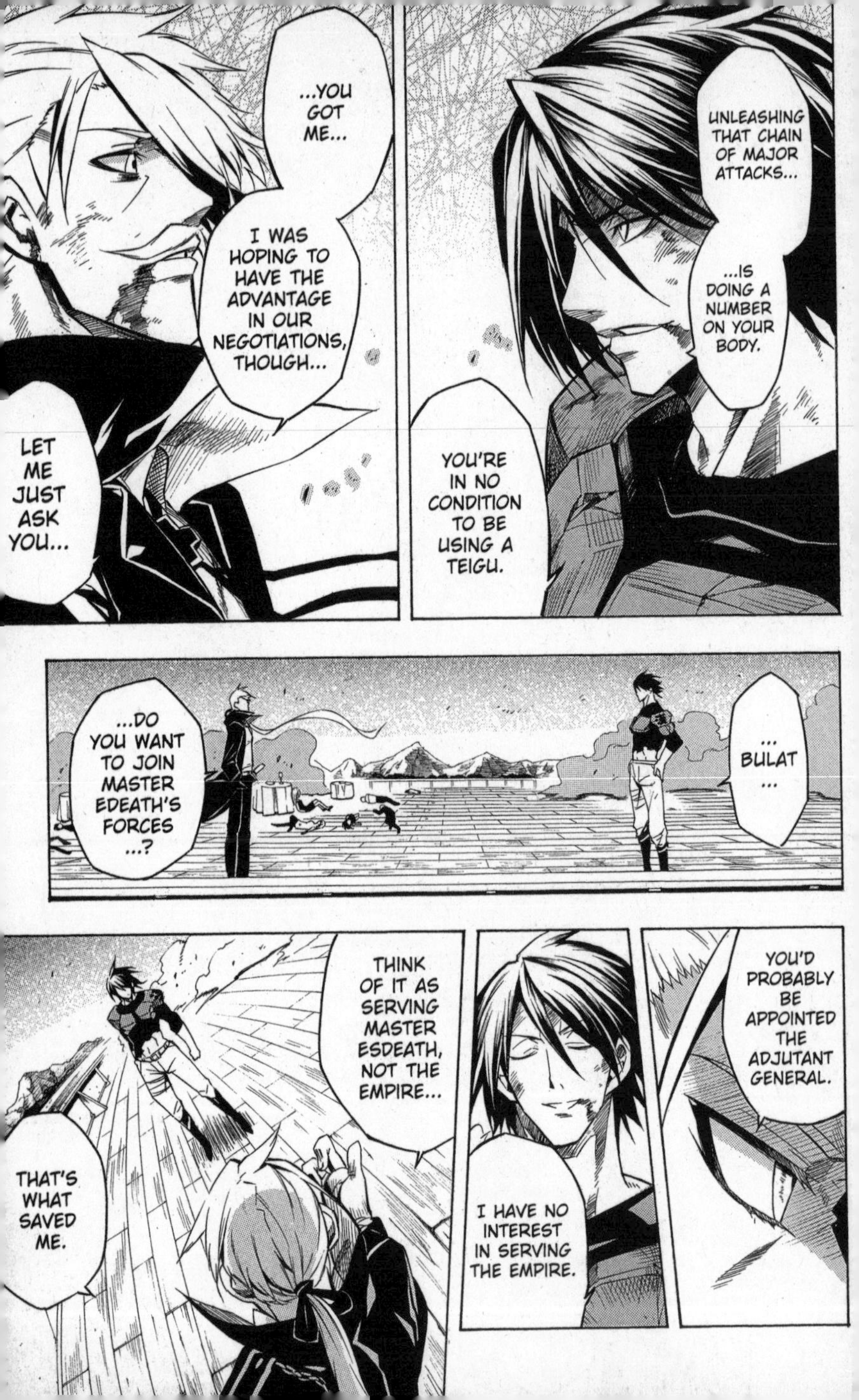
UNLEASHING THAT CHAIN OF MAJOR ATTACKS...
...IS DOING A NUMBER ON YOUR BODY.
YOU'RE IN NO CONDITION TO BE USING A TEIGU.
...YOU GOT ME...
I WAS HOPING TO HAVE THE ADVANTAGE IN OUR NEGOTIATIONS, THOUGH...
LET ME JUST ASK YOU...
... BULAT ...
...DO YOU WANT TO JOIN MASTER EDEATH'S FORCES ...?
YOU'D PROBABLY BE APPOINTED THE ADJUTANT GENERAL.
I HAVE NO INTEREST IN SERVING THE EMPIRE.
THINK OF IT AS SERVING MASTER ESDEATH, NOT THE EMPIRE...
THAT'S WHAT SAVED ME.

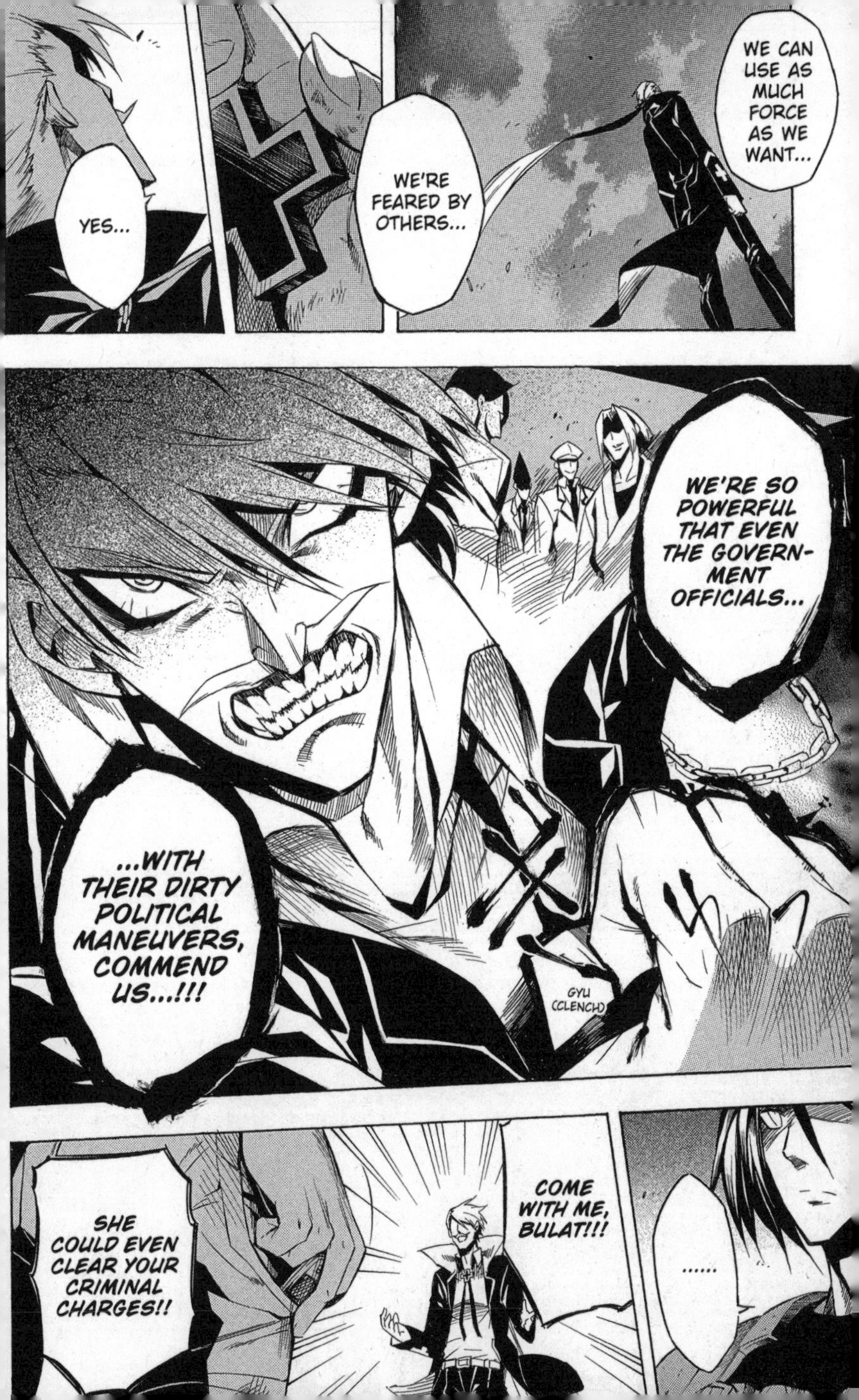
WE CAN USE AS MUCH FORCE AS WE WANT...
WE'RE FEARED BY OTHERS...
YES...
WE'RE SO POWERFUL THAT EVEN THE GOVERN-MENT OFFICIALS...
...WITH THEIR DIRTY POLITICAL MANEUVERS, COMMEND US...!!!
GYU (CLENCH)
......
COME WITH ME, BULAT!!!
SHE COULD EVEN CLEAR YOUR CRIMINAL CHARGES!!

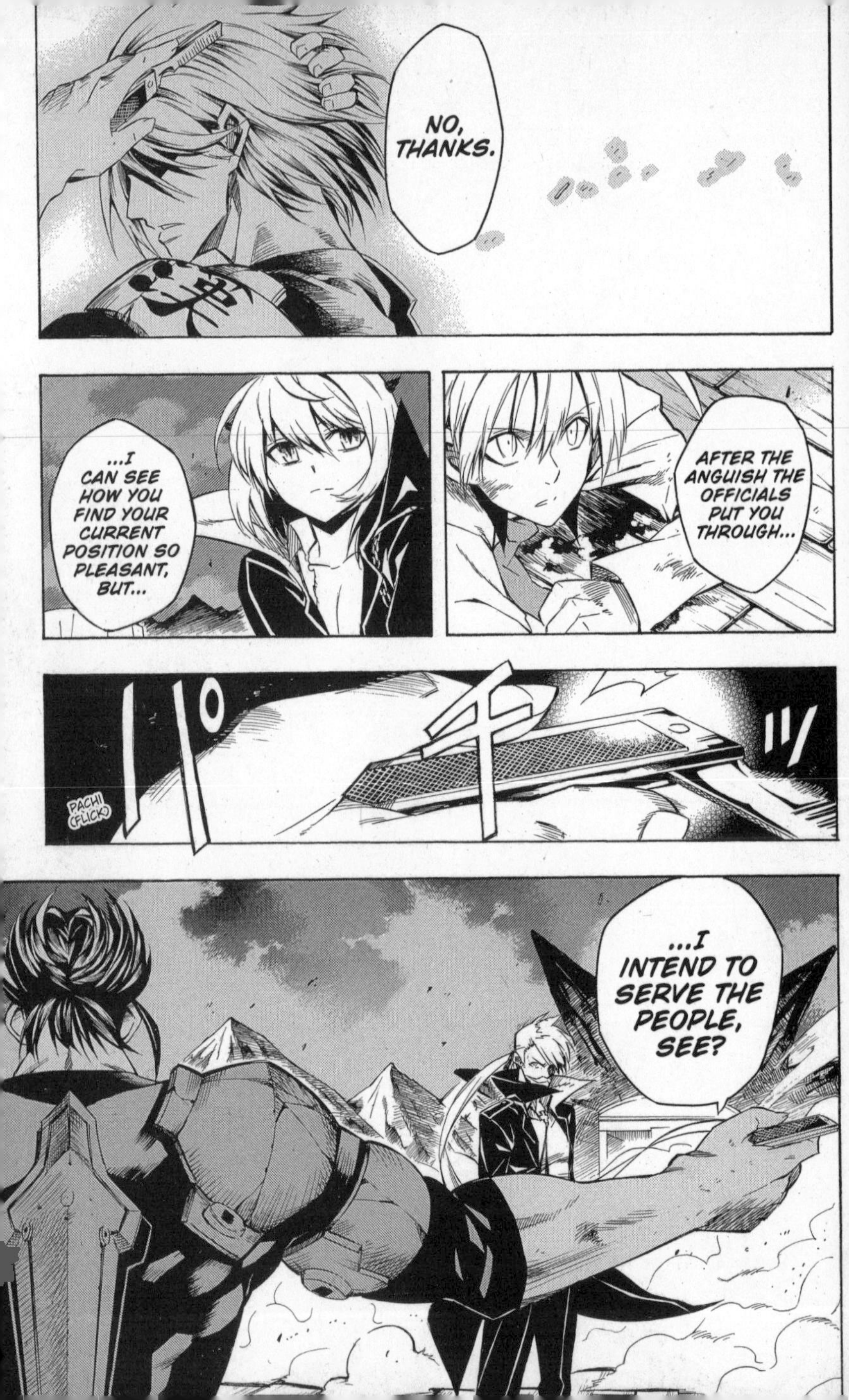
NO, THANKS.
AFTER THE ANGUISH THE OFFICIALS PUT YOU THROUGH...
...I CAN SEE HOW YOU FIND YOUR CURRENT POSITION SO PLEASANT, BUT...
PACHI (FLICK)
...I INTEND TO SERVE THE PEOPLE, SEE?

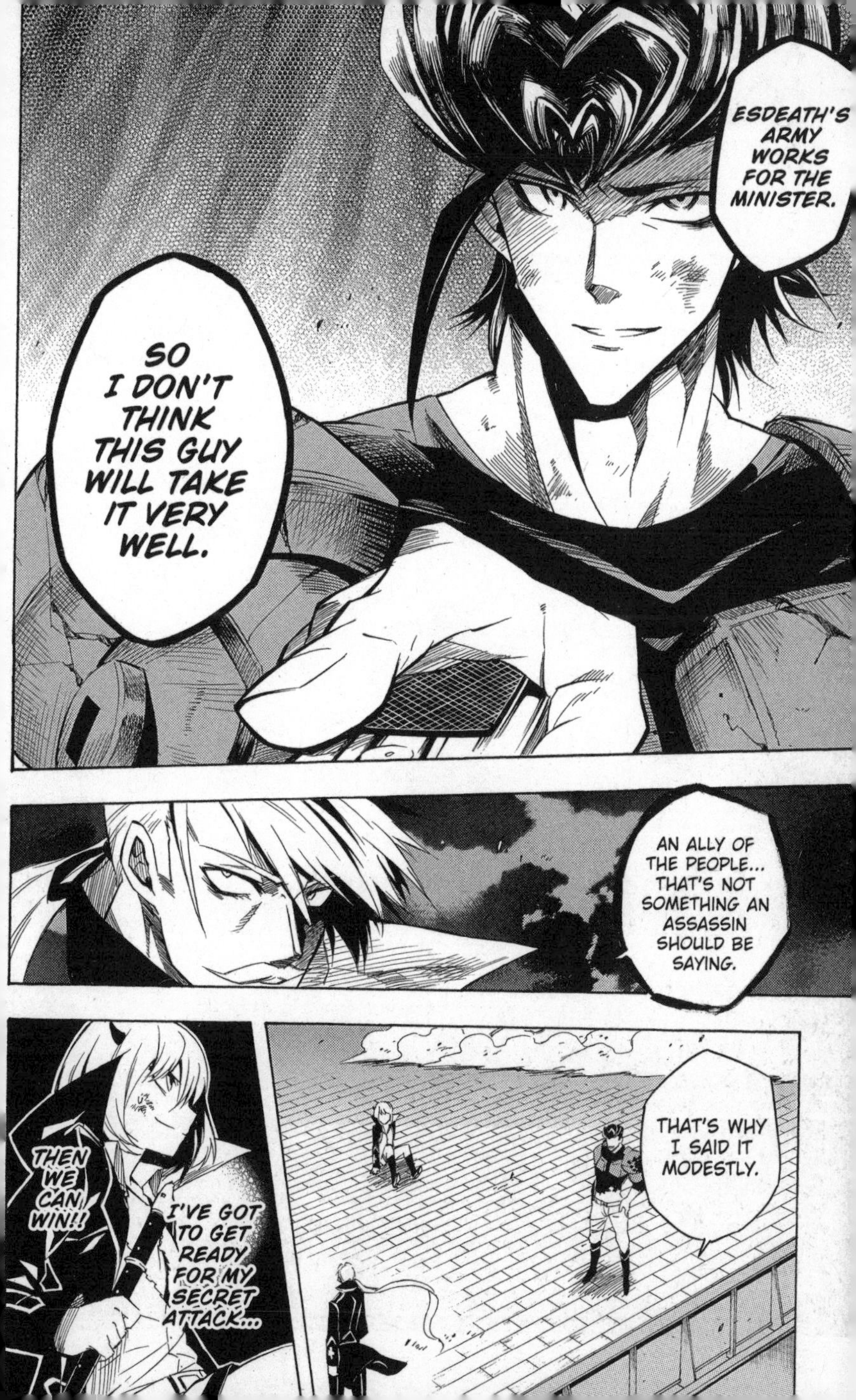
ESDEATH'S ARMY WORKS FOR THE MINISTER.
SO I DON'T THINK THIS GUY WILL TAKE IT VERY WELL.
AN ALLY OF THE PEOPLE... THAT'S NOT SOMETHING AN ASSASSIN SHOULD BE SAYING.
THAT'S WHY I SAID IT MODESTLY.
THEN WE CAN WIN!!
I'VE GOT TO GET READY FOR MY SECRET ATTACK...

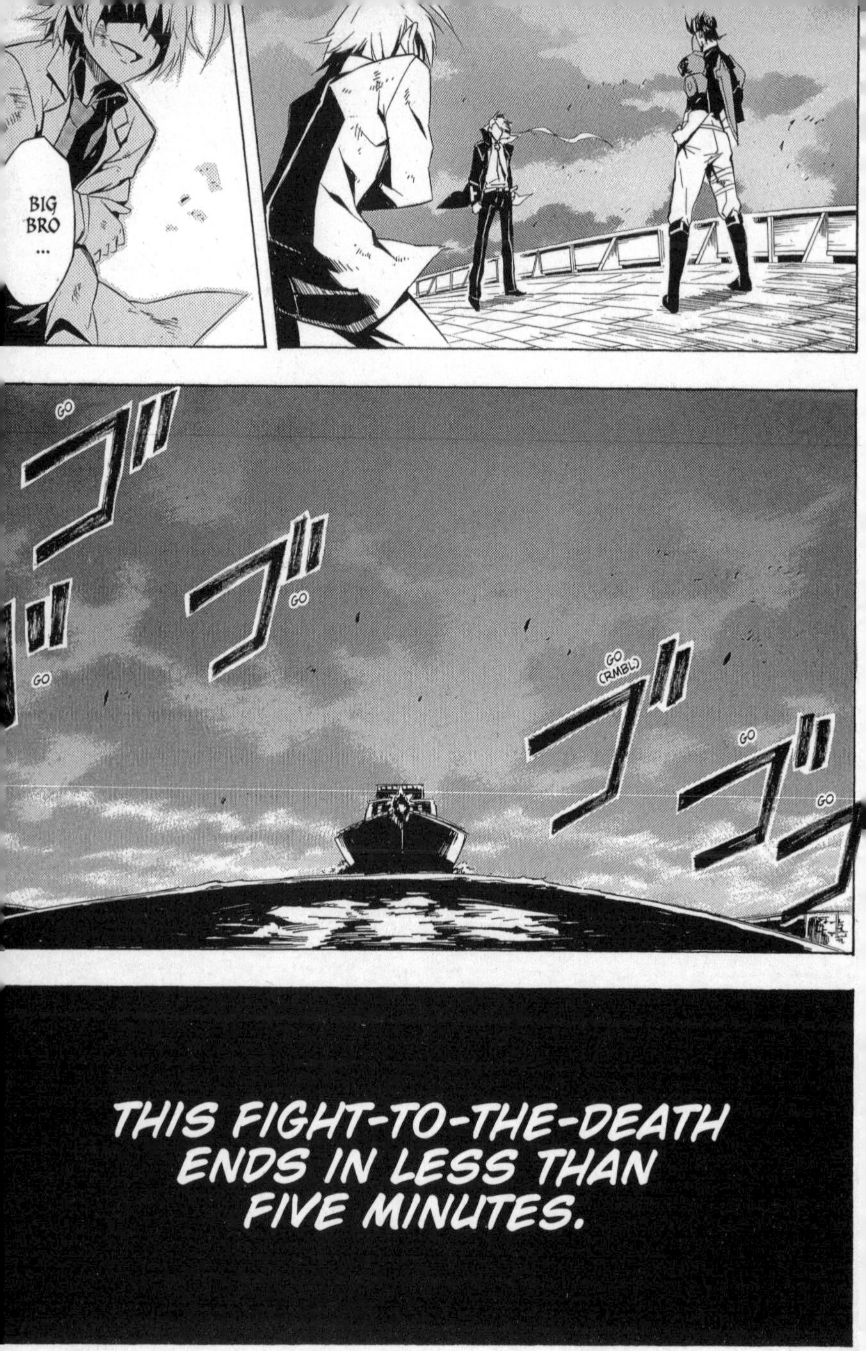
BIG BRO ...
GO
GO
GO
GO (RMBL)
GO
GO
THIS FIGHT-TO-THE-DEATH ENDS IN LESS THAN FIVE MINUTES.

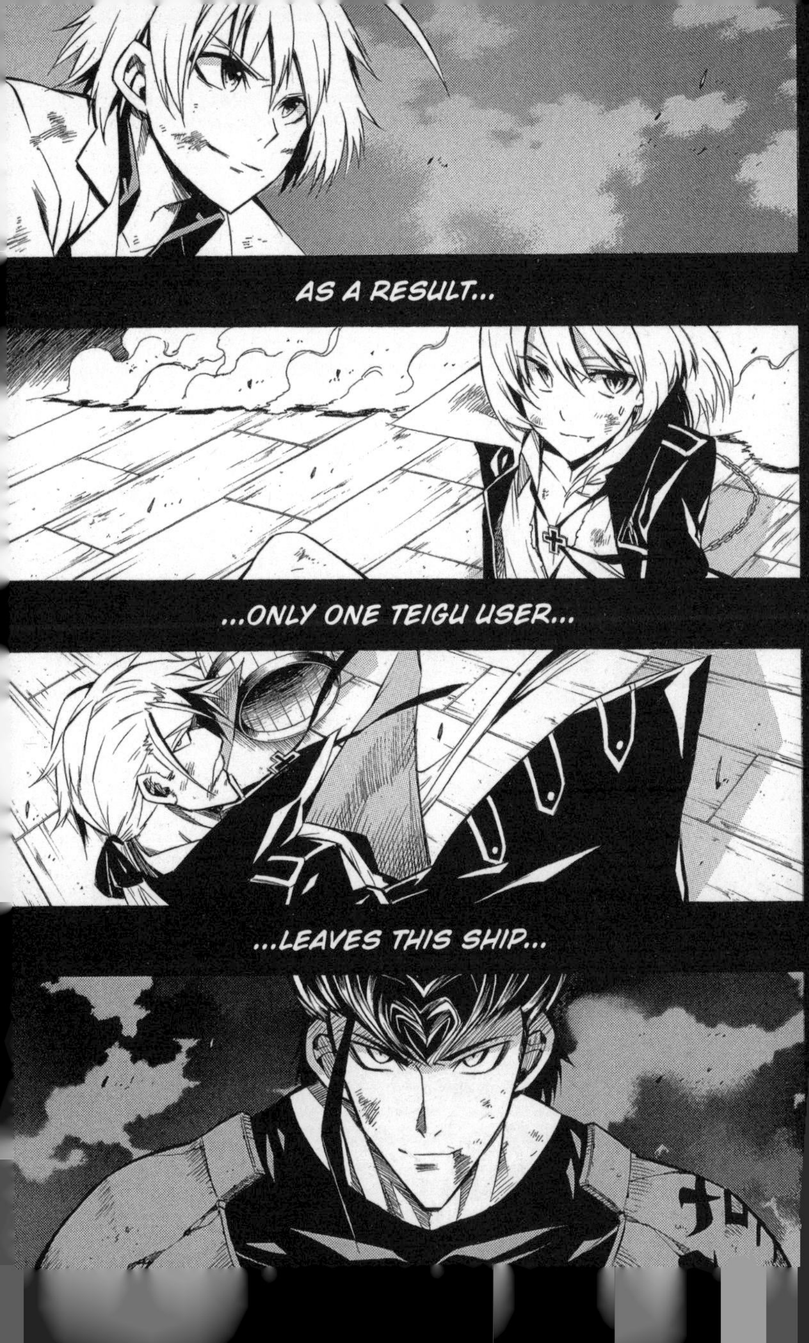
AS A RESULT...
...ONLY ONE TEIGU USER...
...LEAVES THIS SHIP...

CHAPTER 14 KILL ESDEATH'S ARMY (PART 1)

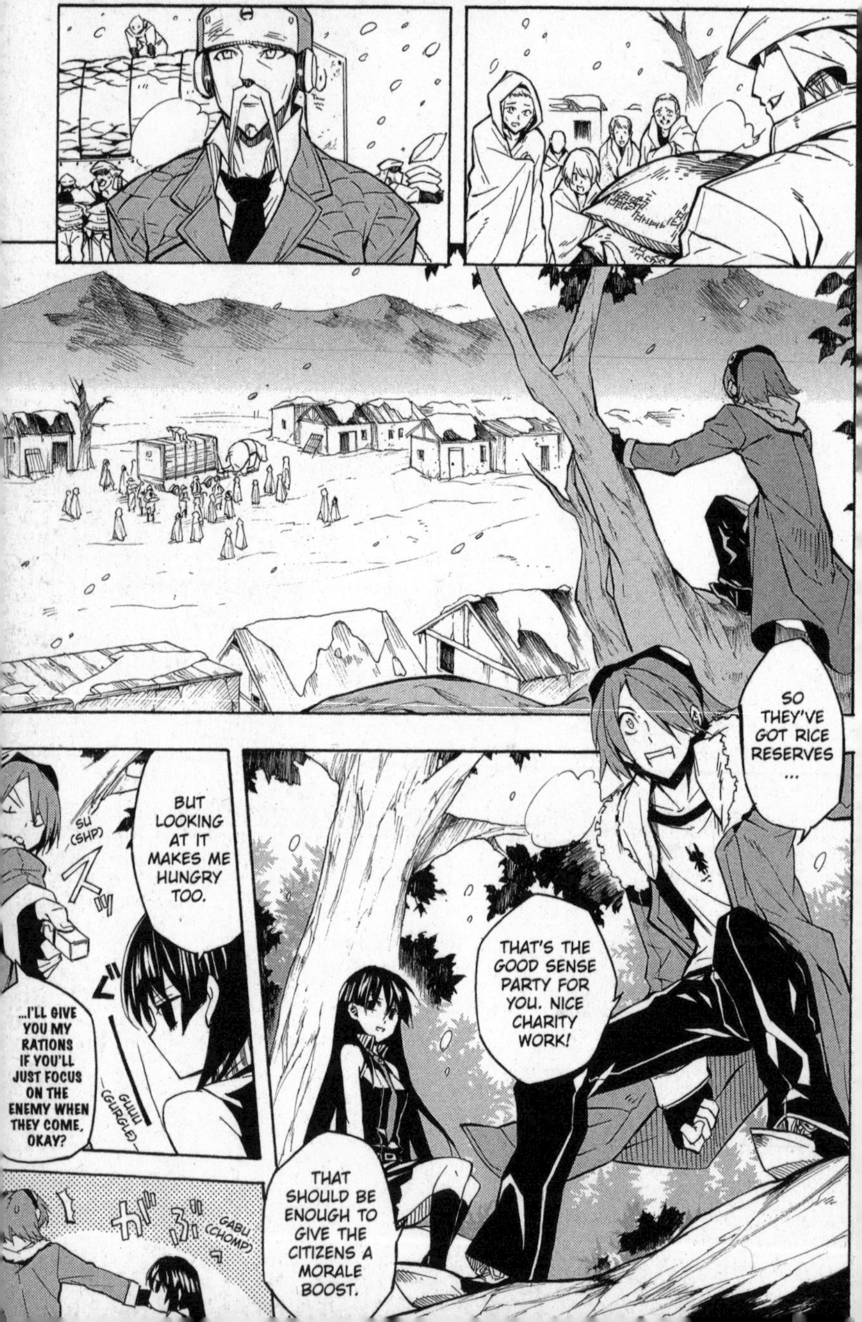
SO THEY'VE GOT RICE RESERVES ...
THAT'S THE GOOD SENSE PARTY FOR YOU. NICE CHARITY WORK!
THAT SHOULD BE ENOUGH TO GIVE THE CITIZENS A MORALE BOOST.
BUT LOOKING AT IT MAKES ME HUNGRY TOO.
SU (SHP)
GULU (GURGLE)
...I'LL GIVE YOU MY RATIONS IF YOU'LL JUST FOCUS ON THE ENEMY WHEN THEY COME, OKAY?
GABU (CHOMP)

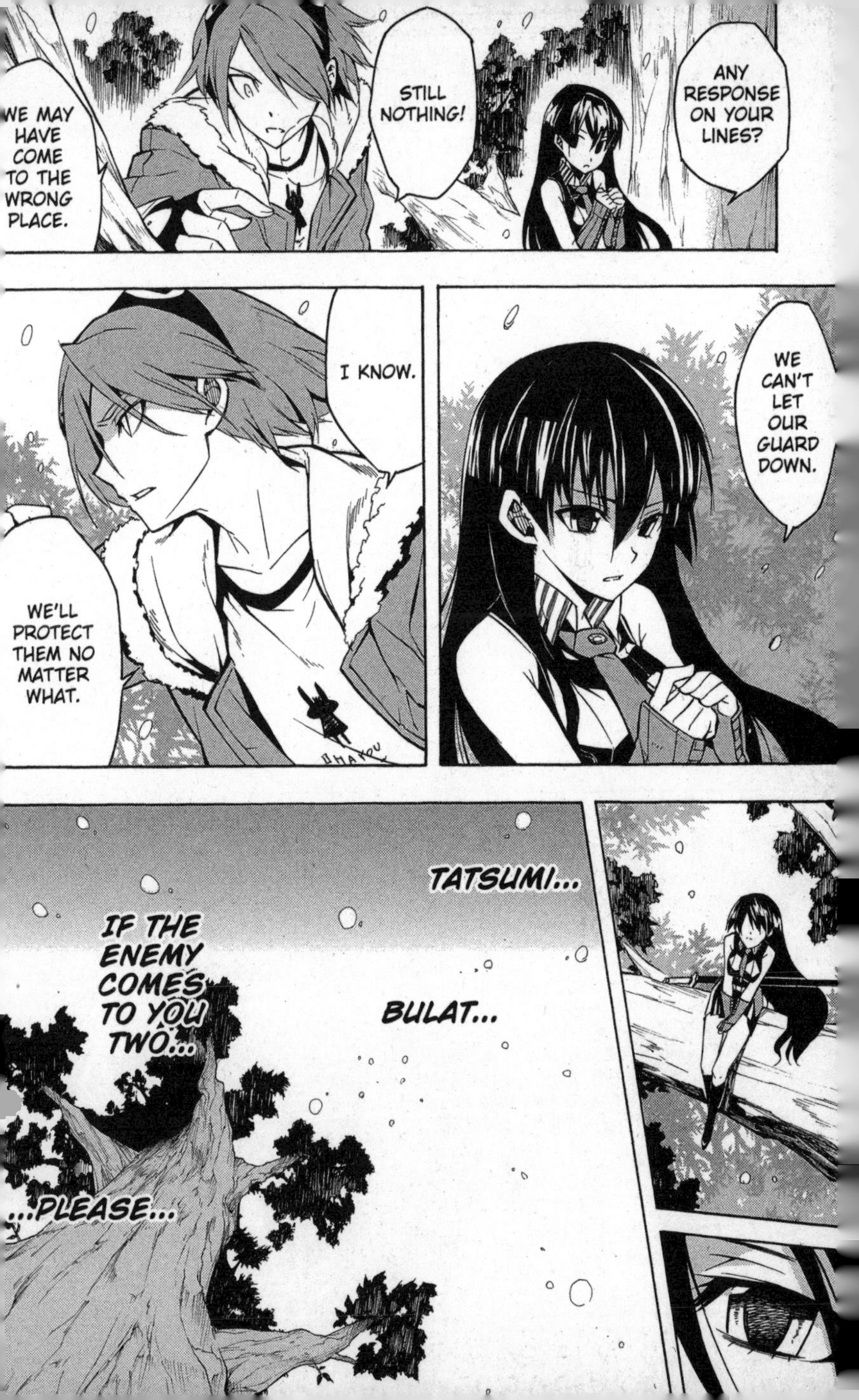
ANY RESPONSE ON YOUR LINES?
STILL NOTHING!
WE MAY HAVE COME TO THE WRONG PLACE.
WE CAN'T LET OUR GUARD DOWN.
I KNOW.
WE'LL PROTECT THEM NO MATTER WHAT.
TATSUMI...
BULAT...
IF THE ENEMY COMES TO YOU TWO...
...PLEASE...

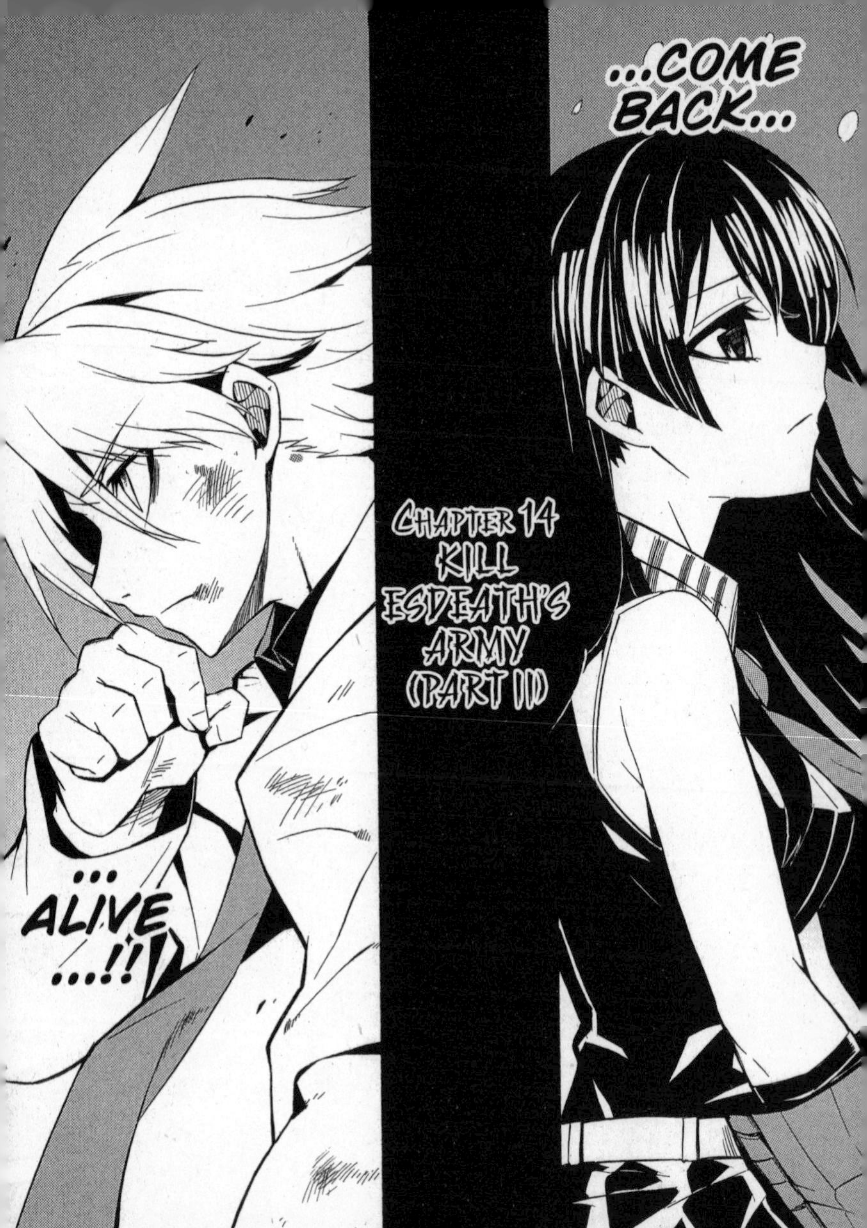
...COME BACK...
Chapter 14 KILL ESDEATH'S ARMY (PART II)
...ALIVE...!!

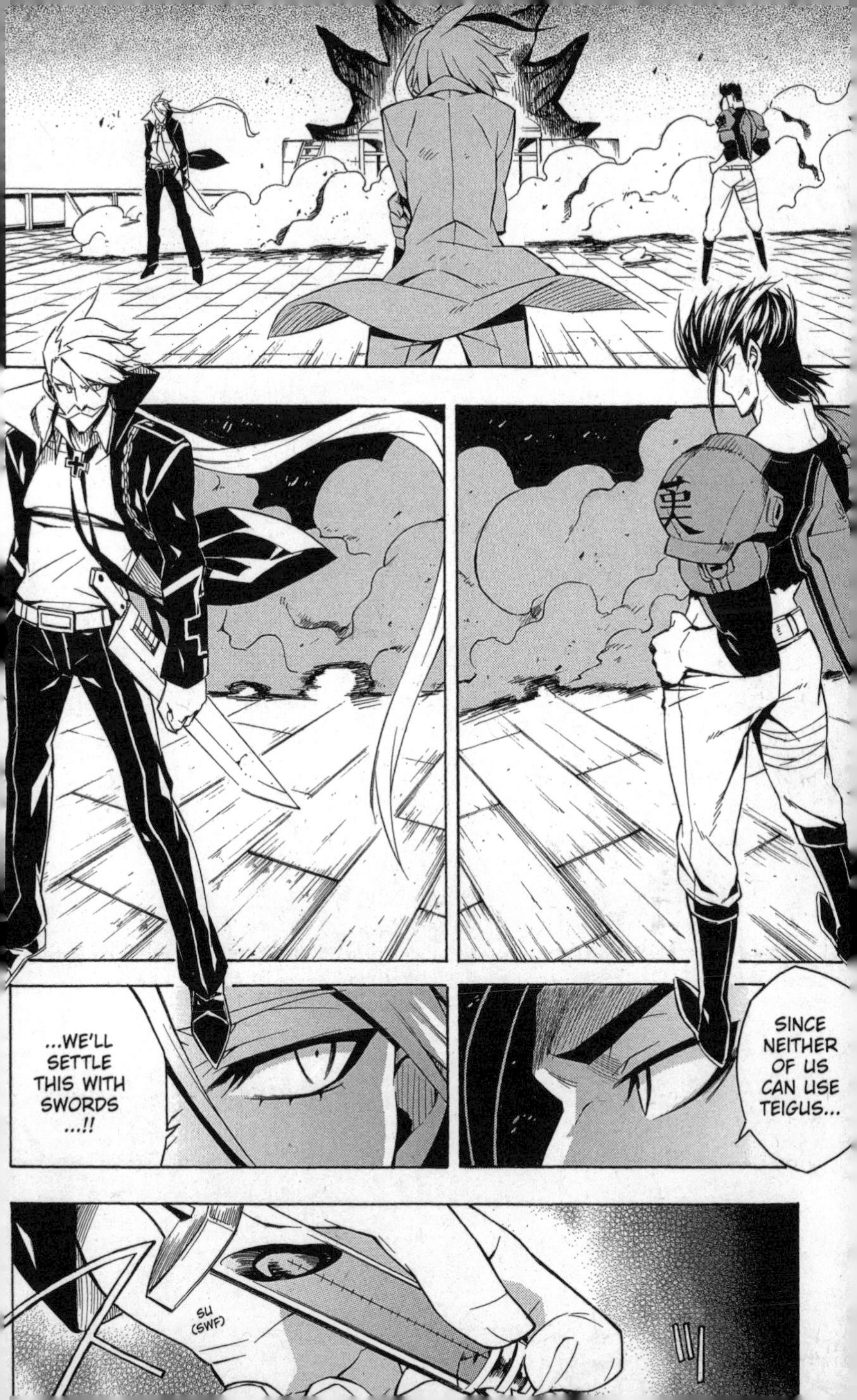
SINCE NEITHER OF US CAN USE TEIGUS...
...WE'LL SETTLE THIS WITH SWORDS ...!!
SU (SWF)

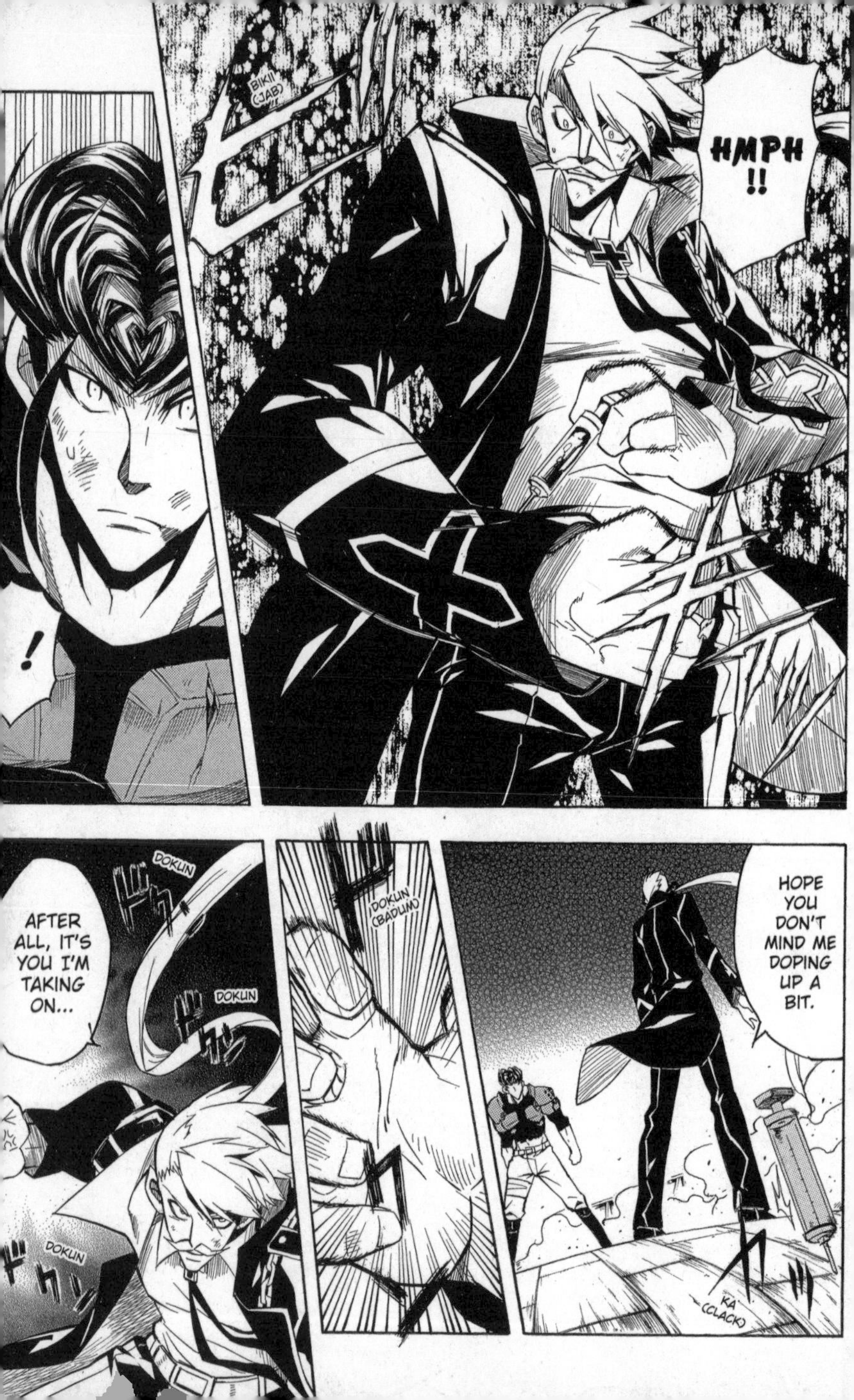
HMPH !!
BIKII (JAB)
!
HOPE YOU DON'T MIND ME DOPING UP A BIT.
KA (CLACK)
DOKUN (BADUM)
AFTER ALL, IT'S YOU I'M TAKING ON...
DOKUN
DOKUN
DOKUN

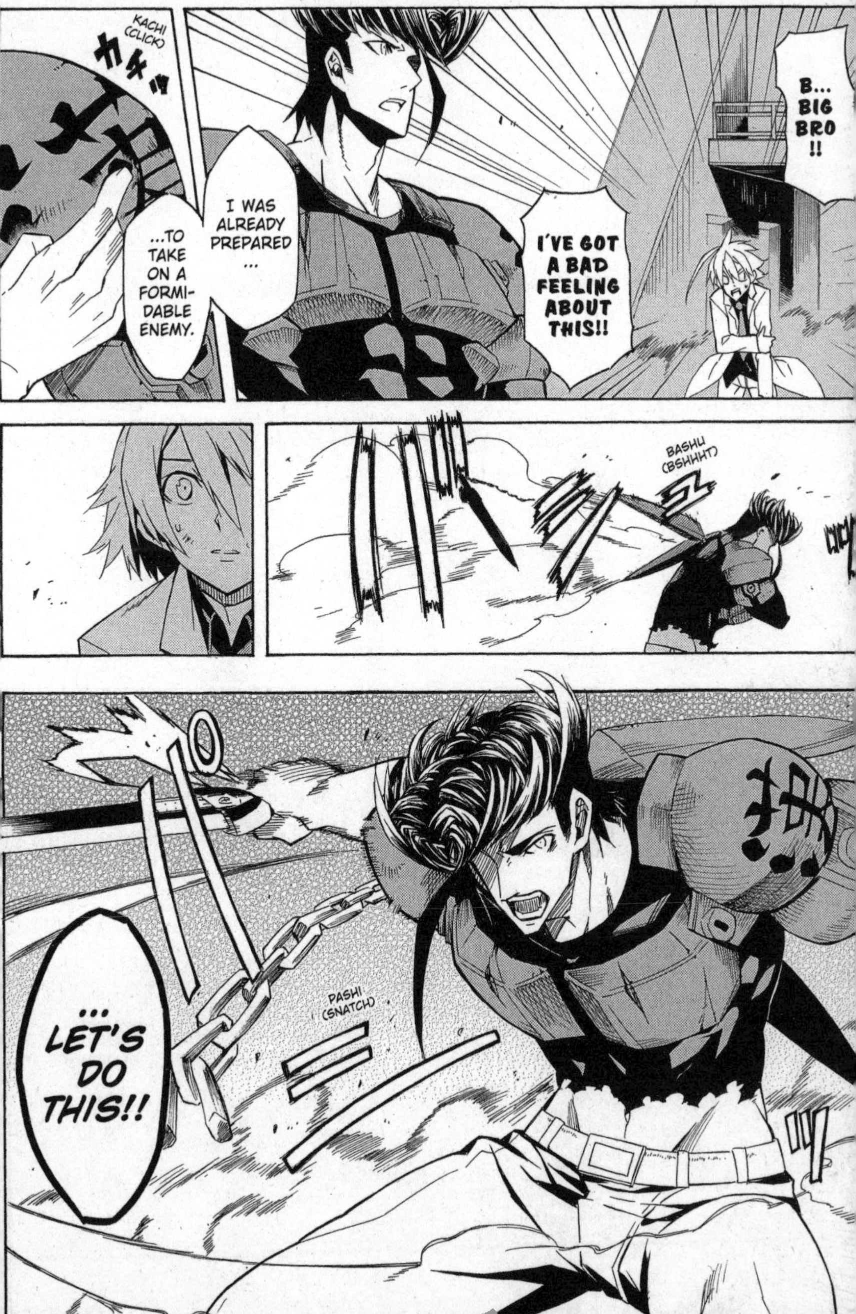
B... BIG BRO!!
I'VE GOT A BAD FEELING ABOUT THIS!!
I WAS ALREADY PREPARED...
...TO TAKE ON A FORMIDABLE ENEMY.
KACHI (CLICK)
BASHU (BSHHHT)
PASHI (SNATCH)
...LET'S DO THIS!!

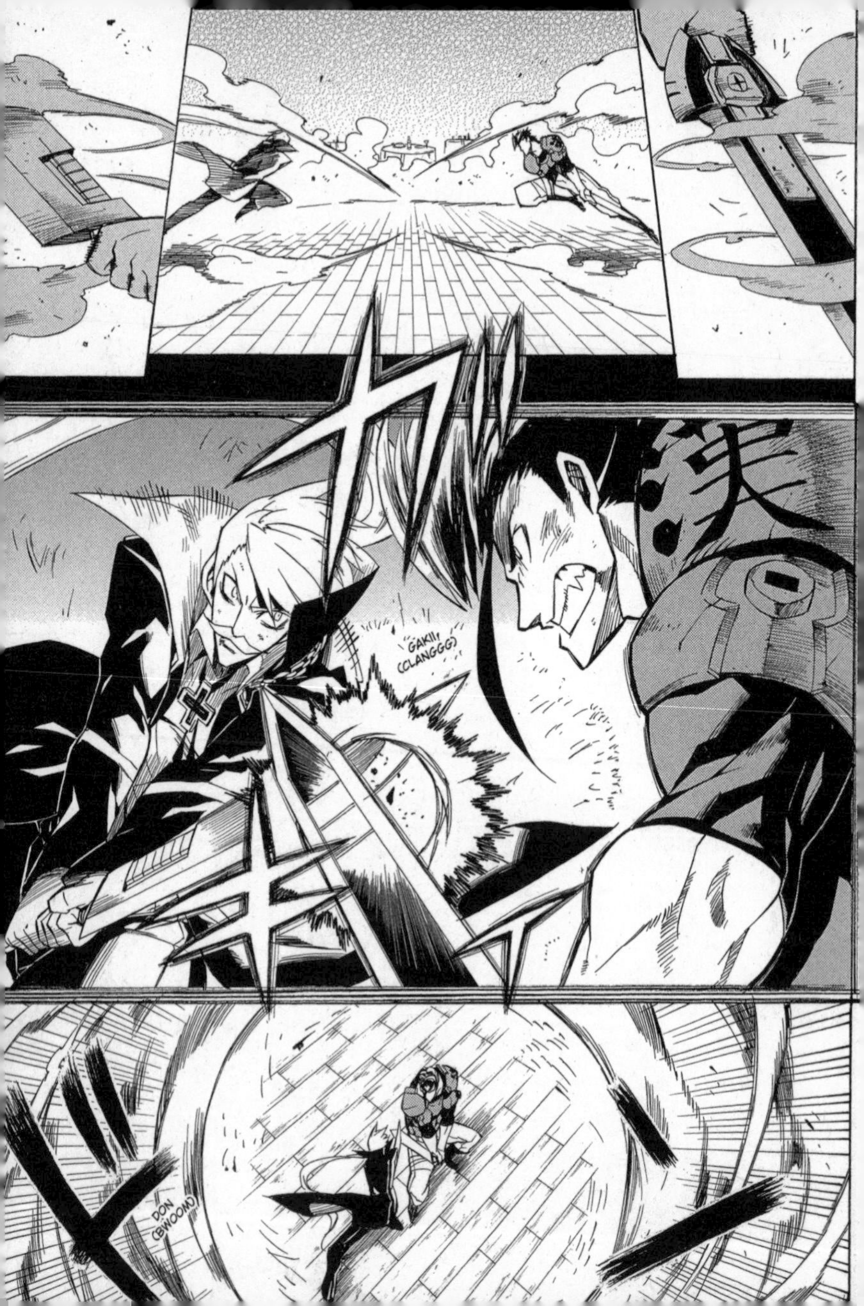
GAKI! (CLANGGG)
DON (BWOOM)

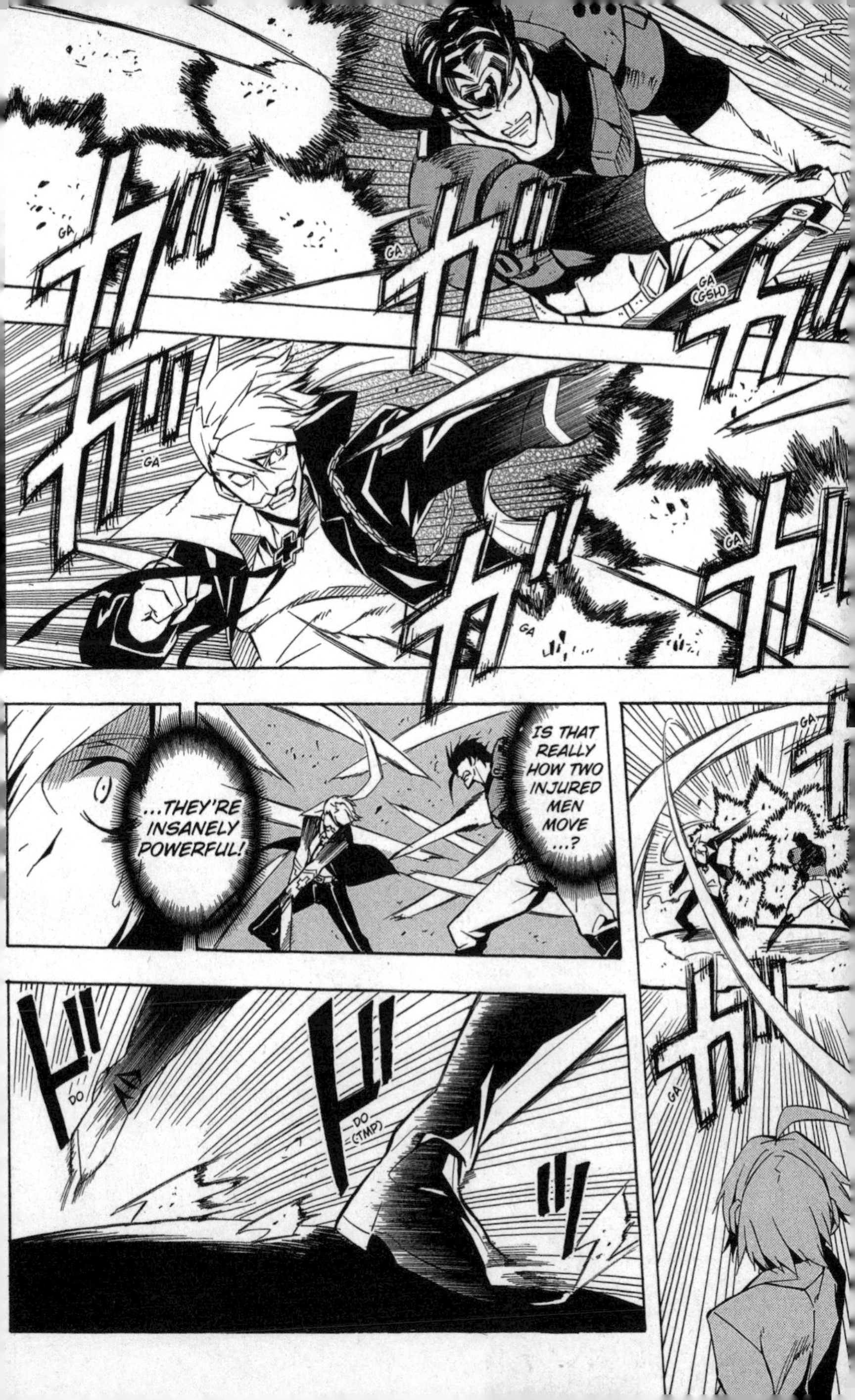
GA
GA
(GSH)
GA
GA
GA
GA
GA
GA
GA
IS THAT REALLY HOW TWO INJURED MEN MOVE ...?
...THEY'RE INSANELY POWERFUL!
DO
(TMP)
DO

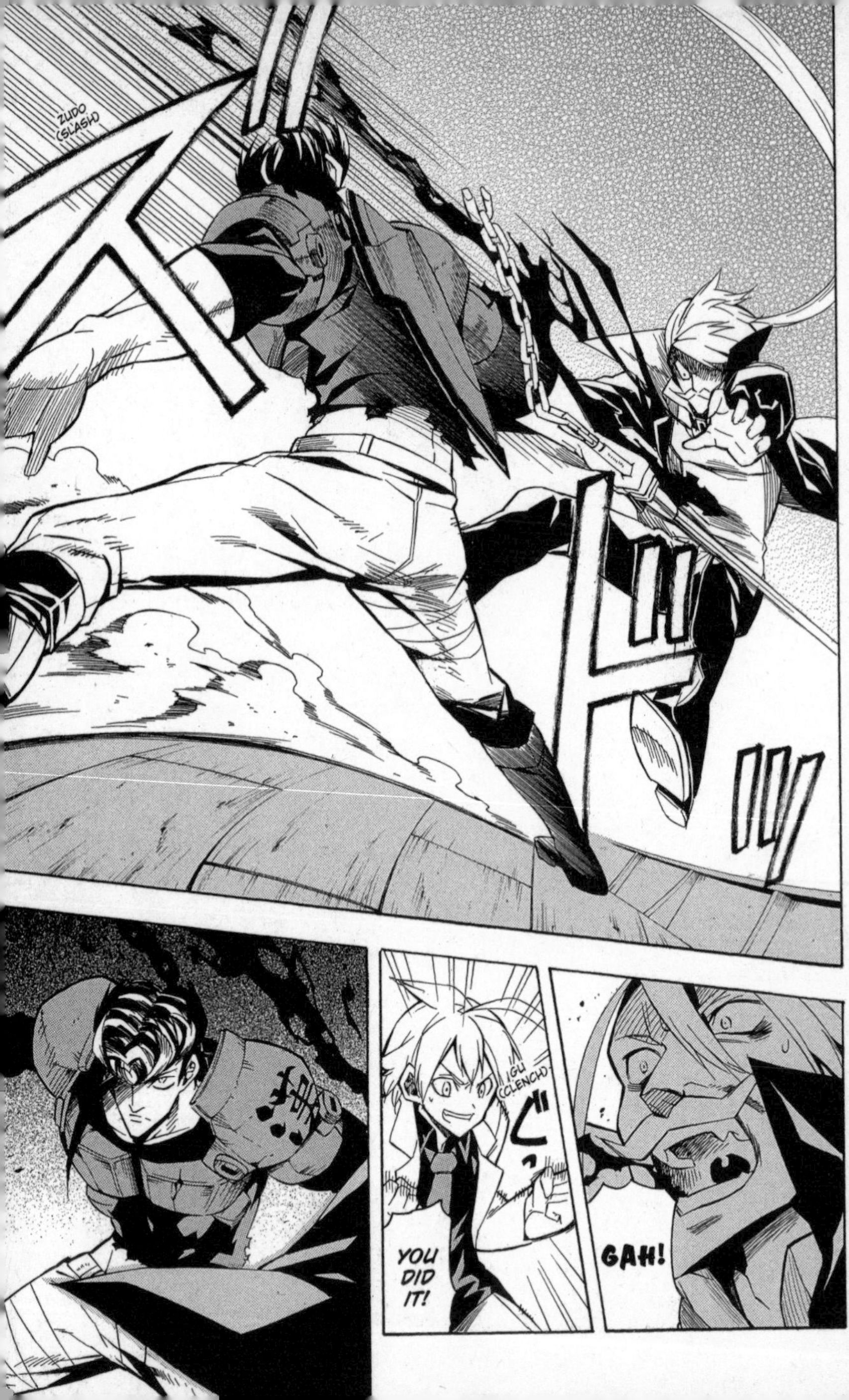
ZUDO (SLASH)
GAH!
GU (CLENCH)
YOU DID IT!

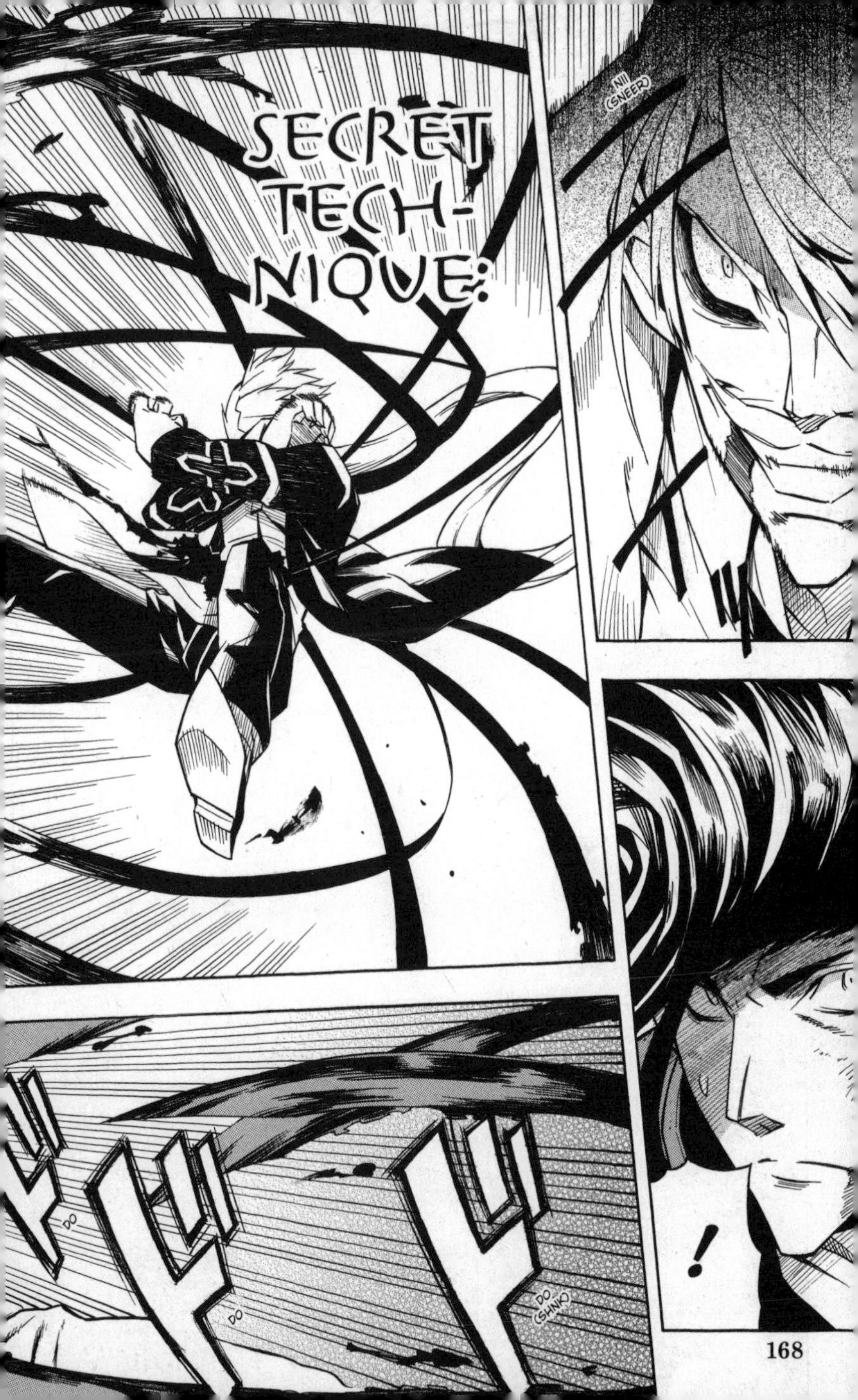

NII (SNEER)
SECRET TECH-NIQUE:
!
DO
DO
DO (SHNK)

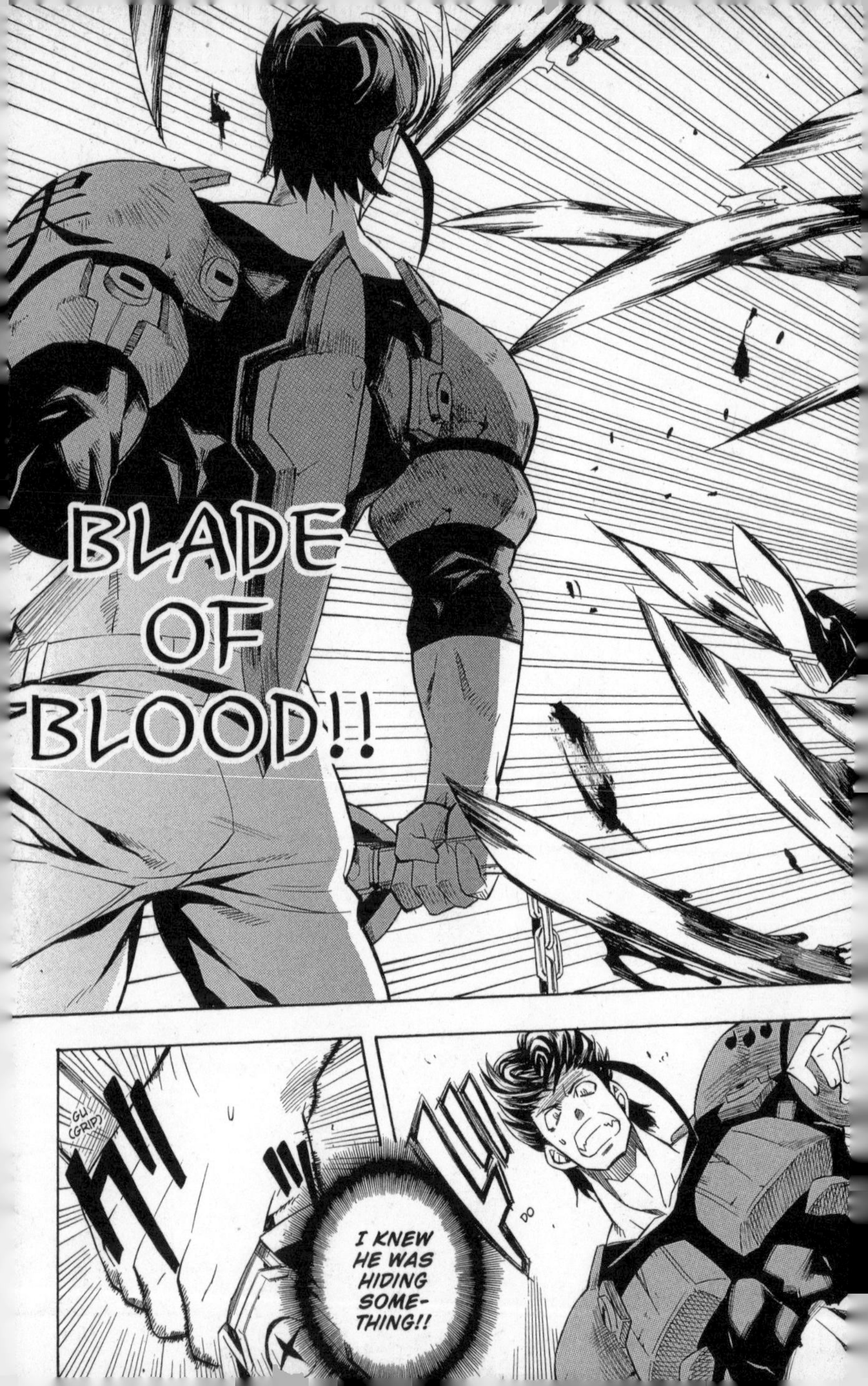
BLADE OF BLOOD!!
DO
I KNEW HE WAS HIDING SOME-THING!!
GU (GRIP)

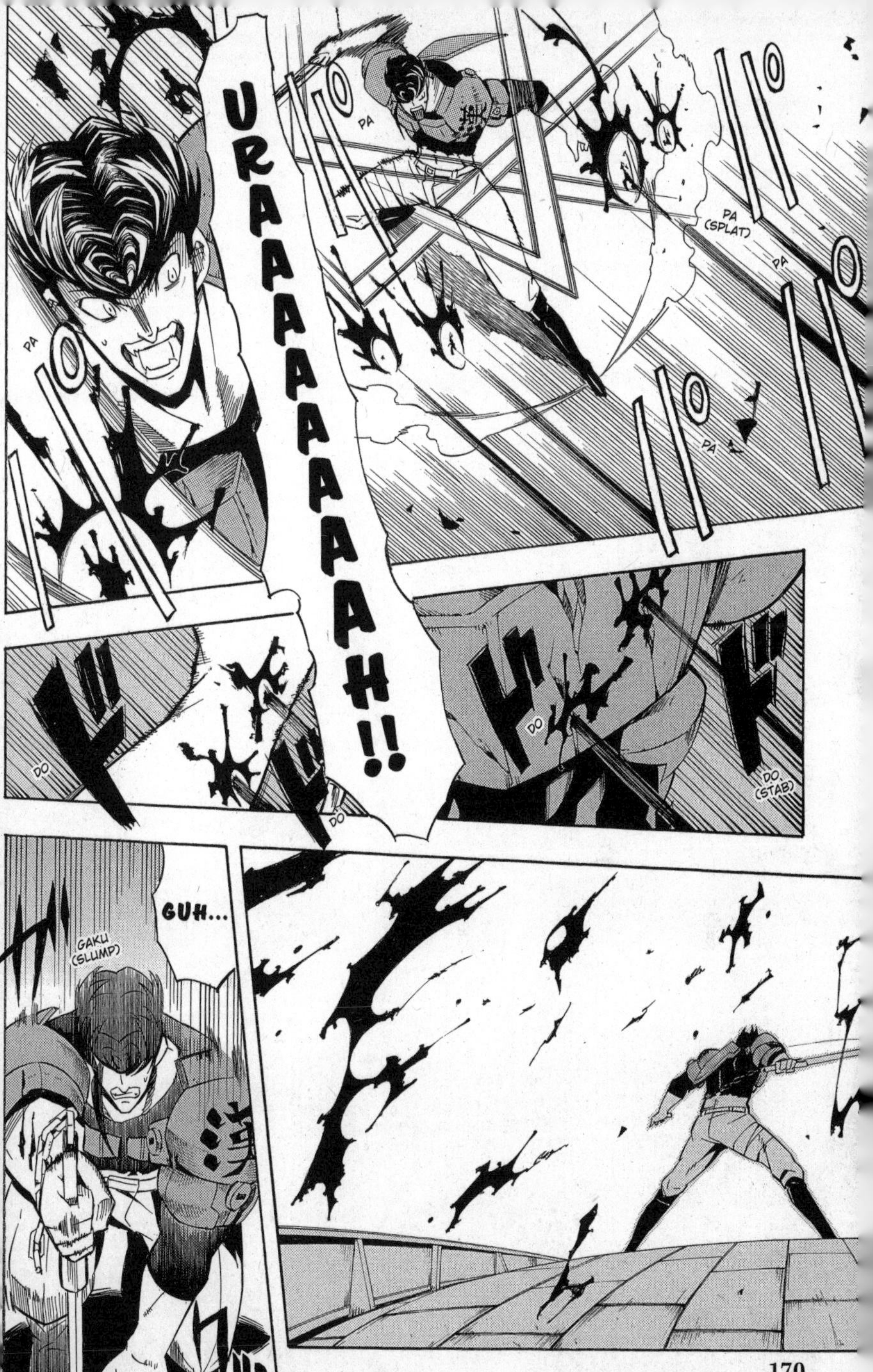
PA
PA
(SPLAT)
PA
PA
URAAAAAAAAH!!
PA
DO
DO
(STAB)
DO
DO
GUH...
GAKU
(SLUMP)

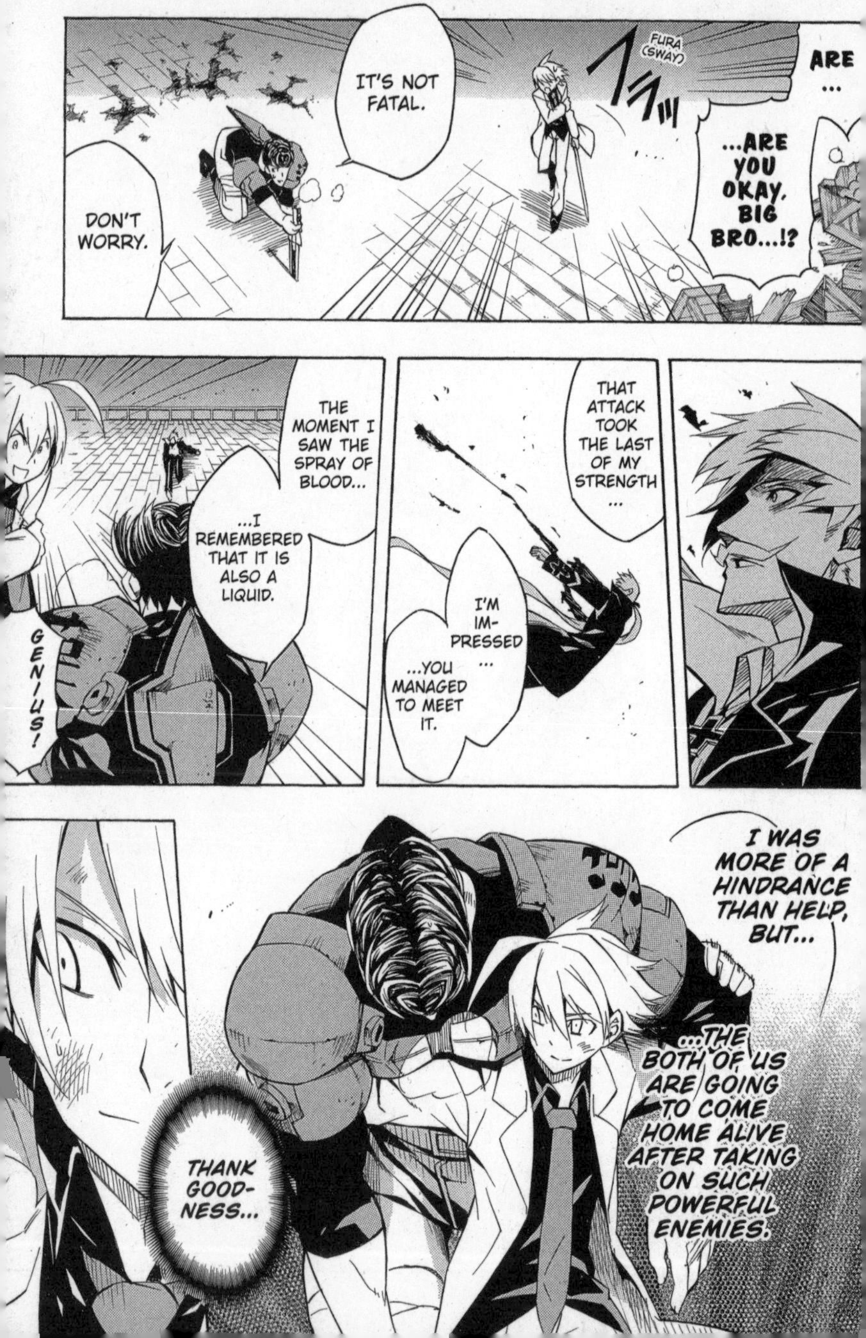
ARE ...
...ARE YOU OKAY, BIG BRO...!?
FURA (SWAY)
IT'S NOT FATAL.
DON'T WORRY.
THAT ATTACK TOOK THE LAST OF MY STRENGTH ...
I'M IMPRESSED ...
...YOU MANAGED TO MEET IT.
THE MOMENT I SAW THE SPRAY OF BLOOD...
...I REMEMBERED THAT IT IS ALSO A LIQUID.
GENIUS!
I WAS MORE OF A HINDRANCE THAN HELP, BUT...
...THE BOTH OF US ARE GOING TO COME HOME ALIVE AFTER TAKING ON SUCH POWERFUL ENEMIES.
THANK GOODNESS...

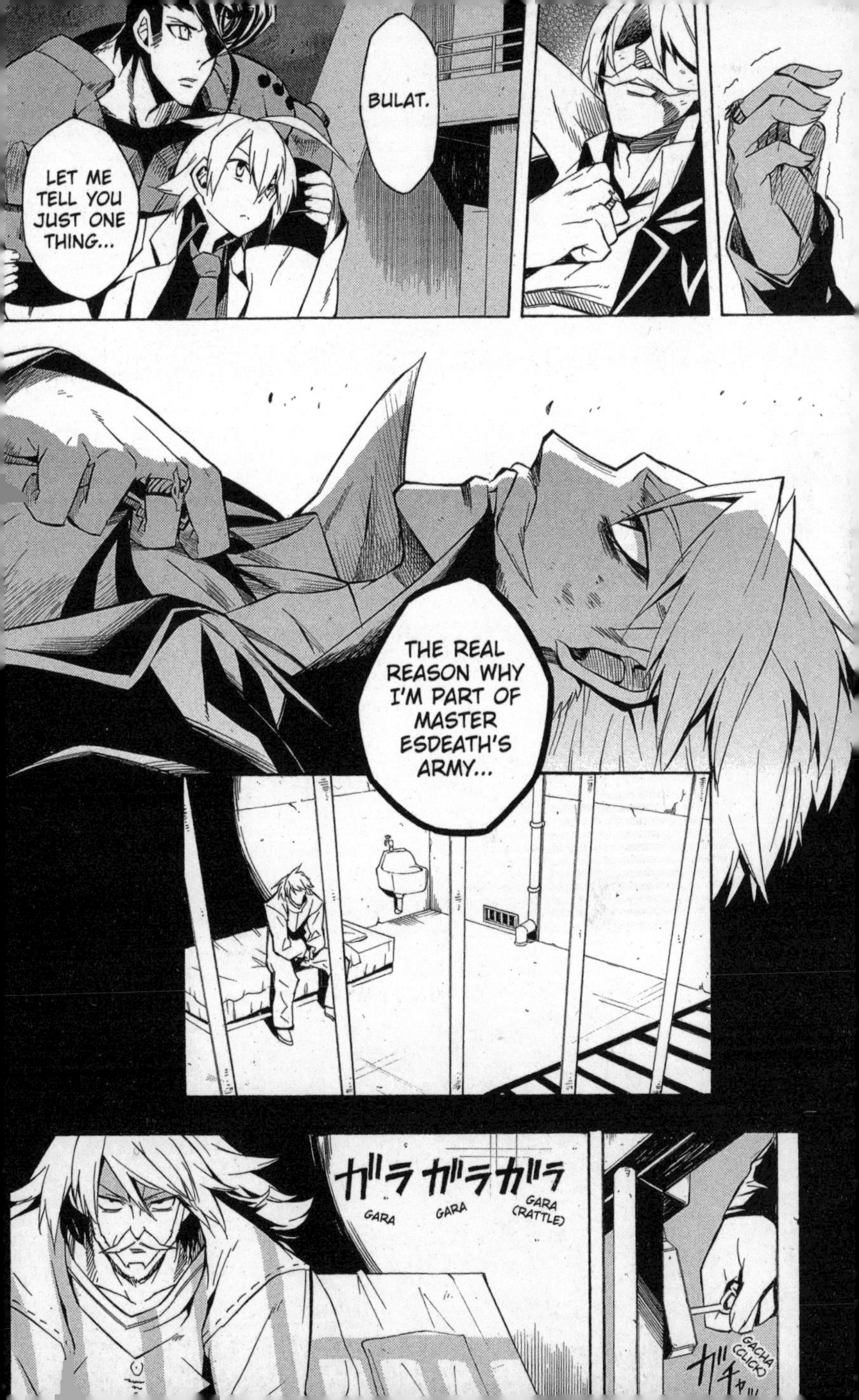
BULAT.
LET ME TELL YOU JUST ONE THING...
THE REAL REASON WHY I'M PART OF MASTER ESDEATH'S ARMY...
ガラガラガラ
GARA GARA GARA (RATTLE)
ガチャ
GACHA (CLICK)

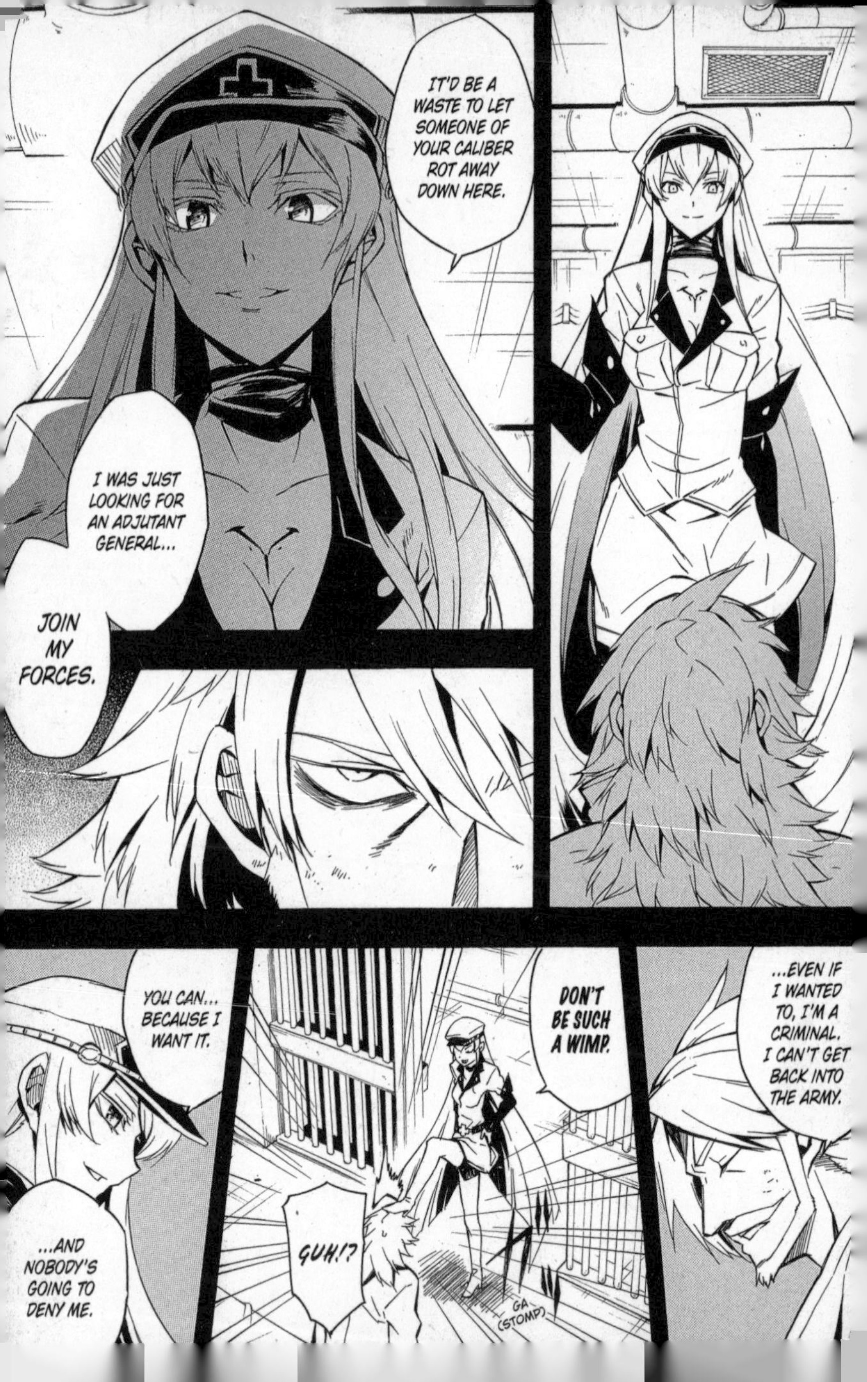
IT'D BE A WASTE TO LET SOMEONE OF YOUR CALIBER ROT AWAY DOWN HERE.
I WAS JUST LOOKING FOR AN ADJUTANT GENERAL...
JOIN MY FORCES.
...EVEN IF I WANTED TO, I'M A CRIMINAL. I CAN'T GET BACK INTO THE ARMY.
DON'T BE SUCH A WIMP.
GUH!?
GA (STOMP)
YOU CAN... BECAUSE I WANT IT.
...AND NOBODY'S GOING TO DENY ME.

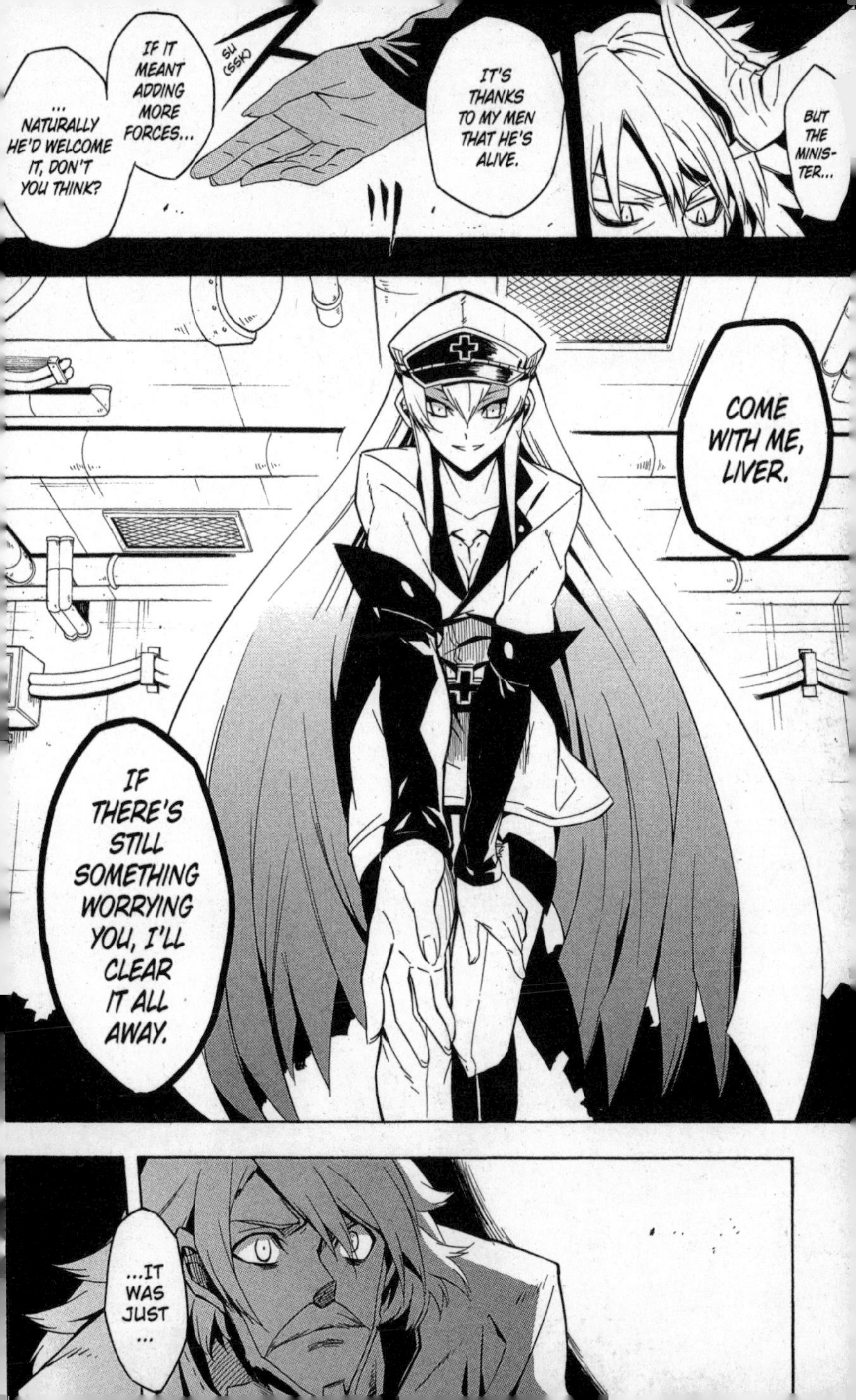
BUT THE MINISTER...
IT'S THANKS TO MY MEN THAT HE'S ALIVE.
SU (SSK)
IF IT MEANT ADDING MORE FORCES...
...NATURALLY HE'D WELCOME IT, DON'T YOU THINK?
COME WITH ME, LIVER.
IF THERE'S STILL SOMETHING WORRYING YOU, I'LL CLEAR IT ALL AWAY.
...IT WAS JUST ...

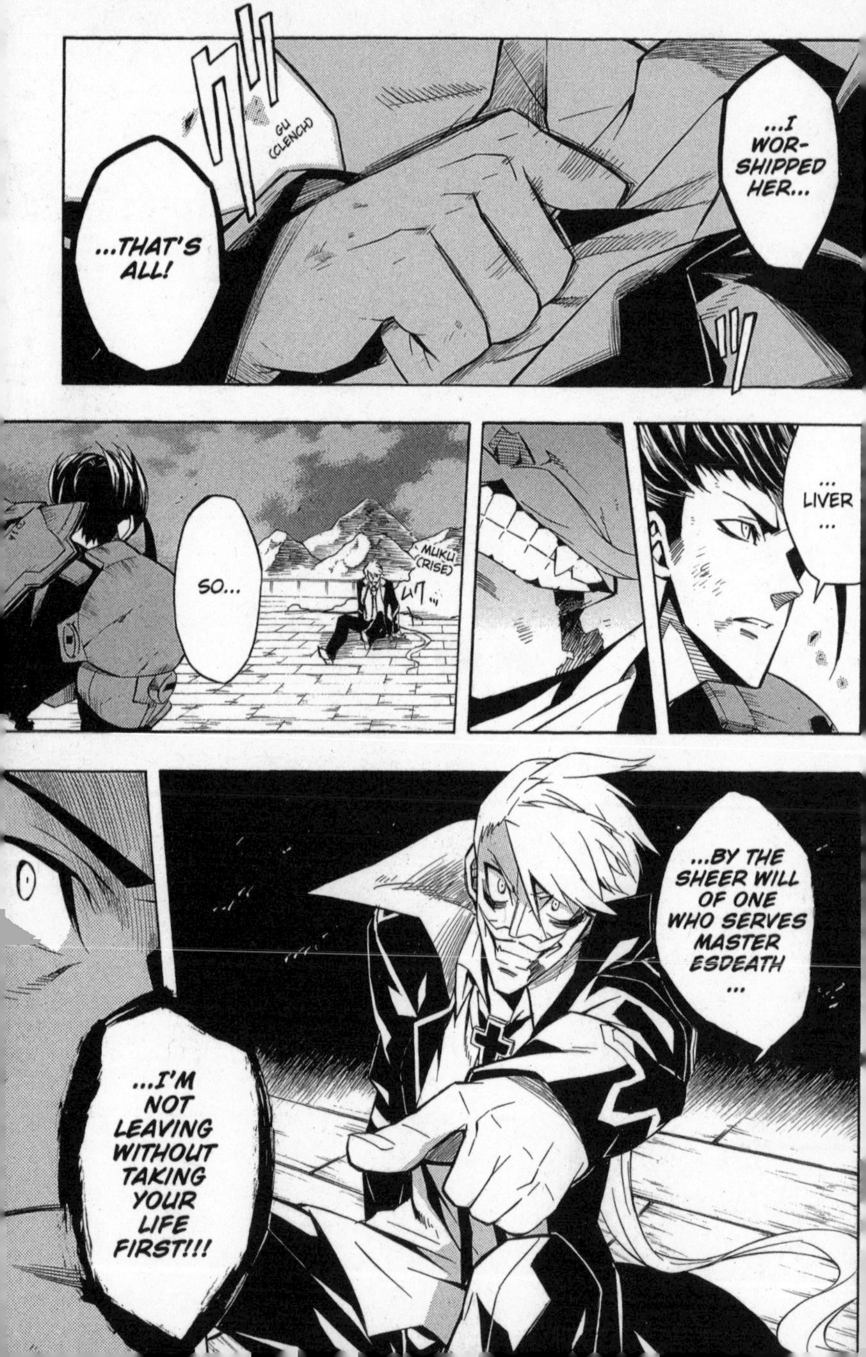
...I WORSHIPPED HER...
GU (CLENCH)
...THAT'S ALL!
...LIVER...
MUKU (RISE)
SO...
...BY THE SHEER WILL OF ONE WHO SERVES MASTER ESDEATH...
...I'M NOT LEAVING WITHOUT TAKING YOUR LIFE FIRST!!!

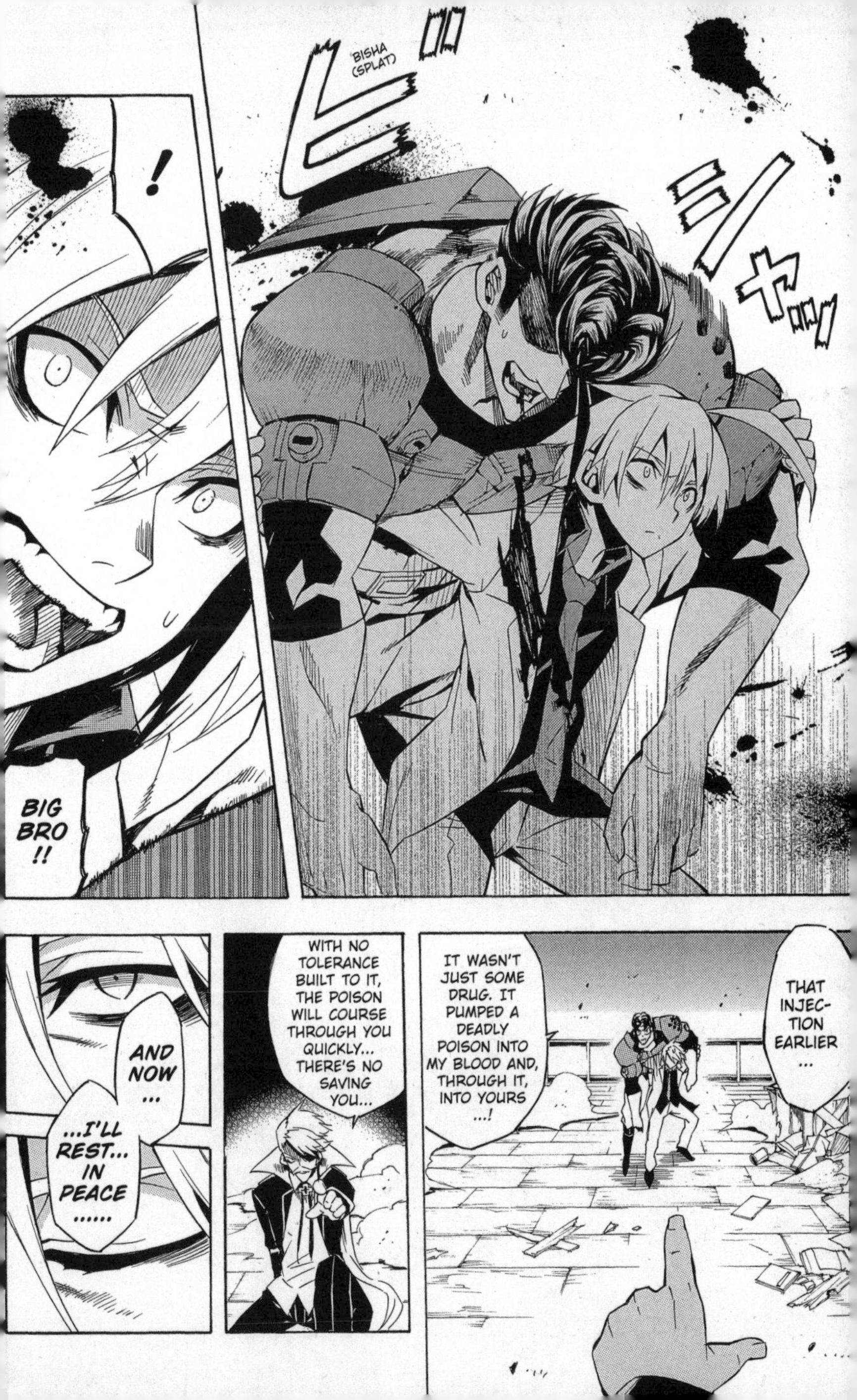
BISHA (SPLAT)
!
BIG BRO !!
THAT INJEC-TION EARLIER ...
IT WASN'T JUST SOME DRUG. IT PUMPED A DEADLY POISON INTO MY BLOOD AND, THROUGH IT, INTO YOURS ...!
WITH NO TOLERANCE BUILT TO IT, THE POISON WILL COURSE THROUGH YOU QUICKLY... THERE'S NO SAVING YOU...
AND NOW ...
...I'LL REST... IN PEACE ......

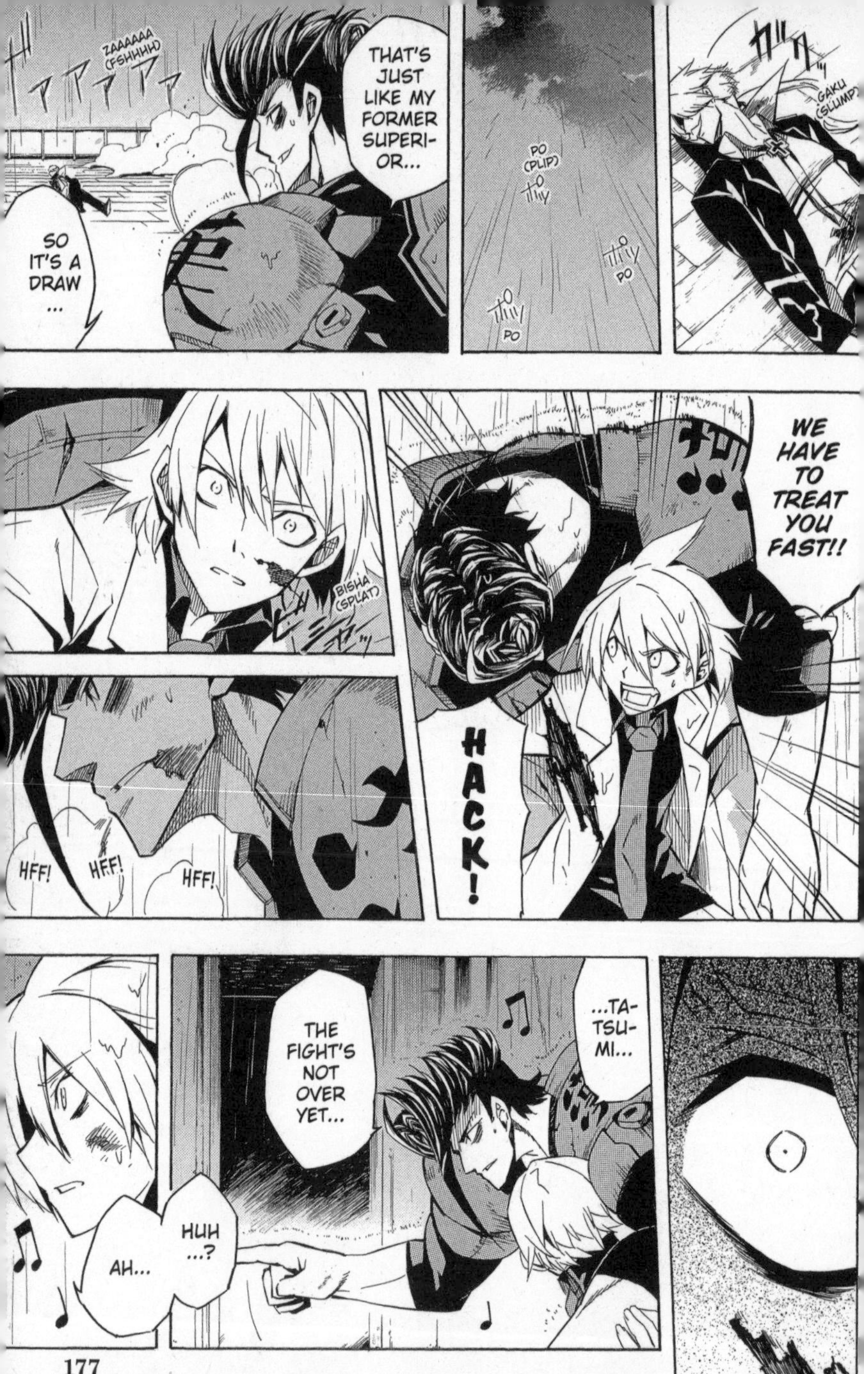
GAKU (SLUMP)
PO (PLIP)
PO
PO
ZAAAAAA (FSHHHH)
THAT'S JUST LIKE MY FORMER SUPERI-OR...
SO IT'S A DRAW ...
WE HAVE TO TREAT YOU FAST!!
HACK!
BISHA (SPLAT)
HFF!
HFF!
HFF!
...TA-TSU-MI...
THE FIGHT'S NOT OVER YET...
HUH ...?
AH...

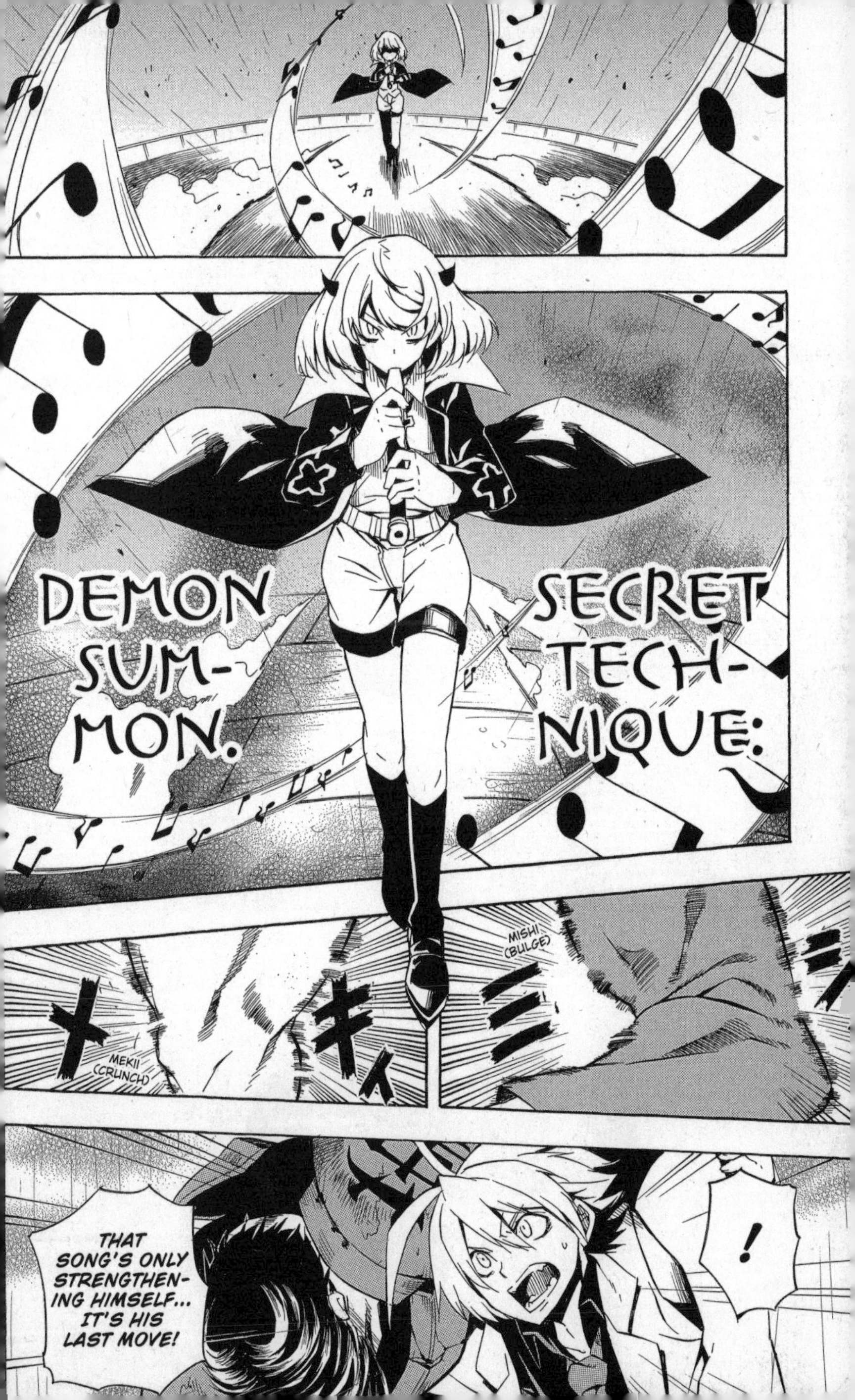
SECRET TECH- NIQUE:
DEMON SUM- MON.
MISHI (BULGE)
MEKII (CRUNCH)
!
THAT SONG'S ONLY STRENGTHEN- ING HIMSELF... IT'S HIS LAST MOVE!

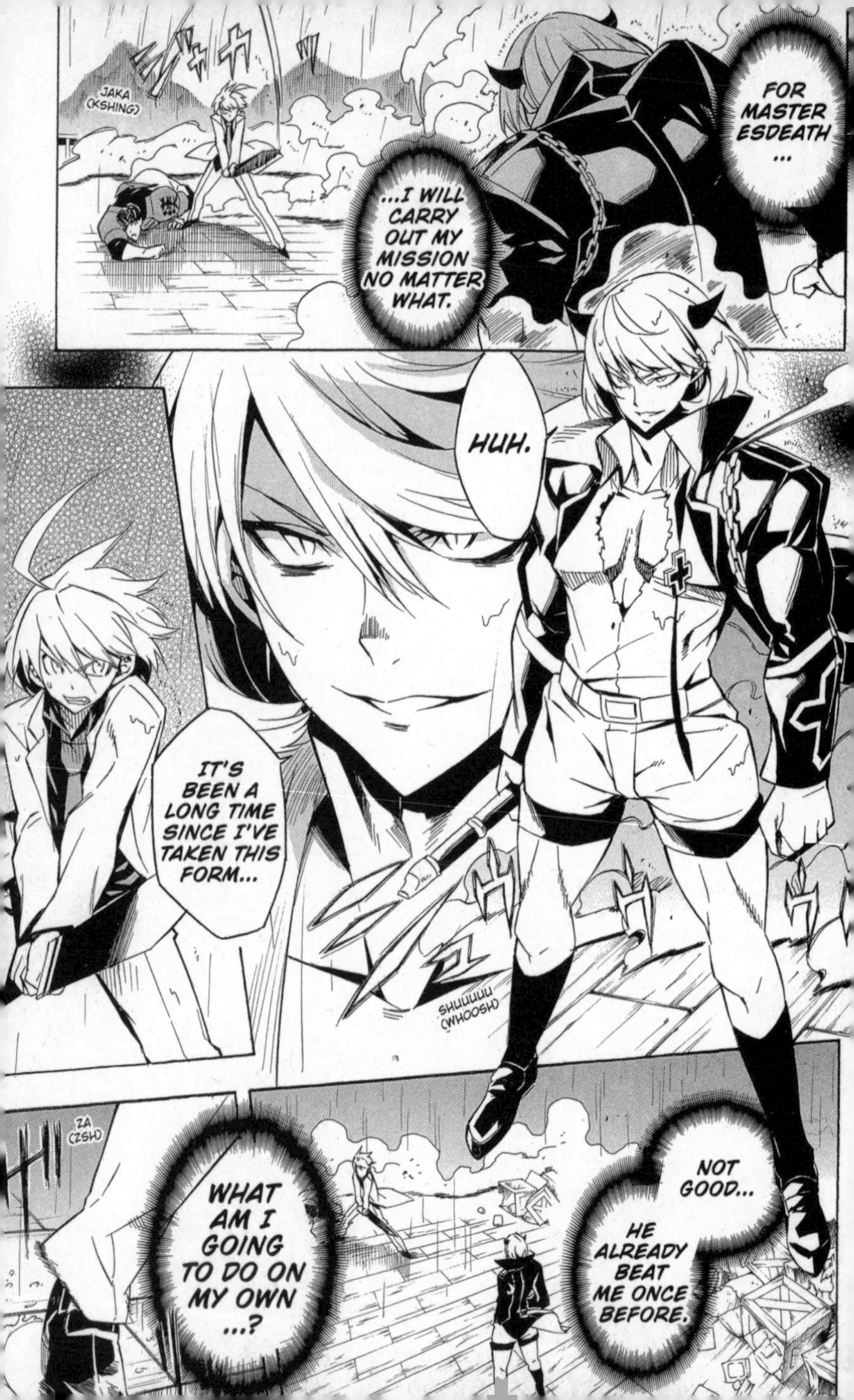
FOR MASTER ESDEATH...
...I WILL CARRY OUT MY MISSION NO MATTER WHAT.
JAKA (KSHING)
HUH.
IT'S BEEN A LONG TIME SINCE I'VE TAKEN THIS FORM...
SHUUUUU (WHOOSH)
NOT GOOD...
HE ALREADY BEAT ME ONCE BEFORE.
WHAT AM I GOING TO DO ON MY OWN...?
ZA (ZSH)

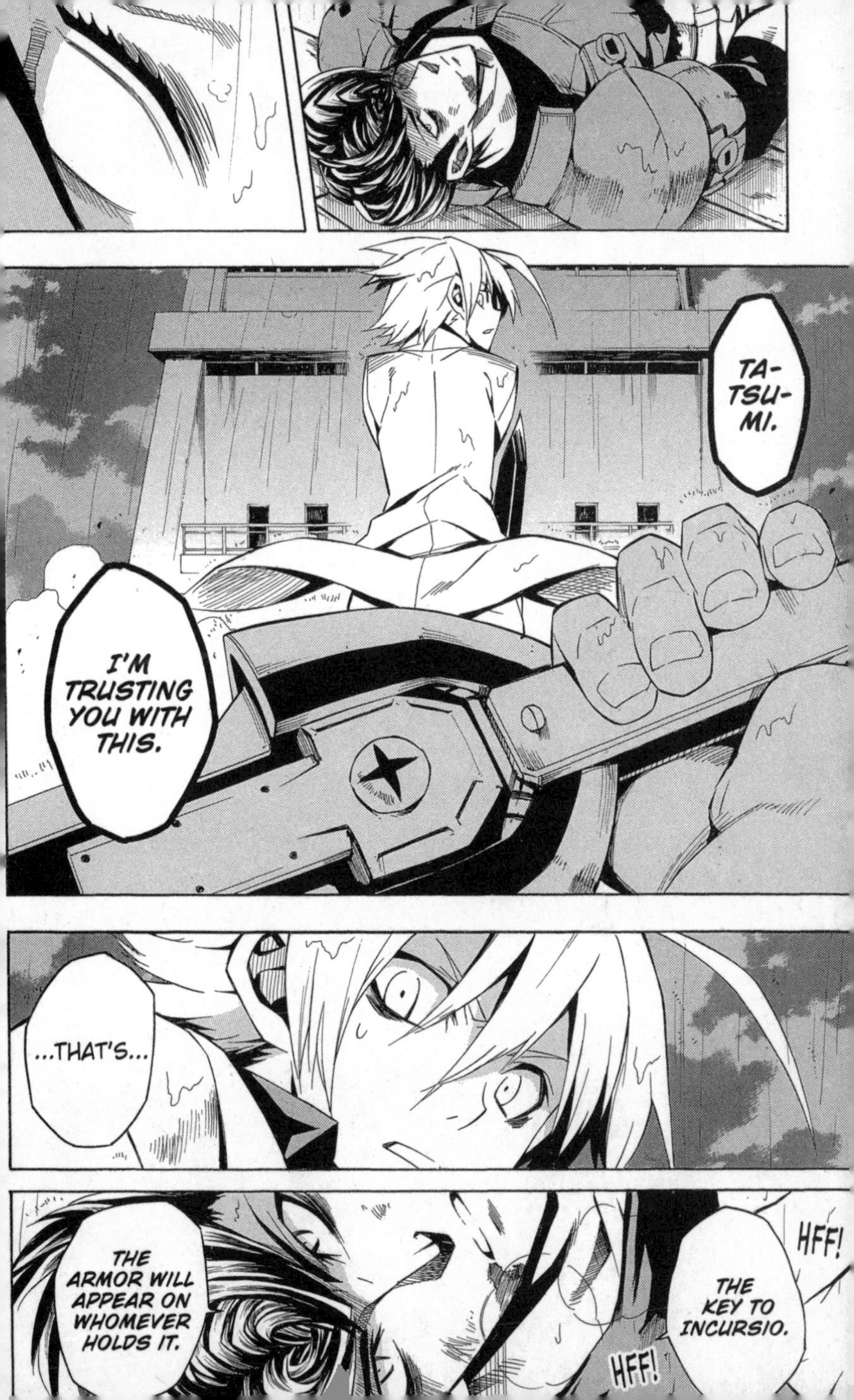
TA-TSU-MI.
I'M TRUSTING YOU WITH THIS.
...THAT'S...
HFF!
THE KEY TO INCURSIO.
HFF!
THE ARMOR WILL APPEAR ON WHOMEVER HOLDS IT.

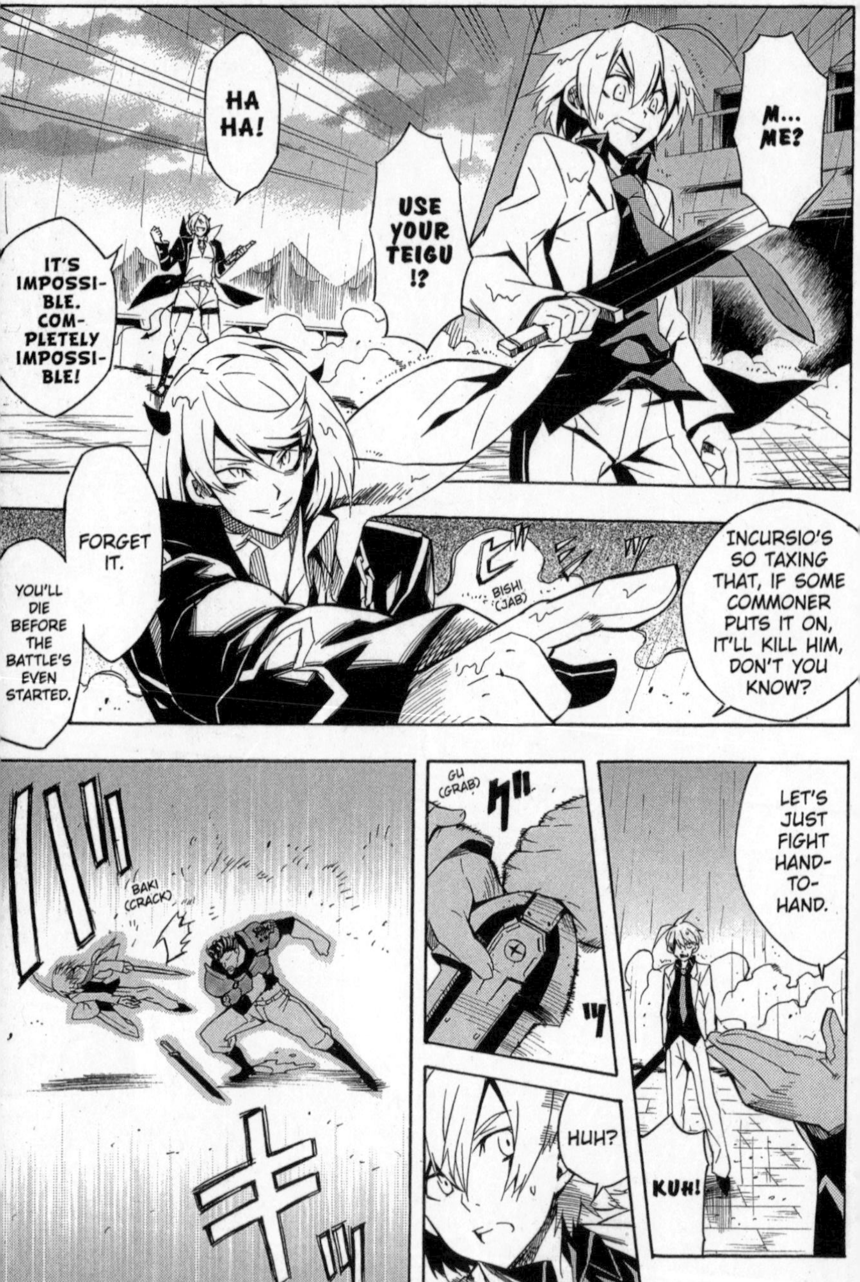
M... ME?
USE YOUR TEIGU!?
HA HA!
IT'S IMPOSSIBLE. COMPLETELY IMPOSSIBLE!
INCURSIO'S SO TAXING THAT, IF SOME COMMONER PUTS IT ON, IT'LL KILL HIM, DON'T YOU KNOW?
BISHI (JAB)
FORGET IT.
YOU'LL DIE BEFORE THE BATTLE'S EVEN STARTED.
LET'S JUST FIGHT HAND-TO-HAND.
KUH!
GU (GRAB)
HUH?
BAKI (CRACK)

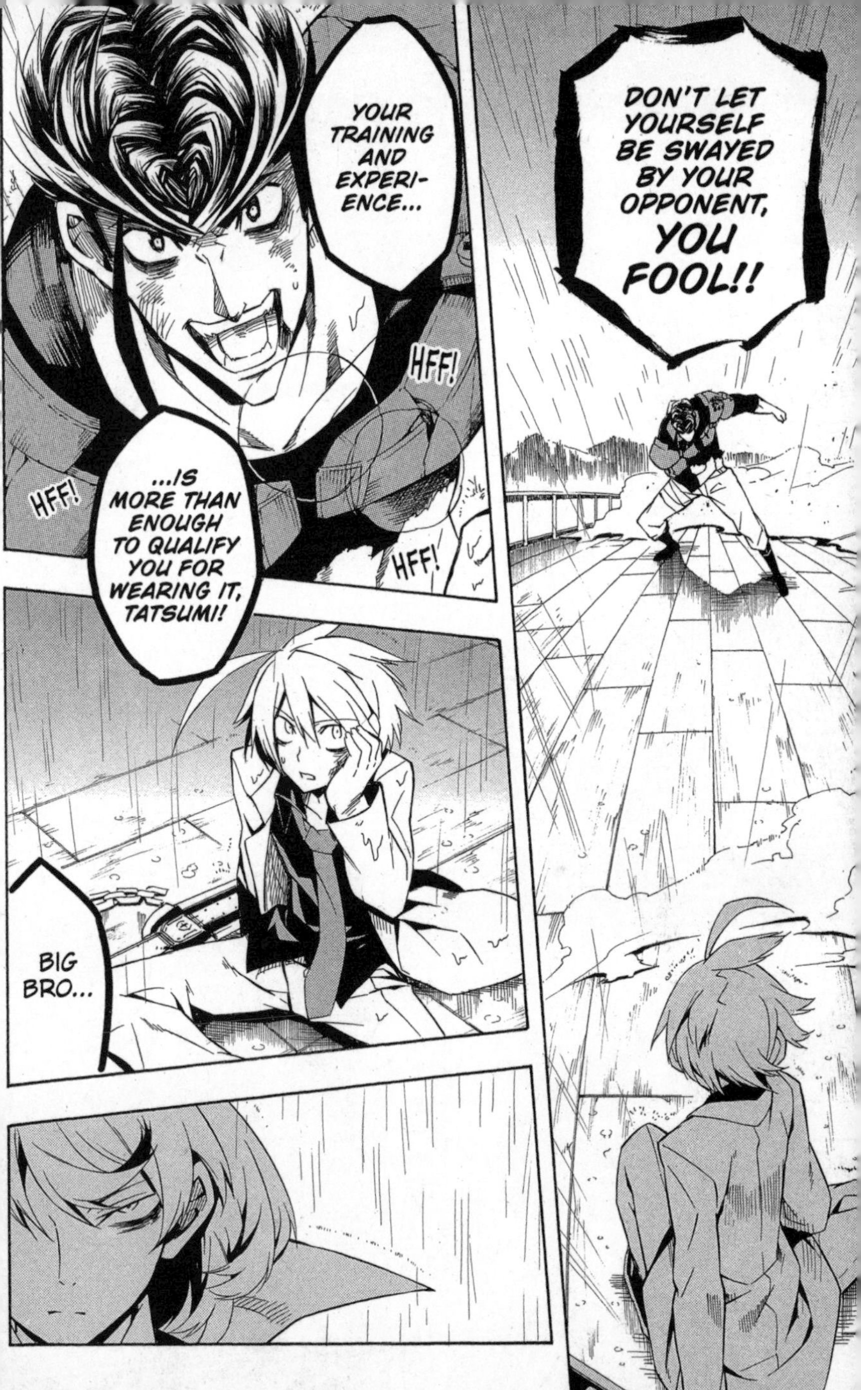
DON'T LET YOURSELF BE SWAYED BY YOUR OPPONENT, YOU FOOL!!
YOUR TRAINING AND EXPERIENCE...
HFF!
...IS MORE THAN ENOUGH TO QUALIFY YOU FOR WEARING IT, TATSUMI!
HFF!
HFF!
BIG BRO...

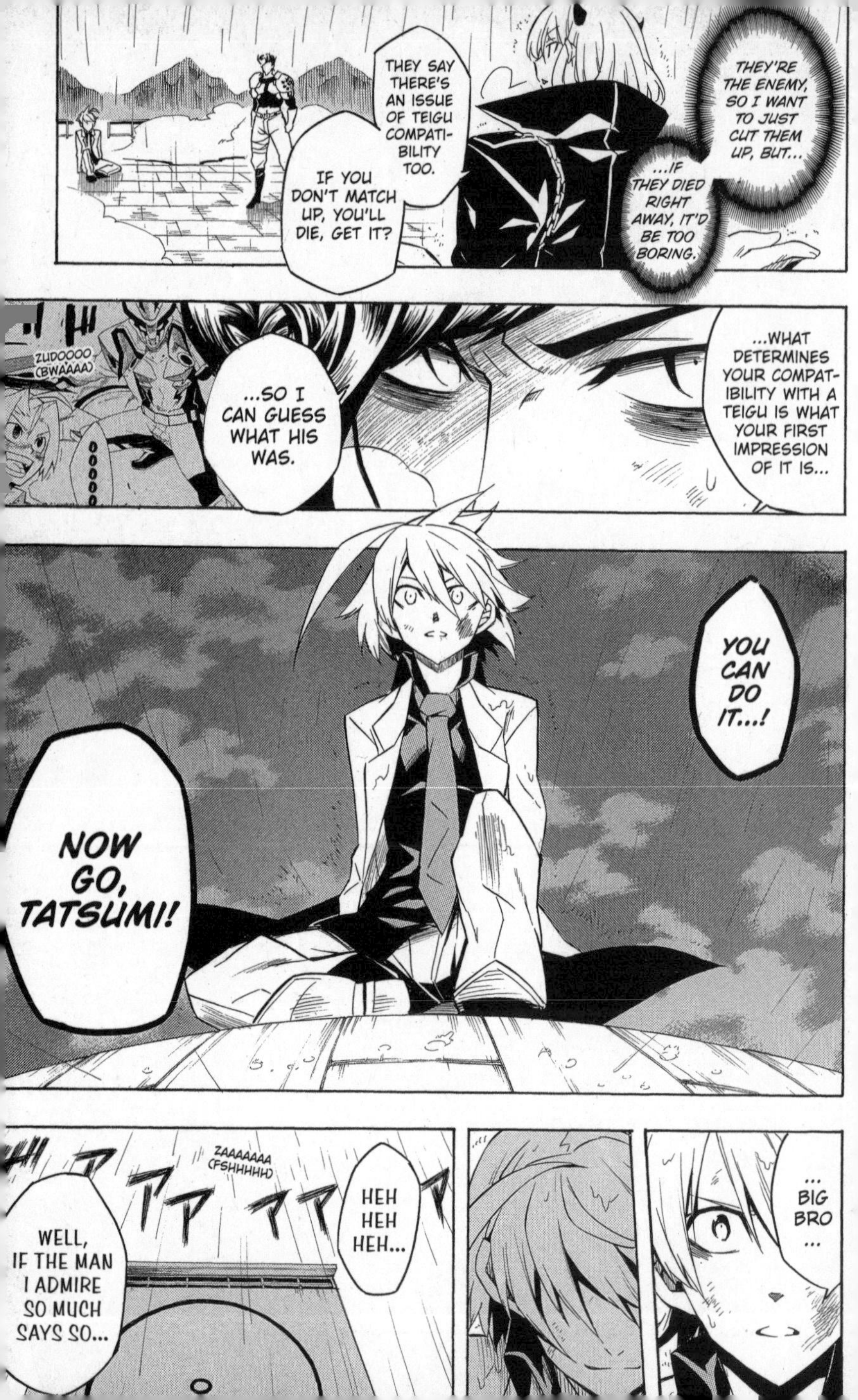
THEY'RE THE ENEMY, SO I WANT TO JUST CUT THEM UP, BUT...
...IF THEY DIED RIGHT AWAY, IT'D BE TOO BORING.
THEY SAY THERE'S AN ISSUE OF TEIGU COMPATIBILITY TOO.
IF YOU DON'T MATCH UP, YOU'LL DIE, GET IT?
...WHAT DETERMINES YOUR COMPATIBILITY WITH A TEIGU IS WHAT YOUR FIRST IMPRESSION OF IT IS...
...SO I CAN GUESS WHAT HIS WAS.
ZUDOOOO (BWAAAA)
YOU CAN DO IT...!
NOW GO, TATSUMI!
... BIG BRO ...
ZAAAAAAA (FSHHHHH)
HEH HEH HEH...
WELL, IF THE MAN I ADMIRE SO MUCH SAYS SO...

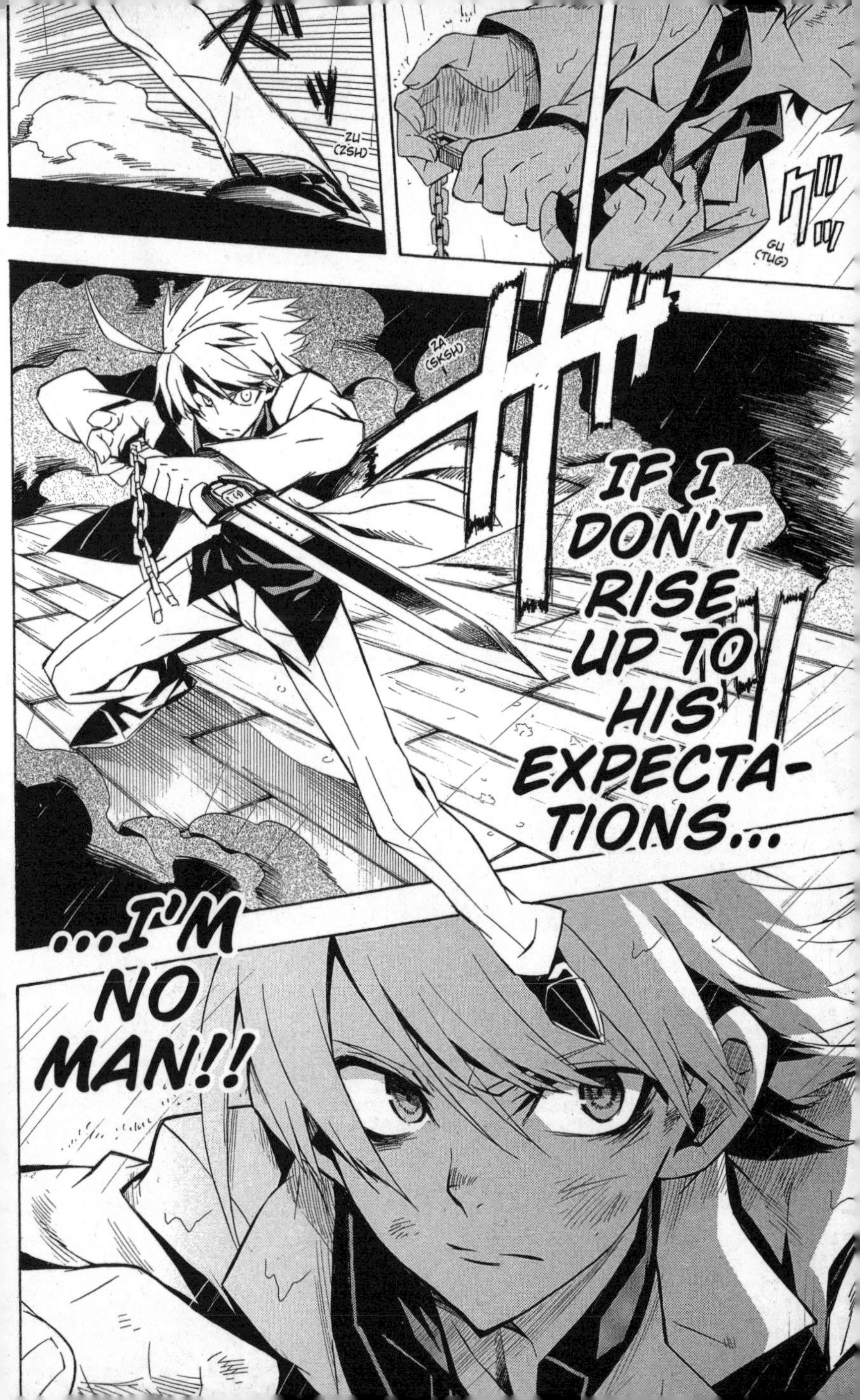
GU (TUG)
ZU (ZSH)
ZA (SKSH)
IF I DON'T RISE UP TO HIS EXPECTATIONS...
...I'M NO MAN!!

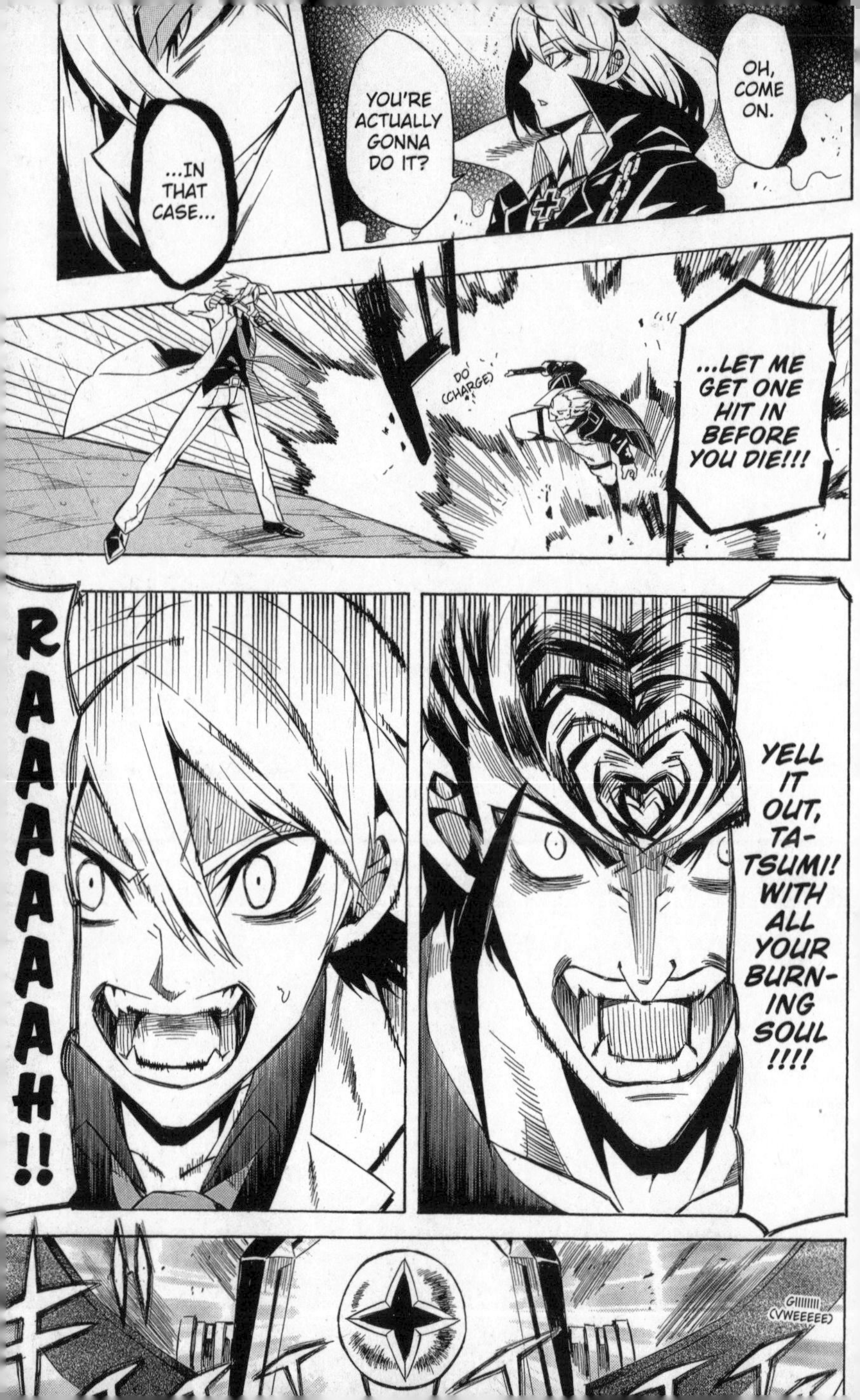
OH, COME ON.
YOU'RE ACTUALLY GONNA DO IT?
...IN THAT CASE...
...LET ME GET ONE HIT IN BEFORE YOU DIE!!!
DO (CHARGE)
YELL IT OUT, TA-TSUMI! WITH ALL YOUR BURN-ING SOUL!!!!
RAAAAAAAH!!
GIIIIIII (VWEEEEE)

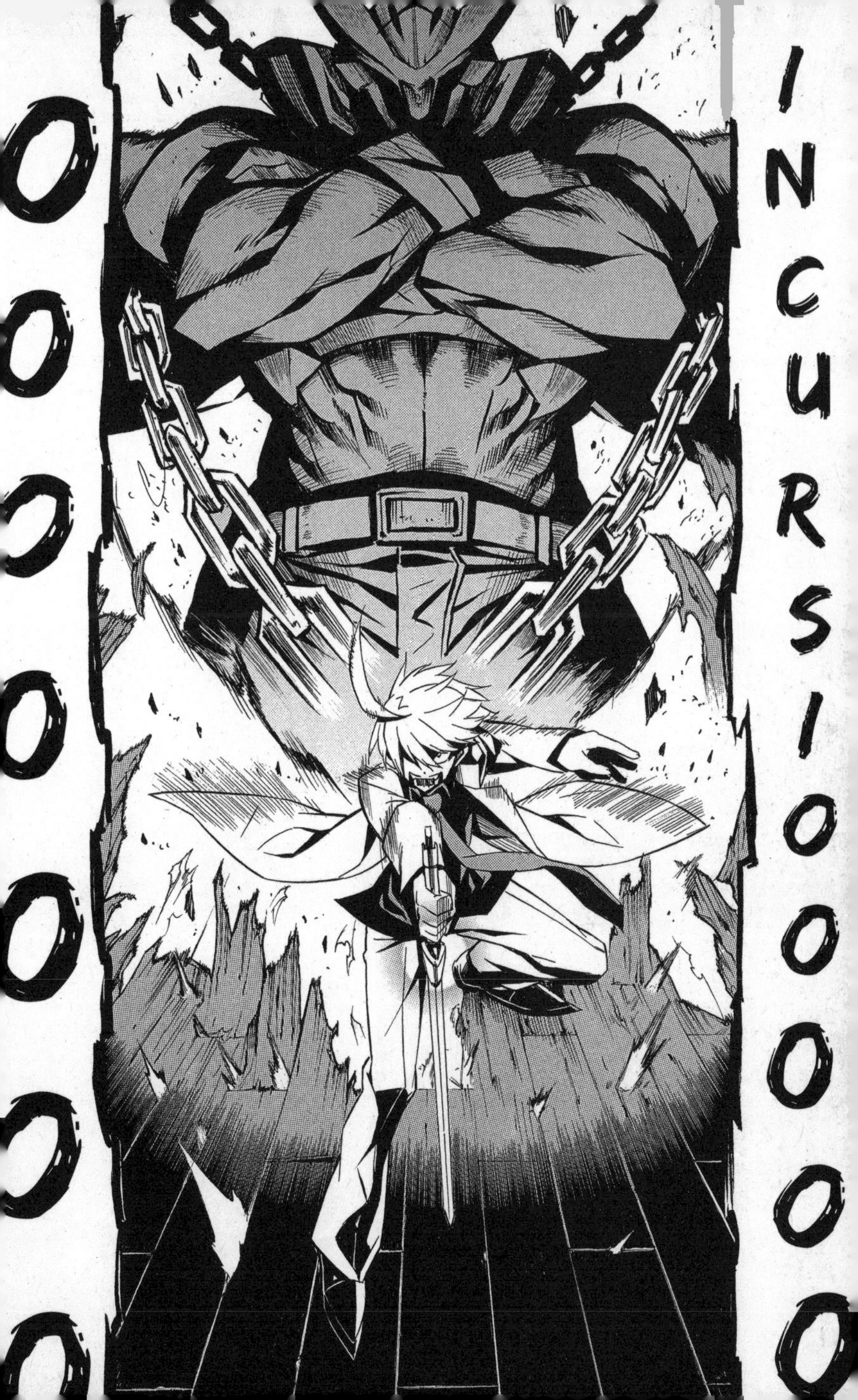
INCURSIOOOOO
OOOOOOOO

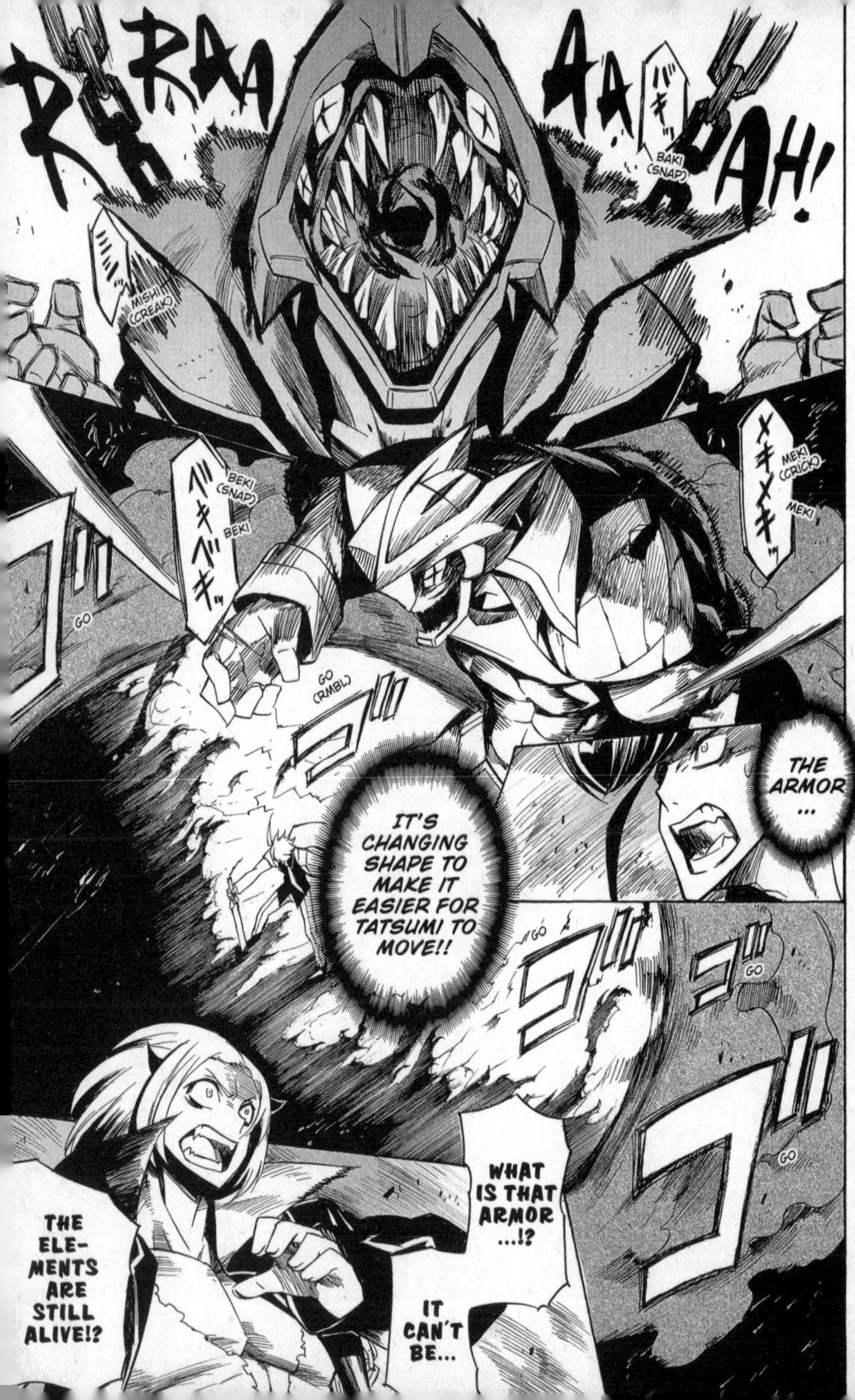
RORAAAAAAH!
BAKI (SNAP)
MISHI (CREAK)
MEKI (CRICK) MEKI
BEKI (SNAP) BEKI
GO
GO (RMBL)
THE ARMOR...
IT'S CHANGING SHAPE TO MAKE IT EASIER FOR TATSUMI TO MOVE!!
GO
GO
GO
WHAT IS THAT ARMOR...!?
IT CAN'T BE...
THE ELEMENTS ARE STILL ALIVE!?

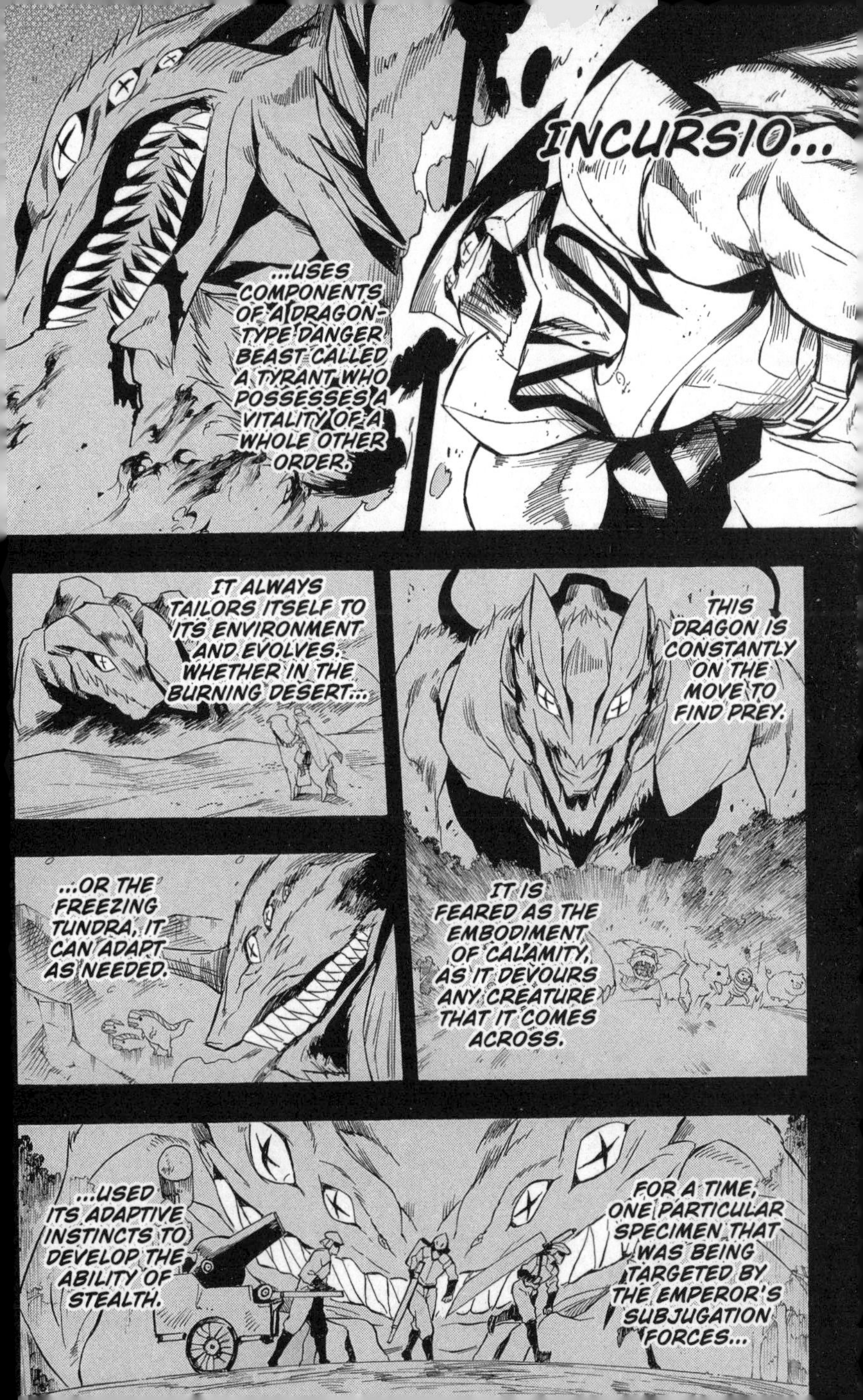

INCURSIO...
...USES COMPONENTS OF A DRAGON-TYPE DANGER BEAST CALLED A TYRANT WHO POSSESSES A VITALITY OF A WHOLE OTHER ORDER.
THIS DRAGON IS CONSTANTLY ON THE MOVE TO FIND PREY.
IT IS FEARED AS THE EMBODIMENT OF CALAMITY, AS IT DEVOURS ANY CREATURE THAT IT COMES ACROSS.
IT ALWAYS TAILORS ITSELF TO ITS ENVIRONMENT AND EVOLVES. WHETHER IN THE BURNING DESERT...
...OR THE FREEZING TUNDRA, IT CAN ADAPT AS NEEDED.
FOR A TIME, ONE PARTICULAR SPECIMEN THAT WAS BEING TARGETED BY THE EMPEROR'S SUBJUGATION FORCES...
...USED ITS ADAPTIVE INSTINCTS TO DEVELOP THE ABILITY OF STEALTH.

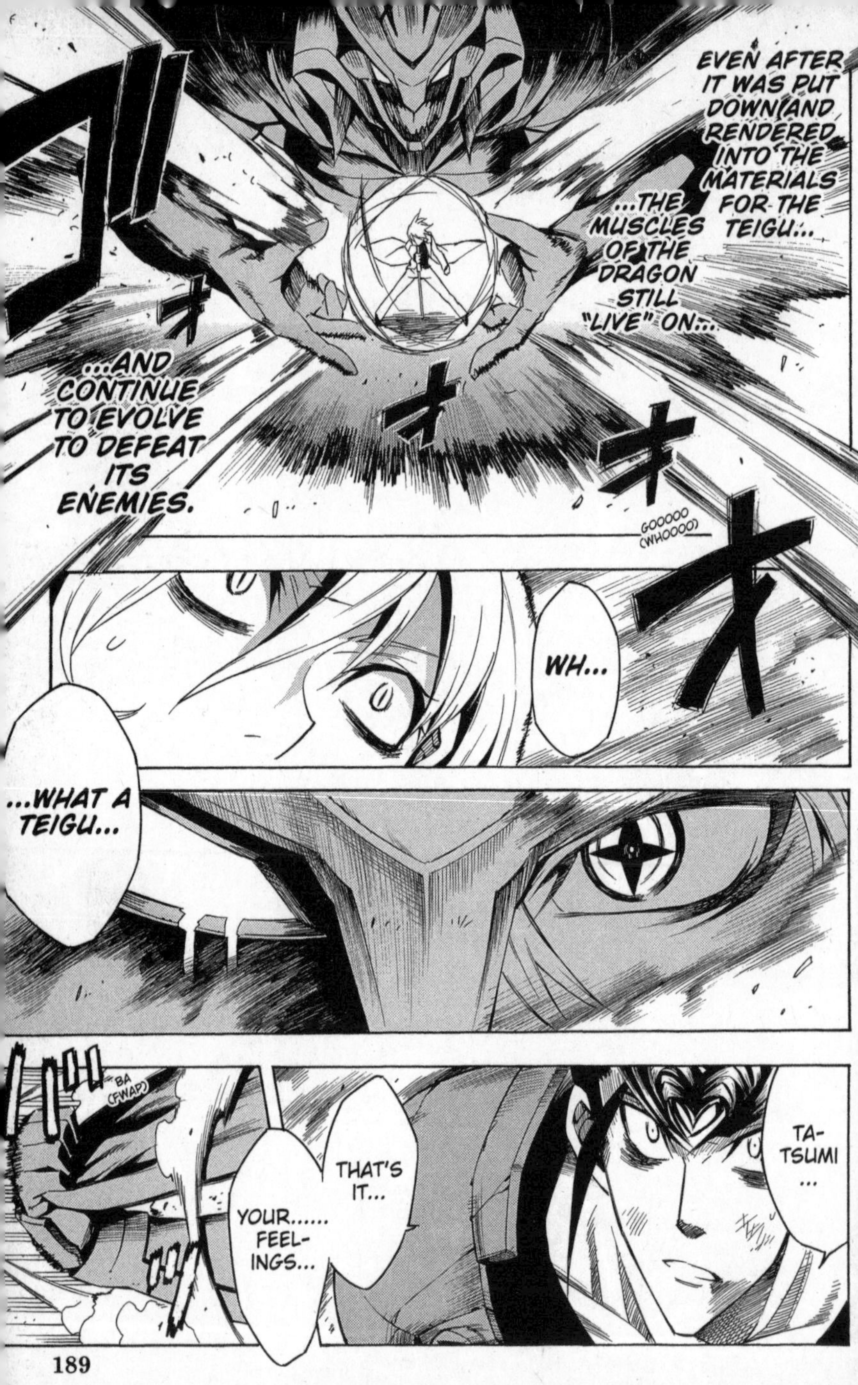
EVEN AFTER IT WAS PUT DOWN AND RENDERED INTO THE MATERIALS FOR THE TEIGU...
...THE MUSCLES OF THE DRAGON STILL "LIVE" ON...
...AND CONTINUE TO EVOLVE TO DEFEAT ITS ENEMIES.
GOOOOO (WHOOOO)
WH...
...WHAT A TEIGU...
TA-TSUMI ...
THAT'S IT...
YOUR...... FEEL-INGS...
BA (FWAP)

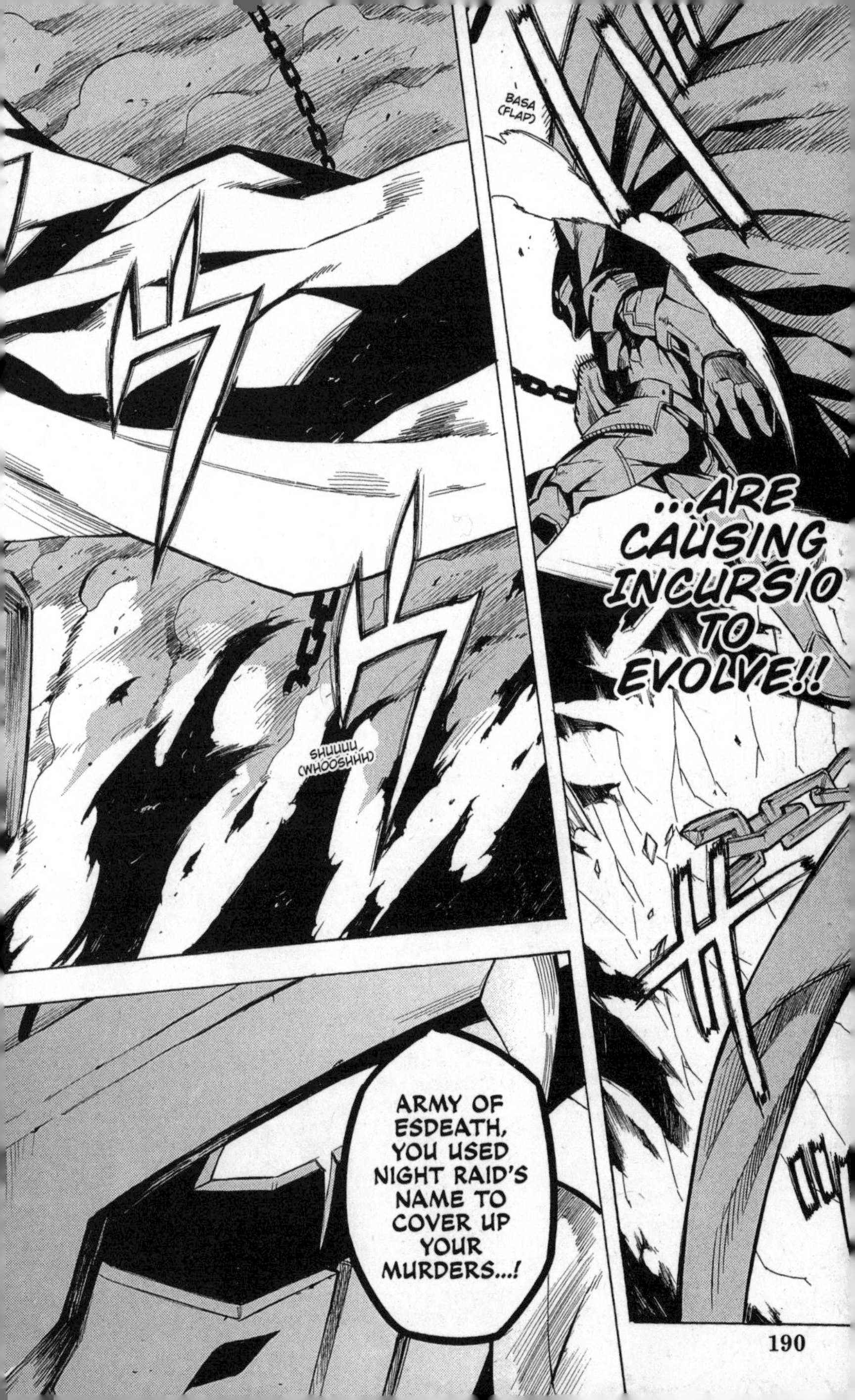
BASA (FLAP)
...ARE CAUSING INCURSIO TO EVOLVE!!
SHUUUU (WHOOSHHH)
ARMY OF ESDEATH, YOU USED NIGHT RAID'S NAME TO COVER UP YOUR MURDERS...!

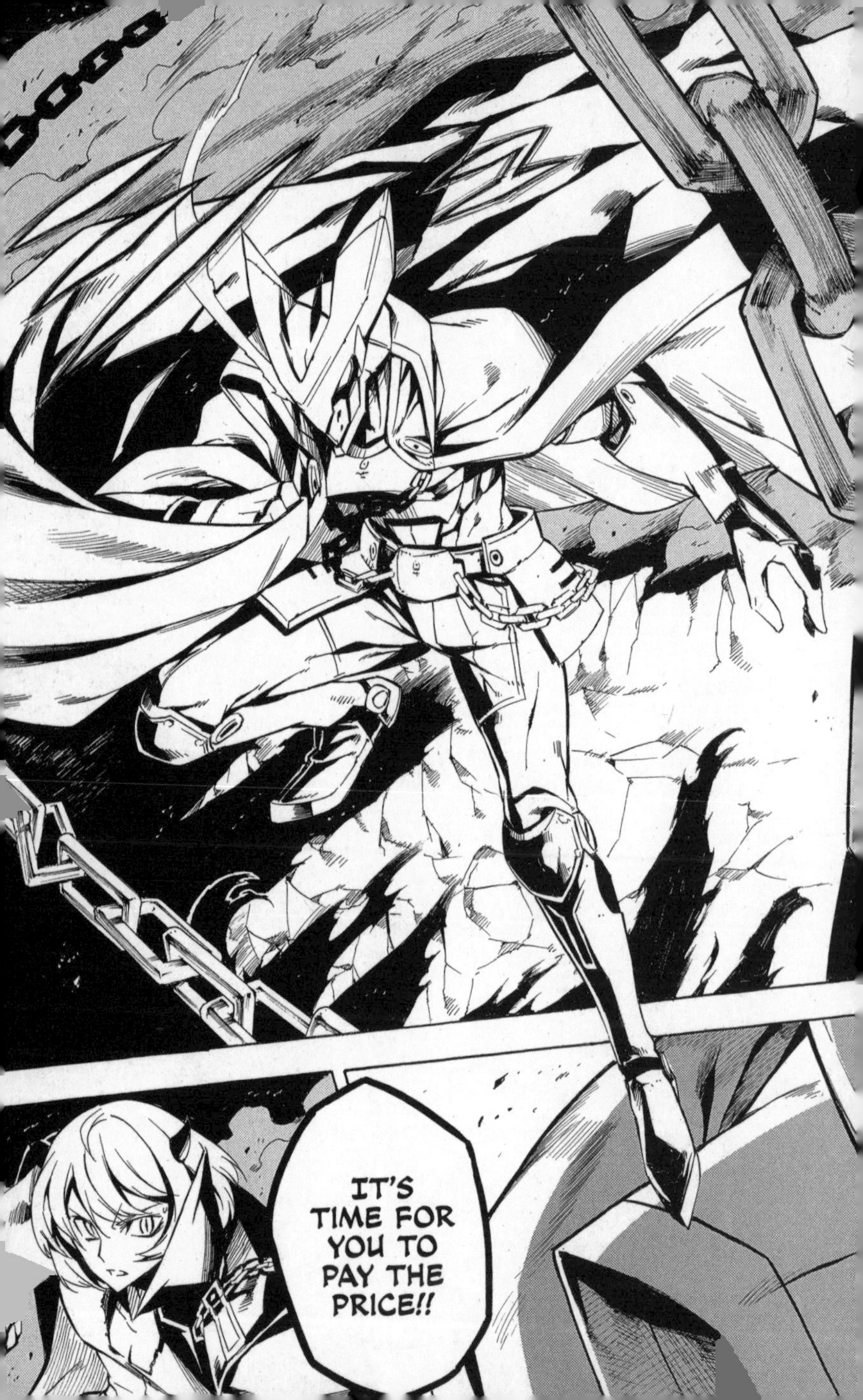
IT'S TIME FOR YOU TO PAY THE PRICE!!

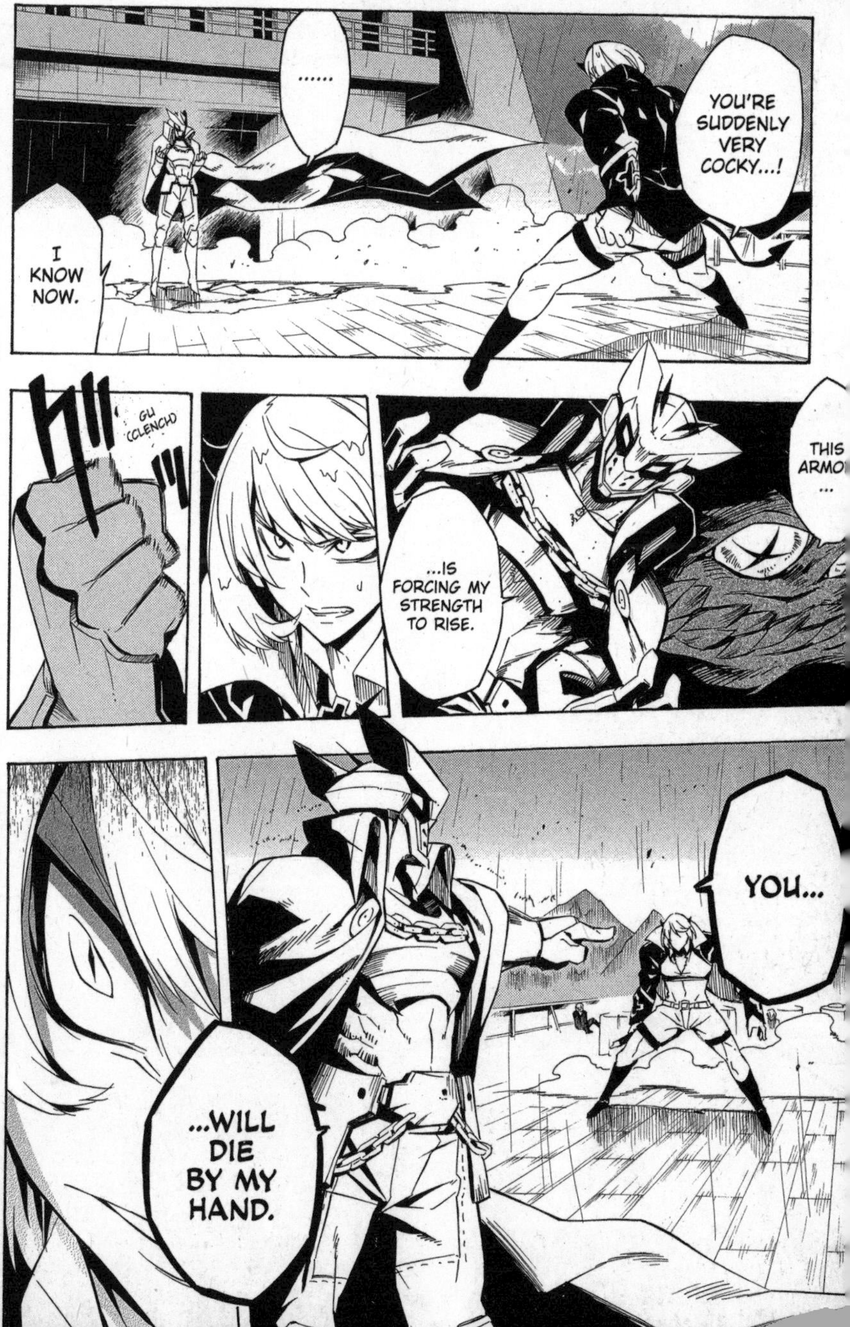
YOU'RE SUDDENLY VERY COCKY...!
......
I KNOW NOW.
THIS ARMO...
...IS FORCING MY STRENGTH TO RISE.
GU (CLENCH)
YOU...
...WILL DIE BY MY HAND.

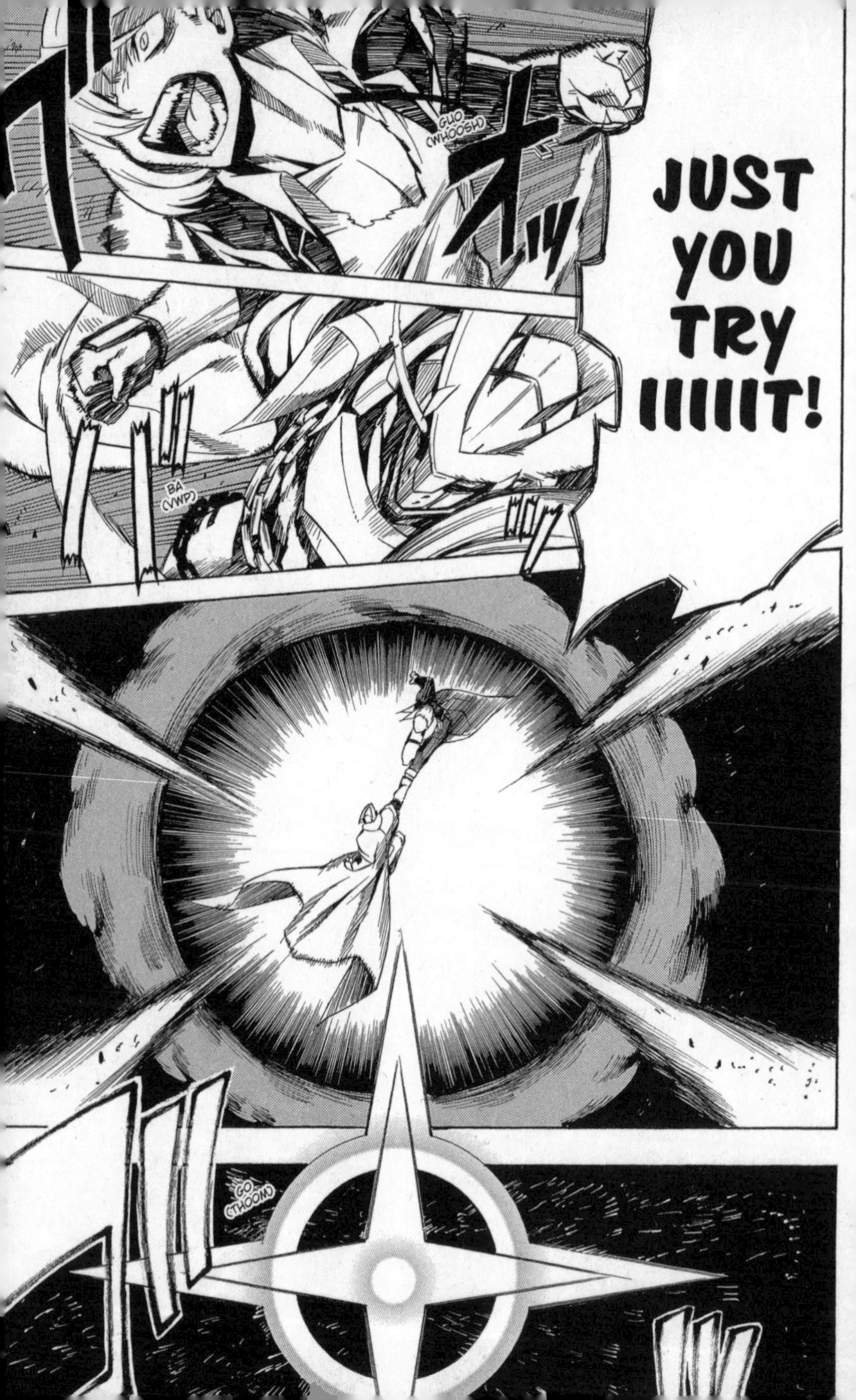
JUST YOU TRY IIIIIT!
GUO (WHOOSH)
BA (VWP)
GO (THOOM)

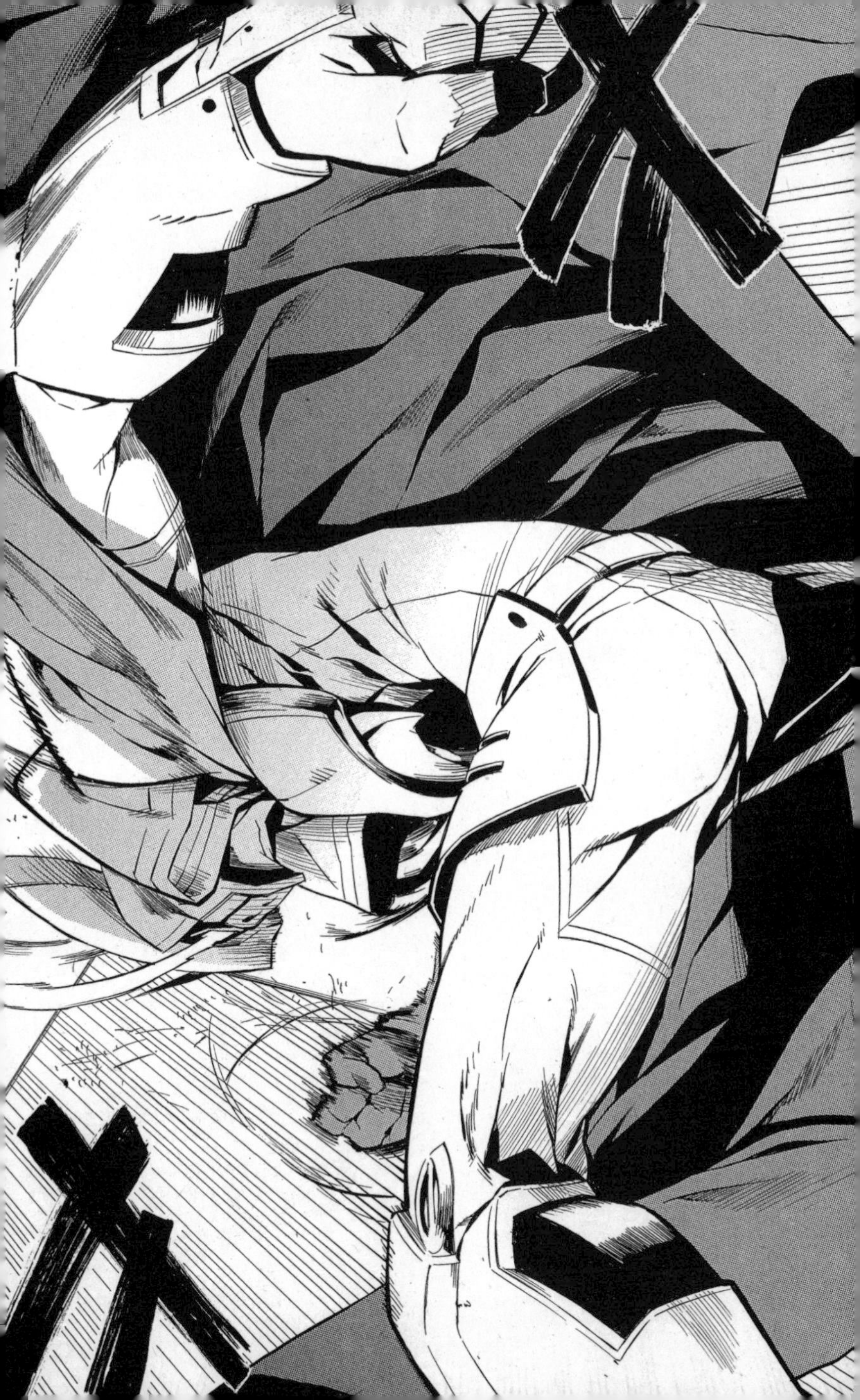

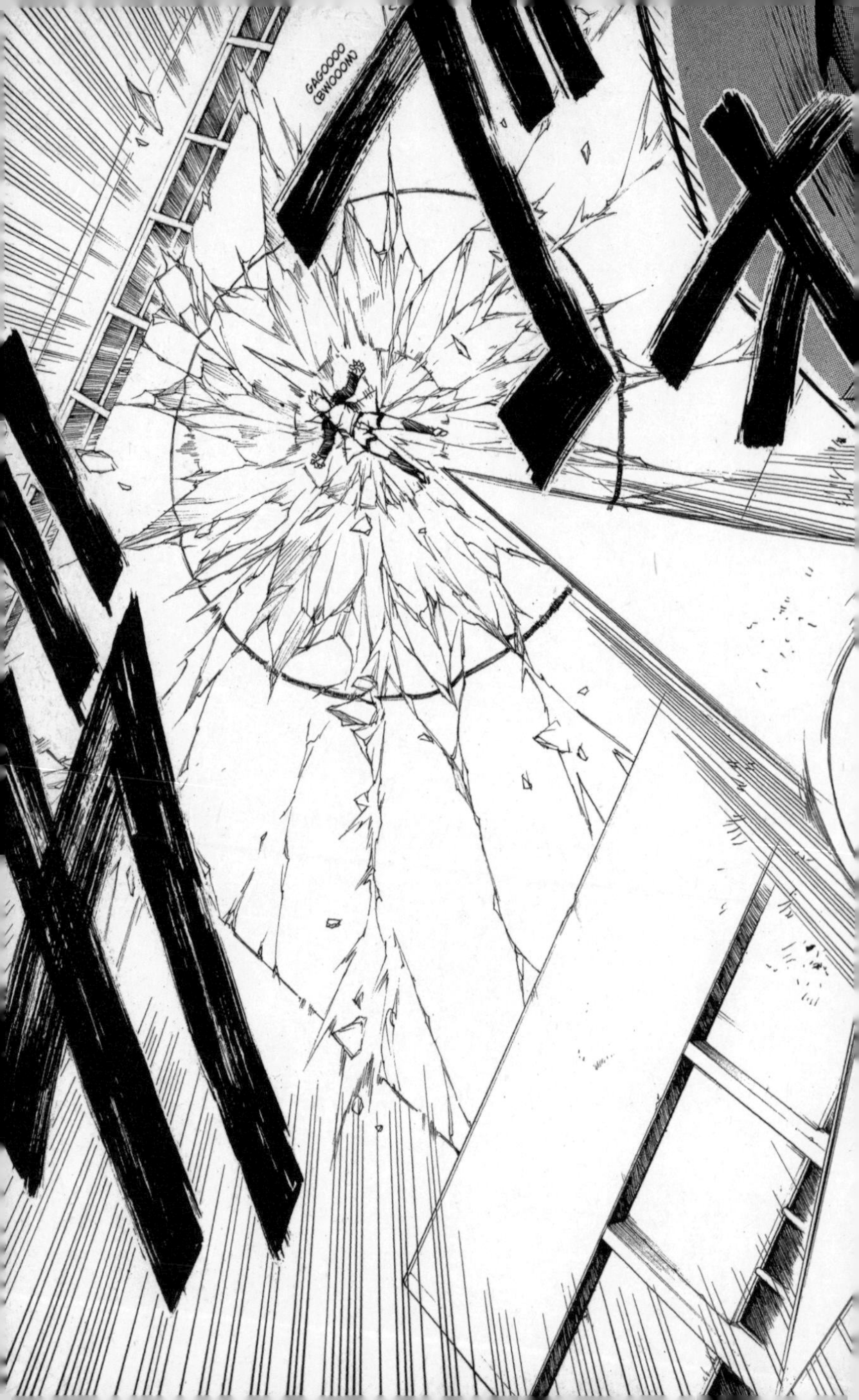
GAGOOOO
(BWOOOM)

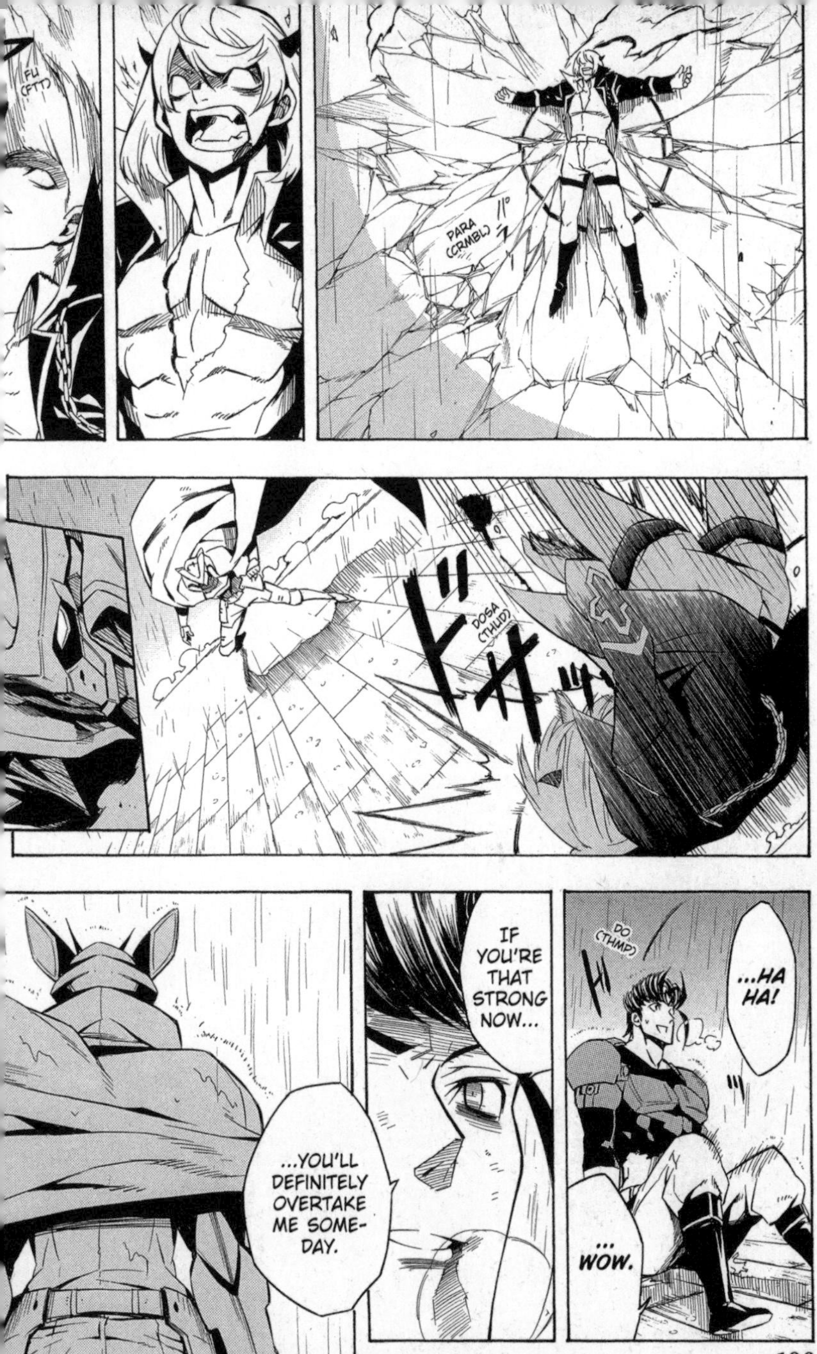
PARA (CRMBL)
FU (FTT)
DOSA (THUD)
DO (THMP)
...HA HA!
...WOW.
IF YOU'RE THAT STRONG NOW...
...YOU'LL DEFINITELY OVERTAKE ME SOME-DAY.

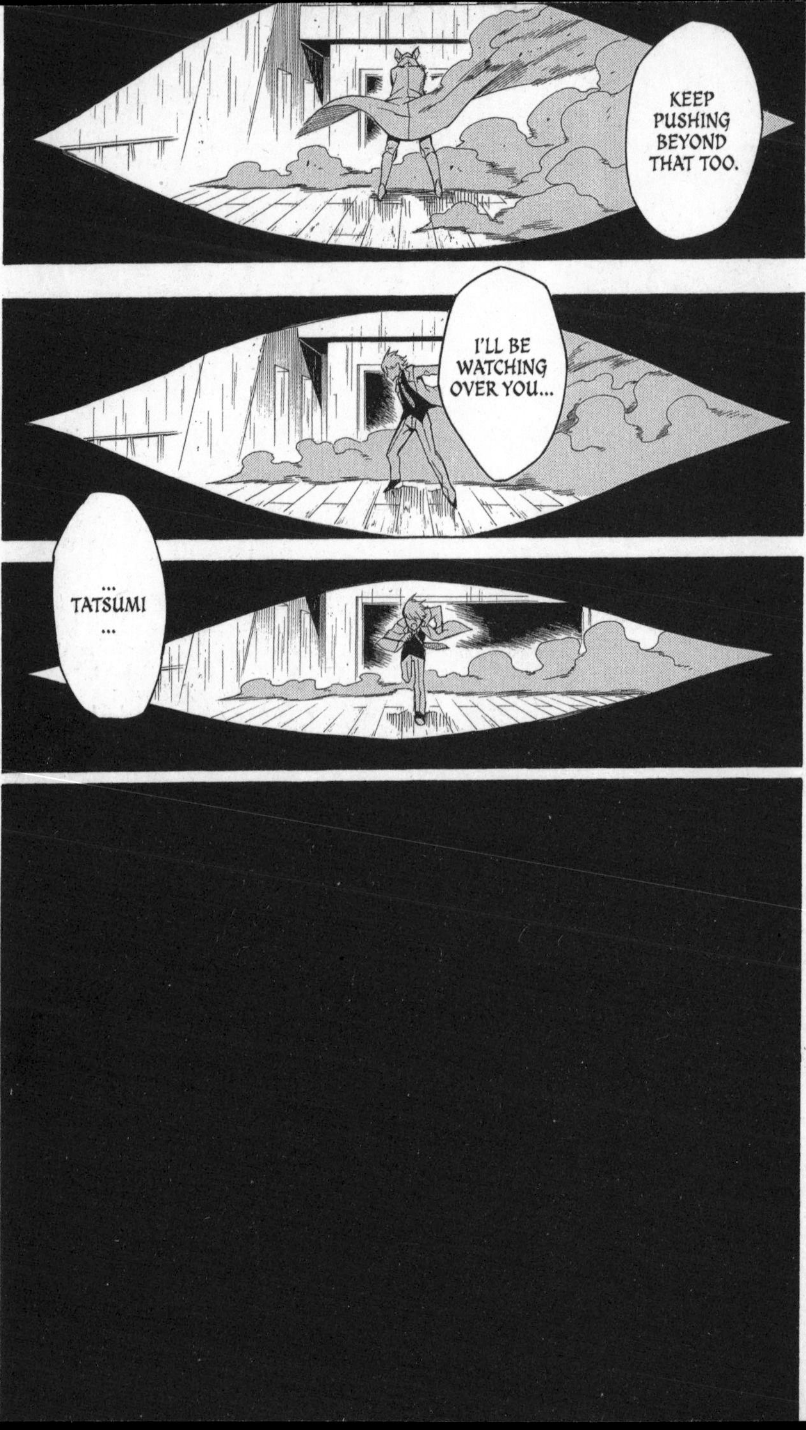
KEEP PUSHING BEYOND THAT TOO.
I'LL BE WATCHING OVER YOU...
... TATSUMI ...

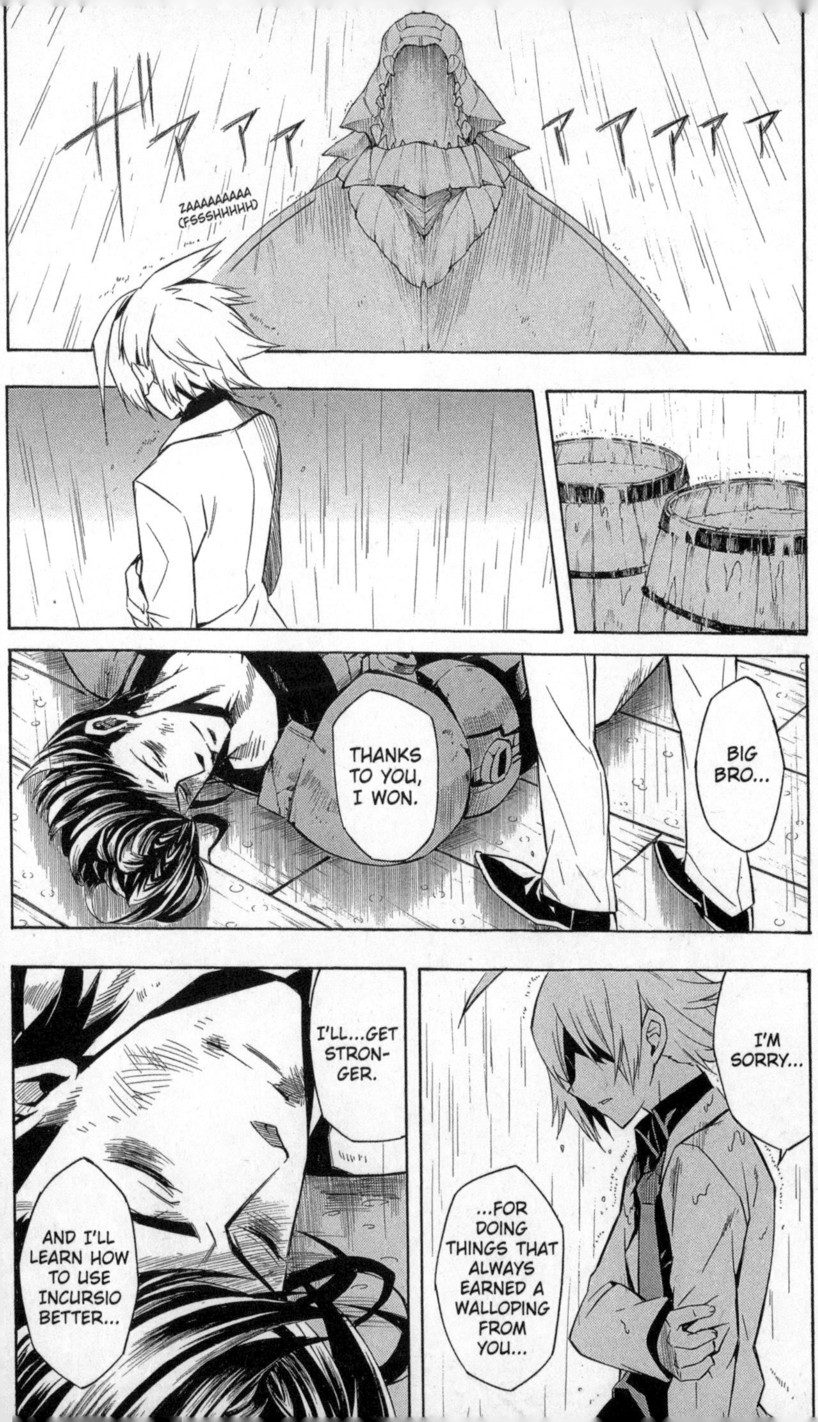
ザアアア アアアアア
ZAAAAAAAAA (FSSSHHHHH)
BIG BRO...
THANKS TO YOU, I WON.
I'M SORRY...
...FOR DOING THINGS THAT ALWAYS EARNED A WALLOPING FROM YOU...
I'LL...GET STRONGER.
AND I'LL LEARN HOW TO USE INCURSIO BETTER...

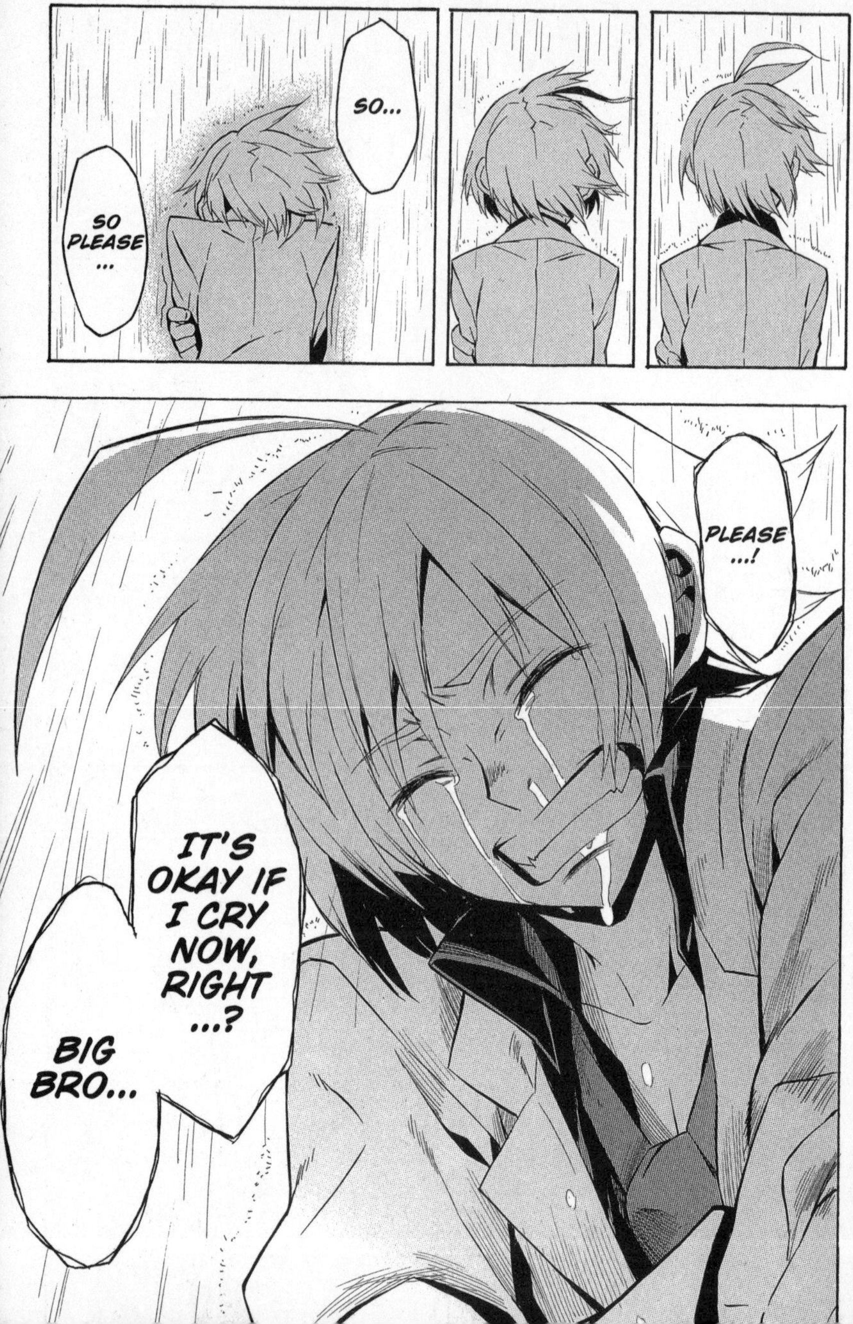
SO...
SO PLEASE ...
PLEASE ...!
IT'S OKAY IF I CRY NOW, RIGHT ...?
BIG BRO...

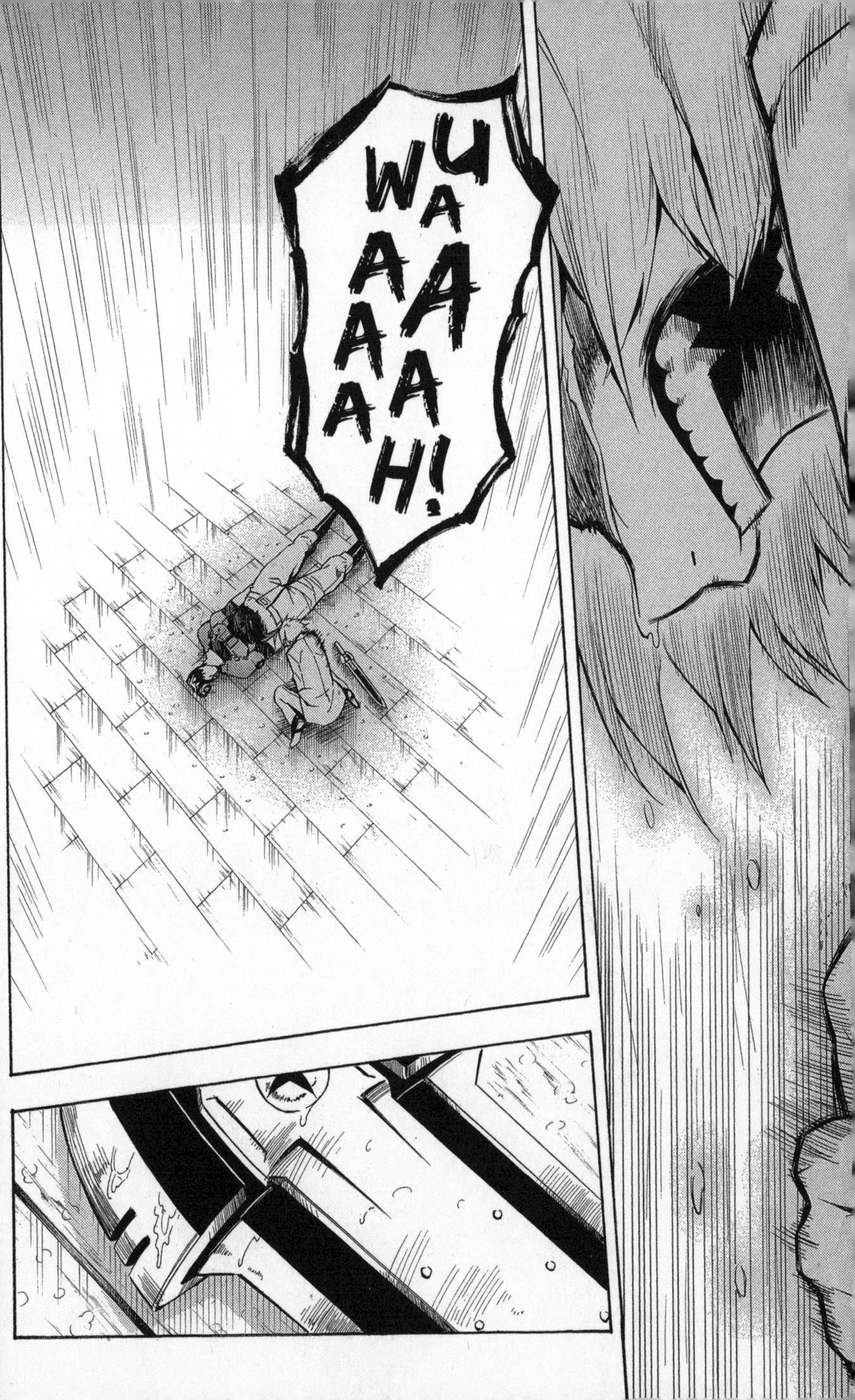
UWAAAAAAAH!

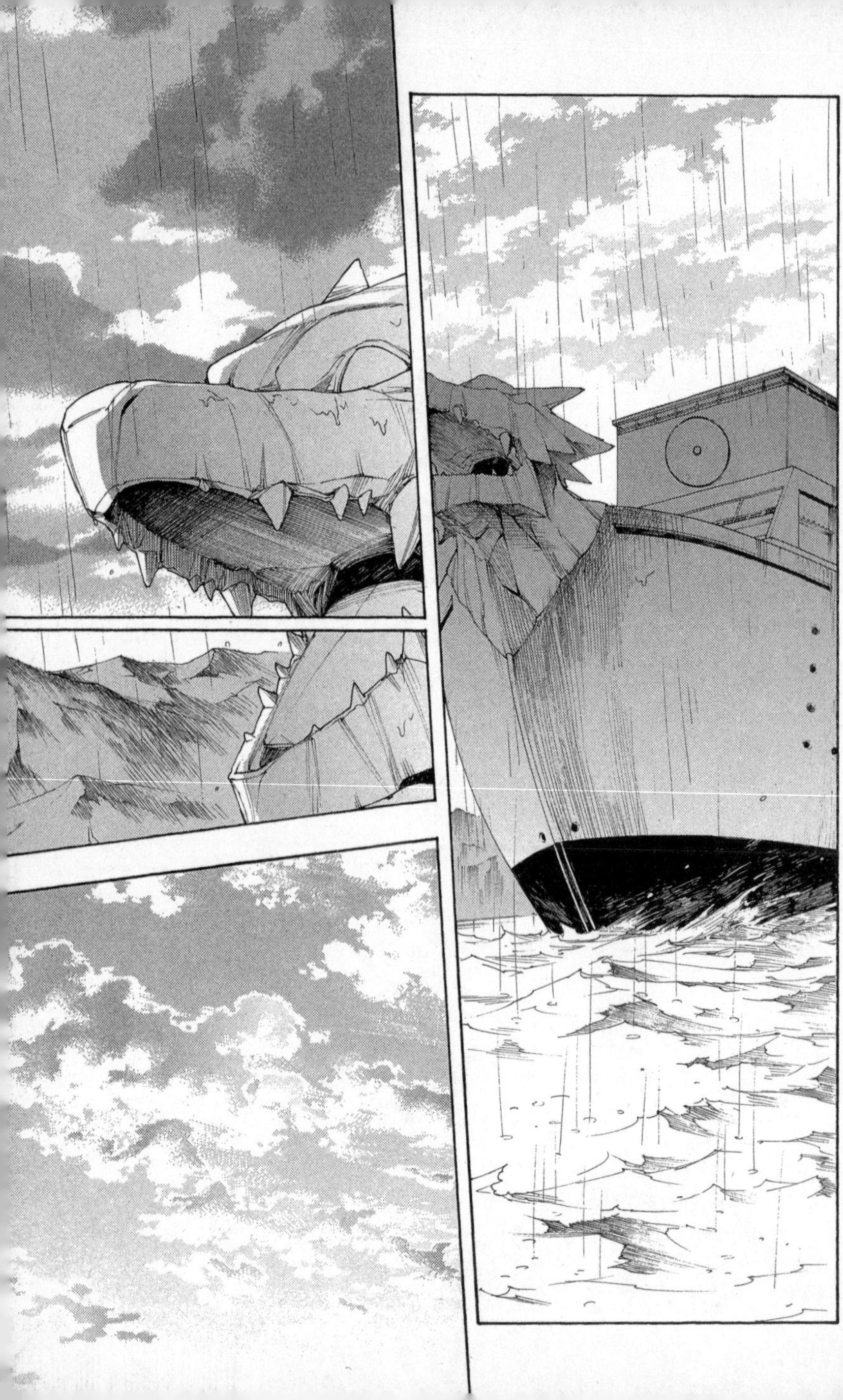

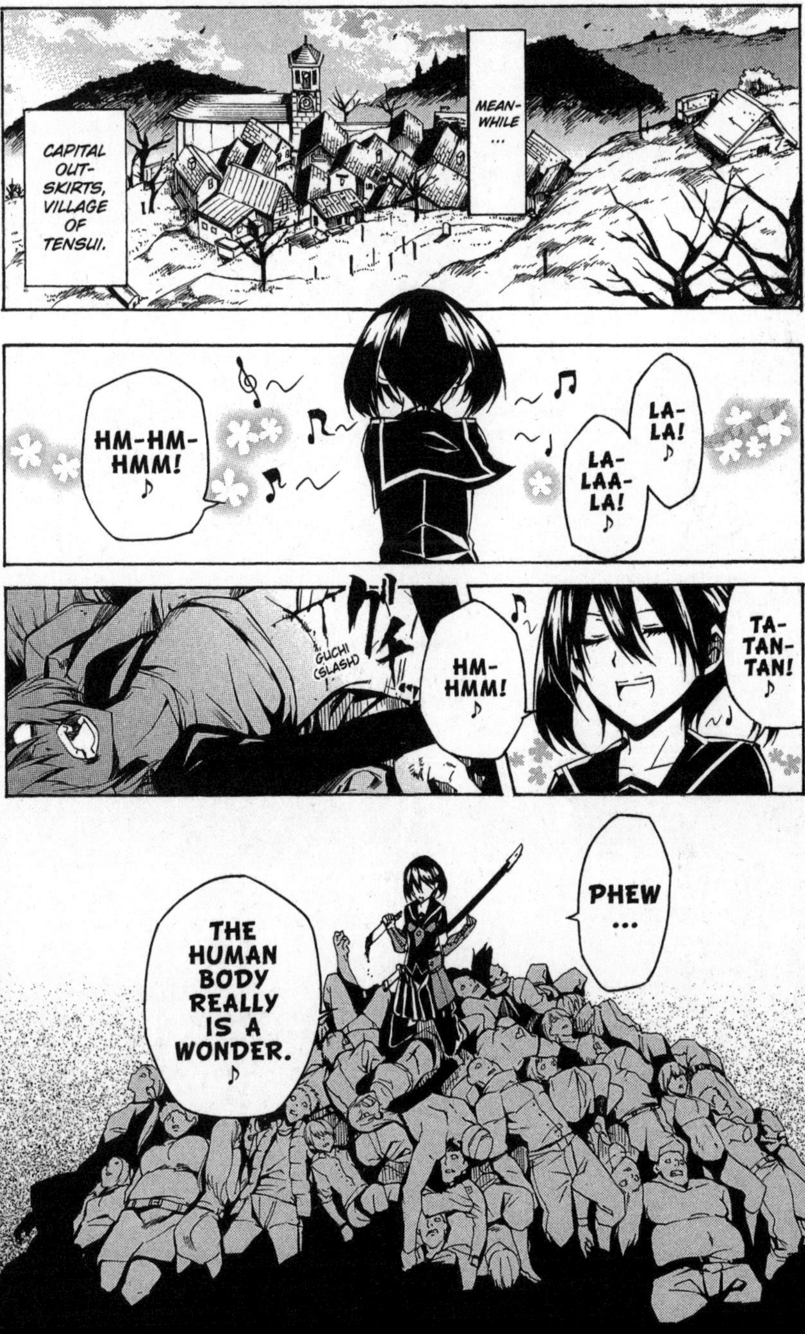
MEAN-WHILE...
CAPITAL OUT-SKIRTS, VILLAGE OF TENSUI.
LA-LA! ♪
LA-LAAA-LA! ♪
HM-HM-HMM! ♪
TA-TAN-TAN! ♪
HM-HMM! ♪
GUCHI (SLASH)
PHEW...
THE HUMAN BODY REALLY IS A WONDER. ♪

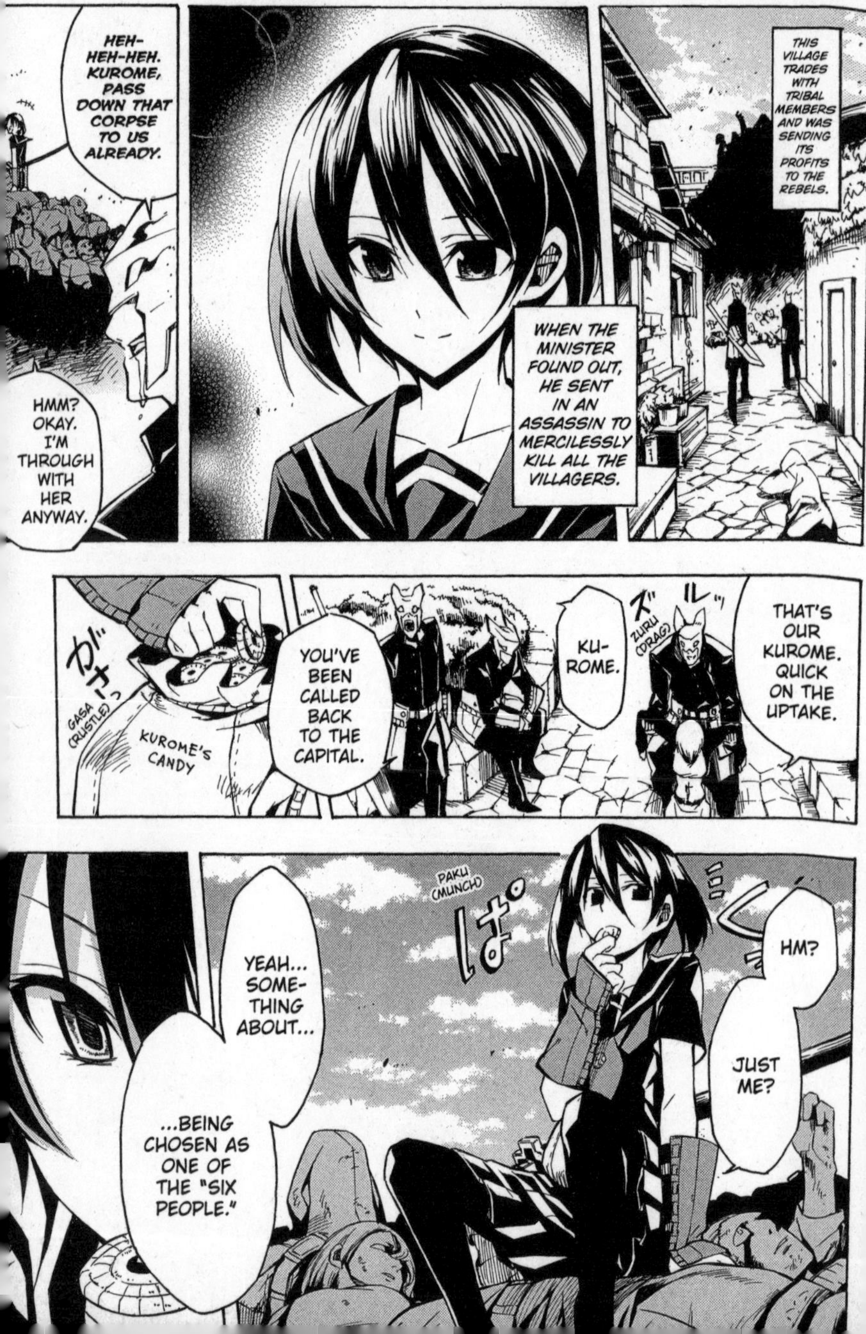
THIS VILLAGE TRADES WITH TRIBAL MEMBERS AND WAS SENDING ITS PROFITS TO THE REBELS.
WHEN THE MINISTER FOUND OUT, HE SENT IN AN ASSASSIN TO MERCILESSLY KILL ALL THE VILLAGERS.
...
HEH-HEH-HEH. KUROME, PASS DOWN THAT CORPSE TO US ALREADY.
HMM? OKAY. I'M THROUGH WITH HER ANYWAY.
THAT'S OUR KUROME. QUICK ON THE UPTAKE.
ZURU (DRAG)
KU-ROME.
YOU'VE BEEN CALLED BACK TO THE CAPITAL.
GASA (RUSTLE)
KUROME'S CANDY
PAKU (MUNCH)
HM?
JUST ME?
YEAH... SOME-THING ABOUT...
...BEING CHOSEN AS ONE OF THE "SIX PEOPLE."

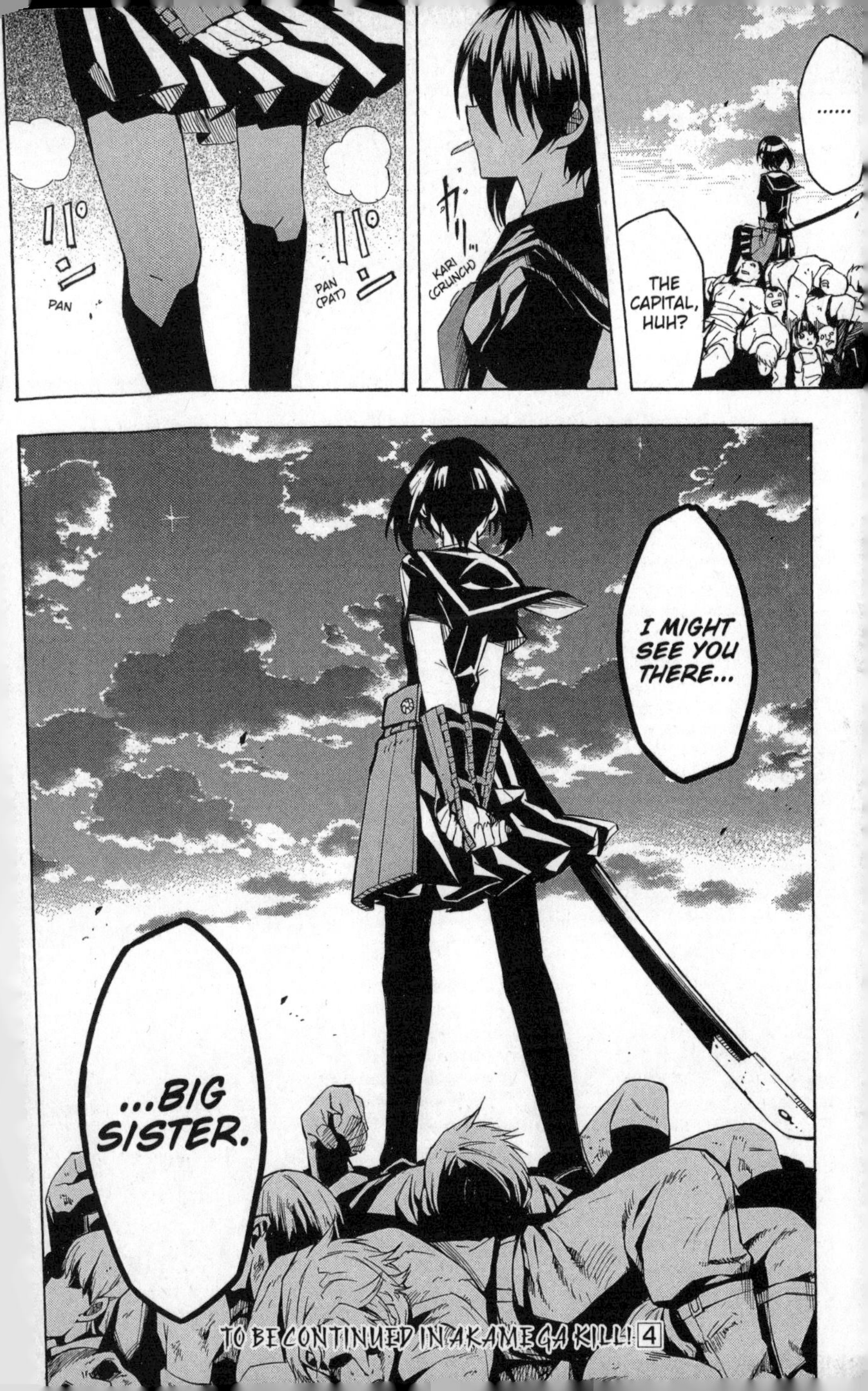
......
THE CAPITAL, HUH?
KARI (CRUNCH)
PAN (PAT)
PAN
I MIGHT SEE YOU THERE...
...BIG SISTER.
TO BE CONTINUED IN AKAME GA KILL! 4

TAKAHIRO's POSTSCRIPT

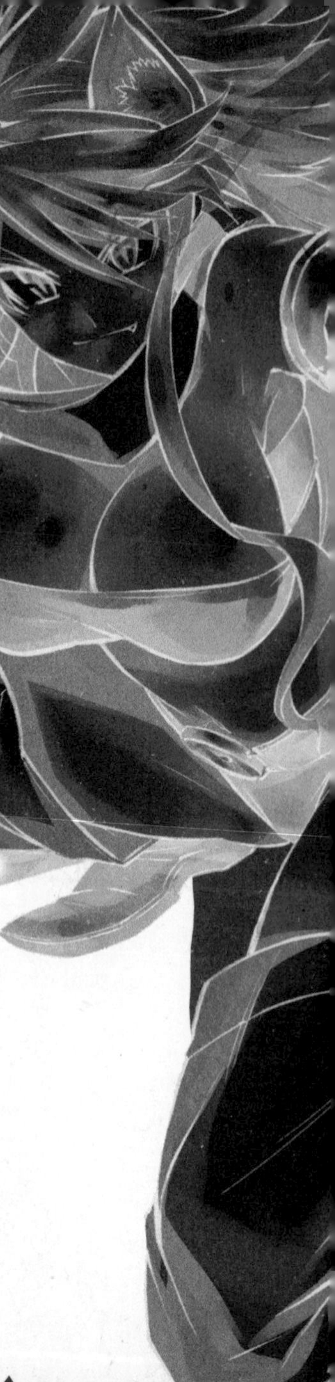

Hello.
It's me, Takahiro, with Minato Soft.
Today I'd like to delve a little deeper into who The Three Beasts are.

[Daidara]
Aiming to win the designation of "strongest," Daidara was on a journey to train in martial arts when he ran into Esdeath. After she beat him in a one-on-one fight, he was inspired by her prowess and agreed to serve under her. He swore his undying loyalty to her but hadn't yet given up on his pathway to strength. Even though he was defeated by Big Bro, it was only because Bulat was so overwhelmingly powerful.
Daidara was plenty strong himself.

[Nyau]
Born into a prestigious aristocratic family, he was a prodigy in every sense of the word, but his family life was unstable, which only aggravated his naturally heartless and twisted nature. He enjoyed dissecting living things for a hobby and thought he was the most sadistic person in the world until he learned about Esdeath. He was embarrassed by how much he still had to learn and became her servant. He is a dangerous character who likes to collect the skins of beautiful women as his war trophies and is the most deviant of all The Three Beasts.

[Liver]
As a wise and brave general, he served the Empire, but as was revealed in this volume, after many complications, he ended up as Esdeath's servant. As a capable army man, he was prized by Esdeath, which he considered an honor greater than any other. In reality, he was the main reason why Esdeath's Army was as capable as it was. He was The Three Beasts' leader, beloved by Nyau and Daidara.

And there you have it.
The backbone of the characters.
Since I couldn't fit it all into this volume,
I wanted to at least showcase it here.
Well, I will be seeing you in Volume 4. Until then!

Takahiro

AKAME GA KILL! 3

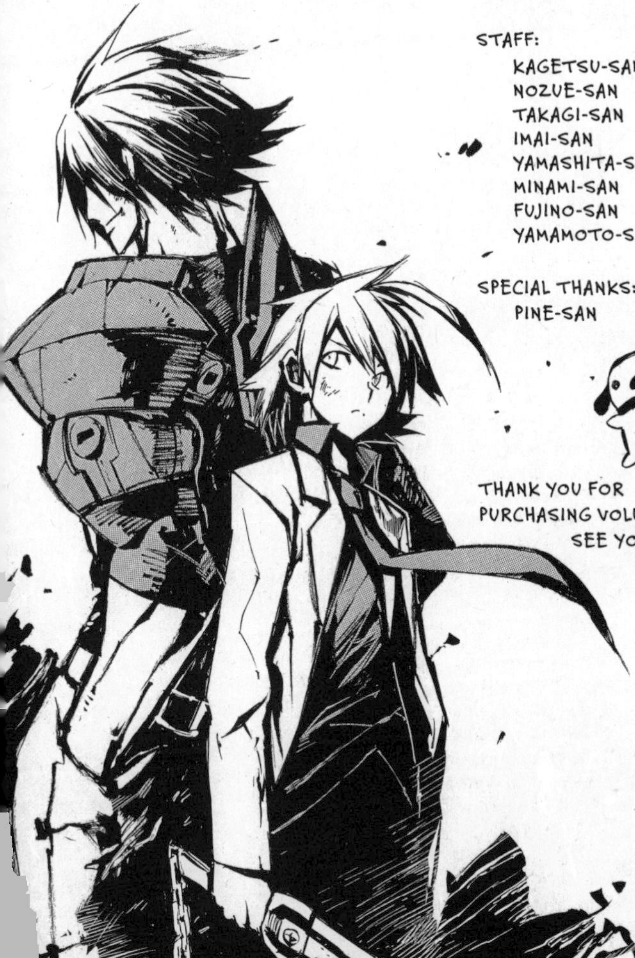

AUTHOR: TAKAHIRO-SAN
EDITOR: KOIZUMI-SAN

STAFF:
KAGETSU-SAN
NOZUE-SAN
TAKAGI-SAN
IMAI-SAN
YAMASHITA-SAN
MINAMI-SAN
FUJINO-SAN
YAMAMOTO-SAN

SPECIAL THANKS:
PINE-SAN

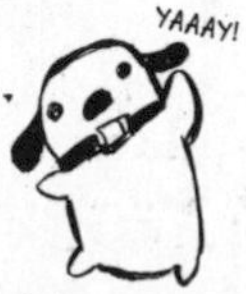
YAAAY!

THANK YOU FOR
PURCHASING VOLUME 3!
SEE YOU IN VOLUME 4!!

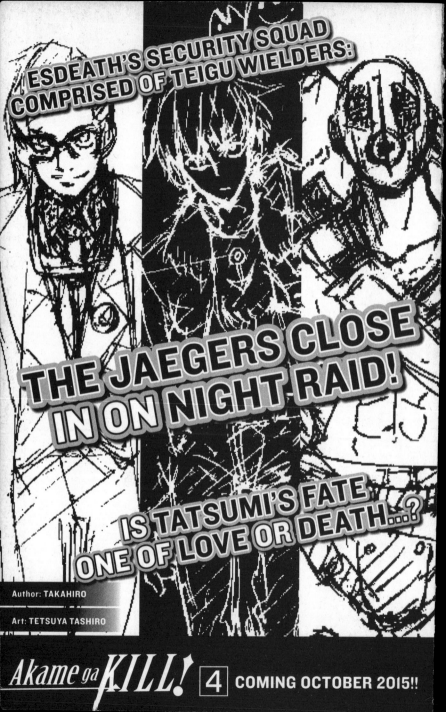

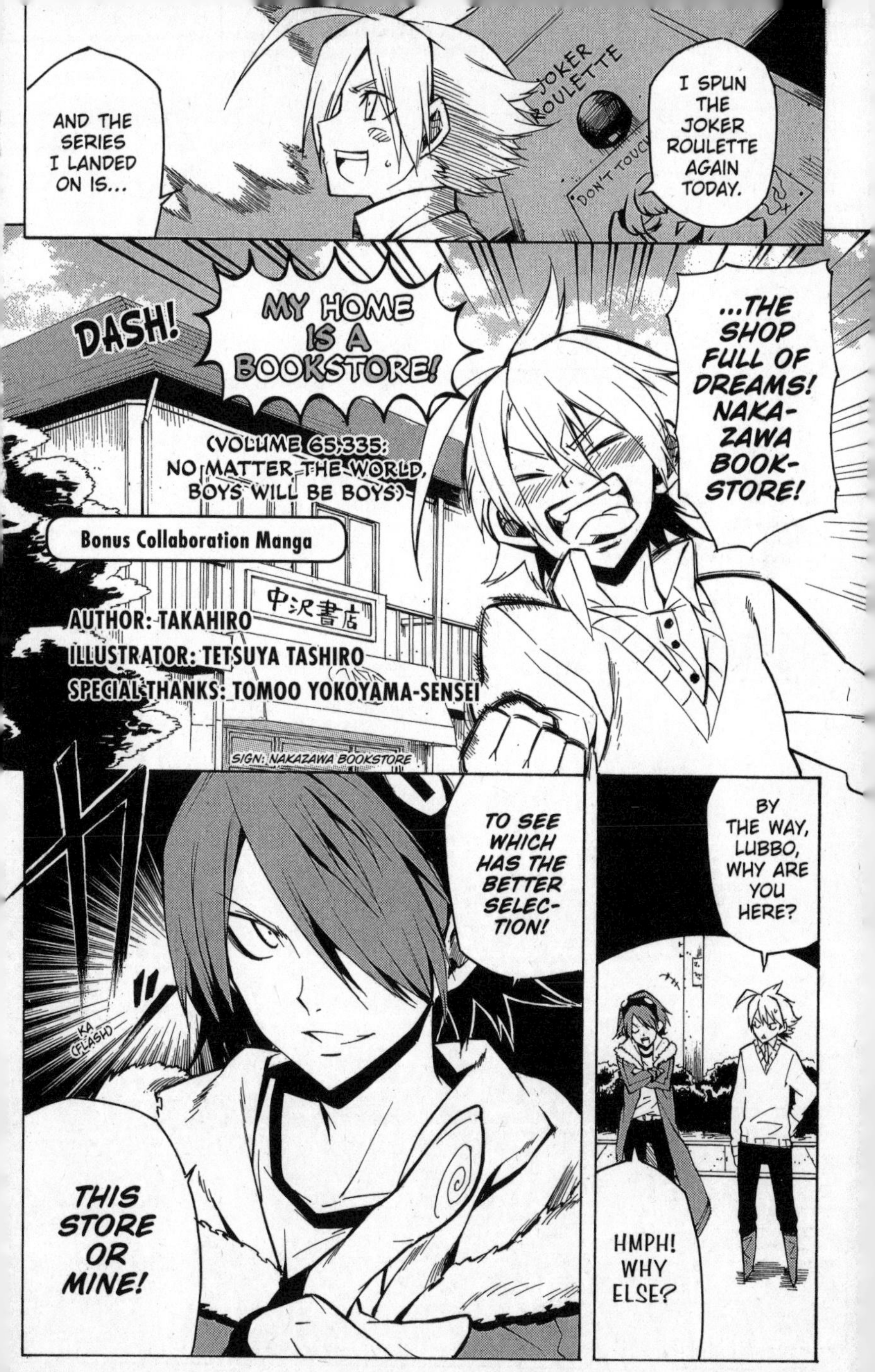
I SPUN THE JOKER ROULETTE AGAIN TODAY.
JOKER ROULETTE
DON'T TOUCH
AND THE SERIES I LANDED ON IS...
...THE SHOP FULL OF DREAMS! NAKAZAWA BOOKSTORE!
MY HOME IS A BOOKSTORE!
DASH!
(VOLUME 65,335: NO MATTER THE WORLD, BOYS WILL BE BOYS)
Bonus Collaboration Manga
AUTHOR: TAKAHIRO
ILLUSTRATOR: TETSUYA TASHIRO
SPECIAL THANKS: TOMOO YOKOYAMA-SENSEI
中沢書店
SIGN: NAKAZAWA BOOKSTORE
BY THE WAY, LUBBO, WHY ARE YOU HERE?
HMPH! WHY ELSE?
TO SEE WHICH HAS THE BETTER SELECTION!
KA (FLASH)
THIS STORE OR MINE!

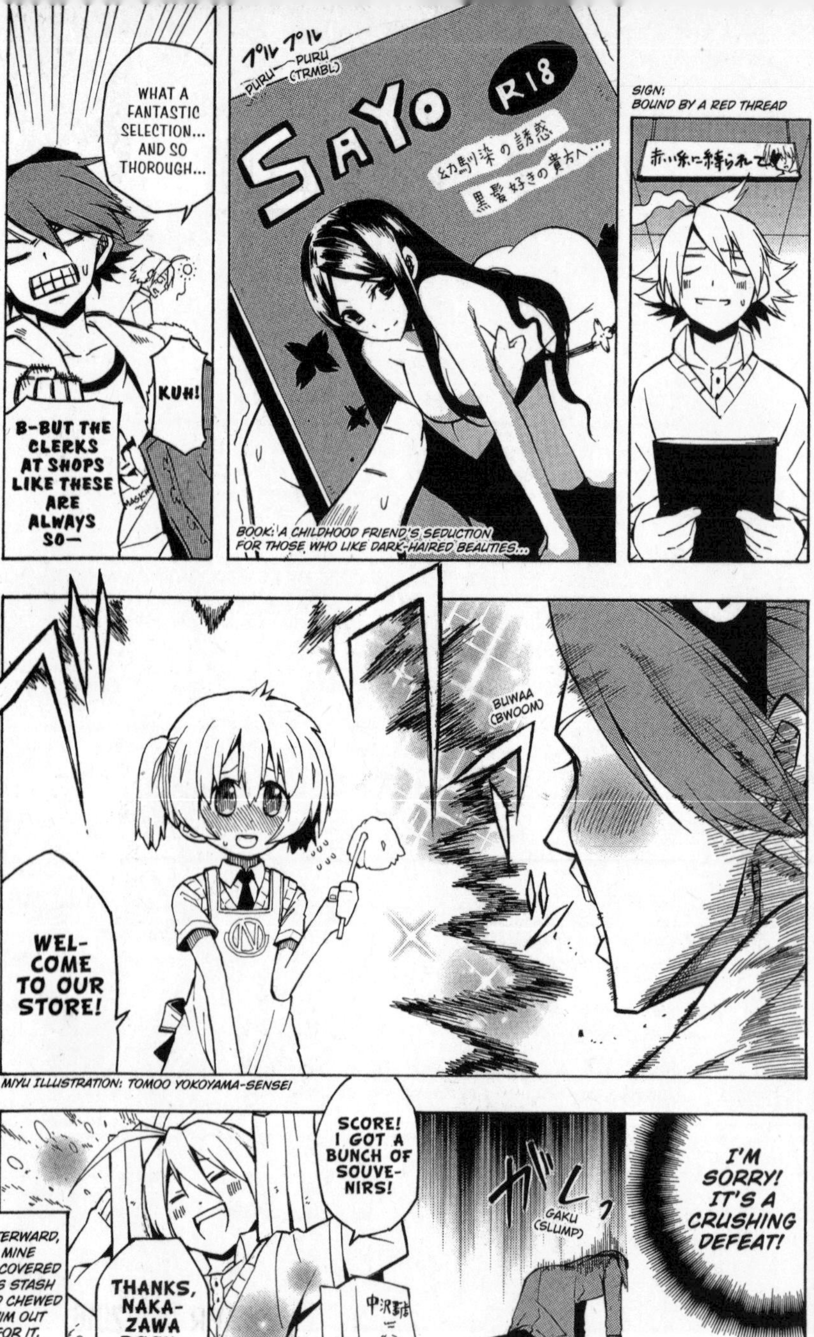
SIGN: BOUND BY A RED THREAD
赤い糸に縛られて
プルプル
PURU PURU (TRMBL)
SAYO
R18
幼馴染の誘惑
黒髪好きの貴方へ…
BOOK: A CHILDHOOD FRIEND'S SEDUCTION FOR THOSE WHO LIKE DARK-HAIRED BEAUTIES...
WHAT A FANTASTIC SELECTION... AND SO THOROUGH...
KUH!
B-BUT THE CLERKS AT SHOPS LIKE THESE ARE ALWAYS SO—
BUWAA (BWOOM)
WEL-COME TO OUR STORE!
MIYU ILLUSTRATION: TOMOO YOKOYAMA-SENSEI
I'M SORRY! IT'S A CRUSHING DEFEAT!
ガクッ
GAKU (SLUMP)
SCORE! I GOT A BUNCH OF SOUVE-NIRS!
AFTERWARD, MINE DISCOVERED HIS STASH AND CHEWED HIM OUT FOR IT.
THANKS, NAKA-ZAWA BOOK-STORE!!
中沢書店
BAG: NAKAZAWA BOOKSTORE

AKAME GA KILL

TAKAHIRO
TETSUYA TASHIRO

Translation: Christine Dashiell • Lettering: Erin Hickman

AKAME GA KILL! Vol. 3
© 2011 Takahiro, Tetsuya Tashiro / SQUARE ENIX CO., LTD. First published in Japan in 2011 by SQUARE ENIX CO., LTD. English translation rights arranged with SQUARE ENIX CO., LTD. and Hachette Book Group through Tuttle-Mori Agency, Inc., Tokyo.

Translation © 2015 by SQUARE ENIX CO., LTD.

Yen Press
Hachette Book Group
1290 Avenue of the Americas
New York, NY 10104

www.HachetteBookGroup.com
www.YenPress.com

Yen Press is an imprint of Hachette Book Group, Inc. The Yen Press name and logo are trademarks of Hachette Book Group, Inc.

The publisher is not responsible for websites (or their content) that are not owned by the publisher.

First Yen Press Edition: July 2015

ISBN: 978-0-316-34004-5

10 9 8 7 6 5 4 3 2 1

BVG

Printed in the United States of America